D0249344

Wings
of
Dawn

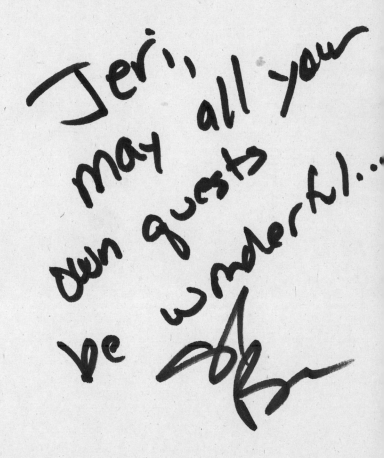

Jeri,
may all your
own quests
be wonderful...

WINGS
of
DAWN

A NOVEL BY
SIGMUND
BROUWER

Chariot Victor Publishing
A Division of Cook Communications

Chariot Victor Publishing,
Cook Communications, Colorado Springs, Colorado 80918
Cook Communications, Paris, Ontario
Kingsway Communications, Eastbourne, England

WINGS OF DAWN
© 1995 by Sigmund Brouwer.
Printed in the United States of America.

Originally published as *Magnus*
First Printing as *Wings of Dawn*, 1999

Editor: LB Norton
Design: Cover and interior by PAZ Design Group

2 3 4 5 6 7 8 9 10 Printing/Year 03 02 01 00

Library of Congress Cataloging-in-Publication Data

Brouwer, Sigmund,
       Wings of Dawn / by Sigmund Brouwer.
       p.   cm.
       ISBN 1-56476-756-6
       1. Knights and knighthood–England–Fiction.   2. Druids and
Druidism—Fiction.   3. Young men—England—Fiction. I. Title.
PS3552.R6825M3   1995   94-13611
                                                   CIP

DEDICATION

To Liz

In all our projects together,
you do what only the best editors are able to do—
nudge, correct, and encourage
with a touch as invisible as it is invaluable.
Thank you.

CHAPTER

1

MARCH 1312
NORTHERN ENGLAND

Since dawn, three ropes had hung black against the rising sun. Enough time had passed for a crowd to arrive and develop a restless holiday mood.

"Hear ye, hear ye, all ye gathered here today." The caller, short and stout with middle age, made no effort to hide the boredom in his voice.

His words had little effect on the people crowded in front of the crude wooden gallows platform.

"Get on with your blathering, you old fool!" The shout came from a hungry-faced woman in the back of the crowd.

"This punishment has been ordered by the sheriff under authority of the earl of York," he continued in a listless tone. "The crimes to be punished are as follows." He unrolled a scroll and held it in front of him at arm's length.

"Andrew, you dimwit!" yelled a fat man. "We all know you can't read. Don't be putting on airs for the likes of us."

The crowd hooted with appreciation, even though none of them realized the scroll was upside down. They grew quiet again, as all stared at those soon to die.

Six burly soldiers stood behind the man with the scroll, holding three prisoners. Even the most weary prisoners made a sudden struggle for freedom when finally facing the thick rope. It was such a struggle the crowd hoped for. Without a final bolt to escape or howlings of despair, a hanging would be a dull event. Indeed, this hanging drew as many as it did because one of the prisoners was an unknown knight.

"John the potter's son. Found guilty of loitering with the intent to pick the pockets of honest men. To be hung by the neck until dead."

Most of the people in the crowd shook fists at the accused boy. He grinned back at them. Ragged hair and a smudge of dirt covered the side of his face. "Intent!" he shouted in a tinny voice at their upraised fists. "Intent is all you can prove. I've always been too fast to be caught!"

The hangman waited for the noise to end and then droned, "The unknown girl who does not speak or hear . . . theft of three loaves of bread. To be hung by the neck until dead."

The crowd quieted as they stared at her. High cheekbones and long dark hair hinted at a beauty to flower. The tragic air about her forced a mumble from the middle of the crowd.

"The baker could have easily kept her for kitchen work, instead of forcing the magistrate on her."

The baker flushed with anger. "And how many more mouths should I support in these times? Especially one belonging to a useless girl who cannot hear instructions?"

Behind all of them lay the town known as Helmsley. Although it was important enough to be guarded by a castle, the town was little more than a collection of wood and stone houses along narrow and dirty streets. The stench of rotting mud and farm animals filled the air.

The crowd fell silent as the strange knight was formally accused. The hangman in the dirty shirt felt their growing excitement, and his voice rose beyond boredom. "Finally, the knight who claims to be from a land of sun. Found guilty of blasphemy and the theft of a chalice. To be hung by the neck until dead."

The people strained to watch for reaction. The knight, clad only in trousers, tunic, and a vest of chain mail, stood with bowed head and showed no curiosity. The bulges of his muscled arms and shoulders revealed a man who had lived by the sword.

Having pronounced all the charges, the hangman intoned, "This on the twenty-eighth day of March in the year of our Lord, thirteen hundred and twelve."

Finished with the memorized words, the hangman rolled the useless paper back into a roll and nodded at the soldiers.

Some of the onlookers had neglected a day's work and traveled as far as six miles. Others had brought their entire families. To their great disappointment, none of the prisoners resisted. With all attention focused on the three figures slowly climbing the gallows, no one saw a figure approaching from behind the town.

Not until he strode amid the crowd did anyone notice him. Then, the awed silence was immediate. The figure was a giant, four hands above the tallest man. The black cloth that swirled around him gleamed and flowed like a river. A hood covered his face; his hands were lost in the deep folds of his robe. He looked like the shadow of death.

He did not break stride until he reached the gallows, then he turned stiffly to face the crowd. The specter let the silence press down upon the people before uttering his first words.

"The knight shall be set free at once." His voice was unearthly, a deep rasping evil that sent the crowd back.

The black specter extended his arms toward the people and hissed, and blue and orange flames shot outward from his right sleeve.

The entire crowd seemed frozen. Then, as if time had resumed, voices broke out.

"Return the knight!" someone shouted, "before we all die!"

"Andrew, save us now!" pleaded another voice. "Set the knight free!"

The hangman blinked twice, then pointed at the figure. "Seize the stranger!" he ordered the soldiers. Two reluctantly stepped forward and drew their long swords.

The specter turned slowly toward them. "For your disobedience," he rasped, "you shall become blind as trees."

He waved his left arm as if invoking a curse. Both fled the gallows, screaming and pressing their faces in agony.

"Do others dare?" The specter asked the crowd, as the soldiers' screams faded.

Andrew was brave and not entirely stupid. He issued fumbling orders to the remaining soldiers to cut the ropes binding the knight.

The specter held his position without motion, his hooded face directed at the crowd.

Before the knight was fully free, a bent, white-haired man in faded rags stepped forth. He limped steadily until he faced the specter with an unfearing upward gaze.

"Your name is Thomas. You are an orphan, reaching manhood," he whispered, staring into the deep shadows of the black cowl. "And you shall give the crowd my instructions as if they came from your own mouth."

The specter did not reply. To the crowd, it was as if each figure were made of stone.

"Do you understand me?" the old man whispered calmly. "Nod your head slowly, or I will lift that robe of yours and expose the stilts upon which you stand."

The nod finally came.

"Good." The old man whispered, "Order the release of the other two prisoners."

Silence.

The old man smiled. "Surely, lad, you have no acid left to blind me. Otherwise you have would done so already. With nothing left to bluff the crowd, you must listen to me." His whispered intensified. "Order their release!"

The specter suddenly spoke above the head of the old man. "Release the others or face certain doom," his harsh voice boomed.

The old man chuckled under his breath. "As I thought. You are poorly equipped."

"Release all three?" the hangman protested, "The sheriff will hang *me*."

"Do as I say," the specter thundered.

Not a person moved.

"You are out of weapons," the old man cackled quietly. "How to you expect to force them now?"

The hangman dared his question again. "All three? Impossible!"

Murmurings came from the people as they too began to lose their edge of fear. A rock, thrown from the back of the crowd, narrowly missed the giant specter. He roared anger, but without flame or the cast of blindness, it was a hollow roar.

Another rock sailed dangerously close.

"Old man," Thomas hissed from the cowl's black shadow, "this is your doing. Help me now."

The old man merely smiled and looked past the specter's shoulder at the sun. "Raise your arms," he commanded.

One more rock whistled past and struck the ground. The murmuring grew.

"Raise them now," the old man repeated with urgency, "before it is too late!"

The specter raised his arms, and the crowd fell silent as if struck.

The old man continued quietly, "Repeat all of my words. If you hesitate, we are both lost. There is less time remaining than for a feather to reach the ground."

The black hood nodded slightly.

"Tell them, 'Do not disobey,' " he whispered.

"Do not disobey." The heavy voice rasped with renewed evil.

"Say, 'I have the power to turn the sun into darkness.' "

"Impossible," Thomas whispered back.

"Say it! Now!" The old man's eyes willed him into obedience.

So the specter's voice boomed in measured slowness. "I have the power to turn the sun into darkness."

A laugh from the crowd.

The old man whispered more words, and the specter repeated each one slowly.

"Say, 'Look over my shoulder. I have raised my arms and even now you will see the darkness eating the edge of the sun.' "

Another laugh, this time cut short. Sudden gasps and assorted fainting spells in front of him startled the specter. He fought the impulse to look upward at the sun himself.

The old man gave him more instructions. The specter forced himself to repeat his words. "Should I wish, the sun will remain dark in this town forever."

He nearly stumbled at the words given him, because already the light of day grew dim. "What kind of sorcerer are you?" he demanded of the old man.

"Say, 'All prisoners shall be released immediately,' " the old man replied in a hypnotic whisper. "Tell them now, while they are in terror."

Thomas did as instructed. In the unnatural darkness, he heard the hangman and the soldiers scurrying into action. Then he repeated the final words given to him by the old man. "Send each prisoner from town with food and water. Tonight, at the stroke of midnight, the town mayor shall place a pouch of gold on these very gallows. The messenger I send for the gold will appear like a phantom to receive your offering. Only then will you be free of the threat of my return."

As the specter finished, trying hard to keep the wonder and

fear from his own voice, an unnatural darkness covered him and the gallows, the crowd, and the countryside.

"You have done well. Go now," the old man spoke. "Drop from your stilts and wrap your robe into a bundle and disappear. Tonight, if you have any brains in your head, you will be able to retrieve the gold. If not . . ."

In the darkness, the orphan named Thomas could only imagine the motion of the old man's hunched shrug.

"These prisoners?" Thomas whispered back. He wanted the knight more than he wanted the gold.

"You desired the knight. As you planned, he will be yours . . . if you prove to him you are his rescuer."

As I planned? How did the old man know?

In his confusion, he blurted, "Why release the others?"

The old man answered, "Take them with you. The boy and girl will guarantee you a safe journey to Magnus. You must succeed, to bring the wings of dawn's light into this age of darkness."

"You cannot possibly know of Magnus."

"Thomas, you have little time before the sun returns."

"Who are you?"

Later, Thomas wondered if there had been a laugh in the old man's reply. "The answer is in Magnus. Now run, or you shall lose all."

CHAPTER

2

Having abandoned his stilts, Thomas now moved lightly on the leather soles strapped to his feet. His crudely sewn tunic fit him almost as tightly as his breeches. Silently dodging branches as he moved from tree to tree in pursuit of his quarry, he was grateful for the brown of the monk's charity cloth, which blended him into the background.

For a man so big, he thought, *the knight cuts through this forest like a roe deer.*

Already they were five miles east of Helmsley and the abandoned gallows. Shortly the Sext bells would mark midday. The half-day of light remaining was ample to continue north and return to the abbey. But were there enough hours left to secure the gold at midnight?

Thomas decided he could not risk a delay. He reckoned the knight's forward progress and began a wide circle through the falling slope of the forest to intercept him.

He did not pause to enjoy the beauty of the surrounding forest. He concentrated on footstep after silent footstep, hoping he had remembered the lay of the land correctly. Fifteen minutes later, he grinned in relief at the expected wide stream at the bottom of the valley. While it blocked him, it would also block the knight. And a thick fallen tree appeared the only way to cross the water.

Thomas reached the tree and scrambled to its center. He sat cross-legged and half hidden among the gnarled branches that reached down into the stream, and waited.

The knight merely raised an eyebrow when he reached the stream's bank and saw Thomas on the fallen tree. His face showed clearly in the midday sun, his brown hair cropped short; his blue eyes as deep as they were guarded.

"For a forest so lonely, this appears to be a popular bridge."

Thomas smiled. "A shrewd observation, sir." He stood and balanced himself on the fallen tree. "I shall gladly make room for you to pass, sir, but I beg of you to first answer a question."

A slight curl of a grin crossed the knight's face. "You are an unlikely troll." He set down his shoulder bag and contemplated Thomas. "That is legend in this country, is it not—the troll beneath a bridge with three questions to anyone who wishes to pass?"

"I am not a legend," Thomas answered. "But together, we may be."

The knight stared at Thomas. He saw a square-shouldered young man dressed in the clothing of a monk's assistant . . . ragged brown hair tied back . . . high forehead . . . a straight nose . . . and a chin that did not quiver at a strange knight's imposing gaze.

He almost smiled again as he noted the lad's hands. Large and ungainly, they protruded from coarse sleeves much too short. A *puppy with much growing to do*, he thought with amusement. *At that awkward age before maturity.*

But there was a steady grace in the boy's relaxed stance, and depth of character hinted by gray eyes that stared back with calm strength. *Does a puppy have this much confidence?* the knight wondered. *This much steel at such a young age?*

Then the knight did grin. This puppy was studying him with an equal amount of detached curiosity.

"I presume I pass your inspection," the knight said with a mock bow.

Thomas did not flush, but merely nodded gravely.

Strange. Almost royal. As if we are equals, the knight thought. He let curiosity overcome a trace of anger and spoke again. "Pray tell, your question."

Thomas paused, weighing his words carefully. He knew his future depended on his words.

"Does your code of knighthood," Thomas finally asked, "make provision for the repayment of a life saved and spared?"

The knight thought back to his tired resignation in front of the gallows, then to the powerful joy that followed as he was spared by the miracle of the sun blotted by darkness.

"If there is nothing in this code you speak of," the knight said slowly, as he pictured the heavy ropes of his death hanging against the dawn sky, "I assure you there certainly should be."

Thomas nodded again. He fought to keep tension from his voice. "Sir William, it was I who saved you from the gallows." Thomas cast his words across the water. "Consider me with kindness, I beseech you, in the regretful necessity which forces me to ask repayment of that debt."

On a normal day, the knight would have merely chuckled at such an absurd claim. But this was not a normal day. Only hours earlier, Sir William had prepared himself to die with dignity. The mix of emotions he had been holding inside after his sudden escape needed release, which they now found in white hot rage.

"Insolent whelp!" he roared.

In one savage movement, he surged onto the log and lunged at Thomas. As his bare hands flashed, fingers of iron tore into Thomas's flesh.

"I'll grind you into worm's dust!" the knight vowed, tightening his fingers around Thomas's neck. "To follow me and lay such a pretentious claim . . ."

Rage prevented Sir William from continuing his words. His biceps bulged as he lifted Thomas by the throat with his war-hardened hands.

Unable to speak, Thomas did the only thing he could do. Eyes locked into eyes, he waited for the knight's sanity to return.

Blackness began a slight veil across Thomas's vision. He brought a knee up in desperation. It only bounced off the chain mail stretched across the knight's belly.

The blackness became a sheet. *I . . . must . . . explain*, Thomas willed to himself. *One . . . last . . . chance.* He reached for one of the gnarled branches of the fallen log. *If . . . this . . . breaks . . . I . . . am . . . dead.*

With his final strength, Thomas pulled hard on the branch. It was not much, but it was enough.

Already in an awkward position with Thomas held extended in midair, Sir William did not anticipate the tug on his balance. Both men toppled sideways into the stream.

Thomas bucked against the water and fought for the surface. He reached his feet in the waistdeep water, and sucked in a lungful of air.

Looking for the knight, he prepared to scramble for land.

Instead of a charging bull, however, he saw only the matted cloth of the knight's half-submerged back. Thomas reacted almost as swiftly in concern as Sir William had moments earlier in anger.

He thrashed through the water and pulled the man upward. An ugly gash of red covered the knight's temple.

Thomas winced as he noted a smear of blood on a nearby boulder. He dragged the man to shore, ripped a strip of cloth from his shirt, and began dabbing at the blood.

Within seconds, Sir William groaned. He blinked himself into awareness and looked upward at the boy.

"By the denizens of Hades," Sir William said weakly, his rage gone. "This cannot mean you now have really spared my life."

As their outer clothes dried on the branches, they began to speak.

"You left the pickpocket and the girl at the road." Thomas made it a statement. "And you seek to hide in the forest."

"You followed me," Sir William countered, as he hopped and slapped himself with both arms against the cold. "And don't think that because I am not strangling you again, I accept your story about the rescue at the gallows."

Thomas moved back to place several more cautious yards between them. "I was that specter," he said.

Sir William laughed. "Look at you. A skinny puppy drenched to the bone. Barely my own height. And you claim to be the specter who brought darkness upon the land."

"I was that specter," Thomas persisted. "I stood on stilts, covered by a black robe, and–"

"Don't bother me with such nonsense. I heard the specter speak. Your voice is a girl's compared to the one that chilled the crowd."

Thomas hugged himself for warmth. "I spoke through a device that concealed my voice," he began to explain.

Again the knight waved him into silence. "I see that none of these inventions are with you."

"I needed to find you quickly," Thomas protested. "I barely had time to hide my bundle."

"You stated you followed me."

"Yes."

"To lay this claim," the knight repeated darkly. His voice rose. "Impossible!"

Sir William paused to let his anger grow. "You try my patience, puppy. No man, let alone a half-grown man, has the power to shoot flame from his hands or cast blindness upon the sheriff's best men."

The knight drew himself up. "And no man," he said with renewed anger, "has the power to bury the sun." He touched his forehead and brought his finger down to examine the blood, then scowled. "If you continue to insist upon these lies, I shall soon forget you pulled me from the stream."

Thomas paused halfway through the breath he had drawn to reply. The forest was silent. Hadn't the muted cries of the birds been a backdrop for most of their time among the trees? He held up a hand and cocked his ear for sound. Any sound.

"Did the hangman suggest that you would be followed?"

Sir William shook his head in irritation, then scowled again at the renewed burst of pain. "None. The man was as cowed as any of the villagers. He fairly cried with relief to see me on my way."

They stared around them. Thomas hugged himself harder to fight the chill of wet skin against spring air.

"I promise you, Sir William," he said in a low voice, "I was that specter. And I beg you to give me the chance to prove it."

"For what reason? I don't even know who you are."

"My name is Thomas. I was raised north of here, in Baxton's Wood, at a small abbey along the Harland Moor."

The knight snorted. "A stripling monk."

Thomas shook his head. "Never a man of the church. And with your help, something much more. The help, I humbly add, that you have already promised to the person who saved you from the gallows."

Sir William waved a fist in Thomas's direction. He dropped it in frustration.

"Thomas of Baxton's Wood," he announced heavily, "here is my word. Show me the pouch of gold to be taken at midnight from the gallows—which I assure you will be heavily guarded—and deliver it to me tomorrow in the guise of the specter. Then I shall be in your debt. Failing that, as you surely shall, give me peace."

Thomas grinned his elation in response. In his careful planning of this day, he had never expected to be shivering and waiting for his clothes to dry as he heard the words he wanted so badly. Still, his quest was about to begin, and only a fool looked a gift-horse in the mouth.

His thoughts turned, as they always did, to the childhood songs repeated evening after evening by the one person at the abbey who had shown him compassion and love.

So much to be fulfilled . . .

A giggle interrupted his thoughts.

Sir William reacted with swiftness and sprang in the direction of a quivering bush. There was a flurry of motion and a short struggle.

Then Sir William straightened. He held the pickpocket and the mute girl by the backs of their shirts.

Thomas reached for his damp shirt to cover his naked chest from the girl's dark eyes. Then he wondered suddenly why he wanted to stare back in return. He had seen village girls before, always ignoring their coy glances as he accompanied the monks to market. But this one . . .

He shook his head at the distraction and fumbled to pull his shirt on. There was barely time to return to the abbey, and he had much more to accomplish by midnight.

Sir William walked forward, carrying his double burden, disgust written plainly across his face.

The pickpocket tried to shake free. "People shouted curses at us along the road. Threw stones and called us devil's children," he said mournfully from his perch in the air. "What had we to do but follow?"

Sir William sighed long and deep and set them down with little gentleness.

CHAPTER

3

"A witch! A witch!" John, the pickpocket boy, scarcely
touched ground as he dashed between trees and skimmed
over fallen logs. "With giant claws and fangs for teeth!"

As the boy plunged into the small clearing, Sir William, who
had been drowsing in the afternoon sun with his back against a
tree, extended his arm.

"Oooof." The boy slammed into it.

"What is this nonsense you wish to share with the entire
valley? If you cry any louder, you'll put the village bells to shame."
Despite his determination to be angry, Sir William smiled, for the
boy had forgotten his panic and now lifted his feet to hang from
the knight's arm as a way to test both their strengths. "And why
did you wander far enough to find this witch?"

The boy dropped and grinned. "You slept, and . . ." he
motioned with his head at the girl, who sat quietly against
another tree ten yards away, ". . . she doesn't speak and barely
moves. Was I too supposed to act as if dead?"

"You have a sharp tongue, lad," the knight warned. "Perhaps I
shall cut it loose and serve it as supper to the witch, if indeed she
exists."

The boy's eyes widened. "It is not my flesh she seeks, but yours.
She pronounced mine too skinny."

"I suppose you informed her that you knew of fatter game and
pointed down the hill to where I slept?"

"How else could I gain freedom?"

Sir William yawned and stretched. "A witch indeed," he said.
"More like an old crone who wanders for herbs and even now
cackles at your terror. Hmmph. Fangs and claws. What

thoughts will you entertain next?"

The boy squatted beside the knight. "Thoughts of money well spent." He held out a grimy palm for the knight's inspection. "I removed this coin from her pocket." Sunlight gleamed from a silver coin thick enough that it represented a month's wages for a peasant.

The knight opened his mouth to admonish the boy, but the bushes parted beside them and before either could react, a heavy wooden cane slashed down at the boy's hand. He pulled away, but not quickly enough, and the tip of the cane slapped his open fingers, spilling the coin to the ground. He danced back, hugging his stung hand under his arm and biting his lip to hold back a cry of pain.

Sir William began to roll to his feet to face the unexpected intruder, but he stopped as the cane stabbed downward into the ground between his legs.

"Move again," screeched a voice, "and you will be less of a man."

Sir William wrapped one hand around the cane and grabbed the intruder's wrist with his other.

"Much as I admire your bravery, milady, it is wasted here. The coin is yours, and it shall be returned with no fight."

"Very well." The screech softened. "As it appears I have no choice, I shall trust you."

The crone lifted the cane, but Sir William did not release his grip until he was standing and able to ensure that he would wake as much a man tomorrow as he had been the previous morning.

He studied his assailant carefully. Black eyes glittered beneath ridged bones plucked free of eyebrows. Her face was greasy, her filthy smudged cheekbones like lumps of blackened dough. Under her ragged shawl were straggles of oily gray hair. A worn cape covered her entire hunched body, shiny where the cloth swelled on her back over the giant lump that marked her deformity.

"Shall I be in your dreams tonight?" she mocked in response to his gaze. Then she leered, showing darkened teeth. "Or is there a reason you travel with the young wench?"

Sir William glanced at the mute girl, who was watching the entire scene with disinterest.

"The girl, it appears, travels in her own world," Sir William replied. "As to my dreams tonight, if you appear, I shall crack that cane across your skull."

"Such a brave man," she crooned, "to bully a helpless old woman."

At that, Sir William laughed. "So helpless that I still tingle to think of that cane."

"My hand," moaned the boy. "It more than tingles."

Sir William frowned. "Give this woman her coin. You were nearly hung for your thievery earlier. A sore hand is hardly enough punishment now."

The boy bent to pick the coin from the dirt, and the old crone cuffed him across the back, then threw her head back and laughed a hideous shriek of delight.

She pocketed the coin, then pointed a bent finger at the knight. "You are an honest man," she said. "Many would have killed for less. I shall favor you with a gift. Follow."

Sir William shook his head.

"It is not far," she said. "Humor an old woman."

With that, she moved to the edge of the clearing and pushed her way through a screen of shrubbery.

Sir William shrugged. "Stay with the girl," he told John.

When he stepped beyond the clearing, the old crone had moved deep enough into the forest that he could barely see her in the shadows beyond.

"Come, come," she beckoned. "Quickly follow."

The knight grinned at his own curiosity. The gift, he was certain, would be of little value. But the old woman showed spirit, and how much harm could there be in a short walk?

When he reached the shadows, she was not to be seen. He paused as his eyes searched the trees.

Her shawl was hung from a branch. A few steps farther, her cape covered a small shrub. And past that, her shabby skirt.

Sir William scrunched his face in puzzlement. Surely the old woman was not coyly disrobing as she walked. Surely, her promised gift was not herself.

Sir William tensed as hearty laughter—deep male laughter— greeted his puzzlement.

The voice's owner stepped out from a nearby tree.

"William, William," the visitor chided. "To see your face as you contemplated the old woman's favors nearly makes our long absence worth the while."

Sir William stared in disbelief. Not at the wig of horsehair that the man held in his left hand. Not at the wax he was pulling from his face. But at the man himself.

"Hawkwood!" Sir William said. "My lord and friend!"

"Whom might you expect? For the prescribed years have passed. As promised, you made your return. Is it not fitting that I too keep my promise?" Hawkwood grinned, then raised his voice to the screech he had used earlier. "Shall I be in your dreams tonight?"

"Scoundrel," William replied. "Few are the hags uglier than you."

"I shall accept that as flattery, for if you can be deceived, then I have retained some skill in the matter!"

They moved toward each other and briefly clasped arms, then stepped back to study each other.

The silver-haired Hawkwood was slightly shorter than the knight. Although older, his face had seen less sun and wind, and his lines did not run as deep. It was a lean face, almost wolflike, but softened by his smile. Stripped of the old crone's clothing, his simple pants and a light vest still gave ample indication of a body used to physical labor. His voice was gentle and low. "It has been far too long, William. The years have treated you well."

"We are both alive," the knight observed dryly. "Anything more is a gift, is it not?"

Hawkwood nodded. "In our fight against the enemy, yes." He removed the last traces of the disguise from his face.

"Would that we had the time for me to cleanse at the stream before we speak," he continued. "And would that we had the time to converse over an ale at a tavern, like the old friends we are. Such luxury however . . ."

"Who is there to hinder us?" William asked. "The forest has no ears. And we have much to discuss."

Hawkwood shook his head in disagreement. "You must return to your young companions shortly. They cannot suspect I was anything other than a wandering old woman."

"They are children!"

"Look more closely at the girl, William. She is almost a woman. And, I'm afraid, more."

"More?"

"More. But hear me later on that subject." Hawkwood began to pace a tight circle. "Were your travels difficult?"

"No, milord. Exile still provides the secrecy and refuge we cannot have here. And in the southern half of England, none questioned me." Sir William shrugged. "I knew, of course, as I traveled north, that word of my arrival would reach the enemy. But also that it would reach you, that you would thus seek me, as you have. This far from Magnus, I thought myself yet safe."

Hawkwood spat. "Nowhere in England is it now safe."

"With the gallows rope around my neck, the same thought occurred to me. For too much time, I wondered if perhaps the plan we laid those years ago had failed, and that you might be dead by now."

Hawkwood spat again. "There have been moments, William. Our enemies' power grows. It was child's play for them to hide the chalice in your horse's saddlebag."

"And child's play for you to arrange the time of the hanging?"

Now Hawkwood laughed. "The years haven't dulled you."

The knight sighed as he recalled his fight with Thomas. "Perhaps. Perhaps not. But I find it difficult to believe that the eclipse occurred when it did because of happenstance or because of a divine miracle that presumes any importance for my scarred hide."

"Tut, tut, William. We are not without our allies among the powerful. I did indeed arrange the time of the hanging based on our ancient charts. But is it not God who arranges the stars? A century will pass before the sky darkens again. We could not have asked Him for more in the spring of this year."

Sir William waved away the protest. "You would have found another method, had there been no eclipse. Perhaps you would have arrived as a specter. . . ."

"Sarah trained the young man well, did she not?"

The knight nodded. "It took all my willpower to pretend surprise when he found me earlier this afternoon. Thomas has grown much since I last saw him."

"Grown enough to topple you into the stream?" Hawkwood laughed at the knight's sudden coughing fit, then moved to a log and sat. His voice became heavy. "Yes, against all odds, the boy has grown to manhood."

Sir William studied Hawkwood's face. "Your countenance suggests a sorrow I do not understand. For I have returned safely, you are here, the boy appeared as Sarah told him to, and Magnus awaits its delivering angel."

Hawkwood closed his eyes and winced in pain. "Sarah is gone. She died four years ago, at Harland Moor."

The knight placed a comforting hand on his friend's shoulder. They remained in silence for several moments before Hawkwood continued. "Because of her death, William, we cannot know whether the enemy have reached Thomas and converted him to their cause."

William raised an index finger. "Is it not significant that he sought me out at the gallows? Only Sarah could have instructed him to expect me."

"I have wondered the same. Yet Sarah died with his teaching barely begun, and him far too young for the passage of rites where a boy is trusted with knowledge of our cause."

William closed his eyes and thought. "If not from her, then, how could he know of me? Magnus fell long before his birth."

"I pray, of course, that he acts upon Sarah's instructions," Hawkwood agreed. "Yet the enemy plays a masterful game. It is equally conceivable that Thomas has been sent forth to lure us out of hiding, that he is one of them. Did you hint anything of our plan to him?"

William shook his head. "I played the fool. As further demonstration of my ignorance, I told him I needed proof he was the specter."

Their conversation was interrupted by a high-pitched cry several hundred yards away. "Sir Wiiiilllliam!"

"The pickpocket," Sir William said. "We do have little time."

"He is a bright one," Hawkwood said. "It served my purpose to let him steal the coin, for I then had reason to visit you. But his fingers are so light I almost did not detect his actions. He is crafty and has spirit. If this were the old days, we could consider teaching him our ways."

"I have affection for him too," Sir William said. "Except for now, because he searches for me, and it seems you have much to say. What of Thomas? What of the girl?"

"Wiilliaammm!" came the boy's voice.

Sir William paused. "Will we meet again soon?"

"In Magnus. I suspect Thomas will take you there."

"The girl? You said the girl—"

"Watch her closely, William. Would not the enemy expect one of us to have you rescued from hanging? Would it suit the enemy's purpose more to guard against the rescue and have you killed, or to let you escape and see where you lead them?"

William took a breath and said in rueful tones, "I am more valuable to them alive and in flight. Thus, they would need some method to track my flight."

"Yes, William. Is it the pickpocket boy who watches you? Or the girl? Or Thomas? That is why I spent long hours waiting for the proper moment to appear as an old hag. I cannot afford to be seen."

"Wiillliamm!" Now the boy was near enough that they could hear the crashing of underbrush.

"Guard yourself, and do what Thomas demands," Hawkwood said with urgency. "If he is not one of the enemy, he will desperately need our help."

"I will guard myself carefully," Sir William vowed, "and wait for you to greet me in Magnus, in whatever guise you next appear."

Hawkwood began to edge into the shadows.

"My friend," Sir William called softly, "what if I discover Thomas belongs to the enemy?"

"Play his game until you have learned as much as you can," Hawkwood whispered back. "Then end his life."

CHAPTER

4

As Thomas reached the summit of the final moor before the abbey, bells rang for None, the service three hours past midday. If one could fly with the straightness of a crow, the Harland Moor Abbey was barely six miles due north of his meeting place with the knight. Winding footpaths and caution against roaming bandits, however, had made his travel seem more like twelve miles. Despite that, he had moved with the quickness driven by urgency.

Below in the valley, Thomas could see the stone walls of the abbey hall through the towering trees. He moved quickly from the exposed summit toward the trees down near the river which wound past the abbey. Years of avoiding the harsh monks had taught him every secret deer path in the surrounding hills. At times he would approach a seemingly solid stand of brush, then slip sideways into an invisible opening among the jagged branches, and later reappear quietly farther down the hill.

His familiarity with the terrain, however, did not make him less cautious, especially since his first destination was not the abbey itself, but a precious hiding place.

Several bends upstream from the abbey hall, comfortably shaded by large oaks, was a jumble of rocks and boulders, some as large as a peasant's hut. Among them, a freak of nature had created a dry, cool cave, its narrow entrance concealed by jutting slabs of granite and bushes rising from softer ground below.

Thomas circled it once. Then he slipped into a nearby crevice and surveyed the area.

Count to one thousand, he said to himself, echoing the instructions given him time and again. *Watch carefully for movement. Let no person ever discover this place.*

Thomas settled into the comforting hum of forest noises, alert for any sign of intruders, as he pondered the power of knowledge hidden within the cave. . . .

Enough time had passed. He circled slowly once more, remembering the love someone had given him with the instructions he had repeated back endlessly.

Always, always, be sure beyond doubt no person sees you slip into the cave. Never, never speak of the existence of the books. The books have the power of knowledge beyond price.

As Thomas entered the coolness of the cave, sadness overwhelmed him, because the place never failed to remind him of the one who had so patiently taught him.

He stood motionless until his eyes adjusted to the gloom. He waited another fifteen minutes. Then he moved forward to the shaft of sunlight that fell in another large crack between two slabs leaning crookedly against another.

Thomas pulled aside a rotting piece of tree that looked as if it had grown into the rock behind it. Dragging out a chest that was as high as his knees and as wide as a cart, he opened the lid, reached inside, and gently lifted out a leatherbound book the size of a small tabletop.

He searched page after page, carefully turning and setting down each leaf of ancient paper before scanning the words before him. Nearly an hour later, he grunted with satisfaction.

Without hurry, he returned the book into the chest, then the chest into its spot in the stone, then the lumber in front of the chest.

He silently counted to one thousand at the entrance of the ruins before edging back into the forest.

"No supper for you tonight," wheezed Prior Jack with vicious satisfaction, as he pinched Thomas's right ear between stubby thumb and forefinger.

Thomas did not move, and Prior Jack seemed disappointed not to find immediate fear in the boy.

"I've changed my mind on your punishment." The monk's eyes became pinpoints of black hatred almost hidden in rolls of flesh. "You're finally to the age which lets us consider flogging, you ignorant peasant orphan."

Thomas closed his eyes and fought pain and anger. *Today is my last day here. It will be fortunate if I don't murder this man.* . . .

Prior Jack's permanent wheeze was the result of the gross fatness which also forced him to waddle sideways through the abbey's narrower doorways.

Most peasants suffered from continuous hunger, and considered themselves fortunate each day to eat more than a bowl of thin cabbage soup and some slices of black wholemeal bread. Yet Prior Jack took advantage of the distance of Harland Moor Abbey from the mother abbey of Rievaulx, becoming a tyrant in relentless pursuit of his gluttony.

It angered him immensely to see Thomas slipping through the back hall of the abbey, because it meant that once again, Thomas had neglected his work in the garden. Worse, no one ever knew where the boy went. Often Prior Jack or one of the other three monks had tried following him, but it was as useless as tracking smoke from a fire. All they could ever do was to punish him on his return.

Not once did they guess how badly the method had backfired. In efforts to escape over the years, Thomas had learned secret ways through the old abbey and hidden paths on its grounds. He had been forced to learn how to move quietly. The continuous punishment had made him the perfect spy and had toughened him to endure anything.

Within the abbey itself, Thomas did not always escape Prior Jack's quick mean hands and silent padding feet.

"Prior Jack." Thomas reached into his shirt and pulled out a knife. "If you don't let go, this knife will slice lard off you in strips."

Prior Jack rattled a gasp from his overworked lungs. "How dare you threaten me? I am a man of God!" But he dropped his grip and stepped back.

Thomas took a deep breath. "You? A man of God? First convince me that God exists. Then convince me you're a man, not a spineless pig of jelly. And, if God does exist, prove to me that you actually follow Him, instead of preaching one thing and doing another."

The fat monk's cheeks bulged in horror. For years, the boy had responded with defiant silence. It curdled his blood to suddenly hear this, and then to realize that the scrawny boy and his corded muscles had grown close to manhood without his notice.

Resolve had changed Thomas's eyes. The gray had become ice, and the knife in his right hand did not waver.

"Philip! Frederick! Walter!" Prior Jack bellowed into the empty stone corridors. He took a step back from Thomas and dropped his voice to its usual strained wheeze. "Put the knife away. Immediate penitence may spare your soul."

Dust danced between them, red and blue in the glow of the light beams from a stained-glass window on the west side of the corridor. It reminded Thomas that the sun was indeed at a sharp angle. Eventide would be upon him soon.

My plan must work, and there is little time to complete it.

The other monks arrived almost immediately, shaved heads faintly pink from exertion.

"The boy has lost his mind," Prior Jack whined. "As you can plainly see, he is threatening to kill me."

Brother Walter, gaunt and gray, frowned. "Put the knife down, boy, and you will only be whipped as punishment. If not, you will lose your hand."

Thomas knew this was no idle threat. Peasants had lost their hands for a simple crime like theft. To threaten members of the clergy was unimaginable.

"Tonight," Thomas said calmly, instead of dropping the knife, "is the night you set me free from this hole that is hell on earth. Furthermore, you will send me on my way with provisions for a week, and also three years' wages."

"Impertinent dog," squeaked Brother Philip. Tiny and shrunken, he quickly looked to the others for approval. "You owe us the best years of your life. Few abbeys in this country would have taken in scum like you and raised you as we did."

"As a slave?" Thomas countered. He lifted his knife higher, and they kept their distance. "Since I was old enough to lift a hoe, you sent me to the garden. When I cried because of raw blisters, you cuffed me on the head and withheld my food. Your filth—dirty, stinking clothing and the slop of your meals—I've cleaned every day for seven years. I chopped wood on winter mornings while you slept indoors, too miserly to give me even a shawl for my blue shoulders."

Brother Frederick rose on his toes and pointed at Thomas. "We could have thrown you to the wolves!"

"Listen to me, you feeble old men." Thomas felt a surge of hot joy. The moment was right, he knew without doubt. The hesitation that had filled him with agony for six months had disappeared.

Yes, he had been ready to leave for some time. The words of his childhood nurse had echoed softly during the dark hours as he lay in bed, night after night, dreaming of the moment. But he had waited and endured until, as his nurse had promised, the day arrived when he could make best use of all the weapons of belligerence and strength she had given him before her death. "You did not take me here as charity. You took me because the prior at Rievaulx ordered that you take me and the nurse. He did so because my parents were not peasants, as you have tried to lead me to believe. My father was a mason, a builder of churches, and he left behind enough money to pay for my education among the clergy. Yet you took advantage of the distance from the abbey at Rievaulx; instead of providing education you used me as a slave."

Brother Philip glanced wildly at the other three. "He cannot know that," he sputtered.

"No?" Thomas's voice grew ominous, and he spoke quietly enough to make them strain for every savage word. "The letters you leave carelessly about speak plainly to me. I've read every report—every false report—that you have sent to the prior at Rievaulx, including the first one in which you promised to do your Christian duty to me. Bah!" Thomas spat at their feet. "Would that I were half as content as you have made him believe."

Brother Walter shook his head. "You cannot read. That is a magic, a gift the clergy give to very few."

Thomas ignored him. "Furthermore, I have written in clear Latin a long letter detailing the history of this abbey over the last years. I have also transcribed the letter into French, with that copy reserved for the earl of York."

"He writes, too?" gasped Brother Philip. "Latin and French?"

"These letters are in the hands of a friend in the village. Unless I appear tonight to ask for them back, he will deliver them to the mother abbey. All of you will be defrocked and sent penniless among the same peasants you have robbed for years without mercy."

"It's a bluff," Prior Jack declared. "If we all move at once, we can lay hold of him and deliver him to the sheriff for hanging."

Thomas waved his knife, and the motion checked any rash action. "Brother Frederick. Your accounting of the wool taken from the sheep that I guarded night after night . . . will it bear close scrutiny when the prior at Rievaulx sends men to examine the records? Or will they discover you have kept one bag of wool for every ten sold, and turned the profit into gold for yourself?"

Frederick's face grew white.

"Don't worry," Thomas said. "The strong box you have hidden in the hollow of a tree behind the pond is safe. But empty of your gold. That has already been distributed among the villagers as payment to hold my letter."

The other monks swiveled their heads to stare at Frederick.

"I see," Thomas said. "It is a secret guarded from the others."

A growl from the prior proved the statement true.

"Prior Jack," Thomas snorted, "the letter also details the food you consume in a single month. I'm sure the prior at Rievaulx will be disappointed to discover that you slobber down nearly four hundred eggs from full moon to full moon. Over fifty pounds of flour. Three lambs. And a side of beef. It will explain, of course, why this abbey has not made a harvest contribution to the mother abbey in five years."

Prior Jack's cheeks wobbled with rage.

"Tut, tut," Thomas cautioned. "Anger, like work, may strain you."

"Enough," Brother Walter said.

"Enough? Is it because you dread to hear what that letter reports of you?"

The lines of Brother Walter's face drew tight. "You shall get your provisions."

"This means, I take it, that your fellow monks don't know your secret vice?"

"You will also receive three years' wages," Brother Walter said.

"He's a male witch," Thomas said simply to the other three. "A practicing warlock. Potions, magic chanting, and the sacrifice of animals at midnight."

The three monks recoiled from Brother Walter.

"Oh, fear not," Thomas said. "He's quite harmless. I've heard the man sobbing into his pillow from failure more times than I care to recall."

In the renewed silence, they could only stare at each other. Four monks in shabby brown and a grown boy with enough calm hatred to give him strength.

"I will take my wages in silver or gold." Thomas was the first to break the impass. "Have it here before the sun is down, along with the provisions. Or I shall demand four years' wages instead."

They hesitated.

"Go on," Thomas said. "I'll keep my word and have the letter returned to you tomorrow, when I reach the village safely."

They turned and scurried, but even before rounding the corner of the hall, they had already begun heated arguments and accusations.

Shortly after the last rays of sun warmed the stained glass, Brother Walter and Brother Philip strode back to Thomas.

Brother Walter held out an oily leather bag. "Cheese, bread, and meat," he said. "Enough to last you ten days."

Brother Philip tossed Thomas a much smaller sack. "Count it," he said. "Two years in silver. Another year in gold."

Thomas regarded them steadily. *Where is the fear with which they departed barely a half hour earlier? Why the gleam of triumph behind Brother Walter's eyes?*

"Thank you," was all Thomas said, as the comforting weight of both sacks dragged on his arms. Yet he waited before leaving. An unease he could not explain filled him.

"Go on, boy," Brother Walter sneered.

Still Thomas waited. Unsure.

Brother Philip gazed at the rough stones beneath his feet. "In the letter," he mumbled, "what have you to tell the prior at Rievaulx about me?"

Thomas suddenly felt pity. The tiny man's shoulders were bowed with weariness and guilt.

"Nothing to damn you," he said gently. "Nothing to praise you. As if you merely stood aside all these years."

"You show uncanny wisdom for a boy," Brother Philip choked, his head still low. When he straightened, he made no effort to hide his tears. "Perhaps that is the worst of all, not to make a choice between good or evil. I'm old now. The terrifying blackness of death is too soon ahead of me, and all I am to the God who waits is an empty man who has only pretended to be in His service."

"Quit your blathering," Brother Walter said between clenched teeth. "Send the boy on his way. Now!"

Brother Philip clamped his jaw as if coming to a decision. "Not to his death. Nor shall I go to meet God without attempting some good." He drew a lungful of air. "Thomas. Leave alone the—"

Brother Walter crashed a fist into the tiny man's mouth. The blow drove Brother Philip's head into a square stone which jutted from the wall. He collapsed to his knees without a moan.

Thomas felt a chill. What had Philip been trying to say?

"Spawn of the devil," Brother Walter hissed at Thomas. "Your soul will roast in hell."

Thomas said nothing and rested the bag of food on his shoulder. He took a half step away, then turned to deliver a promise.

"Brother Walter," he began with quiet deadliness, suddenly guessing the reason for Philip's death. "If indeed there is such a place as hell, your soul will be there much sooner than mine. And your own death shall be upon your shoulders as surely as the death of your brother here."

Thomas then left the hall as silently as a shadow. He paused outside until the noises inside told him that the three remaining monks were struggling with Brother Philip's body. Then, to fulfill his parting promise, Thomas slipped to the rear of the abbey into the cool storage room below the kitchen.

He departed shortly after into the darkness, climbing the valley hills with one sack fewer than he had planned.

CHAPTER

5

Every three hours the small village church rang its bells to mark the passage of time. Each new ringing marked a different devotion for the clergy. Matins at midnight, Lauds at three A.M. and so on. The eighth ringing of the bells meant the last service of the day, Compline, at nine P.M.

That clanging of bronze clappers against bronze bells reached Thomas where he sat, arms hugging knees, beneath a tree halfway between the village and the gallows.

Compline. Already.

Two bundles lay beside him. One, a small sack with gold and silver given by the monks. The second, the bundle of stilts and cloth he had recently recovered from its earlier burial place near the gallows.

Thomas could do no more to prepare himself for his next test. Yet the waiting passed too quickly. He merely had to turn his head to see the distant gallows etched black against the light of moon when it broke through uneven clouds.

If I could pray, Thomas thought, *I would pray for the clouds to grow thicker. Clear moonlight will make my deception more difficult.*

The mayor had not yet deposited the gold beside the gallows. That Thomas knew. He had chosen this place to hide because it was near the road that wound out of Helmsley. It would let him see how many men the sheriff sent from the village to guard the gold on its short journey.

Not for the first time in the last few cold hours did Thomas wonder about the mysterious old man. In front of the panicked crowd in the morning, he had forced Thomas to demand gold that was more money than five men could earn in five years.

Enough to provision a small army.

Almost as if the old man had read Thomas's mind. Thomas shivered, but not because of cold.

How did he know I was not a specter, but an impostor on stilts? How did he know what I wanted? And how did he deceive them all with a trick of such proportion that the sun appeared to run from the sky?

But the question that burned hottest—Thomas wanted to pound the earth with his fists in frustration—was one simple word. *Why?*

If this unknown old man had such power, why the actions of the morning? He could have revealed Thomas as an impostor, yet he had toyed with him, then disappeared. Why would—

Thomas sat bolt upright.

Will the old man suddenly appear again to recapture the gold?

With that final question to haunt him, Thomas discovered that time could move slowly. Very slowly indeed.

"I'll not rest until this gold has been safely borne away by the specter."

The voice reached Thomas clearly in the cold night air.

"Fool!" a harsh voice replied. "The sheriff has promised a third of this gold to the man who brings down the specter. I, for one, have sharpened my long sword."

"I'm no fool," the first voice replied with a definite tremble. "I was there when the sky turned black. The ghostly specter is welcome to his ransom. I only pray we never see him again."

"Shut your jaws!" commanded a third voice. "This is a military operation, not a gathering of old wives."

Thomas counted eight men in the flittering moonlight. Eight men!

Am I a village idiot to think I might overcome the odds of eight well-trained sheriff's men? And if I do succeed, what will I face in the months to come?

Again, Thomas regretted briefly that he could not pray.

Instead, he silently sang lines from a chant that had so often comforted him in his childhood.

Delivered on the wings of an angel,
he shall free us from oppression.
Delivered on the wings of an angel,
he shall free us from oppression.

In the play of moon and clouds, Thomas snatched glimpses of

men setting themselves in a rough circle around the gallows.

The bells for Matins began to ring from the village. Exactly midnight.

The promised phantom did not keep the sheriff's men in suspense. It appeared as if from the ground, not more than a stone's throw from the men circling the gold.

Ghostly white, the phantom moved serenely toward the gallows. In the dim moonlight, it did not show arms. Nor a face. A motionless cowl covered its head.

"All saints preserve us!" screamed the first soldier.

"Advance or you'll lose your head!" countered the commander's voice. "Move together or die in the morning!"

After some moments, all eight men began to step slowly forward with swords drawn.

The phantom stopped and waited. It did not speak.

A cloud blotted the moon completely. The men hesitated, then gasped as an eerie glow came from within the pale body of the phantom. Some stumbled backward on the uneven ground.

"Hold, you cowards," came the tense voice of the commander. The retreating men froze.

"A third of the gold to the one who defeats this apparition!" from someone in the pack.

Still, the phantom said nothing and held its position.

Finally, just as the cloud began to break away from the moon, the one soldier with the sharpened long sword began a rush at the phantom. "Join me!" he shouted. "Show no fear!"

The point of his outstretched sword had almost reached the outline of the phantom when a roaring explosion of white filled the soldier's face and etched sharply for one split heartbeat every ripple of the ground for yards in every direction.

No one had time to react.

The phantom moaned as it became a giant torch. Flames reached for the soldier, who had fallen to the ground, and he crabbed his way backward, screaming in terror.

The other soldiers finally unfroze. They stepped back to huddle in a frightened knot, staring wild-eyed at the flames which outlined the figure of the phantom. They whispered hurried prayers and crossed and recrossed themselves in the anguish of fear.

"A spirit from the depths of hell," one soldier groaned, "spreading upon us the fires which burn eternally."

In response, the flames grew more intense, still clearly showing the shape of the phantom. And it said nothing.

The men stood transfixed. Nearly half an hour later, the last flame died abruptly and the phantom collapsed upon itself. The men did not approach.

One soldier finally thought to glance at the gallows. The large bag of gold no longer rested in the center of the wooden structure.

Sir William stirred as a figure shaded his face from the early morning sun. He had not slept well anyway; the ground was lumpy and cold, and both the pickpocket and mute girl had pressed hard against him to seek warmth during the night.

He blinked open his eyes at a mountain of black that filled the entire sky above him.

"Mother of saints," he said with no emotion. "If you are not the boy Thomas, I am a dead man."

"Your control is admirable," breathed the specter in low rasping tones. "It makes you a valuable man."

With a slight grunt, Sir William sat upright. His movement woke the pickpocket and the girl.

Her hands flew to her mouth, and she bit her knuckles in terror. The pickpocket tried to speak, but no sound came from his mouth.

"Send them down to the stream," the cowled specter said in his horrible voice. "Our conversation must be private."

Neither needed a second invitation to flee, and they were far from sight long before the bushes in their path had stopped quivering.

Sir William stood and measured himself against the specter's height. His head barely reached the black figure's shoulders. A twisted grin crossed his face. "May I?" he asked, motioning at the flowing robe.

The specter nodded.

Sir William pulled back the robe. He snorted exasperated disbelief. "Stilts indeed."

Thomas leaned forward, and as the stilts fell free, hopped lightly to the ground. He peeled back the ominous cowl. Strapped to his face was a complicated arrangement of wood and reeds that looked much like a squashed duck-bill. He loosened the straps. The piece fell into his hands, leaving behind deep red marks across his cheeks.

"Much better," Thomas said in his normal voice. He rubbed his cheeks, then grinned.

In that moment, the knight saw the unlined face of a puppy; but he quickly swore to himself not to forget the puppy had sharp teeth.

The knight shook his head again and gruffened his voice to hide any admiration that might slip through. "And I suppose you can equally explain the fire from your sleeve."

Thomas pulled his sleeves free from his arms to show a long tube running from his wrist to his armpit. "A pig's bladder," he explained, as he raised one arm to show a small balloon of cured leather. "I squeeze," he brought his elbow down and compressed the bag, "and it forces a fluid through this reed. I simply spark it," he flicked something quickly with his left hand, "and the spray ignites."

Sir William nodded.

"Unfortunately," Thomas mumbled, as he remembered how helpless he had felt when the old man challenged him in front of the crowd, "it works only once. Then the bag needs refilling."

"The fluid?"

Thomas shook his head. "I need to keep some secrets."

"How did you blind those sheriff's men?"

Thomas lifted his other arm to show a small tubular crucible of clay strapped to his left wrist. The crucible had a long, tiny neck that pointed almost like a finger.

"Another fluid," Thomas explained. "I sweep my hand and it spews forth. It burns any flesh it touches."

"Another secret, I suppose."

Thomas shrugged. He then said, "I also have the gold from the gallows. Is that enough proof that I was the one who saved your life?"

The knight reminded himself that he must play the role of a skeptic. "Perhaps. Did you use more trickery to get it?"

"Simple trickery. Shorter stilts and a white cape around me, supported inside like a tent by framework of woven branches. The cape was waxed and oiled. I lit a candle inside, stepped back through a flap, and let it burn itself down. It was enough distraction to sneak to the gallows."

Thomas did not mention the mixture of charcoal, sulfur, and potassium nitrate that he had exploded in a flash of white to temporarily rob all the sheriff's men of their night vision. It was another secret which might lead to questions about the precious books.

"You think you have great intelligence," the knight observed dryly.

Thomas thought of the endless hours his childhood nurse, Sarah, had spent coaching him through games of logic, through spoken and written Latin and French, through the intricacies of mathematics. Thomas thought of his greatest treasure—the chest filled with books. But Thomas did not think of his intelligence.

"I have been taught to make the most of what is available," he replied without pride.

Suddenly, the knight sprang forward with blurring swiftness, reaching behind his back and pulling from between his shoulder blades a short sword.

Before Thomas could draw a breath, Sir William pinned him to the ground, sword to his throat.

"You are a stupid child," Sir William said coldly. "Not even a fool would disarm himself in the presence of an enemy."

Thomas stared into the knight's eyes.

Sir William pressed the point of the sword into soft flesh. A dot of blood welled up around the razor-sharp metal. "Not even a fool would walk five miles into a desolate forest with a king's ransom in gold, and offer himself like a lamb to a man already found guilty of stealing a sacred chalice."

Thomas did not struggle. He merely continued to stare into the knight's eyes.

"And," Sir William grimaced as he pressed harder, "lambs are meant for slaughter."

The dot of blood beneath the blade swelled to a tiny rivulet.

"Cry you for mercy?" Sir William shouted.

Neither wavered as they stared at each other.

"Blast," Sir William said, as he threw his sword aside. "I feared this."

He took his knee off Thomas's chest and stood up. Then he leaned forward and grabbed Thomas by the wrist and helped him to his feet. Sir William gravely dusted the dirt off himself, then from Thomas.

It was his turn to grin at Thomas. "The least you could have done was prove to be a coward. Now I have no choice."

Thomas waited.

"For saving my life," Sir William said, "you have my service as required. I ask of you, however, to free me as soon as possible, for I have urgent business."

"Agreed," Thomas said.

Each refrained from showing a secret smile. Yes, Thomas knew that only a fool would have brought a king's ransom in gold to a stranger, so he had not done so. Instead, Thomas had hidden the bulk of it with his precious books. And, of course, the knight did not need to know of the books.

The knight also smiled inside. If Thomas was of the enemy, the bluff with sword against throat would have been the action of a man totally unsuspecting of any intrigue. Thomas now had no reason to believe he was detected.

In the quiet of the woods, they clasped hands to seal the arrangement. Left hand over left hand, then right hand over right hand.

"Now what service do you want of me that was so important to risk your life first as a specter, then as a midnight phantom?" Sir William asked.

Thomas let out a deep breath. "We shall conquer a kingdom," he said. "It is known as Magnus."

CHAPTER

6

Sir William led the way along the narrow path cutting through the low boughs of heather across the top of the moors. The valley bottom offered too much cover for bandits.

Behind the knight, Thomas and Tiny John—as they now called the grinning pickpocket—followed closely. The mute girl, farther back, meandered her way in pursuit, stopping often to pluck a yellow flower from the gorse or to stare at the blue sky patched with high clouds.

Take them with you. It will guarantee you a safe journey to Magnus. Thomas remembered the old man's whisper each time he looked back at the girl. But, distracting as the mystery in her face might be, Thomas had other matters to occupy his mind.

"This must be the valley," he said. "I am certain the last moor was Wheeldale; as marked on my map, Wade's Causeway led us there."

"A remarkable map," murmured Sir William. "Few have the ancient Roman roads so clearly shown."

As Thomas knew from Sarah's patient teaching, Wade's Causeway—a road sixteen feet wide which trailed across the desolate moors from Pickering to the North Sea coast—had been laid by Roman legionnaires. The speed of movement the road allowed them had made them a formidable occupying force.

A thought struck Thomas. "How is it you know Wade's Causeway was Roman built and so very old? You profess to come from far away."

His local knowledge was not the only thing strange about the knight's observation. Because so few could read, most barely knew their family history. To show awareness of the Roman invasion so far back . . .

Silently, Sir William cursed himself. Every second of every minute in the presence of this young wolf demanded vigilance. If Thomas was what he appeared, Sir William could not let him suspect that he was anything more than a knight. Yet if Thomas was of the enemy, he would know Sir William's role, but could not know of the suspicions outlined by Hawkwood. It meant that the knight's every action and every word had to reflect nothing more or less than a fighting man under obligation to Thomas.

So Sir William swung his head slowly to survey Thomas. "England was only a barbarian outpost to the Romans. Where I come from, there are many similar to this."

End of discussion, the knight's face warned.

Thomas decided to look across the valley again.

"Where is Magnus?" Thomas spat out the words at the endless valley.

Sir William sighed. "Three days of hard travel. Three days of rough cold meals, and nothing but silence from you. Now you dance like a child the night before Christmas." He paused to wipe sweat from his forehead. "With the impossible task you have set for us, I should think you would be in no hurry to arrive."

"It's far from impossible," Thomas said. As if to confirm this, he shifted the bundle packed across his shoulders. *Such simple material inside, but enough to conquer a kingdom.*

The knight did not disguise his snort of disbelief, for as a simple fighting man, he would be skeptical. "We are not much of an army. Only in fantasies do two people find a way to overcome an army within a castle."

"I have the way," Thomas replied.

"Thomas, you have much to learn," Sir William said with exaggerated patience. "Castles are designed to stop armies of a thousand. Soldiers are trained to kill."

" 'Delivered on the wings of an angel, he shall free us from oppression,' " Thomas said.

Sir William squinted. "Make sense!"

Thomas smiled. *How many times did Sarah make me repeat the plan? How many times did she promise it would take only one fighting man to win?*

"There is a legend within Magnus," Thomas said. " 'Delivered on the wings of an angel, he shall free us from oppression.' I have been told each villager repeats that promise nightly during prayers. It will take no army to win the battle."

Sir William did not interrupt the rustling sound of the heather for some time. He had questions now, questions that only Hawkwood could answer. The nightly promise had not, of course, existed in Magnus when he was a knight of that kingdom. Had Hawkwood, who foresaw so much, decided long ago that this was how Magnus would be reconquered? But Hawkwood could not foresee Sarah's death; and now, Thomas might be a double-edged sword. Or perhaps not. How should he now react to Thomas's certainty? As one who knew little?

"You presume much," Sir William finally said, in a gentler voice than did not suggest mockery. "Is there oppression within Magnus? And where do you propose to find an angel?"

"I know well of the oppression." Thomas paused to think of a way to phrase it. "It was told to me by someone who escaped from there. Sarah was like a mother and a father. In fact, I believe my parents arranged to send her with me, when they knew the pox had taken them. She was my teacher and my friend at the abbey. The monks endured her presence only because it was stipulated by the money my parents left for my upkeep. She taught me how to read and write—"

Sir William shook his head in the postured amazement such a statement required. "Latin?"

"And French," Thomas confirmed. He said nothing about the necessity of reading the books in a chest hidden in a faraway valley. "Sarah said it was the language of the nobles and that I would need it when . . ."

"When?"

"When I took over as lord of Magnus."

"You sound so certain," Sir William said. "What right have you to take this manor and castle by force?"

"The same right," Thomas said, suddenly cold with anger, "that the present lord had when he took it from Sarah's parents."

During the next half hour of walking, Thomas repeatedly asked one question to break the noise of the wind across the heather. "Where is Magnus?"

The knight remained in front, seeing no need to answer. The girl still trailed them. Only Tiny John showed enthusiasm, as if they were on an adventure.

"Let me get on the man's shoulders!" Tiny John finally piped. "I'll get a good see from there."

Sir William groaned. "I feel like enough of a packhorse without my steed." A cloud of anger passed his face. "First to be arrested falsely for a chalice I didn't steal, and then to lose my horse and armor to those scoundrels . . ."

The knight sighed. "Tiny John, get on my shoulders, then. Without taking a farthing from my pockets. I've had enough trouble with you already."

Tiny John only widened his eternal grin and waved a locket and chain at Sir William, who felt his own neck to reassure himself that it was not his.

"It's the girl's," Thomas said. "Tiny John took it from her this morning. I don't have the heart to make him give it back yet. And she hasn't noticed anything all day."

Sir William kept his face straight. *The only reason Thomas saw the theft is because he spends so much time glancing at the girl*, he thought. *It is almost as if she has riveted his heart, and without a word between them.*

Tiny John tossed the locket to the knight. Sir William glanced at it idly, then felt as if a hand had been wrapped around his throat. *The symbol! The locket shows the symbol!*

Sir William knew now who had been sent to spy. The question remained—was she a partner with Thomas? Or was he ignorant of the danger?

"A peculiar cross emblem," Sir William mumbled as thoughts raced through his mind. He too had learned acting skills. "Nothing I've seen before."

Tiny John did not give him the time to finish wondering. He darted to the knight's back, then scrambled up the broad shoulders and shaded his eyes with his left hand to peer northeast into the widening valley.

Tiny John whistled. "I've caught the spires! Far, far off! But we can make it by eventide."

"Only if I carry you, urchin," Sir William grunted. "And already you're far too heavy for a knight as old as I."

Tiny John dropped to the ground lightly and kept pointing. "That way, Thomas!" he said. "I'm sure I saw the castle that way!"

Sir William glanced at the girl, still several hundred yards back. "Rejoin our silent friend," he told Tiny John as he handed him the thin chain and locket. "Return this to her. Yet do not let her know that it was on my instructions or that I have seen it." The knight thought quickly. "It will appear to her that you have honor, you scoundrel. Then, Tiny John, keep pace! We will do our best to reach Magnus before nightfall."

With the easy downhill walk, it took them less than four hours to reach the final crest which overlooked the castle of Magnus. They paused, not in need of rest, but to comprehend Magnus as it stretched out before them.

"All saints preserve us," breathed Sir William in awe, as if he had never seen Magnus before. "Our mission is surely one of suicide."

Even Thomas faltered. "I have been told the army is not large."

Sir William laughed a strained whisper. "Why maintain an army when you have a fortress like that?" He spread out his arms to indicate the situation. "From afar, I wondered about the wisdom of a castle which did not take advantage of height to survey the valley. Now I understand. A force as large as a thousand might be useless in attack against Magnus."

The valley around Magnus differed little from those they had been seeing for the previous three days. The hills were steeper, perhaps, but the grass and woods in the valley bottom were equally rich, and dotted with sheep and cattle.

But there were two differences. There were no farmers' huts anywhere in the valley, and there was water. Magnus stood on an island in the center of a small lake. High, thick, stone walls ringed the entire island and protected the village inside.

The keep of the castle, home of the reigning lord of Magnus, rose high above the walls, but safely inside and away from the reach of even the strongest catapults.

At the north end, a narrow finger of land approached the island. Just before the castle walls, however, it was broken by a drawbridge no wider than a horse's cart. Even if an army managed to reach the lowered drawbridge, soldiers could only advance three or four abreast—easy targets for the archers on the walls above.

Water, of course, was available in almost infinite amounts to those behind the wall. Lack of food, then, might be the castle's weak point, because siege was obviously the only way to attack

Magnus. With the foresight to store dry foods, however, the reigning lord of Magnus would never suffer defeat.

For several minutes, Thomas could only stare at his impossible task. He forced himself to remember and believe the plan given him by Sarah.

He hoped the doubt in his heart would not reach his words. "If it is so obvious to a military man like you that a host of armies cannot take Magnus by force from the outside," Thomas said, "then the way it must be conquered is from the inside."

Although Sir William told himself not to sigh, he did anyway. "That's like saying the only way to fly is to remain in the air." He frowned at Thomas. "Of course, it must be conquered from the inside. That's the only way to conquer any castle. Our first question is how to get an army. Then we can wonder how to get that army inside."

Thomas ignored him. "There is something wonderful about a castle this impossible to overcome. Once we have it"—Thomas smiled—"it will be that much easier to keep."

He marched forward.

After hiding the bundle he had carried for three days, Thomas returned to the others near the north end of the lake.

"I think," Sir William said in greeting, "it would serve us well to conceal any signs of my trade. The earls and lords of any land guard drastically against threats to their power."

"But against a single man? I would have thought rebellion in the form of a peasant army or a gathering of knights—"

Sir William shook his head grimly and lowered his voice. "Now is not the time to explain. Suffice it to say that serfs and peasants have so little training and so little weaponry that they are considered harmless. So harmless that one man with training or weapons can rise far above an entire village in potential for danger."

Sir William paused. "Aside from the expense of a warhorse, why do you think it is so difficult to reach the status of a knight? And why there are so few in the land? Those in power limit the number for their own safety, should the knights rebel."

On foot without lance or horse, without full armor or following squire to tend his gear, Sir William did not appear to be a knight. After the rescue at the gallows, the sheriff's men had given back to him only his chain mail and one of his swords. Sun's disappearance or not, no sheriff would dare risk an earl's displeasure by sending a knight with unknown allegiance forth into the land with full fighting gear.

He smiled a tight smile of irony. Much as he had regretted the absence of the rest of his equipment, this was one moment he did not mind to be without it.

Even without his usual full range of war gear, however, Sir William did not feel safe from notice. He knew that the guards at the gate would be trained to search for the faintest of military indications in any approaching stranger.

The chain mail covering Sir William's belly, of course, was an immediate giveaway, should it be found. Sir William drew his shirt tighter and checked for any gaps which might betray the finely worked iron mesh. To be totally risk free he should have abandoned the chain mail miles before the castle. But then he would have been as vulnerable to the thrust of a sword as a piglet before slaughter.

His own short sword, of the type favored for close combat since the time of the mighty Roman legions, hung in a scabbard tightly bound to his back between his shoulder blades. Once again, it would have been much safer to leave the sword behind, but next to impossible to find a weapon inside the castle walls. Sir William would have to risk being searched.

And he could lessen the chances of search. Sir William dropped his cloak onto the ground. He wrapped himself in it again without shaking it clean. He smudged dirt into his face and ran debris into his hair.

"Show no surprise when I become a beggar," Sir William warned. He turned to Tiny John with a glare. "Stay behind and hold the girl's hand. One word and you'll become crow bait."

Tiny John gulped and nodded.

The four of them—a full-grown man, a half-grown man, a small boy, and a slave girl—made a strange procession, as they moved from the cover of the trees to the final approach into Magnus.

"No castle is stronger than its weakest part," Sir William grumbled, as they reached the finger of land that stretched from shore to the castle island. "And generally that is the gatehouse entrance. This does not bode well for your mission."

"Expert military advice?" Thomas bantered. Almost in the shadow of the towers of Magnus, he could not be swayed from his high spirits.

Tiny John remained several steps back with the girl, head craned upward to take in the spires. His grin, unlike Thomas's, was finally dampened by those same cold shadows.

"Not advice. Sober fear," replied Sir William. "Unless a man can swim," he snorted, "which is unnatural for any but a fish, the lake is impossibly wide."

"Nobody *swims* across," Thomas argued. "That's why the drawbridge."

"Not swimming *toward* the castle. *Away*. Defenders often force attackers into the water. Those steep banks make it impossible for a man to get out again." Sir William shuddered. "Especially one weighed down with the iron of armor."

Sir William pointed farther. "Worse. This road is the only approach to the monster castle, and I've never seen a barbican which stretches an entire arrow's flight from the drawbridge to the gatehouse. And nearly straight up!"

Lined with small stone towers on each side—small only in comparison to the twin towers of the gatehouse itself—thick walls guarded a steep approach to the castle entry.

"If this gives a hint of the defenses, I can only guess at the treacherousness of the gatehouse itself," Sir William said. He opened his mouth to say something, then paused as a new thought struck.

"Not even Vespers, the sixth hour past noon. Yet this road is as quiet as if it were already dusk. No passersby. No farmers returning from the fields. No craftsmen to or fro. What magic keeps this castle road so quiet?"

"What does it matter?" Thomas shrugged. "All we need to do is get within the walls as passing strangers seeking a night's rest. From there, we shall find the weakness of Magnus and complete my plan."

"Don't be a blind fool," snapped Sir William. "I am bound to you by a vow, but I will not follow you to a certain death. Lords of manors like this have power and wealth beyond your imagination. You think there is no reason he has remained lord since taking it? Inside those walls are soldiers to jump at his every whim. It is a rule of nature that when men have power, they use it to keep it."

"Sir William," Thomas said, unperturbed by the knight's sudden anger, "not once have I given you an indication that I expected you to fight any soldiers. I simply need your military knowledge." He thought of his books, hidden safely three days to the southwest. "With you as adviser, I have ways of using my own powers. . . ."

Sir William checked his objections. For a moment, his military background had caused him to forget his true purpose for remaining with Thomas.

"We shall proceed to the gatehouse," Sir William said. "But slowly. I do not like this situation at all."

As they began the journey across the narrow finger of land to the drawbridge, Sir William began to drag one foot, and he worked enough spit into his mouth so that it drooled from his chin.

A latticed wall of wood meshed with iron bars hung headhigh above the first opening past the drawbridge. Each iron bar ended in a gleaming spike.

"Not good," Sir William whispered. "Someone cares enough to maintain those spikes in deadly order. An indication of how serious they are about security." He motioned his head briefly at the shadows of two men standing against the sunlight at the next gate, at the end of the stone corridor that ran between the portals. "All those soldiers beyond need to do is to release a lever, and those spikes crash down upon us like hammers of the gods."

Thomas held his breath. The gate remained in place as they passed beneath.

Sir William maintained his whispered commentary as he leaned heavily on Thomas. "Look above and beside. Those slots in the stone are called murder holes. They are designed for spear thrusts, crossbow arrows, or boiling liquids from hidden passages on the other side."

Thomas tried not to wince.

With his dragging foot, the knight tapped a plank as wide as two men, imbedded in the stone floor. "It drops to a chute, I'm sure, straight to the dungeon."

The knight took two more slow and weary steps, then paused as if for rest, just before earshot of the two guards. He spoke clearly and softly from the side of his mouth in the dark corridor as he wiped his face of pretended fatigue.

"Thomas, the outside defenses of this castle are as fiendish and clever as I've seen. It does not bode well for any man's chances on the inside." Sir William hesitated. "You may still turn back with honor. And live."

Thomas felt very young as he stared at the broad shoulders of the first soldier at the gate.

Night after night, on the straw bed in the darkness of the abbey, his dreams of glory had seemed so easy. Now, in the harshness of the sunlight and the dust and the noise of the village beyond the stone-faced soldiers, it seemed impossible.

The guards blocked a narrow entrance cut into the large gate. Dressed in brown, with a wide slash of red cloth draped across their massive chests, they stood as straight and tall as the thick spears they balanced beside them.

"Greetings to you," Sir William said in a hopeful, almost begging tone.

The guards barely grunted.

Thomas forced himself to look away from the cold eyes of the soldiers. They were so fierce, so dominating.

Suddenly, the guard on the right whirled and tossed his spear sideways at Sir William!

"Unnnggghh," the knight said weakly. He brought his left hand up in an instinctive and feeble motion to block the spear that clattered across his chest. The effort knocked him back, and Sir William sagged to his knees.

"I beg of you," he moaned, as spit dribbled from the side of his mouth. "Show mercy."

The soldier stood over him and studied the dirty cloak as Sir William cowered.

Even as Thomas held his breath in worry, a thought nudged the back of his mind. A thought written by the greatest general of a faraway land who had lived and fought more than fourteen centuries earlier. *One who wishes to appear to be weak in order to make his enemy arrogant must be extremely strong. Only then can he feign weakness.*

For his unlettered knight to know such wisdom by instinct was truly more amazing than the cowardice he feigned.

Thomas grinned inside, feeling a fraction more confident.

Finally, the soldier sneered downward at Sir William. "Mercy, indeed. It's obvious you need it. Get up, you craven excuse for a man."

Sir William wobbled back onto his feet. The spit on his chin showed flecks of dirt.

"Lodging for the evening, good sir," the knight pleaded. "We are not thieves, but workers seeking employment."

Sir William fumbled through his leather waist pouch and pulled free two coins. "See, we have money for lodging. We ask no charity of the lord of the manor."

The second soldier laughed cruelly. "Make sure it is cleaning and slopping you seek. Not begging as it appears."

The first soldier kicked Sir William. "Up. Get inside before we change our minds."

Sir William howled and held his thigh where the soldier's foot had made a sickening thud. He hopped and dragged his way inside the gate, without looking back to see if Thomas and the two children followed.

Thomas pushed Tiny John and the girl ahead of him.

Not until they had turned past the first building inside did Sir William stop.

Thomas did not let him speak. "Artfully done," he said quickly. "By using your left hand instead of the right when he threw the spear, you made it impossible for them to guess you are an expert swordsman."

Sir William grinned, then motioned for them to continue walking.

"I like this less and less," he said in a low voice. "When I showed those coins, I expected greed would force the soldiers to demand the normal bribe for our entry. They did not."

Thomas raised a questioning eyebrow.

"Corruption shows weakness, Thomas. We are now inside, and everything points to unconquerable strength."

CHAPTER

Thomas woke as first light nudged past the wooden crossbeams of the crude windows high on the dirty stone wall, and was surprised to discover the girl gone.

Thomas did not stop to wonder why his first waking thoughts—and glance—had turned to her. He had not spoken more than a dozen words to her over three days.

The knight could have explained with a knowing smile. At least a dozen times each day, Sir William had hidden his amusement over Thomas's blushing at eye contact with the silent girl. The knight had early decided only the girl's poor rags hindered grown men from staring at her now with unhidden admiration.

Yes, the knight had judged each time Thomas blushed, *the girl will be a woman for whom men become glad fools.* And each time Sir William had made that bittersweet judgment over the last few days, he was torn. *If Thomas makes himself a fool for her, he is not one of the enemy, but will be helpless in their claws. If Thomas is of the enemy, then little sympathy need be wasted upon him.*

Sir William's thoughts were interrupted by slight scufflings as Thomas rose to his feet.

"She's gone," Thomas blurted.

"She is, indeed," Sir William replied. *Is Thomas an actor beyond parallel? Or truly bewildered?*

"We don't even know her name. So many times I wanted to speak, yet . . . "

"It happens that way."

Silence.

I'm in Magnus, Thomas thought, *with a task that threatens my life, that will test everything I have been taught and demand that I use every power available to me. Yet my mind turns to sadness. How could that have happened simply because of . . .*

The girl pushed open the door by walking backward through it. When she turned, the bowls of steaming porridge in her hands gave reason for her method of entry.

She looked shyly at Thomas. For the first time since the gallows, she smiled.

I shall conquer the world, Thomas finished in his mind. *Lead me to the lord of Magnus.*

"The walls of Magnus contain no mean village. There must be nearly five hundred inside the walls," Sir William said. "I'm surprised it has no fame outside this county."

And I'm more alarmed, he thought anxiously, *that there was so little traffic on the road during our approach. Towns this size draw people from two and three days' travel in all directions. Has the enemy so thoroughly taken Magnus that the entire countryside is in his power?*

Thomas was too busy staring in all directions to reply. Already the clamor in Magnus was at a near frenzy.

"Fresh duck!" a toothless shopkeeper shouted, as he dangled it by the feet. "Still dripping blood! And you'll get the feathers at no charge!"

Thomas smiled politely and followed closer behind the knight. He could only trust that Tiny John and the girl would do the same.

Shops so crowded the street that the more crooked buildings actually touched roofs where they leaned into each other. Space among the bustling people between the row of shops was equally difficult to find.

Thomas scanned the buildings for identification. "Apothecary," he mumbled to himself at a colorfully painted sign displaying three gilded pills. He made a note to remember it well. The potions and herbs and medicines inside might be needed on short notice.

He mentally marked the signs of each shop.

A bush sketched in dark shades—the vintner, or wine shop. Two doors farther along, a horse's head—the harness maker. Then a unicorn—the goldsmith. A white arm with stripes—the surgeon-barber. There was a potter. A skinner. A shoemaker. A beer-seller. A baker. A butcher.

"Where is it we go?" Thomas called to the knight's broad shoulders which cleared room, step by step, in front of him.

"A stroll," Sir William said. "I have a few questions which simple observation should answer."

At the end of the first street, they turned left, then left again to follow another crooked street. It took them away from the market crowd and past narrow and tall houses squeezed tightly together.

The girl caught up to Thomas. He remembered what Sarah had taught him about manners and moved so that he walked on the outside. Thus, if a housewife emptied a tub of water or a chamberpot from the upper stories, Thomas would suffer, not the girl.

She seemed content to stay beside him, glancing over to smile whenever Thomas stared at her for too long.

In contrast, Tiny John burned with energy and scampered in circles around them, first ahead to Sir William, then back to Thomas and the girl.

"Check his pockets," Sir William said, without breaking stride. "Make sure they're empty. If that little rogue so much as picks a hair from a villager, all of us are threatened."

Tiny John stuck out his tongue at the knight, but quickly pulled his pockets open to show he'd managed to remain honest.

As they walked on, Thomas began to sniff the air with distaste. He knew they were approaching the far edge of the town—the traditional location of a tannery—because of the terrible smell of curing hides.

Thomas knew the procedure well. How many times had the monks ordered him to scrap away hair and skin from the hide of a freshly killed sheep? As many times as they had then ordered him to rub it endlessly with the normal amount of chicken dung. That, plus the fermented bran and water used to soak hides, made it a terrible task.

The street turned sharply, and they were soon back within earshot of the market.

"Stay with me," Sir William said. "We need to learn more."

Just before reaching the market area, he held up his hand. "Thomas," he said with low urgency. "Look around. What strikes you?"

Thomas had a ready reply. "The crippled beggars. The men with mutilated faces. Far more than one would expect."

The knight's eyes opened wide. "My mind was on military matters. I had not noticed. Surely the lord of Magnus hasn't . . ."

Thomas shrugged. "I have been told many stories of the evil here." And in his mind, Thomas heard Sarah singing gently, *Delivered on the wings of an angel, he shall free us from oppression.*

Sir William said, "Scan the shop signs. Tell me what's missing."

"Missing?"

Finally Thomas answered. "I see no blacksmith."

"You speak the truth. Why is that significant?"

More waiting. This time, Thomas shook his head in apology.

Sir William pursed his lips and added, "Horseshoes and hoes are not the only items a blacksmith will make."

"Swords," Thomas said after a moment. "Blacksmiths also forge swords. Without a blacksmith, there are no weapons, no armor. Whoever controls Magnus takes few chances."

"Well spoken." The knight was impressed.

Before Sir William could comment farther, a small man broke toward them from the fringes of the crowd.

His shoulders were so insignificant they were nearly invisible under his full-length brown cloak. A tight black hat only emphasized the smallness of his head. His wrinkled cheeks bunched like large walnuts as he smiled.

"Strangers!" he cackled. "So brave to visit Magnus, you are! No doubt you'll need a guide. No doubt at all!" He rubbed his hands briskly. "And I'm your man. That's the spoken truth. No doubt. The spoken truth."

Thomas made a move to step around him.

Sir William shook his head at Thomas, then addressed the small man.

"What might be your name, kind man?"

"Ho, ho. Flattery. Always wise. Indeed, you are fortunate. I am a kind man." He paused for breath from his rapid-fire words. "I am called Geoffrey."

"Hmmm. Geoffrey. You are a merchant here?"

"Indeed I am. But strangers are wise to engage a guide in Magnus. And I make a fine guide. A fine guide, indeed."

"Any man can see that." Sir William smiled. "What is it you sell when you are not a guide?"

"Candles. Big ones. Little ones. Thick ones. Skinny ones. The finest in the land. Why, the smoke from these candles will wipe from a window with hardly any—"

"Sold." Sir William jammed his single word into the pause that Geoffrey was forced to take for breath.

"Sold?" Geoffrey's confidence wavered at this unexpected surrender. "I've not shown a one. How can you say—"

"Sold," Sir William repeated firmly. He pulled a coin from his pouch. "Maybe even as many as we can carry." He peered past Geoffrey's shoulders. "Where might your shop be?"

Geoffrey opened and closed his mouth, again and again, like a fish gasping for air. He did not take his eyes away from the coin in Sir William's palm.

"My . . . my shop is away from the market. I only bring enough candles for the morning's sales. I . . ."

"Lead on, good man," Sir William said cheerfully. "It's a pitiable guide who cannot find his own shop."

"He's a blathering fool," Thomas whispered to Sir William, as soon as it was safe. "What do you want from him?"

"Certainly not candles," Sir William whispered from the side of his mouth. "I want a safe location to ask questions."

Thomas could not fault the knight his strategy. Yet, must the information come from an empty-headed babbler like this one?

Every five steps or so, Geoffrey rudely pushed people aside—despite his runtlike size. The resulting arguments proved to be a humorous distraction.

Too much of a distraction. Otherwise Thomas or Sir William might have observed the three soldiers who followed them from a stone's throw back in the crowd.

Just as Thomas began to see clearly the jumble of vats and clay pots in the dimness of the candlemaker's shop, a ghostlike bundle of dirty white cloth rose from a corner and moved toward him.

Thomas brought both of his fists up in protection, then relaxed as he noticed that the worn shoes at the base of the ghost had very human toes poking through the leather.

He backed away, and the bundle of cloth scurried past, bumping him with a solidness that no ghost could give.

"That's Katherine," Geoffrey the candlemaker said. "Daughter of the previous candlemaker. Ignore her. She's surprised because

I've returned early from the market, and she's afraid of people."

Thomas watched her shuffle past a curtain and out of sight in the back of the cramped house.

"The bandages around her head?" Sir William asked.

"It's to keep people from screaming at the sight of her. When she was little, I am told, she reached up and grabbed a pot of hot wax. It poured over her face like water. The foolish child jumped blind into the flame warming the pot. Yes, indeed. As bright as a torch she became. And with half the customers standing in your very spot. The business that was lost because of her screaming!"

The candlemaker waved his hands in dismissal. "It's a curse she did not die. I was stuck with her as part of the arrangement to take over this shop on the owner's death. Who might marry her now? And I'd get no price for her if she did, that's the truth." The candlemaker shrugged. "The will of the Lord, I suppose."

Thomas turned on him with a bitterness he did not know he possessed. "How can you say there is a God who permits this? How can you give the girl less pity than a dog?"

"Thomas." Sir William's calm rebuke drew Thomas from his sudden emotion.

"I give her a home," the candlemaker said in a hurried voice. "It's much more than any dog gets. You've seen the beggars and cripples who gather around. She could be cast loose among them."

Thomas told himself he had no right to interfere. "I ask your forgiveness," he said coldly. "For a moment, her situation reminded me of someone I once knew."

Thomas did not explain that he meant himself. His heart cried for the pain he knew Katherine suffered, yet his brain sadly told him there was no use in caring. The candlemaker was right. In this town alone, there were dozens of beggars and cripples who had less than Katherine.

Thomas added silently to himself, *Such evidence of pain is all the more reason to be angry at this God the false monks so often proclaimed.*

Thomas spoke to move from the subject. "We came for candles."

Relief brightened the candlemaker's face. "Yes. I'll bring my finest."

He clapped his hands twice.

Immediately Katherine appeared with a wooden box.

"She must earn her keep," Geoffrey said defensively, as he glanced at Thomas.

"I'll take the entire box," Sir William said. "You've made mention this is not a town for strangers."

"These are my best candles," Geoffrey said. "I'm surprised you don't know the reputation of Magnus."

Sir William wanted Thomas to believe he knew little about Magnus, and he chose to barter as a way of showing a need for local knowledge.

"Perhaps these are the best candles you have. But compared to London . . ." Sir William shook his head. "In London, the name Magnus stirs no fear into the hearts of good citizens."

"I've not been to London," Geoffrey said, as wistfulness momentarily sidetracked him. "Few of us ever leave Magnus."

He coughed quickly to hide embarrassment at his ignorance, then grabbed the box from Katherine and shook his head as she cowered and waited for instructions.

Thomas felt a comforting hand on his shoulder, even as he winced to see Katherine's fear. The mute girl had seen the pain on his face and moved beside him. Tiny John also seemed subdued at the horror of Katherine's primitive mask. The wrap around Katherine's head was stained with age, almost caked black around the hole slashed for her mouth.

Tiny John clung to the edges of the mute girl's dress. The three companions stayed in a tight cluster, and Thomas felt a great sadness to know their instinctive joining resulted from the status of outcast they all shared.

"I apprenticed from the best master for miles around. I don't need to see London candles to know these burn as bright as any in the land," Geoffrey said, as he forced his voice back to a bartering tone. "And I don't need to see London to know the reputation of Magnus."

"A farthing each dozen," Sir William offered. "And hang this reputation at which you hint of this place."

"Two farthings and no lower," Geoffrey countered. "And strangers as good as you have said less about Magnus and died for it."

Thomas gave the conversation full attention.

"Two farthings for a dozen and a half." Sir William lowered his voice. "And who might be doing the killing?"

Geoffrey shook his head and held out his hand. "The color of your money first. This box holds three dozen candles."

"Four farthings, then. You drive a hard bargain." Sir William counted the coins. "About this fearsome domain . . ."

Even in the dimness, Thomas could see the eager glint of a born gossip in the candlemaker's eyes.

"A fearsome domain, indeed," Geoffrey said. He looked around him, even though he knew every inch of his own shop. "Ever since Richard Mewburn disposed of the proper lord."

"Surely the earl of York would not permit within his realm such an unlawful occurrence as murder."

"Bah." A wave of pudgy fingers. "That happened twenty years ago. Ever since, murder is the least of crimes here in Magnus. The slightest of crimes results in hideous punishment . . . men with their ankles crushed for failing to bow to Richard's sheriff . . . faces branded for holding back crops, even though the poor are taxed almost to starvation."

Geoffrey lowered his voice. "The earl of York is paid rich tribute to stay away. It is whispered that some evil blackmail prevented his father from dispensing justice after Magnus was taken from the rightful earl. A blackmail that still holds his son long after his own death from—"

Katherine gasped. She had not moved since delivering the candles. The first sound of her voice, eerie and muffled from behind the swath of dirty rags around her head, startled Thomas.

"You cannot reveal this to strangers," she protested. "It is enough to sentence them to death!"

Geoffrey brought his hand up quickly, as if to strike the girl.

She stepped back quickly and bumped a table. Two clay candle molds teetered, then fell to the ground and smashed into dust.

"Clumsy wretch!" the candlemaker snarled. He grabbed a thin willow stick from the table beside him and whipped it across the side of her head.

Had Thomas paused to think, he would have decided it was her complete acceptance of the cruel pain that drove him to action. She did not cry, merely bowed her head and waited for the next blow.

Holy rage burst inside Thomas. As the candlemaker raised his arm to strike again, Thomas roared and dived across the narrow space between them. He crashed full force into the candlemaker. Both fell with the blow. Before the candlemaker could react, Thomas pounced on his chest. He pulled the man's head inches form the floor and held it. His arms shook as he fought an overpowering urge to dash the candlemaker's head in one savage motion.

"Foul horrid creature," ground Thomas between clenched teeth. "You shall pay dearly for the abuse—"

He did not finish his threat.

Sir William pulled him upward, and during that motion, soldiers burst into the shop.

Had not Sir William been so helpless with both his arms around Thomas, he might have been able to reach between his shoulder blades and pull the sword free.

Instead, less than a second later, three soldiers had him pinned to the wall.

Two other soldiers grabbed Thomas.

"You hail from the abbey at Harland Moor," the soldier said. It was not a question. "Four monks have been found dead there. One by a blow to the head. Three by poisoning."

The soldier grinned evilly. "You and your large companion here will hang. You for murder. Your companion for aiding a murderer in escape."

CHAPTER

8

Katherine hated crowds. She hated the mockery and taunting of children. She hated the unexpected jostling; the small holes left for her eyes gave her little vision except straight ahead, and most sounds which reached her were muffled and displaced.

So she walked with hesitation through the marketplace, holding her basket as close to her side as possible, and hoped Hawkwood might find her soon.

"Fresh bread! Fresh bread!"

Katherine turned her head to seek the source of the cries. These were not loud enough and insistent enough that . . .

No. This seller of bread was a man with only one arm. The other arm, ending at his elbow, tucked a long loaf of bread against his ribs. Hawkwood was a master of altered appearances, but even he could not give the illusion of a stumped arm.

"Potions! Healing potions! Love potions!"

Katherine turned her head in the opposite direction. It was an old woman, face half hidden in the shadows of a bonnet, leaning over a rough table covered with dried herbs.

Inside her bandages, Katherine smiled. Hawkwood would enjoy the irony of posing as someone with knowledge of herbs and potions.

Katherine moved closer to the old woman and pretended to scan the table as the old woman screamed again, to be heard above the din. "Healing potions! Love potions!"

Katherine waited. Would Hawkwood give her the phrase?

"Scat, girl," the old woman hissed. "You'll turn others away. I've nothing to restore a face like yours."

Still Katherine hesitated. There might be someone standing behind her, forcing Hawkwood to react thus.

"Scat! Scat!" The woman's voice rose to a strained screech. "No love potion would earn you even a blind fool!"

Katherine backed away. Why did people who were weak and hurt take satisfaction in showing cruelty to those even weaker?

Something bumped her ankle.

It was awkward, bending over so far to crane her head that she might be able to see the ground through the eyeholes of her bandage.

The object at her feet was a red ball. Before she could puzzle further, a second ball, blue, rolled past the red one. Then a green ball.

"Ho, ho fair lady! A tiny farthing is all I require." A man danced in front of her, scooped the balls into his hands and began to juggle. "One farthing and laughter is yours."

Katherine shook her head. Whatever reason Hawkwood had for arranging the three lit candles at the altar of the church to wait her morning prayers, it was important enough to have summoned her forth. She could not dally, not even for a jester with a bouncy, belled hat, twinkling eyes, painted face, and ridiculous red and green tights.

The jester spun the balls in a tighter circle so that it was almost a blur. Blue, red, green. "Come, come, fair lady. The Lord loves laughter. Heaven stands open at the sound!"

Heaven stands open.

Katherine did laugh. Again, Hawkwood had managed to arrive unexpected, even as she searched for him. "One farthing then. For when heaven stands open, only fools turn away."

Hawkwood nodded, satisfied from her answer that it was indeed Katherine beneath the bandages. They both knew that should she ever be discovered, two things were certain: her death, and then someone put in her place behind the bandages, to capture Hawkwood.

"Arrange to deliver candles to Gervaise," he said in a lowered voice. "I shall be in the church when the midafternoon bells ring."

The stone walls of the church provided coolness, and as Katherine entered, she set down the cloth bag which held the candles. She pulled her clothes away from her body to enjoy the relief of that cool air against her hot and sticky skin.

"Welcome, Katherine," came a voice from the shadows of a large pillar. "I trust these candles are the same fine quality that our father priest has come to expect."

"Yes, Gervaise," she answered, as her eyes adjusted to the dimness. "Geoffrey complains, of course, that for what payment he receives, he should call the candles a contribution of charity."

Gervaise was an elderly man, gray hair combed straight back. A plain cassock covered his slight body, and he stood with his hands in front of him, folded together.

"Please, Katherine, let me help you with that bundle."

"Thank you," she said.

As he stooped to take the candles, he said, "Will you bring these to the nave? I'll set the others in storage."

Again Katherine nodded. The elaborate acting, she felt, was rarely necessary, but Hawkwood insisted on behaving as if enemy ears were always nearby and open. And, although she didn't know whether to believe him, he said the island was riddled with enough hidden passages that those ears could very well be there.

In the nave, she began to remove from the candelabra the stubs of burnt candles to replace them with new. Not for the first time did it anger her to see the fine wrought gold of the candelabra gleaming in the light which poured in through stained glass high above. How many mouths could this gold feed? How fat must the clergy become?

Something bumped her ankle and rolled over her foot. A red ball.

She smiled, a movement that scraped her skin against the tight bandages. When she turned, she saw the outline of a figure in the shadows behind the beam of light.

Wordlessly, she moved closer.

She saw Hawkwood as he usually was, an old man bent beneath a black cape. "Milord," she whispered, "fare thee well, here where heaven stands open for those who believe."

With this proof that she was behind the mask, Hawkwood relaxed. He pressed farther back, so that he stood in a recess of the wall, invisible in deep shadow. Katherine moved in front of him and bowed her head. Any unexpected visitor would see only her, deep in meditation.

"Katherine, I fare well. Magnus, however, may not."

"Milord?"

"In the candle shop, you were visited yesterday by two men, each now in the dungeons."

"Yes. They were strangely familiar."

Hawkwood wanted to smile. Strangely familiar, indeed. Later, if they lived, he would explain, for to tell her now, with their fate uncertain, was far too cruel.

Instead of smiling, he nodded. "The older is one of us."

Katherine drew in a startled breath.

"The other," Hawkwood continued, "is one I had hoped long ago might take Magnus from the enemy."

"Then if we release them from the dungeon . . ." Katherine began.

"We must, yet the knight is well known to them," Hawkwood said. "He fought hard when Magnus fell, and he was barely able to escape with his life. We must find a way to let them escape without revealing how we have hidden ourselves in Magnus all these years."

"If he is well known to them, why did he return to certain death?"

"Because of the other," Hawkwood replied. He took a moment to gather his thoughts. Katherine did not interrupt.

"We play a terrible cat-and-mouse game with the enemy," he said with a grim smile. "And we are the mouse. They know, as do we, the knight's purpose here. They can afford to let him live while the rest of the game is played. What we do not know is the heart of the other, Thomas."

"Thomas? He is a good man," Katherine said quickly.

Again Hawkwood smiled. This time less grimly. Her defense had been too quick.

"Katherine," he said gently, "do not let his countenance sway you."

She stiffened. "Hardly. Do I forsake what little teaching I have received?"

"My apologies," Hawkwood said.

"He defended me," she said. "A man comely enough that he could chose among maidens fought for a freak behind bandages. What says that of his heart?"

"Would that I could believe it," Hawkwood said. "For in this game, none could suspect that you are of us. Thomas, then, had no other reason to defend you than for what lay in his heart."

"He too is part of this terrible game?"

"Yes, Katherine. As you were hidden here since childhood, so was Thomas hidden in an abbey several days away. He was to be taught in our ways, and given the plan to take Magnus."

"Was?" Katherine said.

Hawkwood smiled at her. She was bright. In happier times, she would already be the best of a new generation.

"Was." he repeated. "The one who was to teach him died. We do not know what happened in the years since. He appeared at the gallows to rescue the knight, and I fear he was sent by our enemy in hopes that we would trust him completely."

"Yet," Katherine said, "he may not be the enemy."

"Is it hope that you express?"

She said nothing.

"Yes, Katherine, he may not be the enemy. And if he acts on his own, he needs our help until we are certain he can be trusted."

"If he acts on his own, he knows nothing of us, or of them," she protested. "It is like sending a sheep into battle against ravenous wolves."

"This too I have considered," Hawkwood said. "Yet, who shall we risk to deliver the knowledge? For the enemy still searches, and if Thomas is one of them, the deliverer is doomed. We are so few that we can spare none."

Katherine sighed. "Yes, milord."

"However," Hawkwood said, "it does not mean we shall abandon him or the knight completely. It is fortunate indeed that Thomas defended you as he did."

"Milord?"

"You now have ample reason to befriend him."

CHAPTER

9

J ailer!" Sir William shouted at the rusted iron door in frustration. "Two days have passed. Surely the lord of this manor must appear to us soon!"

"Shhhhh!" hissed a man hunched in the corner of the cell.

Thomas shrugged and grinned. The man had not spoken since they had been flung into jail.

What light appeared in the cell came from oily torches outside the grated opening in the door. It took Thomas two large steps to reach from side to side of the clammy stone walls, three steps to reach front and back. It was so cramped that had the fetters on the walls been used, one of his wrists could be on either side. Yet there were three of them in this small space, sharing the bedding of trampled straw that soaked up the wet dungeon filth.

Sir William continued, "If we are able to meet the lord of this manor—although I am prepared to believe he is a myth—we can present our case. He will see there is no injustice in the fate of those monks and then release us."

"I regret not sending that letter to the mother abbey at Rievaulx," Thomas said almost absently, as he scratched at a fleabite. "We might have been spared this."

Sir William did not have to ask which letter. In the two endless days of darkness and solitude, interrupted only by the bowls of porridge shoved between the bars of the grate twice daily, he had learned of Thomas's final day at the abbey, including the letter of evidence against the monks.

"How often must I tell you?" Sir William said with gentleness. "They are dead. It makes no difference to our fate how little virtue the monks had. Unless the lord of Magnus learns who truly did poison them, we will hang. He must appear to accuse us so that we can defend ourselves. There is justice in that the monks poisoned themselves."

Thomas smiled, but without much feeling. It gave him little consolation that he had guessed right in his final hour at the abbey.

Quit your blathering, Brother Walter had said between clenched teeth. *Send the boy on his way. Now!*

Brother Philip had clamped his jaw as if coming to a decision. *Not to his death. Nor shall I meet God without attempting some good. Thomas. Leave alone the—*

Leave alone the food, Thomas had realized, as Brother Philip died. It could be nothing else. The monks knew Thomas would immediately retrieve the letter of condemnation upon leaving the abbey. By inserting a slow-acting poison into his requested provision, he would die later and never reveal their crimes.

For that reason, his last act at the abbey had been to replace the food among the other provisions in the kitchen storeroom. If his guess was correct, he would let the monks bring punishment upon themselves. How could he have known the act would send him to the dungeon?

"The lord of Magnus will never appear," crowed the man in the corner.

"Ho, ho! After two days, the man of silence speaks," Sir William observed. "Have you tired of your scavenging friends?"

"My good fellow, in my time here I have seen many like you come, then go to the hangman," the man said. "I have learned not to befriend any. It proves too disappointing."

He gestured at the corner hole. "These furry creatures which make their visits, however, are not so fickle. They require little food, and their gratitude is quite rewarding. And they always return."

Thomas shuddered. He hoped he would not remain so long in the cell that rats would be more attractive than human company. Not when he had the means to conquer Magnus. If only he could escape! All it would take was one clear night and . . .

"The lord of Magnus will never appear?" Thomas prompted.

The man did not rise from his squatting position. He merely swiveled on the balls of his feet to face them.

"Never. It is obvious you know nothing of Magnus."

His cheeks were rounded like those of a stuffed chipmunk. His ears were thick and flappy. Shaggy hair fell from the back of his head to well below his shoulders; his patched clothing was as filthy as the straw which clung to his matted chest hair.

"It is time to introduce myself," he said, with a lopsided grin that showed strong teeth. "My name is Waleran."

He stood, shuffled forward, and extended his empty right hand in the traditional clasp that symbolized a lack of weapons.

"Generally, I do not speak to other prisoners," Waleran said, after Sir William and Thomas had shaken hands with him. "Most arrive alone and learn to ignore me after several days. With two of you, however, the constant talking has given me little peace. I am driven to break my silence."

"Two days of waiting shows remarkable patience," Sir William said.

Waleran shrugged. "I have been here ten years. Time means nothing."

"Ten years!" Thomas examined him again. Although pale, Waleran seemed in good health.

"You wonder what crime sends a man here?" Waleran replied to the frank stare. "Simply the crime of being a villager in Magnus. My son, you see, went to the fields outside the castle one harvest day. Instead of threshing grain, he departed. London, perhaps. I am held here as an example."

Sir William frowned. "How are you an example?"

"To the other families in Magnus. As long as I am here, they know the lord is serious in his edict. No man, woman, or child may leave the village, except to work in the fields and return before nightfall."

"That's monstrous!"

Waleran smiled wanly at Thomas. "Indeed. But who is to defy the lord?"

Sir William began pacing the cell. "It is a strange manor, this Magnus. The lord murders its rightful owner, yet the earl of York does not interfere. Entire families are kept virtual prisoners inside the castle walls, yet the village does not resist."

"Strange, perhaps, but understandable," Waleran said quietly. "You've seen the fortifications of the castle and outside walls. The moors make it unapproachable by an army of any size. Even a man as powerful as the earl of York knows it fruitless to attack. Besides, the lord of this manor is shrewd enough to give no cause for the earl's anger."

Sir William raised an eyebrow.

Now that Waleran had decided to talk, it seemed as if a flood poured forth. "Because the entire village is in vassalage, this manor is extremely wealthy. The lord gives ample homage to the earl of York in the form of grain, wool, and even gold. Simple, don't you see?"

"I do see," Sir William said thoughtfully. "The earl of York is bribed not to attack a castle in his kingdom which he could not successfully overcome anyway."

"Yes, yes!" Waleran nodded quickly. "And with enough soldiers within the gates, the villagers are powerless. Those who do leave to till and harvest the fields know they must return every night, or members of their family will be placed in these very cells. Richard Mewburn may be hated by those inside Magnus, but all are helpless before him."

"What I don't see," Sir William said in the same thoughtful tones, "is why this lord has not appeared to formally accuse us. Strangers that we are, we deserve the justice which must be granted anywhere in the land."

Waleran only shook his head. He returned to his corner, found a crumb to hold above the rathole, then squatted in his former position.

Minutes passed, broken only by the never-ending drips of water onto stones not covered by straw.

Thomas could not stand it any longer. "That is all?" he cried. "You are choosing silence again?"

Waleran slowly craned his head upward. "My silence would be better for you." He sighed heavily. "I tell you with reluctance."

Sir William thought of the empty road leading into Magnus. Strong premonition told him he did not want to hear the next words.

"Magnus has around it black silence," Waleran said. "Traders and craftsmen learned long ago that they risked freedom and all they owned to visit. Whispers of death keep them away. And for good reason."

Waleran looked back to the hole and spoke as if addressing the wall. "Had there not been convenient charges against you, you would still have found yourselves within this dungeon. There are dark secrets in Magnus. Secrets only hinted even to villagers. Secrets which must remain hidden from the entire land."

He paused, and the deadness in his voice spoke chilling truth. "Once inside these walls, strangers are never permitted to leave."

Thomas rolled into a sitting position and wiped straw from his face. *Fear and worry must be exhausting me*, he decided. *The nights pass without dreams. And how is a person to mark the passage of time in this dark hole? No bells to mark the church offices, no sun to mark dawn or nightfall.*

In the dull flickering of torches, Thomas could see that Waleran lay huddled motionless on one side of the cell; Sir William snored gently in his corner. Neither hidden sword nor concealed chain mail seemed to hinder his sleep.

Thomas concentrated on a routine to delay his restlessness. Any thoughts other than questions tortured him with reminders of his helplessness. *My bundle lies outside the castle walls and is capable of winning me a kingdom; yet I am trapped with no hope of leaving.*

So Thomas plucked from his mind the first of many well-worn questions, determined to gnaw it yet again, like an animal searching for the tiniest shred of undiscovered meat. In his four days of captivity, Thomas had concluded nothing new from all his questions. However, all he had was time, and the questions would not leave the cell.

Who is this knight? Thomas asked himself, as another snore reminded him of Sir William. *A man of honor, he has fulfilled his pledge by entering the castle walls of Magnus. He has become a friend, yet he speaks nothing of his past, nothing of his own quest.*

A new question suddenly entered Thomas's mind. *Can the man fight with skill?* Certainly, like any knight, he could defeat a dozen unarmed and untrained peasants. That assumption had lulled Thomas into a sense of security. But was Sir William man enough to fight boldly against other armed and trained men?

Thomas pondered the sword and uncomfortable chain mail that the knight refused to hide beneath the straw, then decided yes. Any man who would endure discomfort day and night to be constantly prepared for any brief chance at escape would be a man to have as an ally.

Thomas then moved to his next question. Tiny John, no doubt, could well find a way to survive. But was the mute girl withstanding the terrors of being alone and friendless in Magnus? It had been four days. The girl could not speak. What work would she find to sustain her? What stranger would treat her with kindness? *Or, will she simply flee Magnus and disappear from my life forever?*

Thomas smiled at his foolishness. Barring a miracle which would give him the chance to use his secret knowledge to win Magnus, he and the knight would never leave this cell for anything but death by hanging. Searching for the girl should not even be a concern.

Stubbornly, despite the only future he could see, Thomas moved to his next question. He was not dead. Yet.

Thus, the next question followed naturally, as it had every time over the last four days. Thomas closed his eyes and pictured himself in the panicked darkness in front of the scaffold.

Again and again, Thomas replayed those few minutes of terror beneath a blackened sky. The old man had known it was Thomas beneath those robes. The old man had known how Thomas had given the illusions of power. And the old man had known of his desire to win Magnus.

How did that mysterious old man know so much—even of my search? And who is he to have the power to block the sun?

Thomas attacked that problem with such intensity that Sir William had to clap hands to get his attention.

"Thomas, you scowl as if we have lost all hope."

Thomas blinked himself free from his trance and answered the knight's easy smile.

"Never!"

In the warmth of their growing friendship, Thomas ached to confide in the knight.

There is so much to tell, Sir William. The chest of books, a source of power as great as any in the land. The gold I have concealed in the cave beside them. The means of winning Magnus. And the promise made at Sarah's deathbed never to reveal these secrets.

Sir William yawned. "My mouth is as vile as goat's dung. Even the water from this roof would be better."

With that, Sir William moved beneath one of the eternal drips and opened his mouth wide. After several patient minutes of collecting water, he rinsed and spat into a far corner of the cell.

Waleran unfolded from his motionless huddle as the door to the cell rattled.

"A visitor," droned the jailer.

"Impossible," Waleran said. "Not once in ten years has a visitor been permitted to—"

The door lurched open, and the jailer's hand appeared briefly as he pushed a stumbling figure inside.

Thomas tried not to stare.

Caked and dirty bandages still suggested mutilated horror. A downcast head and dropped shoulders still projected fear. *Katherine.*

"Who is this wretched creature?" Waleran demanded.

Again it hit him, the instant fury that someone so defenseless might suffer insults. Thomas spun, shoved his palm into Waleran's chest, and drove him backward into the filth.

"Another word and you shall pay—" Thomas began in a low tight voice.

Sir William stepped between the two. "Thomas . . . "

Thomas sucked air between gritted teeth to calm himself as Waleran scrambled backward into his corner.

"Please do not hurt him," Katherine said clearly. "To be called 'wretched creature' is an insult only if I choose to believe it."

Thomas turned to her. She stood waiting, hands behind her back. She was only slightly shorter than he. Her voice, still muffled by the swath bandages, had a low sweetness.

"I beg of you pardon," Thomas said, It pained him to look at her. Not because she was a freak, but because he remembered his own pain and loneliness. It tore at his heart to imagine how much worse was her private agony.

"How is it you are allowed to visit?" Sir William asked.

Katherine's head nodded downward in shyness. "Every day since your capture, I have brought hot meals to the captain of the guards. I have washed his laundry, cleaned his rooms."

"Bribery!" Sir William laughed. "But why?"

Katherine took a small basket from behind her back. "Because of the candle shop. Not once has a person defended me as you did," she answered. "Prisoners here do not fare well. I wished to comfort you."

She pulled back the cloth which covered the basket.

Juices flowed in his mouth as Thomas smelled cooked chicken. Bread. Apples. Chicken. Cheese.

"These luxuries are more than you can afford," Thomas protested.

She ignored him and offered the basket, holding it in front of her until finally he accepted.

"I have a little time," Katherine said. "If it pleases you, Thomas, I wish to speak alone."

"You know my name," Thomas said, as he handed the basket to Sir William.

"Your friend, Tiny John, told me."

Sir William retreated with the basket to a corner to give them privacy.

"Tiny John! He is well?"

"As long as he continues to avoid the soldiers. Many of the shopkeepers take delight in helping that rascal. They like to see the soldiers made fools of."

Thomas pictured Tiny John darting from hiding spot to hiding spot, never losing his grin of happiness.

"And the girl?"

Katherine caught the worry in his voice. She drew a quick breath and turned her head away as she spoke. "The girl truly is beautiful. And you are very handsome. I understand your concern." Katherine faced him squarely again, but her voice trembled. "She has disappeared. But if you ask, I shall inquire for you and search until she is found."

Thomas silently cursed himself. How little affection must be in this poor girl's life if a few moments of kindness from a passing stranger kindles the devotion she now shows. Here she stands, offering gifts she cannot afford, while the passing stranger betrays an obvious concern for another with the beauty she will never have. Thoughtless cruelty.

"No. Please do not look for her," Thomas finally croaked his answer. He blocked thoughts of the mute girl and measured his words carefully. "We might ask instead that you honor us with another visit."

The squaring of her shoulders told him he had answered rightly.

Besides, he consoled himself, *even if Katherine found the mute girl, what good would it accomplish?*

The jailer rapped on the door. "Be quick about leaving."

"Tomorrow," Katherine whispered, "we shall talk of escape."

Thomas woke to the familiar sour taste of heavy sleep. He did not move for several minutes; instead, he stared at the ceiling of the dungeon cell and watched the water drops.

Katherine's visits during the past week had helped to pass the time and to give some hope, but never enough. In her absence, he faced his never-ending questions.

Who is the knight, and can he be trusted with all secrets? Is the mute girl nearby? Who is the old man? And the most pressing question . . . *With Katherine's help, will our plan for escape succeed?*

The water dripped, uncaring about the fate of humans beneath. *Water.* Thomas swallowed and licked dry lips. *Water.* He swallowed the sour taste of sleep again, this time thoughtfully. *Water.* A new realization startled him into sitting bolt upright.

He ran idea after idea through his mind. Much later, he spoke.

"Escape!" he whispered hoarsely.

Sir William muttered from a deep sleep.

"Escape!" Thomas tried again.

Waleran stirred and groaned as he woke. "What's that you say?"

Thomas grinned at Waleran in response, then stepped across the dungeon cell and shook the knight.

"Escape!" He looked over to Waleran. "Yes! I said escape!"

"Back to sleep, you crazed puppy," Sir William said with a thick tongue.

"No. I cannot." Thomas grinned at Waleran, then at the knight.

"I have decided many things," Thomas said. "One is this." He paused and took a deep breath. "Sir William, I have been wrong not to trust you fully. When you threatened my life in the forest, I did not have with me—as you believed—a king's ransom in gold. It was, instead, buried in a safe place. I tell you this now, so that you will trust me completely. I need that trust to ensure that our escape plans will not fail."

Sir William nodded.

"The escape is planned for seven days from now. Katherine, as you have noticed, spends much time in conversation with me. She has received instructions that will let her retrieve some of that gold and bribe the captain of the guards to leave the door unlocked as she leaves."

Thomas paused. "We will need on that day the excellence of a knight who can fight as no other."

Sir William warned Thomas with a glance. "Where do we find such a knight?"

"Trust me." Thomas added urgency to his voice. "Listen, you should know the remainder of the gold is buried directly beneath the gallows rope that nearly hung you outside the village of Helmsley."

Thomas looked the knight squarely in the eyes. "Having revealed my secrets thus, I need from you a demonstration of skill."

"You have me thoroughly puzzled, Thomas." Sir William added his own urgency. *Does Thomas not remember the importance of concealing my fighting profession?* "I have no skills to demonstrate."

"Your sword." Thomas ignored the warning in Sir William's voice. "You have my secret now. I wish to see from you what manner of fighter you might be."

Sir William frowned again and gave another quick shake of his head in the direction of Waleran.

Thomas laughed. "Let Waleran witness this. He too will escape with us if he pleases."

"I have no sword," Sir William hissed between gritted teeth.

"Come, come," Thomas laughed. "Such modesty."

Thomas grinned again at Waleran. "He is a knight."

Waleran's jaw dropped. So did Sir William's.

"Yes. A knight!" Thomas said. "And his fighting skills will lead us to safety."

Thomas gestured impatiently at Sir William. "Please. Impress us with your swordplay."

"You are a fool," Sir William growled. He lurched to his feet and wiped sleep from his eyes. "However, if you insist on playing this game. . . . "

He yawned and shook himself awake. "The basket that Katherine delivered," he said, pointing. "Take from it an apple."

Thomas did as instructed. As Sir William waited, he loosened his shirt, but did not remove it, or the sword.

"Throw it to Waleran," Sir William instructed, from his position halfway between the two.

Thomas shrugged. "As you wish."

He tossed it underhand, slowly, because the distance across the cell was so short.

In a blurring movement that Thomas could not see, Sir William did the impossible. He snapped his hand back and over his shoulders to the sword handle hidden between his shoulder blades. In one motion, he pulled the sword free and slashed the air in front of him just as the apple passed.

"Inconceivable," Thomas breathed.

Waleran could not speak. He merely stared at the apple he had caught in both his hands.

Then Thomas recovered.

"Perhaps few are faster than you," Thomas finally joked. "But your accuracy leaves a little to be desired. That apple passed by unhindered."

"You think so." Sir William's voice had a deadliness that reflected his anger. "You insist in a childish manner on my exhibition, then attempt to mock me. Had you not my sworn pledge, I would strangle you."

He slowly replaced the sword, then spoke to Waleran. "Drop the apple."

Waleran did.

It landed on the bed of straw and fell apart. Cleanly sliced, each half of the apple wobbled to stillness in the silence that followed.

"I cannot believe in God. Not if you tell me He is a God of love," Thomas insisted in a low voice.

"Why is that, Thomas?" Katherine replied calmly.

Thomas welcomed the sound of her voice, especially since Sir William had refused to speak to him since sheathing his sword that morning. Katherine's cheerful sweetness banished the darkness of the dungeon.

Her voice was so expressive that Thomas did not need to read her face to enjoy their discussions. By now, he hardly noticed the covering of bandages around her head.

"It is hard to believe," he said, "when there is so much evidence that He does not love us." Katherine's presence gave such gentle calmness that he wanted to speak of things he had shared with no living soul since the death of his nurse, Sarah.

"Nothing in my life," he said with intensity, "shows such a God.

My parents were taken from me—killed by pestilence before I was old enough to remember them. Then Sarah, my nurse, teacher, and only friend, was gone before I was eleven years of age."

Thomas struggled to keep his fists unclenched. "Surely if this God of yours existed, He would have been there in the abbey when all human love failed me. He was not. Instead, there was only corruption by the very men pretending to serve Him."

"And outside of the abbey," he continued, "is a land where most people struggle to live day to day, servants to the very wealthy earls and lords. Beggars, cripples, disease, and death. There is nothing good in this life."

"Thomas, Thomas . . . " Katherine placed a cool hand upon his.

He shook free. "And you," he blurted with anger. "How could you be so cursed if God truly loved . . . " Then he realized what he was saying. "I'm sorry," he said softly.

"Do not trouble yourself," Katherine said. "I am accustomed to the covering of my face."

She touched her bandages lightly. "This is not a curse. It is only a burden. After all, our time on earth is so short. And God does not see my face."

She moved her hand away from her face and held it up to stop Thomas from protesting.

"Think of a magnificent carpet, Thomas. Thousands and thousands of threads, intertwined in a beautiful pattern. No single thread can comprehend the pattern. No single thread can see its purpose. Yet together, they make the glorious entirety."

She continued with controlled passion. "You and I are threads, Thomas. We cannot see God's plan for us. My scars, your loneliness, the beggars' hunger, and the paths of men in war and peace—all lead to the completion of God's design."

"How do you know this with such certainty?" Thomas almost pleaded, so sure was her voice.

"God grants you peace when you accept Him."

Thomas shook his head slowly. "I wish I could believe. When I left the abbey, I left all pretensions to knowing God. I shall not return."

His statement created a silence between them.

On the other side of the dungeon, Sir William sat in a slouched position, ignoring them. Waleran squatted in his normal position and waited with bread crumbs for the rats.

As the silence between them became uncomfortable, Thomas decided to ask the question he had delayed from fear.

"Tiny John . . . did he succeed?"

"Yes, Thomas. I have made the arrangements."

Gratitude swept warmth across him. For the first time since entering the cell, she replaced in his heart, for a moment, the silent girl with the beautiful face and the haunting eyes.

"Then it is nearly time," he murmured. "Spread the legend among the villagers."

Katherine nodded. "When is it that you wish to escape?"

Thomas thought of the seven days he had promised Waleran.

"In six days, " Thomas said. "On the eve of the sixth day from now."

CHAPTER

10

Thomas recognized the high pitch of Tiny John's voice echoing in the dungeon hallways long before he could understand the boy's words.

Sir William stopped his silent pacing. "That's—"

"Our pickpocket friend," Thomas finished.

The knight squinted and opened his mouth to ask a question, but was interrupted by the clanging of a key in the cell door.

"Horrid fiend!" the guard shouted. "I hope they tear you into pieces!"

A bleeding hand shoved Tiny John into the cell. He tumbled but did not fall. The door slammed shut.

Tiny John surveyed his new home with his hands on his hips and grinned. "Barely nicked him, I did," Tiny John explained. "If only my teeth were bigger, I'd have bitten those fingers clean through."

Sir William shook his head in mock disgust.

Waleran moved closer, not bothering to hide a puzzled expression. "Who are you? And what did that soldier mean, 'I hope they tear you to pieces'?"

"I'm John the potter's son. Some say I'm a pickpocket, but don't believe everything you hear." Tiny John grinned. "I begged him not to throw me in this cell. Told him these two were unforgiving about some jewelry I'd lifted from them, and I'd be killed if he threw me in the same den."

Waleran scowled. "These two would kill you?"

"Of course not," Tiny John said in amazement at Waleran's stupidity. "But how else could I make sure the guard would put me with my friends?"

Waleran sighed.

Tiny John did not notice. He continued in the same cheery voice. "I'm here now, Thomas. Right at eventide as requested. 'Twas no easy task running slow enough for the soldiers to catch me. Especially with so many of my village friends trying to help me escape."

"Right at eventide as requested?" Waleran looked to Thomas for help. "He wanted to be captured?"

Thomas scratched his ear with casualness. "I promised him he would be out tonight."

"Tonight? But the escape is tomorrow!" Waleran blurted.

Thomas ignored that and placed both his hands on Tiny John's shoulders. "The villagers expect an angel?"

"Some believe. Some don't. But all wait for tonight."

"Angel?" Waleran interjected. "Tonight?"

Thomas did not remove his glance from Tiny John's face.

"And Katherine has spread word among the villagers?"

"They wait for angels," Tiny John said. "No other legend could prepare them so."

"Angels?" Waleran stamped the ground in frustration.

"Well done, Tiny John." Then Thomas faced Waleran. "Yes, angels. As one born in Magnus, you surely recall the legend?"

Waleran opened his mouth and snapped it shut.

Sir William was quick to notice.

"Thomas," he said sharply. "What is it you know about this man?"

Waleran edged away from them both.

Thomas replied with a question. "Do you think it strange that one who claims to have been in this cell ten years remains so strong and healthy?"

"The rats," Waleran said quickly. "They provide nourishment when I tire of their friendship."

"Draw your sword, please, Sir William," Thomas continued calmly. "If he opens his mouth again, remove his head. The guards must not hear him shout for help."

Almost instantly, Waleran felt the prick of a sword blade pushing the soft skin of his throat.

"Explain," Sir William told Thomas in a quiet voice. "I do not care to threaten innocent men."

"Waleran is a spy," Thomas said. "Each night as we lie in

drugged sleep, he leaves the cell and reports to his master."

"Drugged sleep?"

"Drugged sleep," Thomas repeated. He thought of the mornings he had licked his dry lips and stared at the ceiling. "I believe it is a potion placed in our water at supper."

"That explains why you asked me not to drink tonight."

Thomas nodded. "Also, these fetters. I began to wonder why we were not manacled to the walls, as is customary. But Waleran needed freedom of movement. We would have suspected if we were bound in iron and he were not."

Sir William added pressure to the sword point. "Is the accusation true? Are you a spy?"

Waleran did not reply.

"Answer enough." Sir William held his sword steady and gazed thoughtfully at Waleran. "The foul taste as I woke. The dreamless nights. How did I not suspect . . ."

"It took me some time too," Thomas said. "Do your arms tire, Sir William?"

"Of holding a sword to this scum's throat? I think not."

"Please. Let me sit," Waleran suggested nervously. His Adam's apple bobbed against the sword point. "If the sword slips . . ."

Sir William nodded. "Sit then. But so much as draw a deep breath and you shall be dead."

Waleran burrowed into the straw.

Sir William did not remove his eyes from Waleran's face. "Thomas, Tiny John said we would escape tonight. Yet nearly a week ago . . ."

"I announced it would happen tomorrow. For the same reason I wanted the demonstration of swordplay for him to see you were a knight. If he thought we trusted him completely, I could plan in safety for escape at a different time."

"You knew then that Waleran was a spy?"

"I suspected as much." Thomas glanced at the ceiling's water drip that had triggered his suspicion. "That night, I poured my water into the straw and pretended to sleep. Shortly after, he answered a soft knock on the door and departed. He returned many hours later."

"Does the lord of Magnus believe we escape tomorrow?" Sir William asked with deceptive calm. His eyes had not wavered from Waleran's face.

"You expect me to reply?"

Sir William brought his sword point up again. "These are your choices. You answer to me, and merely risk punishment from him. Or you refuse to answer to me, at the certainty of immediate death. After all, I stand to lose nothing by slaying you."

"Yes," came the quick reply. "He intends to arrest Katherine tomorrow."

"They know, of course, of the plan to bribe the guards?"

"Yes. Tonight, as you slept, he intended to remove your sword, and tomorrow to arrest Katherine."

"Where," Thomas asked, "will we find Richard Mewburn, Lord of Magnus, tonight?"

Waleran smiled. "If I tell you that, I am no longer merely risking punishment. Should you actually escape and reach him, he will know you could only have discovered that knowledge from one source. And if you don't escape, which is much more likely, then you don't need the knowledge anyway."

"Why were you placed here as a spy?" Sir William asked. Although he knew the answer, Thomas had proven himself too capable at unraveling mysteries. He did not want Thomas to suspect him at all, and he needed to continue to act as if he were merely a knight. "Why would Richard Mewburn think Thomas and I were important enough to need watching in this cell? I came in as a beggar, and Thomas as—"

"And why were you placed here ahead of our arrest?" Thomas asked, as a sudden new thought shocked him.

"Your arrival and mission were expected."

The old man at the gallows! There was no other way possible for anyone in Magnus to know! Thomas almost swayed as he fought the rush of adrenaline that swept him. *Why help me and the knight escape, only to imprison us at Magnus?*

"Tell me who foretold of our arrival!" he said, in a voice hoarsened by urgency. "And where he is now!"

Waleran shrugged. "I am simply a spy. I only know there are many dark secrets in Magnus."

Sir William lowered and rested the blade of his sword against Waleran's throat. "Explain yourself."

"That is all I will reveal. Death itself is a more attractive alternative."

Thomas felt chilled. *Dark secrets of Magnus?* Then he clamped his jaw. *The only magic in any kingdom is the power held by the lords. And if the moor winds continue to blow, morning will find me holding that power.*

"Ignore his blathering," Thomas said, as his adrenaline subsided. "Sir William, there is much I need to tell you before we leave this cell tonight."

Waleran laughed. "You still think you might leave?"

Thomas nodded at Tiny John. "Pickpockets do have their uses," he said.

Tiny John grinned and pulled from his coat a large key.

Sir William frowned. "Any moment the guard will discover it missing and return!"

"Not likely," Thomas said. "Just as Katherine instructed, Tiny John lifted it three days ago when the guard strolled through the marketplace. Katherine waited at the candle shop, then made a impression of it, so that Tiny John could return it within minutes. What you now see is a duplicate."

Sir William began to grin as widely as Tiny John, then stopped abruptly. "How do you propose we silence this spy? We have no rope. No gag. As soon as we leave the cell, he'll call for help."

Thomas smiled. "He should sleep soon. I switched cups during supper. Waleran drank the drugged water intended for me."

They encountered the first guard within ten heartbeats of easing themselves from the dungeon cell.

Startled, he stepped backward and placed a hand on the hilt of his sword.

Sir William was faster. Much faster. Before the guard could flinch, Sir William's sword point pinned his chest against the wall. The guard dropped his hand and waited.

"Run him through!" Tiny John urged.

"Spare his life," Thomas said in a voice that allowed no argument.

"Thomas, I'm not fond of killing people, believe me. Yet, this man has been trained to do the same to us. At the very least, he will sound the alarm."

In the yellow light cast by smoking torches, the man's fear was obvious by the sweat that rolled down his face.

"You have children?" Thomas asked.

The guard nodded.

"Spare him," Thomas repeated. "I would wish a fatherless life on no one."

Sir William shrugged. Then in a swift motion, he crashed his free fist into the guard's jaw. The guard groaned once, then sagged.

"We'll drag him back into our cell," Thomas instructed. Then he spoke to Tiny John through a smile that robbed his words of rebuke. "This isn't a game, you scamp. Would you care to have a sword through your chest?"

Tiny John squinted in thought. "Perhaps not."

Thomas laughed. "Get on with helping us."

Within moments, they left the guard as motionless as a sack of apples beside the snoring Waleran.

Ten minutes later, they reached the cool night air and low murmur of a village settling down at the end of evening.

Thomas smiled at the wind that tugged at his hair.

CHAPTER

11

In the early darkness outside the castle walls, Thomas forced away his fear.

Planning in the idle hours, he told himself, *is much too easy. In grand thoughts and wonderful schemes, you never consider the terror of avoiding guards on the battlements and dropping by rope into a lake filled with black water.*

He shivered in his dampness.

Katherine must be here. Or all is lost.

Sir William must rally the village people. Or all is lost.

The winds must hold. Or all is lost.

Sarah's patient voice echoed in his memory. *Cast not your thoughts toward the fears, but focus on your wishes.*

Thomas grinned in the moonlight. "I want to fly like an angel," he whispered. "Wind, carry me high and far."

As if reading his mind, the wind grew. And with it, his chill in his wet clothing.

Five more minutes, he told himself. *If Katherine doesn't appear within five minutes, then I'll call out.*

He counted to mark time as he walked. "The winds blow from the north," Katherine had said. "Once you reach the open moors, mark the highest point of the hills against the horizon and move toward it. I shall appear."

Without warning, she did.

"You have retrieved your bundle?" she whispered.

"Yes. Undisturbed. Everything remains in it."

"Then wrap this around you."

With gratitude, Thomas slipped into a rough wool blanket.

"I've also brought you dry clothing," she said.

Without thinking, Thomas drew her into the blanket, hugged her, and kissed lightly the bandage at her forehead. It surprised him as much as her, and she pulled back awkwardly.

"Please, dress quickly. Time is short."

Thomas changed his clothes with numbed fingers, and soon his skin began to glow with renewed warmth.

"When I am lord," he promised, "you shall have your heart's desire."

"You do not know my heart's desire," she whispered so softly that her words were lost in the wind.

Thomas would have not heard anyway. He was scrambling forward, searching for the sheets and wooden rods he had removed from his bundle.

"I did this as a young child to pass time after my nurse died." Thomas spoke as he worked. This far from the castle walls there was no danger of being overheard. "But I confess, it was on a smaller scale."

He tied two rods together at one end, then propped and tied a cross member halfway down, so that the large frame formed an A.

"However, I have no fear of this failing." He did, of course, but showing that fear to Katherine would not help.

"In a strange land, far away, men build these to test the gods for omens before setting sail to voyage."

"How is it you know of these things?" Katherine stood beside him, handing him string and knives and wax as requested.

Surely there is no harm in telling her? Thomas asked of his long-dead Sarah. *I will not mention the books.*

"You must vow to tell no person." Thomas waited until she nodded. "What I am building comes from the land known as Cathay."

"Cathay! That is at the end of the world!"

Thomas nodded. His hands remained in constant motion. He tested the frame. Satisfied, he moved it to a sheet of cloth, spread flat across the grass.

"It is a land with many marvels. The people there know much of science and medicine. I expect they would be called wizards here."

"'Tis wondrous strange," Katherine breathed.

Thomas nodded. "Their secrets enabled me to win the services of a knight. And now, through the legend of Magnus, a kingdom."

He knelt beside the frame. "Needle and thread."

Instantly she placed it in his hands. He began to weave the sheet to the frame. For the next hour, he concentrated on his task and did not speak.

In silence, Katherine placed more thread in his hands as required. The moonlight, bright enough to cast shadows across their work, hastened their task.

Finally, Thomas stood and arched his back to relieve the strain. He set the structure upright. The wind nearly snatched it from his hands, and he dropped it again. Satisfied, he surveyed it where it lay on the ground. As wide as a cart and as high as a doorway.

He found the loose end of the twine and tied it in the middle of the crossbar. There still remained the sewing of bonds that would attach him to the structure. And after that, the flight.

Katherine interrupted his thoughts. Her voice quavered. "You are certain the men of Cathay use such a thing?"

Thomas kept his hands busy as he replied. "There is a man in Italy named Marco Polo. He spent many years among the people of Cathay.

"This Marco Polo recorded many things. Among them, the custom of sending a man aloft in the winds before a ship sailed from shore. If the man flew, the voyage would be safe. If he did not stay in the air, the voyage was delayed."

Katherine spoke quickly. "There were times he did not stay in the air?"

"Tonight will not be one of them," Thomas vowed. "Too much has happened to bring me this far."

"Then it is God's will that you triumph," Katherine replied.

For the first time since Sarah's death, Thomas permitted a crack in his determined wall of disbelief.

"If that is indeed truth, begin a prayer," he said. "Begin it from both of us."

The winds held steady.

Will I succeed? Or will all my dreams and plans and preparations at the abbey end here with my death?

He tied leather shoulder straps to the cross members of the structure, and another leather band that would secure his legs.

Do not think of failure.

He drove a peg into the ground with the hammer Katherine had smuggled out earlier.

My death here would be of no matter. Should I fail, life will not be important to me. I will never have a chance like this again.

To the peg, he attached one end of a roll of twine, the last object from his bundle.

Do not think of failure.

He tied the other end of twine to a belt of leather around his waist. Between both ends, the remaining twine was rolled neatly on a large spool. Small knots every three feet thickened the twine.

Will the knight be inside waiting with the new army? Or has he been captured already?

Thomas looped the handles of a small, heavy bag around his neck. The cord of the bag bit fiercely into his skin and brought tears to his eyes.

Do not think of failure.

Finally, he slipped his hands into crudely sewn gloves of heavy leather.

Will the winds be strong enough? Katherine, pray hard for me.

"I will lie down on this," he said. "Attach the straps around my shoulder. That will leave me movement with my arms. When I am ready, please help me to my feet. Then stand aside. The wind should do the rest."

Moving onto his back relieved some of the pressure of the cords around his neck. Thomas fastened himself securely and took a deep breath.

You have dreamed long enough of this moment. Sarah promised you again and again that this kite was the only way into Magnus. Wait no longer.

"I am ready."

Katherine reached for his outstretched hand. She braced herself, then heaved backward. Thomas lurched to his feet with the huge structure on his back.

"Wings of an angel," Katherine breathed in awe.

The wind snatched at Thomas. He grabbed the twine where it was secured to the peg. It took all his strength to hold the ground.

"Thomas!" Katherine pointed behind him at the castle. "Soldiers! At the gate!"

He could not turn to see. That was the worst of it. He was bound to a kite that would let him see only into the wind—not where it took him, leaving him driven at a brutally high and hard castle wall which was impossible to watch during his approach.

Two hundred carefully paced steps to reach the walls. *Will that give me enough time to soar out of reach?*

The wind screamed at the sail on his back.

"Flee, Katherine! Away from the castle. Rejoin me tomorrow!"

She shook her head. "Go! God be with you!" With that, she pushed him, and a gust of wind pulled the twine through his hands.

Airborne!

The kite picked up momentum so quickly that the twine sang through his fingers. Even through heavy leather gloves, Thomas felt the heat.

The moon cast his shadow on the ground and from his height, it appeared like a huge darting bat. The soldiers below him shouted and pointed upward.

Thomas forced them from his mind and concentrated instead on counting each knot. His mind became a blur of numbers. He reached one hundred once, then began over. At eighty again, he clutched hard and the kite swooped upward even more sharply. His fingers froze.

Katherine!

While he could not see the castle wall, facing into the wind let him glance at Katherine, already far away. The same moon which cut such clear black shadows showed too clearly that the soldiers had reached her.

Why does she not flee?

Thomas understood immediately.

She protected the peg!

Katherine had grabbed one of the remaining sticks of wood to advance on the soldiers. Once the soldiers reached it, a single slash of sword would sever Thomas from the ground. She knew it. And the soldiers, if they did not know it yet, would realize it at once upon reaching the peg.

Thomas wailed. *Why did I not tell her the twine was needed only briefly?*

"Flee!" he screamed. But his words were lost to the wind.

Thomas tore his eyes from the scene below. There was nothing he could do now for Katherine except get over the castle walls on the wings of an angel. He ached to see behind him. How far was he from the castle walls? He only knew he was not high enough yet to get over the rough stone.

He willed his fingers to release the cord. Eighty-one. Eighty-two. Eighty-three . . .

A scream pierced the darkness. The soldiers had reached Katherine.

Concentrate!

At ninety-nine, he stopped the unraveling by swiftly lashing the twine around his wrist in two loops. It felt as if the sudden stop tore his hand loose. With his other hand, he fumbled with the sack at his neck and pulled free a heavy grappling hook.

It too was attached to twine, and Thomas dropped it, knowing there was ample cord attached to the sack around his neck.

Without the extra weight of the grapple, the kite bobbed upward, high enough to clear the castle wall.

At the same time, the tremendous pressure on his lashed wrist ceased.

The rope at the peg's been cut! Katherine!

"Please, God. Be with us now!" Thomas cried into the black wind.

The grappling hook hit the surface of the drawbridge and bounced upward as the wind took the kite.

Savagely, with all the anger he wanted to direct at the soldiers, Thomas wrapped his fingers around the twine which unraveled from the sack around his neck.

"Please, God. Let it hold!"

The grapple hopped upward again and clacked against the wall of the gate before spinning away.

By then, Thomas was over the walls and in sight of everyone within Magnus.

A great shout arose to meet him. Sir William had gathered the army!

Clank. The grapple's first bounce against the lower part of the walls.

Thomas held his breath.

The kite tore upward so quickly that barely any wall remained between the grapple and the night sky. If it did not catch, the wings of an angel would carry Thomas far, far away from Magnus. Without Thomas there, Sir William's army would scurry homeward. Never would Magnus be freed from . . .

Thud.

Despite all the strength he possessed, twine spun through his gloves from the sudden lurch of kite against wind as the grapple dug into the top of the castle wall.

The shout of people below him grew louder.

Thomas still did not dare look downward.

He fought the twine to a standstill, then looped it around his belt. Then and only then did he survey Magnus.

The kite hung as high as the highest tower. Suspended as it was against the moon, the people gathered below could only see the outspread wings of white. They roared, "Delivered on the wings of an angel, he shall free us from oppression!"

Thomas nearly wept with relief. He pulled his crude gloves free and tucked them among the remaining twine in the sack around his neck.

"Delivered on the wings of an angel, he shall free us from oppression!"

Thomas could see them, all armed with hoes and pitchforks, protected by rough shields of tabletops and helmets of pots. As they shouted, they pumped their hands upward in defiance.

That was the secret to conquering Magnus. Not to find a way to bring an army into it, but to form one from people already inside. One knight to lead them. One angel to inspire them.

The roar of their noise filled the sky. There were enough to pack the market space and spill into the alleys. Thomas could see no soldiers foolish enough to approach the roiling crowd.

"Delivered on the wings of an angel, he shall free us from oppression!"

The pounding of noise almost deafened Thomas. He blinked away tears of an emotion he could not understand.

It was time to return to earth.

Thomas found the knife in his inner shirt. He twisted against the shoulder straps and reached behind him.

Slash. He tore open a slit in the white cloth. Wind whistled through and the kite sagged downward. Another slash. Slowly, the kite began to drop, as its resistance to the wind lessened.

As Thomas neared the ground, he began to loosen the straps around his shoulders. Just before the kite could die completely, he released himself and cut through the twine. The kite bobbed upward as Thomas fell. He rolled with the impact and stood immediately.

The crowd, with Sir William at the front and Tiny John at his side, advanced in a wave toward him.

"Delivered on the wings of an angel, he shall free us from oppression!"

Thomas held up his right hand.

The instant silence at the front of the crowd rolled backward, as each wave of villagers took its cue from the wave in front.

Within a minute, it was quiet enough for Thomas to hear his own thudding heart. *What do I say? None of my dreams prepared me for a moment like this!*

Sir William rescued him.

"Thomas," he called. "Thomas of Magnus!"

In a great chant, the crowd took up those words. "Thomas of Magnus! Thomas of Magnus!" Like thunder, his name rolled inside the castle walls.

Then Thomas remembered. *Katherine!*

He held up his hand again.

Again, the silence sifted backward from him.

"Sir William," Thomas cried, "the gate is open with half the soldiers outside. If you take the gate now, they will be unable to return inside."

Sir William understood immediately. It took little urging for him to gather a hundred men.

"Wait!" Thomas cried again. "They have the girl Katherine. Bargain for her life."

The knight nodded briskly and moved forward. One hundred angry men followed.

Thomas closed his eyes briefly. What had he seen from his perch in the sky? Soldiers scurrying to their last retreat, the keep itself, four stories tall and unassailable.

Tonight, these villagers were an army, unified by emotion and hope. Tonight, the remaining soldiers would not fight. They knew, as did Thomas, that tomorrow, or the day after, these fierce emotions would fade.

When that happened, these villagers would no longer be a solid army, prepared to die in a fight for freedom. Then, once again a handful of trained fighters would be able to conquer and dominate seven hundred people.

The battle must be won tonight! Thomas thought hard. Then it struck him. *If the soldiers cannot be reached for us to fight them now, they must not be able to reach us later.*

Thomas cast his eyes toward the keep. Unlike the castle walls, it had not been designed for soldiers to fight downward from above. The solution, once it hit him, was obvious.

"Good people of Magnus!"

Whatever shuffling of impatience there was in the crowd stopped immediately.

"Enough blood has been shed within these walls. Enough cruel oppression. Enough pain and bitterness. Tomorrow's dawn brings a new age in Magnus!"

The roar began, "Delivered on the wings of an angel, he shall free us from oppression!"

Thomas held up his hand again. "Our captors, now captive, shall be treated with kindness!"

To this, there was low grumbling.

"Do you not remember the pain inflicted on you?" Thomas shouted. "Then do not double the sin, knowing full well the pain, to inflict it in return."

Immediate silence, then murmurings of agreement. "We have a wise and kind ruler!" a voice yelled.

"Wise and kind! Wise and kind!"

Again, Thomas requested silence. "Furthermore," he shouted, "we shall not inflict injury upon ourselves by attempting to storm the keep."

A hum of questions reached him.

"Instead," Thomas shouted, "we shall wait until the remaining army surrenders." Before he could be interrupted again, Thomas picked a large man from the front of the crowd. "You, my good man, gather two hundred. Arm yourselves with spades and shovels and meet me in front of the keep in five minutes."

He pointed at another. "You, gather fifty men and all the tar and kindling in the village."

With that, Thomas turned and strode toward the keep. He did not have to look behind him to know that hundreds followed in a large milling crowd.

A quarter-hour later, the two smaller groups joined Thomas and the main crowd in front of the keep. Not one soldier had even ventured to stick his head outside a casement.

With the arrival of all the village's men, Thomas quickly began to outline his plan. The men grasped it immediately. Many grinned in appreciation. But Thomas had no time to savor his victory.

Sir William approached him with long strides. "Our men have barricaded the remaining soldiers outside the walls," he said. "There is no sign of Katherine. Alive or dead."

Thomas beat his side once with his right fist. *This is no time to show pain or mourning*, he told himself. *Those around me must feel nothing but joy.*

He made his face appear expressionless under the bright lights of hundreds of torches.

"We cannot forsake the kingdom for one person," he told Sir William. "Not until this battle is complete shall I begin the search for her." He gave his final command. "The rest must follow me and remain as guards. We do not want to tempt the soldiers to leave the keep and fight. Enough blood has been shed within the walls of Magnus!"

CHAPTER

12

It took until noon the next day to complete Thomas's plan for bloodless warfare. When they finished, the keep had effectively been isolated from the rest of the village.

The men had dug a shallow moat around the keep, throwing the dirt to the village side as a barricade. Thomas then had the moat filled with tar and pitch and kindling. Standing guard every twelve paces were men armed with torches.

After the final barrel of pitch had oozed into the moat, Thomas called upward at the keep, "Who wishes to speak to the new lord of Magnus?" All of the village stood gathered behind him. Tomorrow or the day after they might resume normal life, if the siege dragged on. Today, however, was a day to behold. A new lord—one who had already shown wisdom and consideration— was about to dictate terms of surrender to the old lord.

A single face appeared from the third floor. "I am the captain."

Thomas said, "Not a single soldier shall die. But we will not provide food or water. You may surrender when you wish. Be warned, however. Should you decide to counterattack, the moat will impede any battle rush upon the village. And if you struggle to cross the pitch, it shall be set aflame!"

"We have heard that you deal with fairness," the captain replied.

Thomas frowned in puzzlement.

"One of our men thanks you for his life," the captain explained.

Yes. The prison guard we left with Waleran. And what has become of that spy?

"When you are prepared to surrender," Thomas instructed, "one of your men must deliver all your weapons to the edge of the moat. Then, and only then, will we build you a bridge to the safety of the village and to food and water." Thomas paused. "Your lord will also be granted his life upon surrender."

The captain said, "That will not be necessary. Nor will a prolonged siege."

"What is that you say?"

"There is a tunnel that leads to the lake. The former lord of Magnus fled with two others during the night. We wish to surrender immediately."

"Fare thee well, Thomas."

"I wish that it were not this way," Thomas replied to Sir William.

The knight smiled his ironic half smile. Beside him, his horse, a great roan stallion given from the stables of Magnus, danced and shook its mane with impatience.

"Thomas," Sir William said, "we are both men of the world. We do not *wish*. We attempt to change what we know can be changed, we accept what cannot be changed, and we always strive for the wisdom to know the difference. In this case, my departure cannot be changed."

Thomas held his head straight. He must fight the lump in his throat. "After a month in Magnus, you still dispense advice."

"Listen, puppy," the knight growled. "You may be lord of Magnus, and a good one, I might add, but you are never too old for good advice."

The new lord of Magnus squinted into the morning sun to blaze into his memory his last look at the knight. Not for the first time did he wonder from where Sir William had come. Or where he went.

"I thank you for all your good advice," Thomas said in a quiet voice. "Without it, I would have foundered."

A month earlier, within hours of forcing the soldiers to surrender, Thomas had discovered that a position as lord meant much more than simply accepting tribute. He was also administrator, sometimes judge, sometimes jailer.

Sir William had first guided Thomas through the task of selecting his army from the soldiers. Usually those who swore loyalty remained, and those who didn't were skinned alive by flogging, or worse. Thomas did not want any men pretending loyalty merely to escape death. As a result, most of the men had been eager to serve.

Day by day, Sir William had taken Thomas through his new tasks as lord. Day by day, Thomas had grown more confident and had earned the confidence of the villagers. If any of them had doubts about their new lord because of his youth, those doubts quickly disappeared.

Thomas truly was lord of Magnus. And as lord, he hid from public view his grief. Katherine had not been found. Nor was there any trace of the mute girl. Even Tiny John could not find a clue to her disappearance.

"You brood once more." Sir William's voice interrupted his thoughts. "Perhaps the time is not ready for my departure."

Thomas forced a grin. "So that I must endure more of your nagging? I think not. Be on your way, and may, may . . ."

"May *God* be with me?" Sir William teased. "At least progress has been made. You are now ready to consider Him as a friend?"

Thomas smiled tightly. He had spent much time considering Katherine's strong faith. And he could not forget that during his worst moment in the air, he had cried out to the God he thought he did not believe in.

Before the moment could become awkward, Sir William mounted his horse.

"I thank you for my life," he said with a salute. The drumming of the horse's hooves remained with Thomas all of that day.

One mile past the crest of the hill that overlooked the valley of Magnus, the knight reined his horse to a halt. He hobbled its front feet and let it find grass among the heather and gorse.

While a few hundred yards farther down there began isolated stands of trees, it was open here. Here, against the horizon, he was in plain view. And here, against the horizon, none would be able to approach him without being equally in plain view.

Hawkwood did not keep the knight waiting long. Sir William saw him first as a small black figure stepping out from the trees below, a figure that grew quickly as Hawkwood covered ground with long, vigorous strides.

"My friend," the knight called, "you wear the guise of an old man, but move as a puppy. Merlin himself would find it a performance sadly lacking."

Hawkwood shook his head and raised his voice to be heard above the moor winds. "Merlin himself would rest beside a fire when the cold begins to move across the hills. If I walked like an old man, I would soon feel like one."

"I feel like one now," Sir William said. "It was no easy task to leave the young lord."

"He does inspire affection," Hawkwood agreed. "Katherine too does not want to believe he serves a different cause."

"Katherine. She is well?" The knight could not keep sharp anxiety from his voice. "All that Gervaise could relay was that she had escaped the soldiers."

Hawkwood nodded. "She suffered one blow, but the bandages softened the club's impact. It helped that I was able to run horses through the midst of them; the commotion from inside the walls accomplished the rest."

Sir William relaxed. "And now?"

"Now we have the luxury of time and privacy so that she can be taught in our ways."

"The luxury of time? You fear not the fate of Magnus?"

"Always," Hawkwood said. The wind plucked at his hood, and he threw it back to expose his silver hair. "But I fear it will be unwise to force whatever happens next. It will serve us better to wait and watch. Gervaise, of course, is there, and I hope to continue to find ways to wander freely throughout Magnus when necessary. Over twenty years have passed; another few months will not hurt."

"No? If Thomas is not one of theirs, they will double their efforts. Who will protect him from an enemy he cannot see?"

Hawkwood leaned forward, both hands on the head of his cane. "If he is not one of theirs, they will assume he is ours and will play the waiting game too. Besides, if they truly wanted him dead, there is nought we could do. As you well know, dealing death is too simple . . . poison, an asp beneath his bed covers, a dart from a passageway."

"Your task is to wait and watch," the knight said heavily, "while I return to exile, to rely on messages which take months to receive. I do not know which is more difficult."

CHAPTER

13

The next morning, at sunrise, two soldiers escorted the mute girl into the keep of the castle.

"My name is Isabelle," she said with a bow.

"Isabelle," Thomas repeated softly. He did not rise from his large chair in the front hall, despite his flood of joy. No lord rose during an audience.

She stood in front of him in the front hall of the keep. Tapestries hung on the walls. The fireplace crackled, for even in the summer, early mornings were cool. Two soldiers guarded the entrance, stiffly unmoving with eyes straight forward.

Tiny John bobbed into the room. All guards knew he had privilege at any time.

"I heard she was back," he blurted. He glanced her up and down and whistled. "She's a marvel of beauty, she is!"

"She can also hear every word you say," Thomas observed with a dry smile.

"Aaack!" Tiny John spun on his heel and ran.

Tiny John had spoken truth. The mute girl—no, Isabelle, Thomas told himself—did not wear rags. Instead, her slim body was covered from neck to ankle in a clean white dress. Her long dark hair now gleamed with health. The same beautifully etched high cheekbones . . . the same mysterious eyes . . . and the same haunting half smile.

He wanted to weep with joy; instead, too conscious of the dignity required as lord, he dismissed the soldiers.

When they were alone, he whispered it again. "Isabelle."

"Yes, my lord."

"Please, 'Thomas.' "

She lowered her head, looked upward, and said shyly, "Yes, Thomas."

He wanted to throw himself into her arms. His heart pounded at the strange feelings he had tried to forget.

"Isabelle," he started. Although he could will himself to remain in his chair, he could not keep the hushed wonder from his tone. "Your return is a miracle. Yet I am flooded with questions. Where have you been? How is it you prospered while away? And how is it you now speak and hear?"

She straightened her shoulders and looked him directly in the eyes. "There is much to tell. Will you listen, lord?"

He smiled. "Gladly."

Her smile, a promise and a reward all in one, drew from him a silent inward gasp, yet he managed to keep his face motionless.

"I am from a village far south of here. My parents perished in a fire when I was a baby. I am told the villagers did not think it worth their while to preserve me. I was only a girl. But a lonely old woman, one who was truly mute and deaf, fought for me. The villagers, who suspected she was a witch, dared not disagree. She died when I was ten. With her gone, the villagers were free to chase me away."

Thomas nodded. His heart ached with growing love for her. She was an outcast too. Together, they might . . .

"Because the old lady could not hear, I learned early to speak with my hands. And when I was forced to travel from village to village, seeking food and shelter, I soon discovered the advantages of posing as mute and deaf. It earned pity. Also, I learned not to trust, and being mute and deaf put me behind walls that no person could break."

Isabelle faltered and looked down at her hands. "Not even you, Thomas, wanted me. You saved us all from death by hanging, but you wanted only the knight."

"That is no longer true," he said quickly.

"So I chose to remain mute and deaf. Yet often, I would see you glancing at me, and my heart would wonder."

Thomas finally moved from his chair. He approached her and took her hands in his. "Perhaps," he said gently, "your heart was hearing mine."

"When you were arrested," she continued, "I fled Magnus.

After three days of travel, with no food and little sleep, I reached the dales near the town of York. I threw myself at the mercy of the first passing carriage. The lady inside took pity. She fed and clothed me, and arranged for me to work as a maid in her kitchen. When word reached me of the fall of Magnus—"

"Word had reached the outer world?" Thomas interrupted sharply.

She bowed her head again. "Yes."

The earl of York will arrive soon, Thomas realized with a pang of urgency. *Am I prepared to keep this small kingdom against the forces of the larger one?*

He kept his face still. "So you braved the moors and returned."

"Yes," Isabelle said. "My heart could not rest until it discovered the answer."

"Answer?"

She tightened her grip on his hands. "Yes. Did I belong to you? Or had I been fooling myself about your glances?"

"I am the only fool," Thomas said gallantly. "Not to have searched the world for you."

She did not hesitate. She threw her arms around his neck.

Thomas felt on his neck her warm skin and the cool circle of her medallion.

Take them with you. The old man's words at the hanging. *It will guarantee you a safe journey to Magnus.*

Even as Thomas held her, his mind raced with thoughts and questions. Slowly, ever so slowly, he released her. A single tear dropped from his eye.

"Isabelle," he croaked, "I wish it were not so."

What had Sir William said upon departure? *We do not wish. We attempt to change what we now can be changed, we accept what cannot be changed, and we always strive for the wisdom to know the difference.*

"You must answer me these further questions," Thomas continued in the same pained voice. "Who are you? And who placed you among us? Was it the old man at the gallows?"

"I . . . I do not understand."

Do not wish. Attempt to change what you know can be changed.

He forced the words from his mouth. "If you do not answer, you shall spend your remaining days condemned to the same dungeon you arranged for me and the knight."

It took five days for Isabelle to realize that Thomas was not bluffing. Five days of darkness, solitude, and the endless rustling of rats in the straw.

When she next appeared in front of him in the halls, her hair was matted, and her eyes held a wildness of fear.

Thomas too had dark circles under his eyes. Sleep did not come easily in the anguish of doubt.

Yet there was the medallion. . . .

Thomas again dismissed the guards at the entrance and rose to shut the doors behind them.

He waited for her to speak.

The silence stretched. Still, he waited behind her and said nothing.

Finally, she spoke without turning. Her voice broke upon the words. "How is it you know?"

At that, Thomas sighed. A tiny hope flickered that he was wrong, that he could still trust her.

"Your medallion," he said. "What a blunder to leave it around your neck upon your return."

She clutched it automatically.

"Do not fear," Thomas said heavily. "I had seen it already, the day that Tiny John lifted it from you on the moors. The strange symbol upon it matches the symbol engraved in the scepter I found below the former lord's bed, now mine. I forgot seeing it, until your return reminded me."

"Moreover," Thomas continued, "there was the soldier's attack outside the walls of Magnus the night I was delivered on 'the wings of an angel.' How did they know to venture outside the walls? I had not been followed. No sentry could have seen me or Katherine. You or the knight or Tiny John were the only ones to know that I had with me on my way here a bag filled with the means to conquer Magnus. You or the knight or Tiny John were the only ones to know I had left it outside the castle walls."

Isabelle turned to face him.

"And our arrest," Thomas said, "could not have been a coincidence. Or the fact that a spy had already been planted in the dungeon ahead of us. The knowledge of our presence in Magnus could only have come from you, the person who disappeared our first morning here to return with a bowl of porridge to explain your absence."

Isabelle nodded.

The implications staggered Thomas. *Isabelle's nearness had already been planned before the hanging and the rescue of Sir William! Again, it circled back to the old man at the gallows and his knowledge!*

"Why? How?" Thomas said, almost quiet with despair. "My plans to conquer Magnus were a dream, kept only to myself. How did the lord know—"

"Why?" she said calmly. "Duty. I am Lord Richard's daughter."

"Daughter! You were one of the three figures to escape the night of my conquering!" Thomas stopped, puzzled. "No one recognized you here when you arrived with us."

"Do you think the lord of Magnus would dare let his daughter wander the streets among a people who hated him? No one recognized me because I spent so little time among them."

Thomas shook his head. "And duty dictated you return and pretend love for me?"

She nodded.

"How were you to kill me?" Thomas asked with bitterness. "Poison as I drank your health? A ladylike dagger thrust in my ribs during a long embrace?"

A half sob escaped Isabelle. "Those . . . those were my father's commands. I am unsure whether I could have fulfilled them."

Thomas shrugged, although at her admission the last pieces of his heart fell into a cold black void. "No matter, of course. I cared little for you."

She blinked, stung.

"Go on," Thomas said with the same lack of expression. "From the beginning. At the gallows."

"As you have guessed," she said, "it was arranged I would be on the gallows. My father feared a threat to his kingdom. And he did not believe the knight would die."

That was the greatest mystery. From the beginning, the lord of the very kingdom Thomas intended to take had foreseen his every move.

"How did your father know? Did he instruct the old man to appear at the gallows? Or is it reversed—did the old man instruct your father of my intentions?"

"Old man?" Isabelle stared at Thomas for long moments. Then she threw her head back in laughter. When she finished, and found her breath again, she said, almost with disbelief,

"You truly do not know."

Thomas gritted his teeth. "I truly do not know *what?*"

"I was not there because of you. You were not the threat my father feared. I was there because of the knight."

Because of Sir William . . . the knight with the unknown background.

Isabelle kept her voice flat. "My father sometimes used cruel methods to maintain his power. I did not approve or disapprove. This is a difficult world. I am told that when my father first overthrew the lord of Magnus . . ."

Thomas gritted his teeth again. *Sarah's parents.*

" . . . that he publicly branded each opposing soldier and knight. Then he had them flogged to death. One escaped . . . the most loyal and most valiant fighter of them all."

She let those words hang while Thomas grasped the truth.

"Sir William!"

"Yes, Sir William. When my father received word that Sir William had returned to this land, he paid a great sum of money to have the sacred chalice stolen and placed among his belongings."

"You were sent to the hanging to be a spy, should he be rescued. How did your father know it would happen?"

"He guessed it might, and he wanted to be safe. The hangman had instructions to release me if the knight died on the gallows."

Thomas paced to the far side of the room. "Why? Why did he foresee a rescue?" Nothing could be more important to Thomas than this. If Isabelle could explain why, it would lead to the old man, and how anyone knew Thomas would be at the hanging.

"Thomas," she began, "there is a great circle of conspiracy that is much larger than you and I. My father also acted upon the commands of another. And there is much at stake."

"You are speaking in circles."

"I know only what I have guessed after a lifetime in Magnus. Haven't you wondered why this castle is set so securely, so far away from the outer world? Why would anyone bother attacking a village here? Yet an impenetrable castle was founded. And by no less a wizard than—"

The door exploded open.

Time fragmented before Thomas's eyes. Geoffrey the candlemaker! At a full run with short club extended! Startled guards in half motion behind him! Club thrown downward!

Thomas beginning to dive! Too late!

Much too late. And Thomas, half-stunned by his full-length dive, raised his head in time to see the first guard with an uplifted sword.

"No!" Thomas roared. "He must not be killed!"

Too late again. Geoffrey fell into a limp huddle. Beside him, in a smaller huddle, Isabelle.

Geoffrey's arm and hand scraped the floor in a feeble twitch.

Thomas could only stare at the fingers and ring now inches from his face.

He finally rose in the horrified silence shared by both guards.

"My lord, we did not know—"

Thomas waved a weary hand to stop the soldier's voice. He bent and gently took the medallion from Isabelle's neck. Then he matched it to the ring on Geoffrey's hand.

They were identical.

CHAPTER

14

Dawn found Thomas on the eastern ramparts of the castle walls. The guards knew by now to respect his privacy; each morning the sentry for that part of the wall would retreat at the sight of the new lord of Magnus approaching.

This hour gave Thomas what little peace he could find. The wind had yet to rise on the moors. The cry of birds carried from far across the lake surrounding Magnus. First rays of sun edged over the top of the eastern slope and began to reflect off the calm water. The town lay silent.

It was the time of day that he searched his own emptiness.

"Sarah," he spoke to his long-dead friend, "the castle has been taken from the brutal conqueror who killed your parents. That was my promise to you as you lay dying. Now it is fulfilled. Yet, why do I feel so restless?"

The morning did not answer.

He could keep a brave and resolute face as the new lord of Magnus, and he always did during the busy days with the villagers. Yet in the quiet times, there were too many questions.

There is so little that I know, Thomas thought.

An old man cast the sun into darkness and directed me here from the gallows. The old man knew Isabelle was a spy; the old man knew my dream of conquering Magnus. Who was that old man? Will he ever reappear?

A valiant knight befriended me and helped me win the castle that once belonged to his lord. Then he departed. Why?

A crooked candlemaker and the daughter of the lord we vanquished remain in the dungeons of Magnus, refusing to speak, though long since recovered from the blows which rendered them unconscious. What conspiracy was Isabelle about to reveal? Why is she silent now? Why do they share the same strange symbol?

And what fate has befallen Katherine?

There is so much I must do.

There are books filled with priceless knowledge, able to give a young man the power to conquer kingdoms. They must be brought safely to the castle.

The earl of York has heard that Magnus has fallen to me. He will arrive to exact tribute or begin a siege. All of Magnus must be prepared.

And I must not cease in searching—without the villagers being aware—for the secrets of Magnus.

For a moment, Katherine's voice echoed in his mind. *You and I are threads, Thomas. We cannot see God's plan for us.*

Thomas smiled. *Oh, that there were a God with enough love and wisdom to watch over all our follies.*

He speculated with wonder on that thought for many long minutes. He thought of Katherine's bravery and conviction. He thought of his own confusion.

Suddenly, Thomas spun on his heels and marched from the ramparts. He strode through the village streets and came to a small stone building near the center market square. There, he banged against the rough wooden door.

A strong voice answered, and the door opened to show an elderly man with gray hair combed straight back.

"My lord," he said without fear. "Come inside, please. We are graced with your presence."

They moved to the nave at the front of the church. Sunlight streamed through the eastern windows and cut sharp shadows across both their faces. In the man's eyes, Thomas saw nothing of the greed he had witnessed for many years at the abbey. It was enough for Thomas to finally speak.

"Father," Thomas said. "Help me in my quest."

CHAPTER

15

JUNE 1312
NORTHERN ENGLAND

Thrust! Thrust! Slash sideways to parry the counterthrust! Thrust again! A few hardened soldiers watched impassively as Thomas weakened slowly in defense against their captain.

Ignore the dull ache of fatigue that tempts you to lower your sword hand, Thomas commanded himself. *Advance! Retreat! Quickly thrust! Now parry!*

Above Thomas, gray clouds of a cold June day. Around him, a large area of worn grass, and beyond, the castle keep and village buildings within the walls of Magnus.

Right foot forward with right hand. Concentrate. Blink the salt sweat from your eyes. And watch his sword hand!

A small boy struggled to push his way through the wall of soldiers who blocked him from Thomas.

He can sense you weakening. He pushes harder. You cannot fight much longer. Formulate a plan!

"Thomas!" the boy cried. One burly soldier clamped a massive hand around the boy's arm and held him back.

Thomas began to gasp for air in great ragged gulps. His sword drooped. His quick steps blurred in precision.

The captain, a full hand taller than Thomas, grinned.

The death thrust comes soon! Lower your guard now!

Thomas flailed tiredly and relaxed one moment too long.

His opponent stretched his grin wider and—overconfident because of the obvious fatigue in his opponent—brought his sword high to end the fight.

Now!

Thomas focused all his remaining energy on swinging his sword beneath that briefly unguarded upstroke. The impact of sword on ribs jarred his arm to the elbow. He danced back, expecting victory.

Instead, the captain roared with rage as he fell backward onto the dirt and scrabbled to his feet.

"Insolent puppy! Now learn your lesson!"

Among the soldiers, a few faces showed amusement. The small boy among them kicked his captor in the shins, but did not free himself.

The captain rushed forward and waved his sword.

Intent on saving what energy he could, Thomas merely held his own sword carefully in front to guard.

"Fool!" the captain shouted, still waving the sword in his right hand as distraction, while his left hand flew upward in an arc that Thomas barely saw. At the top of that arc, the captain released a fistful of dirt into the eyes and mouth of his opponent.

Thomas caught most of the dirt as he sucked in a lungful of air. The rest blinded him with pain. The choking retch brought him to his knees, and he did not see the captain's sword flash downward.

Once across the side of the ribs. Then a symbolic point thrust in the center of his chest.

Over.

The soldiers hooted and clapped before dispersing to their daily duties. The small boy broke loose as his captor joined the applause. He darted to Thomas.

"That dirt was unfair, it was!" the boy said.

Thomas coughed twice more, then staggered to his feet.

"Wooden swords and protective horsehide vests or not, my lord," the captain said to Thomas, "I expect you'll be taking a few bruises to your bed tonight."

Thomas spit dirt from his mouth. "I expect you'll have one yourself, Robert. It was no light blow I dealt to your ribs. By our rules, I thought the fight would end." He wiped his face and left a great smudge of sweat-oiled dirt.

The boy tugged on his sleeve. "Thomas."

"Later, Tiny John."

"Rightfully so. By our rules, you were the winner." Robert of

Uleran replied. The man's scarred and broken face was a testimony to decades of rough living.

"I continued to fight, however, for two reasons."

Thomas spit more dirt from his mouth and waited.

"I was angry you had fooled me by pretending tiredness so effectively. In a month you have learned far more than most. I should have expected that move from you."

"Thomas!" Tiny John said.

"Later, Tiny John." He turned his attention back to Robert of Uleran. "Anger has never been part of the rules," Thomas observed.

"Neither has mercy. And do not deny it." Robert's eyes flashed beneath thick dark eyebrows. "When you landed that first blow, you should have moved in to finish me. Instead, you paused. That hesitation may some day cost you your life."

Robert drew his cloak aside and began to unbind the thick horsehide padding around his upper body. "I will not impart to you all I know about fighting, only to have you lose to a lesser man with more cruelty."

"Thomas!" Tiny John blurted.

Thomas good-naturedly placed a hand over Tiny John's mouth. He knew this was the proper time to make his announcement.

"Robert," he said, "I do not wish for you to remain captain of all these soldiers. Pick your replacement."

"My lord, have I offended you?"

"Pick your replacement," Thomas ordered. As lord of Magnus, he could not allow anyone to question him lightly.

"Yes, my lord."

Tiny John considered biting the hand over his mouth. But even he recognized the steel in Thomas's voice and decided there would be a better time later.

"David of Fenway, my lord," Robert said. "He shows great promise, and the men respect him."

"Please remove your possessions from the soldiers' quarters," Thomas said.

For a moment, Robert's face expanded with rage at the further insult. He drew a deep breath and stared at Thomas.

Neither flinched.

Then Robert's shoulders sagged. "Yes, my lord."

Thomas drew his own breath to speak, but was interrupted

by the drumming of horse hooves.

A great white beast rounded the buildings. On it, a man in a flowing purple cape, sword sheathed in scabbard.

Thomas removed his hand from Tiny John's face and placed it on Robert's shoulder to hold his presence.

"It's the earl of York," Tiny John blurted. "That's what I was trying to tell you. He asked permission at the gates to enter alone and unguarded. Twenty of his men remain outside."

The earl of York! Thomas had known it was only a matter of time until he faced this visit. Magnus, tucked as it was in the remotest valley of the North York moors, still lay within jurisdiction of the earl of York. *Will the earl accept a new pact of loyalty? Or is he here to declare war?*

The horse arrived at their feet, and the man dismounted with an easy grace.

He immediately moved forward to Robert and extended his right hand to show it bare of weapons. "Thomas of Magnus. I am the earl of York."

Robert was in no mood to enjoy the mistake. "The lord of Magnus stands beside me."

The earl's eyes widened briefly with surprise. He recovered quickly and extended his right hand to Thomas.

"I come in peace," he said. "I beg of you to receive me in equal manner."

"We shall extend to you the greatest possible hospitality," Thomas answered. "And I wish for you to greet Robert of Uleran, the man I trust most within Magnus, and . . . " Thomas paused to enjoy the announcement he had been about to make " . . . newly appointed sheriff of this manor. He may be busy, over the next few hours, as he moves his possessions to his new residence in the keep."

If the earl of York did not understand the reason for Robert's sudden and broad smile, he was polite enough not to ask.

Thomas, with Robert, led the earl of York and his horse to the stables. There he summoned a boy to tend to the horse.

It took great willpower not to bombard the air with questions. Thomas, however, remembered advice that he had been given by an old friend. *The one who speaks first shows anxiousness, and in so doing, loses ground.*

Instead, Thomas contented himself with a very ordinary observation. "The clouds promise rain," he said, as they left the shelter of the stables.

The earl of York looked up from his study of the nearby archery practice range. "I fear much more than rain."

Thomas waited, but the earl said nothing more until their walk brought them to the keep of Magnus.

"A moat *within* the castle walls?" he asked.

In front of them lay a shallow ditch. Had it only been two months since Thomas had filled it with tar and crackling dry wood and threatened to lay seige to the former lord unless his soldiers gave up without bloodshed?

"Temporary," Thomas commented.

The earl paused and looked upward at the keep. Four stories high and constructed of stone walls more than three feet thick, it was easily the most imposing structure within the walls of Magnus. Not even the cathedral compared in magnificence.

Thomas also gazed in appreciation. From its turrets, Thomas watched each morning as Magnus began to stir. There was the street of shops, each with a large painted sign that showed in symbol its trade. And the narrow, curved streets with houses so cramped together and leaning in all directions they were like crooked dirty teeth.

And of course, the cathedral. Thomas would smile to turn his eyes upon the steeple that rose from the depths of the village. He smiled because of an old man given the task of sweeping the stone floors there, an old man Thomas had once confused for a priest, an old man who truly believed in the God that Thomas struggled to find and seemed to live in a manner that showed belief. Not like monks who preyed upon the poor and innocent.

Thomas glanced at his guest to see if he had finished his inspection of the keep. The earl nodded.

Thomas almost smiled at the demonstration of power. Subtle . . . this man appearing to give me permission to allow him to enter my hall.

They climbed the outside steps with Robert following. The entrance to the keep was twenty feet from the ground, to make it difficult for attackers to gain entrance.

The ground level, reached by descending an inside stairway, contained the food stores and the kitchen on one side, and the open hall for eating and entertainment to the middle and rest of the other side.

Above were the three residential stories, with the lord's rooms on the top. Each level was open in the center and looked down upon the hall, so that all rooms were tucked against the four outer walls. Below, reachable only by a narrow passageway and deep enough below the stone that cries of prisoners would never reach the hall, was the dungeon.

Thomas always shuddered to think of that hold of endless night. He had spent much too long there, almost doomed before he could even start the events which led to his conquering Magnus. And now the dungeon held two silent and cowed prisoners who were proving to be among his thorniest problems.

Until the arrival of the earl.

"I shall leave, my lord?" Robert asked.

"As you wish," Thomas said. He would have appreciated the man beside him during a discussion with the earl. But the need for help might show weakness. Thomas was glad that Robert knew it too.

Thomas gestured at two leather padded chairs near the hearth. Before they had time to sit, a maid appeared with a steaming mixture of milk, sugar, and crushed barley.

"No wine?" The earl raised an eyebrow.

Disdain?

"No wine. It tends to encourage sloth."

The earl grinned. "There's gentle criticism if I ever heard it. And from someone so young."

They studied each other.

Unlike many of the men in Magnus, Thomas had kept his hair long. Tied back, it seemed to add strength to the impression already given by his square shoulders, high intelligent forehead, straight noble nose, and untrembling chin.

Surely this youth must be frightened, the earl of York thought. *He knows I have almost as much power as the king of Britain himself. Yet those gray eyes remain calm, and everything in the way he sits is controlled and relaxed.*

Thomas repeated to himself, "Never show fear. Nor hesitation." He wanted to close his eyes briefly to silently thank

Sarah, the one who had spent many hours drilling him on how to act. She had believed he would someday rule Magnus. And now he faced his first great test.

The earl did not know whether to frown or laugh. *How long will this youth remain silent? Will he not break and utter the first words?*

Thomas lifted his thick clay cup in a wordless salute. The earl responded in turn and gulped the thick, sweet broth.

Still Thomas waited. His eyes did not leave the earl's face. He saw a man already forty years old, but with a face quite different than one would expect of nobility. The chin had not doubled or tripled with good living. There were no broken veins on his nose to suggest too much enjoyment of wine. No sagging circles beneath his eyes, evidence of sleepless nights from poor health or a bad conscience.

Instead, the face was broad and remarkably smooth. Neatly trimmed red-blond hair spoke of Vikings among his ancestors. Blue eyes matched the sky just before dusk. Straight, strong teeth now gleamed in a smile.

"Do you treat all visitors this harshly?" the earl asked.

"Sir! I beg of you forgiveness. Do you wish to dine immediately?"

"It is hardly the food, or lack thereof. Surely you have questions, yet you force me to begin!"

"Again, I beg of you forgiveness."

"If you want me to believe that, you have to stop hiding that smile." The earl laughed at the discomfort he produced with that statement. "Enough," he then said. "I see you and I shall get along famously. I detest men who offer me their throats like craven dogs."

"Thank you, my lord," Thomas said quietly. He coughed. "I presume you are here to inspect me."

The earl nodded.

"I thought as much," Thomas said. "Otherwise, you would not have made such a show of mistakenly greeting my sheriff, Robert."

This time, the earl had enough grace to show discomfort. "My acting was so poor?"

Thomas shook his head. "Only a fool would have entered Magnus without knowing anything about his future ally—or opponent. Between Robert and me, you should have easily guessed which one was young enough to be the new lord of

Magnus." Thomas held his breath.

The earl of York decided to let the reference to ally or opponent slip past them both.

"Do your men practice their archery often?"

"With all due respect, my lord," Thomas answered, "I think you mean to question me about the distance between the men and their targets."

This time, the earl did not bother to hide surprise.

"I saw your eyes measure the ground from where the grass was trampled to where the targets stand. I would guess a man with experience in fighting would think it senseless to have practice at such great distance."

"Yes, I wondered. But I reserved judgment."

"I am having the men experiment with new bows."

"New bows? How so?"

Thomas showed that the question had been indiscreet by ignoring it. "In so doing, I also wish to let them understand it is my main desire that they survive battles, not die gloriously. Distance between battle lines ensures that."

The earl took his rebuke with a calm nod. "Truly, that is a remarkable philosophy in this age."

Thomas did not tell the earl it was a strategy already fourteen hundred years old, a strategy from a far land, contained in the books of power which had enabled him to conquer Magnus.

"Not one soldier died as Magnus fell," Thomas said instead. "That made it much easier to obtain loyalty from a fighting force."

"You have studied warfare?"

"In a certain manner, yes." Thomas also decided it would be wiser to hide the fact that he could read, and that he could do so as well in French, the language of the nobles, and in Latin.

The earl of York was a man who believed strongly in hunches. And everything told him that Thomas showed great promise.

"When I arrived," he said, "I had not decided what I might do about your new status. I feared I might be forced to waste my time gathering a full force and laying a dreadfully long siege."

"Again, I thank you."

"You may not," the earl said heavily.

Thomas raised an eyebrow to frame his question.

"Because of what my heart believes," the earl said, "I wish

to seal with you a loyalty pact. You may remain lord here with my full blessing."

Thomas hid his joy. A siege, a protracted war, would not occur!

"That sounds like reason for celebration, not concern," Thomas said carefully.

The earl pursed his lips, shook his head slowly and spoke with regret. "I am here to request that you go north and defeat the approaching Scots."

Thomas didn't dare blink. To say yes might mean death. To refuse might mean death.

"Come," the earl said, holding up a thick, strong hand to prevent Thomas's reply. "Let us walk through your village."

Thomas, still stunned, managed a weak smile. *At least he calls it my village.*

They retraced their steps through the keep and were soon swallowed by the crowded and hectic action of the village market. They walked untouched through the push and shove of the crowd, their rich purple robes badges of authority. People parted in front of them, as water does for a ship's bow.

"This battle . . . "

"Not yet." The earl held a finger to his lips.

They walked through the market . . . past the church in the center of the village . . . past the whitewashed houses.

Finally, at the base of the ramparts farthest from the keep, the earl of York slowed his stride.

"Here," he said. He pointed back at the keep. "Walls tend to have ears."

Thomas hoped his face had found calmness by then. "You are asking me to risk my newly acquired lordship by leaving Magnus immediately for battle?"

"You have no one you can trust here in your absence?"

"Can anyone be trusted with such wealth at stake?" Thomas answered.

The earl shrugged. "It is a risk placed upon all of us. I too am merely responding to the orders of King Edward." Darkness crossed his face. "I pray my request need not become an order. Nor an order resisted. Sieges are dreadful matters."

Unexpectedly, Thomas grinned.

It startled the earl to see that response to his scowl of power, an action which often made grown men flinch.

"That is a well-spoken threat." Thomas continued his grin. "A siege of Magnus, as history has proven, is a dreadful matter for both sides."

"True enough," the earl admitted. He thoughtfully steepled his fingers below his chin. "But Magnus cannot fight forever."

Sunlight glinted from a huge gold ring. Thomas froze.

The ring! Its symbol matches those belonging to the prisoners in the dungeon!

"This request for help in battle comes for a twofold reason," the earl said. "First, as you know, earldoms are granted and permitted by order of the king of England, Edward II, may he reign long. The power he has granted me lets me in turn hold sway over the lesser earldoms of the north."

"Earls may choose to rebel," Thomas said.

Another scowl across the earl of York's wide features. "It has happened. But they are fools. The king can suffer no traitors. He brings to bear upon them his entire fighting force. Otherwise, further rebelling by others is encouraged. You have—rightly or wrongly—gained power within Magnus. You will keep it as long as you swear loyalty to me, which means loyalty to the king."

Thomas nodded. *But does loyalty include joining forces with one who carries the strange symbol?*

Once again, Thomas forced himself to stay in the conversation. "Loyalty, of course, dictates tribute be rendered to you."

"Both goods and military support, which I in turn pledge to King Edward," the earl said. "Magnus is yours; that I have already promised. Your price to me is my price to the king. We both must join King Edward in his fight against the Scots."

Thomas knew barely thirty years had passed since King Edward's father had defeated the stubborn, tribal Welsh in their rugged hills to the south and east. The Scots to the north, however, had proven more difficult, a task given to Edward II on his father's death. They had a new leader, Robert Bruce, whose counterattacks grew increasingly devastating to the English.

Reasons for battle were convincing, as the earl quickly outlined. "If we do not stop this march by our northern enemies, England may have a new monarch—one who will choose from among his supporters many new earls to fill the

English estates. Including ours."

Thomas nodded to show understanding. Yet behind that nod, a single thought transfixed on him. *The symbol. It belongs to an unseen, unknown enemy. One the prisoners in the dungeon refuse to reveal.*

"Couriers have brought news of a gathering of Scots," the earl explained. "Their main army will go southward on a path near the eastern coast. That army is not our responsibility. A smaller army, however, wishes to take the strategic North Sea castle at Scarborough, only thirty miles from here. I have been ordered to stop it at all costs."

Thomas thought quickly, remembering what his childhood tutor had explained of the North York moors and its geography. "Much better to stop them before they reach the cliffs along the sea."

The earl's eyes widened briefly in surprise. "Yes. A battle along the lowland plains north of here."

"However—"

"There can be no 'however,' " the earl interrupted.

Thomas too could match the earl in coldness. "However," he repeated, flint-toned, "you must consider my position. What guarantee do I have this is not merely a ploy to get my army away from this fortress, where we are then vulnerable to your attack?"

The earl sighed. "I thought you might consider that. As is custom, I will leave in Magnus a son as hostage. I have no need of more wealth, and his life is worth more than twenty earldoms. Keep him here to be killed at the first sign of my treachery."

Thomas closed his eyes briefly in relief. The earl was not lying.

Uncontested by reigning royalty, and given officially by charter, Magnus will remain mine. If I survive the battle against the Scots. If I survive the mystery behind the symbol on the ring.

CHAPTER
16

By *this time tomorrow, I will be committed to war.* Despite a thrill of fear at the thought, Thomas also felt a shiver of joy. The earl of York had departed with his twenty men to the main battlecamp "a halfday's ride east" to a valley adjoining the territory of Magnus. Thomas now paced in the privacy of his room on the highest floor of the castle keep.

Every morning as an orphan in a faraway abbey, Thomas had awakened to one thought: "*Conquer Magnus.*" Every night the same thought had been his last before entering sleep.

Yet, after succeeding in a way that had mesmerized an entire kingdom, Thomas did not feel complete. Was it the need for action, or an emptiness caused by the loss of the two friends who had made it possible?

Unlike the battle of Magnus a few months ago, this war against the Scots could not succeed without loss of life. Would he be numbered among the dead? Or would he see through the fog surrounding the strange symbol of evil that the earl of York displayed on a ring of gold?

Thomas clenched his jaw with new determination. One answer, he suddenly realized, might wait for him in the dungeon. He reached it a few minutes later.

"Our prisoners fare well?" Thomas asked the soldier guarding the dank passageway to the cells.

"As well as can be expected. Each day, an hour of sunshine. But they are never allowed out together."

Thomas waited for his eyes to adjust to the hazy torchlight, then he continued behind the guard through the narrow passageway. He heard the same rustling of bold rats, felt the same feeling of cold air that clung damply. Thomas hated the dungeon, hated the need to use it.

There were four cells, iron-barred doors all facing each other. Two held prisoners. A girl, nearly a woman, in one and a candlemaker who had tried to murder her in the other.

"I wish to see the candlemaker," he told the guard. "Wait outside." He stepped into the cell.

Geoffrey the candlemaker sat against the far wall, chained to the rough stone blocks. He was a tiny man, with tiny rounded shoulders and a wrinkled compact face. His cheeks puffed as he grinned mockery at his visitor.

Thomas did not waste a moment in greeting. "Answer truth, and you shall be free to leave this cell."

The mocking grin only became wider.

Thomas began his usual questions. "Why do you and the girl, Isabelle, share the strange symbol?"

The usual reply. Nothing.

"She spoke of a conspiracy before you stopped her," Thomas continued. "Who conspires and what hold do they have on you?"

Only the dripping of water from the ceiling of the cell broke the silence.

"Your answers no longer matter," Thomas said with a shrug. "Today I have pledged loyalty to the earl of York."

Geoffrey laughed—the last reaction Thomas had expected. Yet a reaction to give hope. Either the earl of York did not belong to those who held the symbol, or the candlemaker excelled as an actor.

"The earl has as little hope as you do, when already the forces of darkness gather to reconquer Magnus," Geoffrey snorted. "You are fools to think Magnus will not return to . . ."

The candlemaker snapped his mouth shut.

"To . . . ?" Thomas pressed.

That mocking grin shone again in the flickering light. "To those of the symbol," Geoffrey said flatly. "You shall be long dead by their hands, however, before those behind it are revealed to the world."

Thomas stood at the rear of the cathedral. Late afternoon sun warmed the stone floor and etched shadows into the curved stone ceiling above.

He waited until the elderly man came close enough to hear him speak softly.

"Father, I leave tomorrow. I wish to bid farewell."

That was the joke they shared. Gervaise served the church as a custodian. Shortly after conquering Magnus, Thomas had finally broken a vow to reject God and the men who served Him. He had entered the church and mistaken Gervaise for a priest.

The questions Thomas asked, and the answers Gervaise provided, forged the beginning of a friendship between a lord and the man who swept floors.

"Yes," Gervaise nodded. "You will lead the men of Magnus into battle against the Scots."

"The procession leaves at dawn—" Thomas stopped himself, then blurted, "How is it you knew?"

Gervaise laughed. His voice matched the strong lines of humor that marked his old skin. His eyes had prompted Thomas to immediate trust on their first meeting. They held nothing of the greed he had seen the monks, who took advantage of their power among superstitious peasants.

"Thomas, you should not be amazed to discover that men find it crucial to put their souls in order before battle. I have seen a great number enter the church today for confessions."

Not for the first time did Thomas wonder at the educated mien of the older man's speech. Why would someone of his obvious intelligence settle for a lifetime of cleaning duties?

Gervaise saw that doubt flash across Thomas's face and mistook it for something else.

"Again the disbelief," he chided with a smile. "Simple as these men may be at times, they have the wisdom to acknowledge God. Someday, Thomas, the angels will rejoice to welcome you to the fold."

"I am not convinced there are angels."

The wry smile curved farther upward. "Despite the legend you so aptly fulfilled the night you conquered Magnus?"

"Gervaise . . ."

" 'Delivered on the wings of an angel, he shall free us from oppression.' I shall never forget the power of that chant, Thomas. The people gathered beneath torchlight. The appearance of a miracle on white wings. Yet you yourself doubt angels?"

"Gervaise!" Thomas tried to inject anger into his voice.

"Tomorrow you'll be gone, Thomas. Have you any other miracles to astound the Scots?"

"Gervaise! Are you suggesting I arranged the miracle of angel wings?"

"Of course. Our Heavenly Father has no need to stoop to such low dramatics."

Thomas sighed. "You would be kind to keep that belief to yourself. As it is, I am able to hold much sway over the rest of Magnus, despite my youth. Leaving this soon would be much less safe for me were it otherwise. I do want to be welcomed back as rightful lord."

"Rightful lord? This is indeed news. Has it to do with a certain visitor who entered Magnus earlier in the day?"

"Little escapes you," Thomas commented, then explained much of his conversation with the earl. But Thomas did not mention the symbol, or his fear of it. Some secrets could not be shared.

Gervaise listened carefully, aching to believe that Thomas was not a tool of the enemy. When Thomas finished, Gervaise spoke with simple grace. "And your prisoners, my friend? Has Geoffrey revealed who told him to murder the former lord's daughter?"

Thomas shook his head. He could not escape the ache in being reminded of the other prisoner. One who had loved, then betrayed him, almost at the cost of his life.

"Time will answer all," Gervaise said. He walked with Thomas to the cathedral doors. "I shall continue praying for you, Thomas. The angels *will* rejoice when you accept His most holy presence in your life."

Thomas almost nodded. Yet how could he believe what he did not see?

CHAPTER
17

Gathered in a small circle beneath a towering oak were fourteen of the most powerful earls and barons in the north.

"David, will you permit such a puppy to remain with us in council?" The fat man did not hide his contempt and surprise at seeing Thomas present among them.

"Aye, Frederick, the puppy remains."

"But these are matters of war!" exploded the questioner.

Some nodded agreement. Others waited for the earl of York to respond. All stared at Thomas.

Around these men of power, the army swelled as soldiers marched in from all directions.

Huge warhorses clothed in fighting colors stood patiently, attended by anxious squires. Knights, dressed only in tights and light chain mail, rested in the shade; mules and servants would carry the heavy armor and swords and lances to the battle site.

The bulk of the army, however, were men of farms and villages who owed the knights and earls and barons a set number of days of military service each year.

Many were poorly equipped and carried only crude leather shields and sturdy, sharpened wooden poles called pikes. These men would form stationary front lines of battle while the faster moving knights would charge ahead or retreat on their warhorses, according to the earl's command.

More ably equipped than pikesmen were the yeomen, armed with longbows and capable of raining arrows far beyond the opposing front lines. The longbows could be reloaded almost instantly; some men could fire two arrows per second.

Others carried crossbows, which fired short bolts with enough fury to pierce even a knight's armor. Crossbows were expensive, however, and difficult to reload. Even strong men were forced to brace the bow with their feet and draw the string back with the full strength of both arms. With the much shorter arrow length, crossbows were less accurate than a longbow.

Thomas's own army held six fully equipped knights, a reflection of the moderate wealth of Magnus; many earls with more property could support only two or three knights. Each warhorse alone was worth five years' wages; each set of armor, two years' wages; and each knight, nearly the ransom worth of a king. As superb fighting machines, knights were held loyal by the reward of estates; many of the outlying valleys of Magnus had been deeded for that purpose.

Thomas's army also held twelve men with crossbows, and another forty with longbows. His remaining men were pikesmen who already sweated with fear, even this far from the lowland plains of future battle.

Most of the earls and barons around Thomas had contributed larger armies. The sum of them made for the noise and confusion of thousands of fighting men, plus an almost matching number of cooks and servants and hangers-on. With banners and flags of fighting colors waving like a field of flowers, and with the constant movement of people, the gathering around this council of war lent the valley a carnival-like atmosphere.

Before the army's return, thought Thomas, *many men will die, to leave behind widows and orphans.*

The fat man yelled to repeat his challenge. "These are matters of war!"

Thomas surveyed the other men in the circle.

Show no fear. Lose respect here and my own men will never follow me. Lose my men, and I lose control of Magnus.

Thomas fought the impulse to lick his suddenly dry lips. If the earl of York did not vouch for him, he could be forced to prove himself immediately. A fight perhaps. These were solid men, who had scrabbled for power on the strength of steel nerves and iron willpower. Would Robert of Uleran's training be enough to overcome?

Then he replied with quiet authority. "Frederick, this 'puppy' you so casually address had the intelligence to conquer alone the ultimate fortress, Magnus itself. Could you have done the same, even with an army of a thousand?"

Then he laughed to break the discomfort of his rebuke. "Besides, Frederick, this 'puppy' is taller than you already. When he fills out to match the size of his hands, he'll be a terrible enemy. Treat him well while you can."

The others joined in the laughter.

Thomas realized that if this meeting were to end now, he would simply be regarded as a special pet, favored by the earl of York. Yet could he risk the earl's anger?

"I need no special treatment," Thomas suddenly declared, then felt the thud of his heart in the immediate silence.

Is it too early to reveal the weapons my men have mastered in secrecy?

He hoped the narrowing of the earl of York's eyes meant curiosity, not anger at the insult of publicly casting aside his approval.

I've gone too far to turn back.

"Tomorrow, when we rest at midday," Thomas said, "I propose a contest."

It took the remainder of the day for all the stragglers to gather. By dusk, the valley was full of men and horses.

As Thomas stood in the growing dusk and watched the countless campfires begin to tremble their light, he felt a hand on his shoulder.

"Friend or foe?" Thomas asked with a laugh.

The earl of York's voice sounded from behind him. "Friend. Most assuredly a friend. And one surprised to hear humor from so serious a man."

"All you and I have discussed is war. It's hard to find humor in the killing of men."

"Spoken well, Thomas," the earl said. "And I'm here to offer apology. You were indeed right to earlier cast aside my vouch for you. I may think of you as an equal, but others choose only to believe what their eyes see."

Thomas barely heard the rest of the earl's encouraging words.

"Others choose only to believe what their eyes will see." Must God follow me even among the camps of war?

Dawn broke clear and bright. Before the sun grew hot, all tents had been dismantled and packed. With much confusion and

shouting, the earls and barons directed their men so that the
entire army formed an uneven column nearly half a mile in
breadth, and so long that the front banners began forward motion
nearly twenty minutes before those in the rear.

The army marched only three miles before an eerie noise
began, like the faraway buzzing of bees. The whispering became a
hum, and the hum gradually became a babble, till it finally broke
into pieces of excited conversation.

"Demons upon us!"

"We are fated to doom!"

"Pray the Lord takes mercy upon us!"

Then, like the eye of an ominous storm, the voices
immediately in front died. That sudden calmness chilled Thomas
more than the most agitated words.

Within sixty more paces, he understood the horrified silence.
To the side of the column stood a small clearing. Facing the
column, as if ready to charge, and stuck solidly on iron bars
imbedded into the ground, were the massive heads of two white
bulls. Blood had pooled beneath the heads, and swarming flies
gorged on the thick brown-red liquid beneath the open and
sightless eyes. Thomas fought the urge to retch.

The remains of a huge fire scarred the grass between the heads,
with the charred hooves carefully arranged outward in a circle.

Thomas looked upward. Hanging from the branches of a
nearby tree, swaying lightly in the wind like heavy ribbons, were
the entrails of the bulls. Carved clearly into the trunk was the
strange symbol of conspiracy, the one that matched the ring of the
earl of York.

Thomas closed his eyes in cold fear. Words spat with hatred by
Geoffrey echoed through his head. *Already the forces of darkness
gather to reconquer Magnus.*

Thomas shivered again beneath the hot blue sky.

"This had better be good," growled Frederick. His jowls
wobbled with each word. "Anything to make these peasants forget
this morning's unholy remains of two white bulls." White bulls,
rare and valuable beyond compare, suggested a special power that
appealed to even the least superstitious peasants. What spirits
might be invoked with such a carefully arranged slaughter?

Thomas felt the pressure as he faced the barons and earls around him. "If each of you would please summon your strongest and best—"

"Swordsmen?" Frederick sneered. "I'll offer to fight you myself."

"Yeomen," Thomas finished.

"Bah. An archery contest. Where's the blood in that?"

"Precisely," Thomas said, wondering briefly how the fat man had ever become an earl. "How does it serve our purpose to draw blood among ourselves when the enemy waits to do the same?"

The reply drew scattered laughs. Someone clapped Thomas on the back. "Well spoken, puppy!"

The fat man would not be deterred. "What might a few arrows prove? Everyone knows battles are won in the glory of the charge, the nobility of holding the front line against a countercharge. Man against man. Beast against beast. Bravery against bravery until the enemy flees."

Thomas noticed stirrings of agreement from the other earls and barons. He *did* feel like a puppy among starving dogs. Yet he welcomed the chance to argue a method of warfare which had served generals two oceans away, nearly two thousand years earlier.

"Man against man? Beast against beast?" Thomas countered. "Lives do not matter?"

"*We* command from safety," Frederick said smugly. "Our lives matter and are well protected. It has always been thus."

Thomas drew a breath. Was it his imagination, or was the earl of York enjoying this argument? The thought gave him new determination.

"There are better methods," he said quickly, removing all emotion from his voice. "The bulk of this army consists of poorly trained farmers and villagers, none with armor. How they must fear the battle!"

"The fear makes them fight harder!" Frederick snorted.

"Knowing they are to be sacrificed like sheep?"

"I repeat," Frederick said, "it has always been done in this manner."

"Listen," Thomas said, now with urgency. If he could present his argument clearly . . . "If these men knew you sought to win battles and preserve their lives, loyalty and love would make them far better soldiers than fear of death."

"But—"

Thomas would breach no interruption. "Furthermore, man against man, beast against beast, dictates that the largest and strongest army will win."

"Any simpleton knows that," Frederick said scornfully.

"And should we find ourselves the lesser army?"

Silence.

Thomas quoted from a passage of one of his secret books.

" 'The art of using troops is this. When ten to the enemy's one, surround him; when five times his strength, attack him; if double his strength, divide him; if equally matched, you may engage him; if weaker in numbers, be capable of withdrawing; and if in all respects unequal, be capable of eluding him.' "

The earl of York smiled openly at the slack-jawed response of the listeners, but Thomas did not notice. Instead, he searched his memory for the final quote. " 'All war is deception. What is of supreme importance in war is to attack the enemy's strategy. And the supreme art of war is to subdue the enemy without fighting.' "

More silence.

The fat one recovered first. "Bah. Words. Simply words. What have they to do with an archery contest?"

"Let me demonstrate," Thomas said, with much more confidence than he felt. "Gather, each of you, your best archer."

The opposing fourteen bowmen lined up first. Each had been chosen for height and strength. Longer arms drew a bowstring back farther, which meant more distance. Stronger arms were steadier, which meant better accuracy.

Seven targets were set two hundred yards away. People packed both sides of the field, so that the space to the targets appeared as a wide alley of untrampled grass.

Without fanfare, the first seven fired. Five of the seven arrows pierced completely the leather shields set up as targets. One arrow hit the target but bounced off—yet even a good enough feat to be acknowledged with brief applause. The other arrow flew barely wide, and quivered to a rest in the ground behind the targets.

The results of such fine archery drew gasps, even from a crowd experienced in warfare.

The next seven archers accomplished almost the same. Five more arrows pierced the targets. The other two flew high and beyond.

Then Thomas and his men stepped to the firing line.

In obvious contrast, Thomas had chosen small men with shorter arms. He stood at the line and spoke in low tones only to them. "You have practiced much. Yet I would prefer that we attempt nothing which alarms you."

He paused and studied them. Each returned his look.

"You enjoy this?" Thomas asked.

They nodded. "We know these weapons well," one said. "Such a demonstration will set men on their ears."

Thomas grinned in relief. "Then I propose this. We will request that the targets be moved back until the first of you says no farther. Thus, none of you will fear the range."

More smile and nods.

Thomas then turned and shouted down the field. "More distance!"

He noted with satisfaction the renewed murmuring from the crowd. The men at the targets stopped ten steps back and began to position them.

"Farther!" Thomas commanded.

Louder murmurs. The best archers in an army of thousands had already shot at maximum range!

Five steps, ten steps, twenty steps. Finally, one of the archers whispered the range was enough. By then, the targets were nearly a quarter of the distance farther then they had been set originally.

The crowd knew such range was impossible. Expectant silence replaced disbelieving murmurs.

Thomas made no person wait. He dropped his hand, and a flurry of arrows hissed toward the leather shields. Few spectators were able to turn their head quickly enough to follow them.

Eleven arrows thudded solidly home. One drove through the shield completely, spraying stripped feathers in all directions. The final two arrows overshot the targets by twenty yards.

Thomas turned calmly to his archers and raised his voice to be heard. He smiled. "Survey the crowd and remember this for your grandchildren. It's not often in a lifetime so few are able to set so many on their ears."

The northward march began again. Memory of the two white bulls faded quickly, as all tongues spoke only of the archery contest. But Thomas and his men had little time to enjoy their sudden fame. Barely an hour later the column of people slowed, then stopped.

Low grumbling rose. Some strained to see ahead, hoping to find reason for the delay. Those older and wiser flopped themselves into the shade beneath trees and sought sleep.

Thomas, on horseback near his men, saw the runner approaching from a distance ahead. As the man neared, Thomas saw his eyes rolling white with exhaustion.

"Sire!" He stumbled and panted. "The earl of York wishes you to join him at the front!"

"Do you need to reach more commanders down the line?" Thomas asked.

The man heaved for breath and could only nod.

Thomas nodded at a boy beside him. "Take this man's message," he instructed. "Please relay it to the others and give him rest."

With that, Thomas wheeled his horse forward and cantered alongside the column. Small spurts of dust kicked from the horse's hooves; the sheer number of people, horses, and mules passing through the moors had already worn the grass to its roots.

Thomas soon spotted the earl of York's banners at the front of the army column. About half of the other earls were gathered around, their horses grazing nearby.

Thomas swung down from his horse and strode to join them. For the second time that day, a chill prickled his scalp. Three men stood in front of the earls, dressed in torn and filthy pants, no shoes or shirt. Each was gray with fear and unable to stand without help.

The chill that shook Thomas, however, did not result from their obvious fear or weakness, but from the circular welts on the flesh of their chests.

"They've been branded!" he blurted.

"Aye, Thomas. Our scouts found them bound to these trees." The earl of York nodded in the direction of nearby oaks.

Thomas stared with horror at the three men. The brand marks nearly spanned the width of each chest. The burned flesh stood raised with angry, dark puffiness.

Thomas sucked in a breath. Each brand shows the strange symbol.

"Who . . . who . . ."

"Who did this?" the earl of York finished for Thomas.

Thomas nodded. He fought the urge to glance at the earl's hand to confirm what he didn't want to believe. *The symbol that matched the earl's ring. The symbol burned into the grass between two white bulls' heads. The symbol of conspiracy.*

"It is impossible to tell," the earl of York answered his own question. "Impossible to understand why they have been left for us to find."

"Impossible?" Thomas could barely concentrate. *Already the forces of darkness gather. . . .*

"Yes. Impossible. Their tongues have been removed." The earl shook his head sadly. "Poor men. And of course they cannot write. We shall feed them, rest them, and let them return to their homes."

Can the earl of York be this fine an actor, to stand in front of these tortured men and pretend he had no part of the symbol? Or is his ring simply a bizarre coincidence?

The earl wiped his face clean of sweat.

His ring was gone; a tiny band of white marked where he had worn it.

Thomas shook off the feeling of being utterly alone.

CHAPTER
18

Frederick proved to be a gracious loser. "This puppy has the teeth of a dragon," he toasted at council of war that evening.

Thomas accepted the compliment with equal graciousness. "As you rightly guessed," he said to Frederick, "the power lies within the bows, not the archers."

"I erred to judge you on size or age," Frederick continued.

Thomas shrugged. Not necessarily from modesty, but because the idea for the ingenious modification of the bows had been taken straight from one of his ancient books.

Running the length of the inside of each bow, Thomas had added a wide strip of thin bronze, giving more strength than the firmest wood. His biggest difficulty had been finding a drawstring which would not snap under the strain.

"But such archery will prove little in this battle." An earl sitting beside Frederick interrupted Thomas in his thoughts. "You have only twenty such bows."

Thomas laughed. "Do the Scots know that? They will understand only that arrows are suddenly reaching them from an unheard-of distance, far beyond their own range."

The earl of York strode to the campfire, and all rose in respect.

"I have just received word from our scouts," he said. "The Scots' army numbers over four thousand strong."

Silence deepened as each man realized the implications of that news. Outnumbered by a thousand. They would be fortunate to survive.

As was his due, the earl of York spoke first. "Perhaps our warrior, Thomas of Magnus, has a suggestion."

The implied honor nearly staggered Thomas. To receive a

request for counsel among these men. . . . Yet was the earl of York a friend or foe? And if a foe, why the honor?

"Thank you, sire," he replied, more to gain time and calmness than from gratitude. He thought hard. *These men understand force and force alone. This much I have learned.*

Another thought flashed through his mind, a story of war told him by Sarah, a story from one of the books of ancient knowledge.

He hid a grin in the darkness. Each man at the campfire waited in silence, each pair of eyes studied him.

"We can defeat the Scots," Thomas said. "First, we must convince them we are cowards."

Thomas awoke in the night to the scent of perfume and the softness of hair falling across his face.

He drew breath to challenge the intruder, but a light finger across his lips and a gentle shushing stopped him.

"Dress quickly, Thomas. Follow without protest," the voice whispered. Thomas saw only a silhouette in the dimness of the tent.

"Fear not," the voice continued. "An old man wishes to see you. He asks if you remember the gallows."

Old man! Gallows! In a rush of memory as bright as daylight, Thomas felt himself at the gallows. The knight who might win Magnus for him about to be hung, and Thomas, through disguise and trickery attempting a rescue. Then the arrival of an old man, one who commanded the sun into darkness.

"As you wish," Thomas whispered in return, with as much dignity as he could muster. No mystery—not even the evil terror of the strange symbol—was more important to him than discovering the old man's identity.

The silhouette backed away slowly, beckoning Thomas with a single crooked finger. He rose quickly, wrapped his cloak around him, and shuffled into his shoes.

How did she avoid the sentries outside my tent?

Thomas pushed aside the tent flap and followed. Her perfume hung heavy in the night air.

Moonlight showed that both sentries sat crookedly against the base of a nearby tree. Asleep! It was within his rights as an earl to have them executed.

"Forgive them," the voice whispered, as if reading his mind.

"Their suppers contained potions of drowsiness."

He strained to see the face of the silhouette in the light of the large pale moon. In response, she pulled the flaps of her hood across her face. All he saw was a tall and slender figure leading him along a trail which avoided all tents and campsites.

It felt like a dream to Thomas, but he did not fear to follow. Only one person had knowledge of what had transpired in front of the gallows—the old man himself. Only he could have sent the silhouette to his tent.

At the farthest edge of the camp, she turned and waited.

When Thomas arrived, she took his right hand and clasped it with her left.

"Who are you?" Thomas asked. "Show me your face."

"Hush, Thomas," she whispered.

"You know my name. You know my face. You hide from me."

"Hush," she repeated.

"No," he said with determination. "Not a step farther. The old man wishes to see me badly enough to drug my sentries. He will be angry if you do not succeed in your mission."

She did not answer. Instead, she lifted her free hand slowly, pulled the hood from her face, and shook her hair loose to her shoulders.

Nothing in his life had prepared him for that moment.

The sudden ache of joy to see her face hit him like a blow. For a timeless moment, it took from him all breath.

It was not her beauty which brought him that joy, even though the curved shadows of her face would be forever seared in his mind. No. Thomas knew he had learned not to trust appearances, that beauty indeed consisted of heart joining heart, not eyes to eyes. Isabelle, now in the dungeon, had used her exquisite features to deceive, while gentle Katherine, horribly burned and masked by bandages, had proven the true worth of friendship.

Thomas struggled for composure. What then drew him? Why did it seem as if he had been long pledged for this very moment?

She stared back, as if knowing completely how he felt, yet fearless of the voltage between them. Then she smiled and pulled the hood across her face once again.

Thomas bit his lip to keep inside a cry of emotion he could barely comprehend. Isabelle's betrayal at Magnus now seemed a childish pain. He drew dignity around him like a shield.

"The old man wishes to see me," he finally answered.

She led him by the hand and picked faultless footsteps through the valley stream.

They walked—it could have only been a heartbeat, he felt so distant from the movement of time—until they reached a hill which rose steeply into the black of the night.

An owl called.

She turned to the sound and walked directly into the side of the hill. As if parting the solid rock by magic, she slipped sideways into an invisible cleft between monstrous boulders. Thomas followed.

They stood completely surrounded by granite walls of a cave long hollowed smooth by eons of rain water. The air seemed to press down upon him, and away from the light of the moon. Thomas saw only velvet black.

He heard the returning call of an owl, and before he could react, he saw a small spark. His eyes adjusted to see a man holding the small light of a torch which grew as the pitch caught fire.

Light gradually licked upward around him to reveal a bent old man wrapped in a shawl. Beyond deep wrinkles, Thomas could distinguish no features; the shadows leapt and danced eerie circles from beneath his chin.

"Greetings, Thomas of Magnus." The voice was a slow whisper.

"Who are you?"

"Such impatience. One who is lord of Magnus would do well to temper his words among strangers."

"I cannot apologize," Thomas said. "Each day I am haunted by memory of you. Impossible that you should know my quest at the hanging. Impossible that the sun should fail that morning at your command."

The old man shrugged and continued in the same strained whisper. "*Impossible* is often merely a perception. Surely by now you have been able to ascertain that the darkness was no sorcery, but merely a trick of astronomy as the moon moves past the sun. Your books would inform a careful reader that such eclipses may be predicted."

"You know of my books!"

The old man ignored the urgency in Thomas's words. "My message is the same as before. You must bring the winds of light into this age, and resist the forces of darkness poised to take from you the kingdom of Magnus. Yet what assistance I may offer is little. The decisions to be made are yours."

Thomas clenched his fists and exhaled a frustrated blast of air. "You talk in circles. Tell me who you are. Tell me clearly what you want of me. And tell me the secret of Magnus."

Again Thomas's words were ignored.

"Druids, Thomas. Beware those barbarians from the isle. They will attempt to conquer you through force or through bribery."

"If I do not go insane because of your games," Thomas said through gritted teeth, "it will be a miracle. Tell me how you knew of my quest. Tell me how you know of the books. Tell me how you know of the barbarians."

"To tell you is to risk all."

Thomas pounded his thigh in anger. "I do not even know what is at risk! You set upon me a task unexplained and give me no reason to fulfill it! I must have knowledge!"

Even in his frustration, Thomas sensed sadness from the old man.

"The knowledge you already have is worth the world, Thomas. That is all I can say."

"No," Thomas pleaded. "Who belongs to the strange symbol of conspiracy? Is the earl of York friend or enemy?"

The old man shook his head. "Thomas, very soon you will be offered a prize which seems far greater than the kingdom of Magnus."

The torch flared once before dying, and Thomas read deep concern in the old man's eyes.

From the sudden darkness came his final whispered words, "It is worth your soul to refuse."

CHAPTER

19

In the daylight, Thomas took advantage of the frenzied preparations to break camp. He slipped away and scrambled along the valley stream, searching for the cleft in the rock that had led him to the midnight meeting.

He had no success. The daylight disoriented him and nothing seemed familiar. He walked back, wondering if the night before had been a dream, and hoping it had not. He only had to close his eyes to remember her face and her gently whispered farewell.

Thomas was given little time to ponder the event. Immediately upon his return, a servant led his horse to him. Thomas mounted, trotting alongside his army as the massed march moved forward, creaky and bulky, but now with a sense of urgency. The enemy waited three days ahead.

Repeatedly during the day, the earl of York brought his horse alongside Thomas and relayed new battle information, or confirmed old. It was a clear sign to the other earls that Thomas was fully part of the council of war. Yet Thomas wondered, *Does the earl of York have other reasons for pretending friendliness?*

Thomas noticed how little laughter and singing there was in the marching column. No one had forgotten the grisly sights of the previous day.

Druids, the old man had said. *Beware those barbarians from the isle.*

Were they the ones of the strange symbol and the terrifying acts of brutality?

As Thomas swayed to the gentle walk of his horse, he decided there was a way to find out, even if the old man of mystery never appeared again.

First, however, there was the formal council of war, as camp was made that evening. The earl of York wasted no time once all were gathered. "After tonight, there are only two nights before battle. You have reduced by a third the fires in your camps?"

In turn, each earl nodded, including Thomas.

"Good, good," the earl of York said. "Already their spies are in the hills. Observing. Waiting."

" You know this to be true?" Frederick asked.

The earl of York snorted. " Our own spies have been reporting for days now. Only a fool would expect the enemy not to do the same."

"Their fires," Thomas said. "What word?"

"The valleys they choose for camp are filled as if by daylight."

Silence, as each contemplated the odds of death against such an army.

The earl of York did not permit the mood to lengthen, but continued his questions in the tone that made them sound like orders. "All of you have brave volunteers ready to desert our army?"

Again, each nodded.

"Tomorrow is the day. Let half of them melt away into the forest. The rest on the following day." He paused. "Slumber in peace, gentlemen. Dream only of victory."

While all began to leave, the earl moved forward and discreetly tugged on Thomas's sleeve.

"If this battle plan works, friend, your reward will be countless. If not . . ." The earl smiled the smile of a fighter who has won and lost many times. " . . . If not, it shall be man against man, beast against beast. What say you to that?"

"Then I shall fight bravely, milord."

"No, Thomas. What say you to a reward? Let us prepare ourselves for the best. Ask now. What is your wish?"

Thomas thought of the ring. The symbol. And Druids.

Is the earl of York part of the conspiracy to reconquer Magnus? If so, will he still honor a promise made?

"Reward?" Thomas repeated quietly. "I would wish simply that you spoke truth to a simple question."

The earl's jaw dropped, but he recovered quickly. "You have my word of honor." Then he dryly added, "My friend, in fairy tales most men ask for the daughter's hand."

Thomas snorted at that unexpected reply. During that moment, he felt at ease with the older man. "I would fear, milord, that the daughter might resemble too closely her father."

The earl slapped his belly and roared laughter. "Thomas!" he cried. "You are a man among men. I see a destiny for the likes of you."

Surely, Thomas told himself, *this man cannot be one of them.*

She was the oldest woman he could find during a hurried search of the other campsites as dusk quickly settled.

She sat, leaning her back against a stone which jutted from the flattened grass. Her shabby gray cloak did not have a hood, and her hair had thinned enough so that her scalp stretched shiny and tight in the firelight; the flesh on her face hung in wattles from her cheeks and jaw.

"Ho! Ho!" she cackled, as Thomas stopped in front of her. "Have all the young women spurned your company? Tsk, tsk. And such a handsome devil you are."

She took a gulp from a leather bag. "Come closer, dearie. Share my wine!"

Thomas moved closer, but shook his head as she offered the wine. She smelled of many days of squatting in front of a cookfire, and of many weeks without bathing.

She cocked her head. "You'd be Thomas of Magnus. The young warrior. I remember from the archery contest." Another gulp. "I'll not rise to bow. At my age, there is little to fear. Not even the displeasure of an earl." She finished her sentence with a coughing wheeze.

The old, instinct had told Thomas, *will know the tales you need, the tales you did not hear the night before.*

So he asked. "Druids. Would you fear Druids?"

The old crone clutched her wine bag, then took a slower swallow and gazed thoughtfully at Thomas. "Druids? That is a name to be spoken with great care. Where would someone so young get a name so ancient and so forgotten?"

"The burnings of two white bulls," Thomas guessed. He was still working on instinct. "Three men now tongueless and branded."

"Nay, lad. That's not how you conjured the dreaded name. A host of others have seen the same. Not once have I heard the name of those evil sorcerers cross any lips."

Evil sorcerers!

"So," she continued, "it is not from their rituals you offer that name, although none have guessed so true. Confess, boy. How is it you know what no others perceive?"

He was right. Druids were behind the symbol. That meant then that Druids were behind the conspiracy to take Magnus. What might this old, old woman know of their tales?

Thomas did not flinch at her stare. *Keep her speaking,* he commanded himself. He tried to bluff. "Perhaps one merely has knowledge of their usual activities."

The crone revealed her gums in a wide smile. "But, of course, you're from Magnus."

Thomas froze and every nerve ending tingled. Magnus . . . Druids. As if it there were a natural connection between the two. "What," he asked through a tightened jaw, "would such imply?"

"Hah! You do know less than you pretend!" The crone patted the ground beside her. "Come. Sit. Listen to what my own grandmother once told me."

Slowly Thomas moved beside her. A bony hand clutched his knee.

"There have been over a hundred winters since she was a young girl," the old crone said of her grandmother. "Generations have passed, common knowledge of those ancient sorcerers has disappeared. Even in my grandmother's youth, Druids were rarely spoken of. And now . . ."

The crone shrugged. " . . . Now *you* come with questions." The bony hand squeezed and she asked abruptly, "Do you seek their black magic?"

"It is the farthest thing from my desires."

"I hear truth in your words, boy. Let me then continue."

Thomas waited. So close to answers, it did not matter how bad she smelled. His heart thudded, and for a moment he wondered if she heard it.

"Druid means 'Finder of the Oak Tree.' It is where they gather, deep in the forests to begin their rituals. I was told that their circle of high priest and sorcery began long ago in the mists of time, on the isle of Celts. They study philosophy, astronomy, and the lore of the gods."

Astronomy! The old man in the cave had known enough astronomy to predict the eclipse of the sun!

Thomas stood and paced, then realized her voice had stopped.

"I'm sorry," he said. "Please, please continue."

"They offer human sacrifices for the sick or for those in danger of death in battle." The crone crossed herself and swallowed more wine. "And the legends still persist. It is said that when the Romans overran our island—before the time of the Saxons and before the time of the Viking raiders—they forced the Druids to accept Christianity. But that was merely appearance. Through the hundreds of years, the circle of high priests held on to their knowledge of the evil ways. Once openly powerful, they now remain hidden."

Thomas could not contain himself longer. "Magnus!" he said. "You spoke of Magnus."

Her hand clutched his knee one final time, then relaxed. She gave a soft laugh. "Bring me a feast tomorrow. Rich meat. Cheese. Buttered bread. And much wine. That is my price for the telling of ancient tales."

After a cackle of glee, she dropped her head to her chest and soon began to snore.

Thomas washed back the last of his mutton stew with ale as he finished supper. Tomorrow, the army would travel until late afternoon, camp behind hastily constructed palisades, and prepare for battle the following day.

Much was on his mind. His men respected his quiet mood and gave him peace. They stood or sat in small groups around the fire, trading oft-repeated stories which were not as loud as the night before. The older men especially—those who had seen friends die in battle—said little this close to the lowland plains north of the moors.

"Your provisions, sir," a dirt-streaked servant girl said, with her head down.

"Thank you," Thomas said. He accepted the cloth bag, and noted with satisfaction its heavy weight. The old crone would be well paid for her tales. He walked through the graying light to seek her.

Thomas smiled grimly to see that there were fewer campfires than the night before. The earl of York's orders had been carried out with precision. The area of the camp had been reduced too, and it took little time for Thomas to recognize the banners of the earl whose army held a grumpy, dirty crone with tales that stretched back six generations.

Thomas strode around the fires once, then twice. No one called out to him. His colors clearly marked him as an earl, and avoiding the eye of those in power usually resulted in less work.

Finally, he was forced to attract the attention of a man carrying buckets of water hanging from each end of a pole balanced across his shoulders.

"Tell me, please," Thomas said. "Where rests the old cook?"

"A day's travel behind us, milord." The man grimaced. "Just more duty for some of us now."

"She deserted camp?"

"No, milord. She was found dead this morning." The man crossed himself quickly. "Rest her soul."

"That cannot be!"

The man shrugged. "Too much wine and too much age. It came as no surprise."

Thomas clamped his mouth shut, then nodded his thanks.

What had the crone said? *Druids. That is a name to be spoken only with great care.*

Surely her death was coincidence. Still, Thomas glanced around him often at the deepening shadows as he hurried to his tent and the welcome sentries.

CHAPTER

20

Late afternoon the next day, Thomas joined the earl of York at the head of the army column. Astride their horses, they overlooked yet another moor valley.

"Thus far, our calculations have served us well," the earl of York said. "Scouts report the Scottish army is barely a half day away. And beyond here, the moors end at the plains."

Thomas nodded. "This does appear to be the perfect place to ambush an army. High sloping hills—impossible to climb under enemy fire. Narrow entrances at both ends—easy to guard against escape. An excellent choice."

"Well, then. We have chosen." The earl of York sighed. "Any army trapped within it is sure to be slaughtered." He turned and called to the men behind him. "Send a runner back with directions. We shall camp ahead." He pointed. "There. In the center of the valley."

Quietly he spoke again to Thomas. "Let us pray the valley does not earn a new name in our honor," he said with a shudder. "The Valley of Death."

Thomas shuddered with him, but for a different reason. Even after several days of travel, it still seemed too bright, the pale band of skin on his finger where the earl had so recently worn a ring.

Dawn broke with a thunder of impending war, as a deep drumroll of thousands of hooves shook the earth. The screams of trumpets ordered the direction of the men and beasts which poured into both ends of the valley. High banners proudly led column after column of foot soldiers four abreast, every eye intent on the helpless encampment of tents and dying fires in the center of the valley.

It immediately became obvious that much thought had gone into the lightening-quick attack. Amid shouting and clamor men and horses moved into rocks that were hundreds wide.

Like a giant pincer, the great Scottish army closed in on the camp. First, a deep front row of pikesmen. Behind them, hundreds of archers. Behind the archers, knights on horses.

At first light and with stunning swiftness, it was a surprise attack well designed to catch the enemy at its most vulnerable—heavy with sleep.

Finally, a great banner rose upward on a long pole. Every man in the Scottish army became silent.

It made for an eeriness that sent shivers down the backs of even the most experienced warriors. An entire valley filled with men intent on death; yet in the still air of early morning, the only sound was the occasional stamping of an impatient horse.

Then a strong voice broke forth. "Surrender in the name of Robert Bruce, king of the Scots!"

The tents of the earl of York's trapped army hung limp under the weight of dew. Not one flap stirred in response. Smoke wafted from fires almost dead. A dog scurried from one garbage pit to another.

"We seek to deal with honor!" the strong voice continued. "Discuss surrender or die in the tents that hide you!"

Moments passed. Many of the warriors found themselves holding their breath. Fighting might be noble and glorious, but to win without risking death was infinitely better.

"The third blast of the trumpet will signal our charge. Unless you surrender before then, all hell will be loosed upon you!"

The trumpet blew once. Then twice.

At the edge of the camp, a tent flap opened and a figure stepped outside, to begin striding toward the huge army. From a hundred yards away, the figure appeared to be a slender man, unencumbered with armor or weapons. He walked without apparent fear to the voice which had summoned him.

Thomas could barely comprehend the sight as he walked. Filling the horizon in both directions were men and lances and armor and horses and banner and swords and shields and pikes.

Directly ahead, the men of the opposing council of war. Among them, the man who had demanded surrender in his strong, clear voice.

Thomas tried driving his fear away, but he could not. *Is this my day to die?*

He could guess at the sight he presented to the men on horseback watching his approach. He had not worn the cloak bearing the colors of Magnus. Instead, he had dressed as poorly as a stable boy. Better for the enemy to think him a lowly messenger. Especially for what needed to be done.

There were roughly a dozen gathered. They moved their horses ahead of their army, to be recognized as the men of power. Each horse was covered in colored blankets. Each man was in light armor. They were not heavily protected fighters, they were leaders.

Thomas forced himself ahead, step by step.

The spokesman identified himself at once. He had a bristling red beard and eyes of fire to match. As he stared at Thomas with the fierceness of a hawk, his rising anger became obvious.

"The earl of York hides in his tent like a woman and sends a lad?"

"I am Thomas. Of Magnus. I bring a message from the earl of York."

The quiet politeness seemed to check the Scot's rage. He blinked once, then said, "I am Kenneth of Carlisle."

Thomas was close enough now that he had to crane his head upward to speak to the one with the red beard.

Sunlight glinted from heavy battle-axes.

"Kenneth of Carlisle," Thomas said with the same dignity, "the earl of York is not among the tents."

The earl spoke almost with sadness. "I am sorry to hear he is a coward."

"Milord, may we speak in private?"

"There is nothing to discuss," Kenneth said. "Accept our terms of surrender, or the entire camp is doomed."

"Sir," Thomas persisted, hands wide and palms upward, "as you can see, I bear no arms. I can do you no harm."

Hesitation. Then a glint of curiosity from those fierce eyes.

"Hold all the men," Kenneth of Carlisle commanded, then dismounted from his horse. Despite the covering of light armor, he swung down with grace.

Thomas stepped back several paces to allow them privacy.

Kenneth of Carlisle advanced and towered above Thomas. "What is it you can possibly plead which needs such quiet discussion?"

"I mean no disrespect, milord," Thomas said in low tones, "but the surrender which needs discussing is yours."

Five heartbeats of silence.

The huge man slowly lifted his right hand as if to strike Thomas, then lowered it.

"I understand." Yellow teeth gleamed from his beard as he snorted disdain. "You attempt to slay me with laughter."

"No," Thomas answered. "Too many lives are at stake."

Suddenly Kenneth of Carlisle clapped his hands down on Thomas's shoulders and shook him fiercely. "Then play no games!" he shouted.

His surge of temper ended as quickly as it had begun.

Thomas took a breath. "This is no game."

He looked past Kenneth of Carlisle at the others nearby on their horses. They stared back with puzzled frowns.

"I am here to present you with a decision," Thomas continued. "One you must consider before returning to your horse."

"I shall humor you." Kenneth of Carlisle folded his arms and waited.

Thomas asked, "Did you believe our army was at full strength?"

After a moment of consideration, the Scottish earl replied, "Certainly not. Our scouts brought daily reports of cowards fleeing your army. The deserters we captured all told us the same thing. Your entire army feared battle against us. We saw proof nightly. Your—"

"—campfires," Thomas interrupted. "Each night you saw fewer and fewer campfires. Obvious evidence of an army which shrunk each day, until last night when you may have calculated we had fewer than a thousand remaining."

Kenneth of Carlisle laughed. "So few men we wondered if it would be worth our while to make this short detour for battle."

"It was the earl of York's wish," Thomas said. He risked a quick look at the tops of the hills, then hid a smile of satisfaction.

"Eh? The earl of York's wish?"

"Again, with much due respect, milord," Thomas swept his arm wide to indicate the valley, "did it not seem too easy? A crippled army quietly camped in a valley with no means of escape?"

Momentary doubt crossed the man's face.

Thomas pressed on. "The deserters you caught had left our army by the earl of York's commands. Each man had instructions to report great fear among the men left behind. We reduced the campfires to give the impression of mass desertion. While our fires are few, our men remain many.

The news startled Kenneth of Carlisle enough that he flinched.

"Furthermore," Thomas said, "none of those men are here in the valley. Each tent is empty. In the dark of night, all crept away."

Five more heartbeats of silence.

"Impossible," blurted Kenneth of Carlisle. But the white which replaced the red of flushed skin above his beard showed that he suddenly considered it very possible, and did not like the implications.

Thomas kept his voice calm. "By now," he said, resisting the urge to look and confirm what he already knew, "those men have reached their new positions. They block the exits at both ends of this valley and line the tops of the surrounding hills."

"Impossible." This time, his tone of voice was weaker.

"Impossible, milord? Survey the hills."

This was the most important moment of the battle. Would the huge man be stunned at their desperate bluff?

What he and Thomas saw from the valley floor seemed awesome. Stretched across the entire line of the tops of the hills on each side of the valley, men were stepping into sight in full battle gear. From the viewpoint below, those men were simply dark figures, made small by distance. But the line was solid in both directions and advancing downward slowly.

The earl of York had timed it perfectly.

"Impossible," Kenneth of Carlisle said for the third time. There was, however, no doubt in his voice.

Murmuring rose from around them as others noticed the movement. Soon word had spread throughout the entire army. Men started shifting nervously.

"The earl of York's army will not advance farther," Thomas promised. "Not unless they have reason."

Thomas also knew that if the earl of York's army moved any closer, the thinness of the advancing line would soon become obvious. The row was only two warriors deep; as many as possible had been sent away from the line to block the escapes at both ends of the valley.

"We shall give them reason," Kenneth of Carlisle swore intensely, as he drew his sword. "Many will die today!"

"And many more of yours, milord."

Kenneth of Carlisle glared, and with both hands buried half the blade of the sword into the ground in front of Thomas.

Thomas waited until the sword stopped quivering. "Milord," he said, hoping his fear would not be heard in his voice. "I requested a discussion in privacy so that you and I could reconsider words spoken in the heat of anger."

Kenneth of Carlisle glared harder.

"Consider this," Thomas said. "The entrances to the valley are so narrow that to reach one of our men, twenty of yours must fall. Nor is it possible for your men to fight upward against the slope of these hills."

"Warfare here in the center of the valley will be more even," Kenneth of Carlisle stated flatly. "That will decide the battle."

Thomas shook his head. "The earl of York has no intention of bringing the battle to you."

"The earl of York is a coward!" Kenneth of Carlisle blustered.

"A coward to wish victory without killing his men or yours? All your supplies are behind at your main camp. His men, however, will be well fed as they wait. In two or three days, any battle of our rested men against your hunger-weakened men will end in your slaughter."

Kenneth of Carlisle lost any semblance of control. He roared indistinguishable sounds of rage. And when he ran out of breath, he panted a declaration of war. "We fight to the bitter end! Now!"

He turned to wave his commanders forward.

"Wait!" The cry from Thomas stopped him in midstride. "One final plea!"

The Scottish earl turned back, his fiery eyes flashing hatred. "A plea for your life?"

Thomas realized again how close he was to death. And again, he fought to keep his voice steady.

"No, milord. A plea to prevent the needless slaughter of many men." Thomas held out his hands. "If you will permit me to hold a shield."

The request was so unexpected that curiosity once more replaced fierceness. Kenneth of Carlisle called for a shield from one of his men.

Thomas grasped the bottom edge and held it above his head so that the top of the shield was several feet higher than his hands.

Let them see the signal, Thomas prayed. *For if a battle is declared, the Scots will too soon discover how badly we are outnumbered.*

Moments later, a half dozen men broke from the line on the hills.

"Behind you, milord." Thomas hoped the relief he felt was not obvious. "See the archers approach."

Kenneth of Carlisle half turned and watched in silence.

The archers stopped three hundred yards away.

"So?" Kenneth of Carlisle said. "They hold back. More cowardice."

"No, milord," Thomas said, still holding the shield high. "They need come no closer."

The Scottish earl snorted. "My eyes are still sharp, puppy. Those men are still a sixth of a mile away."

Both watched as all six archers fitted arrows to their bows.

"Fools," Kenneth of Carlisle continued in the same derisive tone. "Fools to waste their efforts as such."

Thomas said nothing. He wanted to close his eyes, but did not. *If but one arrow strays . . .*

It seemed to happen in slow motion. The archers brought their bows up, drew back the arrows and let loose, all in one motion. A flash of shafts headed directly at them, then faded into nothing as the arrows became invisible against the backdrop of green hills.

Whoosh. Whoosh.

The sound arrived with the arrows and suddenly Thomas was knocked flat on his back.

For a moment, he thought he'd been struck. Yet there was no piercing pain, no blood. And he realized he'd been gripping the shield so hard from fear that the force of the arrows had bowled him over as they struck the target above his head.

Thomas quickly moved to his feet and looked down to follow the horrified stare of Kenneth of Carlisle. Behind him on the ground lay the leather shield, penetrated completely by six arrows.

Thomas took full advantage of the awe he felt around him. "That, milord, is the final reason for surrender. New weaponry. From the hills, our archers will shoot at leisure, secure that your archers will never find the range to answer."

A final five heartbeats of suspense.

Then the huge Scottish earl slumped. "Your terms of surrender?" he asked with resignation.

"The earl of York simply requests that you surrender your

weapons. Some of your earls and dukes will be held captive for
ransom, of course; but as tradition dictates, they will be well
treated. The foot soldiers—farmers, villagers, and peasants—will
be allowed to return immediately to their families."

Kenneth of Carlisle bowed his head. "So it shall be," he said.
"So it shall be."

"Would that I had a daughter to offer," the earl of York said.
"She and a great portion of my lands would be yours."

Thomas flushed. The earl believed it was a blush of
embarrassment. But mention of marriage simply reminded
Thomas of his ache to see again the midnight messenger who had
led him to the old man.

"Ah, well," the earl of York sighed, "if I cannot make you my
son, at least I can content myself with your friendship."

Another flush of red. The earl believed it was a blush of
modesty. Once more, Thomas knew differently. This time, he
reddened to remember his suspicions. *Is this man one of the symbol?
Will he betray me? Or I him?*

"Yes, yes," the earl of York said, letting satisfaction fill his slow
words. "The legend of the young warrior of Magnus grows. Even
during the short length of our journey back from the Valley of
Surrender, tales of your wisdom have been passed repeatedly from
campfire to campfire."

Thomas said nothing. He did not wish credit for strategy taken
from the secret knowledge which was his source of power. As well,
other worries filled his heart.

Magnus lies over the next hill, he thought. *Will the earl of York
now honor his reward promised with victory?*

They rode slowly, Thomas returning home with his small army
in an orderly line behind, the earl to retrieve his son left at
Magnus as a guarantee of safety for Thomas.

All the worries washed over Thomas. *Who are these Druids of
the symbol? What games did the old man play—he who, like the
Druids, knew astronomy—and where did he gain such intimate
knowledge of my life? The castle ahead—will it provide safety against
the forces of darkness which left such terrifying sights for all to see on
the march northward?*

"Your face grows heavy with dread," the earl of York joked. "Is it because of the question which burns so plainly in your restlessness over the last few days? Rest easy, my son. I have not forgotten your strange victory request."

"My son." Surely this man is not part of the darkness.

Thomas steeled himself.

From the marchers behind him, voices grew higher with excitement and anticipation. Within an hour, they would crest the hill above the lake which held the island castle of Magnus.

There can be no good time to ask, Thomas told himself. He forced his words into the afternoon breeze.

"Your ring, milord. The one which carries the evil symbol burned upon the chests of innocent men, the one you removed before battle. I wish to know the truth behind it."

The earl abruptly reined his horse to a halt and stared Thomas full in the face.

"Any question but that. I beg of you."

Thomas felt his heart collapse in a chill of fear and sadness. "I must, milord," he barely managed to whisper. "It carries a darkness which threatens me. I must know if you are friend or foe."

"Friend," the earl said with intensity. "I swear that upon my mother's grave. Can that not suffice?"

Thomas slowly shook his head.

The earl suddenly slapped his black stallion into a trot. Within seconds, Thomas rode alone.

At the entrance to the valley of Magnus, Thomas saw the earl of York sitting on his horse beneath the shade of a tree well aside of the trail.

The earl waved once, then beckoned. Thomas slowly trotted his own horse to the tree.

The noise of travel faded behind him. Blue of the lake surrounding Magnus broke through gaps of the low-hanging branches, and dappled shadows fell across the earl's face. It was impossible to read his eyes.

"I suspect you would not force me to honor my vow," the earl finally said. "You have the mark of a man who lets other men live their lives as they choose."

Thomas gazed steadily in return. "The man who betrays another also betrays himself. Often that is punishment enough."

The earl of York shook his head. "From where do you get this wisdom?"

"What little I have was given by a dear teacher, now dead."

Almost the entire small army had passed along the trail. Then final puffs of dust fell to rest as the last straggler moved on; in the quiet left behind, the earl began again.

"I have waited here in deep thought and anguish," he said. "The ring is a shameful secret passed from father to son through many generations."

He smiled weakly. "Alas, the debt I owe and a promise made justly demands that now the ancient legend be revealed to one outside the family."

Thomas waited.

"The symbol belongs to a group of high priests with dark power. We know only their name, not the men behind the name," the earl almost whispered.

"Druids," Thomas said.

"Impossible to guess!"

"From the isle of Celts. Men now hidden among us."

"Thomas, your knowledge is frightening," the earl of York said quickly. "Most who speak that name soon die."

Thomas smiled grimly. "That promise has already been made. Why else do I drive you to answer me all?"

The earl of York sighed. "Then I shall tell all."

He climbed down from his horse and motioned for Thomas to do the same; then he gazed at the far lake of Magnus as he spoke in a flat voice.

"In our family, the ring is passed from father to eldest son, the future earl of York. With it, these instructions: Acknowledge the power of those behind the symbol or suffer horrible death. And our memory is long. Three centuries ago, the earl of York refused to listen to a messenger—one whose own ring fit into the symbol engraved upon the family ring. Within weeks, worms began to consume the earl's still living body. No doctor could cure him. Even a witch was summoned. To no avail. They say his deathbed screams echoed through out the castle for a week. His son—my great-great-grandfather—then became the new earl of York. When he outgrew his advisers, he took great care to acknowledge the power of the ring which had been passed to him."

Thomas felt the chill of the earl's voice. "Acknowledge the power?"

"Yes," came the answer. "A favor asked. A command given. Rarely more than one in an earl's lifetime. Sometimes none. My great-grandfather did not receive a single request. My father . . ."

The earl's voice changed from flat to sad. "My father obeyed just one command. It happened over twenty years ago. I was old enough to understand his pain.

A thought clicked within Thomas. *Over twenty years ago . . .*

"Your father stood aside while Magnus fell!" Thomas said. "Despite allegiance and protection promised, he let the new conquerors reign."

The earl of York nodded.

It explained much! Thomas had sworn to Sarah on her deathbed that he would reconquer Magnus to avenge the brutal death of her parents, the former and rightful rulers of Magnus, who had been dethroned over twenty years ago.

Then Thomas drew a deep breath as he realized the implications. It could not be. But he knew it was.

"Having lost it," Thomas gritted, "these Druids now demand that Magnus be returned. Horrifying rituals plain to see along the march. A message for me, perhaps." Then the implication he dreaded. "Or a message for you."

The earl of York slowly turned to face Thomas. His face showed the gray pallor of anguish.

"Thomas, I call you friend. Yet twice along the march, in the dark of the night, I was visited by one of the ring."

Thomas did not blink as he held his breath against the words he did not want to hear.

The earl's voice dropped to little more than a croak. "Each time, Thomas, I received warning to expect that payment for my family's power is soon due."

CHAPTER
21

Two others also traveled to Magnus, but with much less fanfare than the triumphant army returning home. These two avoided the main path through the moors.

The first figure remained well wrapped in black cloth, shoulders stooped over his cane. The second figure, however, walked tall and confident with youth. When the wind rose, it swept her long blond hair almost straight back.

They moved so steadily that the casual observer would have marveled at the old man's stamina—or urgency. They finally rested at a secluded spot in the hills directly above the lake and castle of Magnus.

"I have no desire to risk you there," Hawkwood said, pointing his cane downward at the village. "But Thomas will learn both his prisoners have escaped the dungeon. That, I fear, is the bold move which marks the Druid attempt to reconquer Magnus."

"There is little risk for me," the young woman said. "My disguise will continue to serve me well."

The old man arched an eyebrow. "Katherine, you were a child during most of your previous time in Magnus, not a young woman now in love."

She blushed. "Is it that apparent?"

Hawkwood shook his head. "The joy on your face as we discussed a method to reach Thomas during his march to the lowland plains of battle. Your sighs after our midnight meeting, when we followed the army to the Valley of Surrender. And your trembling that morning on the hillside as we waited the outcome of his plan against the Scots."

Her blush deepened. "Thomas is worthy. I had much

opportunity to watch him in Magnus. And now, perhaps, my feelings will give me courage to help him as he needs."

Hawkwood suddenly struck a slab of rock with his cane. "No!"

He looked at the broken cane, then at her. His voice softened. "Please, no. Emotions are difficult to trust. Until we are certain which side he chooses, he cannot know of you, or the rest of us. The stakes are far too great. We risk your presence back in Magnus for the sole reason that despite all we've done, he is or might become one of them. Love cannot cloud your judgment of that situation."

"You were not there," she whispered, almost to herself, "the day he attacked a man for insulting a poor, hideous freak. You did not see the rage in his eyes that someone so helpless should suffer. Thomas will not sell his soul. He will not be seduced by a promise of Druid power."

Hawkwood sighed. "Beneath your words, I hear you saying something else . . . that you don't want to be his executioner."

Four tall trees cast shadows along the main path where it became a narrow bridge of land leading across the waters of the lake to Magnus.

Katherine approached the water alone, and instead of continuing across to the drawbridge of Magnus, walked to the base of the trees and bound her hair into a single tail, then slowly bowed to her knees out of sight of the path.

Grass pressed lines into her knees through the fabric of her dress. A travel bag weighed against her hips. She cleared her mind of awareness even of the sounds of insects in afternoon sun or of the breeze which swayed the leaves above her.

There, she began to pray silently. *Lord of love, I am selfish to wish for his love when so much is at stake. Yet if it is Your will, please spare both our lives in the madness which might overcome Magnus. Please give strength to Thomas, so that he chooses the path of good. And should he choose the evil of that madness, please help me with my terrible task. In the name of Your Son, our Savior, I pray. Amen.*

She stood, and for long minutes simply stared across the water at the cold stone walls of Magnus. Despite the peace of her trust, she shivered.

Then she fumbled with the wide tongue of leather which held

her travel bag closed. She reached inside and pulled loose a bundle of filthy bandages.

With practiced movements, she flipped her hair upward and pushed the long tail into a flat bundle against her head and held it there as she wrapped the cloth around her jaws, then her nose and eyes and forehead.

When she finished, only a large, black hole for her mouth and two dark, narrow slits for her eyes showed any degree of humanity.

Katherine woke in the gutter to hands reaching roughly within her blanket. Sour breath, heavy garlic, and the odor of unwashed skin pressed down.

Katherine almost screamed in rage, then remembered her role—burned and scarred too horribly to deserve any form of kindness.

Her voice became a low, begging moan instead.

"Awake? Bad luck for you!" From the darkness, a broad hand loomed to block out the light of the stars, and the blow that followed shot white flashes through her closed eyes. Her left cheek swelled immediately tight beneath the bandage.

Katherine bit back a yelp of pain and resigned herself to being robbed of what little she owned.

Another voice interrupted the figure above her.

"My good man," it called cheerfully from just down the street, "you show kindness to assist strangers during this dangerous time of night. Here, now, let me help you get this poor woman from the gutters."

"Eh?"

The voice from behind its candle moved closer. "And probably not a moment too soon. Why, any common gutter thief might have swooped in like a pest-ridden vulture."

The startled man above Katherine swore under his breath, then fled.

She drew herself upright into a sitting position and hugged her knees. Through the narrow slits of the constricting bandages, it was difficult to see her rescuer as he approached. It was easy, however, to hear his warm chuckle.

"Like a rat scurrying away from a torch. And with not a shred of good humor."

The candle flared and moved downward with the man's slow,

stooping motion. Katherine, still wrapped and hidden in a thin blanket, flinched at his touch.

"I have no money," Katherine replied.

Another warm chuckle. "You are a stranger here. Otherwise, you would know the lord of Magnus provides a generous allowance to the church for the purpose of sheltering those in need."

His hand found her elbow and guided her to her feet.

She could not see his face behind the candle. But she heard his gasp as he pushed aside the blanket which covered her face.

That familiar sound tore at her heart. It reminded her again of the nightmare of living as a freak. Freedom from that life— traveling with the old man and watching the joy in his eyes as he drank in the youth and beauty of her uncovered face—had been so precious after years imprisoned beneath the filthy bandages. And for a moment, she could not sponge away the bitterness inside.

"Horror?" She mocked his gasp. "You were expecting an angel perhaps?"

Long silence. Then words she would never forget. "Not horror, my child. Surprised relief. Thomas of Magnus has spoke often of his friend Katherine. It will give him great joy to see you."

Katherine woke again to the touch of hands. But these were gentle, and plucked at the bandages on her face.

"No!" Her terror was real, not feigned as so much of her life beneath bandages had been.

The servant woman misunderstood the reason.

"Shhh, my child. Thomas has instructed that you be bathed and given fresh wraps and new clothing."

"No!" Katherine clutched the servant woman's wrists. "My face!"

"Hush, little one. You shall not be mocked in the lord's home."

Katherine did not have time to appreciate the irony; after a lifetime of abuse, kindness itself finally threatened the secrecy of her disguise. Should those of the darkness discover she had been among them all these years . . .

Katherine pushed herself into an upright position. "Please, milady. Lead me to the bath. Leave the fresh wrap nearby. But I beg of you, grant me the solace of privacy."

The servant woman felt the urgency in Katherine's plea, and

compassion almost rendered her speechless. *This poor child, to have a face so hideously burned and scarred that her entire life must be spent in hiding. . . .*

"Of course," the woman said softly.

Katherine let strong, calloused hands guide her from the warmth of the bed. Before she could barely notice the coldness of the floor, the servant woman stooped and fitted on her feet slippers of sheepskin.

As Katherine relaxed and turned to accept help into the offered robe, she smothered a cry of delighted surprise. The previous night had been too dark for her to see her new sleeping quarters in the castle. What she saw explained why sleep had been so sound.

Her bed was huge, and canopied with veils of netting. Her mattress of straw—what luxury!—hung from the canopy on rope suspenders. The mattress was covered with linen sheets and blankets of wool and fur. Feather pillows too!

Such softness of sleep. Such softness of robe against her skin.

Katherine suddenly realized how she must appear to a servant accustomed to waking royalty. Her arms and legs were smeared with grease and dirt; her clothes were little more than torn rags. And in the cool freshness of the room, she suddenly became aware of the stink of the streets upon her body.

She faltered slightly. The servant woman ignored that.

"Come, milady," the woman said. "Your bath awaits. And you shall greet Thomas of Magnus like a queen."

He appears so serious, she thought. *Already, the weight of his power bends him.*

She began with an awkward bow. As her heart thudded, she wondered in the anguish of knowing she could never ask, *Does he feel for me the way I do for him? Or was that simply wishful imagination during those few moments he stared at me beneath the moonlight?*

Katherine forced herself to remember she was beneath bandages and was not the midnight messenger. "You overwhelm me with these gifts of—"

Thomas frowned and shook his head slightly.

Katherine stopped.

Thomas stared straight ahead, every inch of his seated body the ruler of an earldom. Behind Katherine, each side of the huge double wooden door slowly swung closed under the guidance of the sentries just outside the room.

The doors thudded shut.

Thomas let out a great sigh.

"They seem to prefer it when I am solemn," he grinned. "Apparently earls are not allowed to have fun. Especially when dispensing wisdom and justice from this very chair."

Thomas stepped down lightly.

"Katherine, you've returned." He knelt, took one of her hands, and kissed the back of it. He stood and placed both his hands on her shoulders. "I missed our conversations."

Katherine smiled beneath her bandages. *To go from formidable man to a sweet boyishness in such a short time. Not bragging about the Valley of Surrender. Not boasting of his new wealth. But to spend effort setting me—a person he believes to be a freak—at ease. It would not be difficult to remain in love with such a person.*

Keeping those thoughts to herself, she replied, "Thank you, milord."

"Milord! Not 'Thomas'? After you rescued me from the dungeon? After you made it possible to conquer the walls of Magnus? You gravely disappoint me with such an insult."

Grave disappointment, however, did not show on his face. Only warmth.

Would that I could tear these bandages from my face, Katherine thought. *Only to watch his eyes and hope he would recognize me.*

She tried to keep the conversation safe so that nothing in her actions might betray her thoughts. And that her questions would reflect ignorance. "How fares that rascal Tiny John? Or the knight Sir William?"

"Tiny John still entertains us all," Thomas told her. Then his smile turned to frown. "The knight bid farewell too soon after Magnus was conquered. There was much about him which cannot be explained."

He tried a half smile in her direction. "Much, also, is a mystery to me here in Magnus. Perhaps you have not heard. I left Magnus to battle the Scots. During my absence, two prisoners escaped, including the evil man Geoffrey who purchased you as a slave when he became a candlemaker. Impossible that they could escape without help from someone within Magnus. I feel there is no one here I can trust."

He looked at her strangely. "Even your disappearance the night we conquered Magnus—"

Katherine bowed her head. "Thomas—"

"No," he said, as if coming to a quick decision. "I was not seeking an explanation. You assisted me to this earldom. I am happy that you have returned. Furthermore, urgent matters press upon me."

"Oh?"

"Strange evil generated by an ancient circle of high priests known as Druids. And worse."

Thomas stared into space. "News has reached me. Barely days after returning to his home, the earl of York again leads an army into the moors. His destination is Magnus."

"No!" Katherine's surprised horror was not feigned. *Does Hawkwood know of this? What action must we take now?*

"As you know," Thomas said, "when I first arrived in Magnus, the former lord, Richard Mewburn, had me arrested and thrown into the dungeon because of the deaths of four monks. My explanation to you was truth. They had killed themselves by eating the food meant for me, food they had poisoned to murder me."

Katherine nodded.

Thomas responded to her nod by starting to pace back and forth across the room . . . brows furrowed, hands clenched behind his back.

"After Mewburn fled in defeat," he continued, "all in Magnus accepted that the charges of murder had been false, merely an excuse to imprison me and the knight."

Katherine nodded again.

"Yet," Thomas said, "messengers now bring me word that the earl of York has sworn an oath of justice, that he is determined to overthrow Magnus and imprison me for those same murders."

"That is an impossible task!" Katherine finally spoke. "You are lord within these walls. Over hundreds of years, Magnus has never been taken by force alone."

"Only by treachery," Thomas agreed. "Or, as I did, with the help of the people of Magnus."

"So," Katherine asked quietly, "why are you worried?"

"A prolonged siege will do neither side any good," he answered, "and another matter, more subtle, also disturbs me."

Katherine waited. She was grateful that her old bandages had been changed to new, because even so, it was hardly possible to bear her prison of freakishness while near Thomas.

"There was enough time during the march to the battle against the Scots for the earl of York to accuse me of murder. There was enough time then for him to arrest me. Why did he not?"

"His son was being held captive as a guarantee of your safety?" Katherine asked.

Thomas glanced at her briefly, then shook off a strange expression.

"No," he said a moment later. "If the charges were as true as the earl of York obviously now believes, no one inside Magnus would have harmed his son to protect a murderer."

Long silence.

"Had the earl of York heard of the deaths before the march?" Katherine started.

"That is what puzzles me. If so, why suddenly decide to act upon them later?" Thomas stopped pacing and stared directly at Katherine.

"However," he said, "the monastery of my childhood was obscure, and I as an orphan even more so. Thus, it is easy to think that the earl of York had not heard of the deaths."

Thomas frowned. "But how did Mewburn, the former lord of Magnus in those isolated moors, know of those deaths soon enough to cast me into the dungeon, while others in power remained uninformed until much later?"

CHAPTER
22

The chamber was so narrow and tight that Katherine was forced to stand ramrod straight. Even so, the stone of the walls pressed painfully against her knees and elbows.

She had stood like this, fighting cramps of pain, in eight-hour stretches each of the previous two days. The slightest movement chafed the bandages against her face. Raw skin and rigid muscles were the price she paid to spy on Thomas.

The tiny chamber was hidden in a hollowed portion of the thick rear wall of the throne room. Tiny vents in the cracks of stone—at a height barely above Katherine's waist and invisible to anyone inside the room—brought air upward into the space. The vents did not allow any light into the chamber, only sound, carried so perfectly that any word spoken above a whisper reached Katherine's ears.

She had no fear of being detected. Whenever Thomas left the throne room, she abandoned the hiding spot, with enough time to return to her bedchamber to clean away the dirt smudged into her by the walls, before he might invite her for conversation or a meal.

Just as Hawkwood had described it to her before sending her back to Magnus, the entrance to the chamber was fifty feet away, hidden in the recesses of a little-used hallway. To slip in or out, she need simply stand in the recess until enough quietness convinced her that entry or exit was safe.

Remember Hawkwood and his instructions, she told herself as yet another cramp bit into her left thigh. *This is a duty we have performed for generations.*

Two days of petitions and complaints. Two days of the slowly considered words given in return by the earl, Thomas of Magnus.

Two days of exquisite torture, listening and loving more the man who might never discover the secret of her hidden face. But not once, the expected Druid messenger.

Yet the Druid would arrive. Hawkwood had so promised, and Hawkwood was never wrong.

"Milord. One waits outside," a sentry called into the throne room.

The voice Katherine heard moments later sent an instinctive fear deep inside her.

"Thomas of Magnus." Not a question, but almost a sneer. The voice was modulated, and had no coarse accent of an uneducated peasant.

"Most extend courtesy with a bow," Thomas replied, immediately cold.

"I will not prolong this through pretense," the voice replied. "I am here to discuss your future."

A pause. Then the voice spoke quickly. "Don't! You draw breath to call for a guard, but if you do, you will never learn the secrets of this symbol, or of Magnus."

The Druid messenger.

Katherine no longer felt the ache of stiff limbs, no longer noticed the wraps of cloth which muffled her breath. Every nerve tingled to listen further.

"I grant you little time," Thomas replied.

"No," came the triumphant voice. "I have as long as I like. Dread curiosity is plain to read on your face."

"Your time slips away. What is your message?"

The sneering voice came like a soft caress. "The message is simple. Join our circle, remain earl, and gain great power beyond comprehension. Or deny us and lose Magnus."

"Why should I not have you seized and executed?" Thomas asked after a long silence.

"For the same reason that you still live. After all, we have a thousand ways to kill you. An adder perhaps—that deadly snake slipped into your bedsheets as you sleep. Undetectable poisons, a dagger in the heart. You still live, Thomas, because your death does not serve our purpose. Just as my death now would not serve yours."

"No?" Thomas asked.

"No. You and I, of course, are merely representatives. Your

death would only end your life. It would not return to us the power over the people of Magnus who, before your arrival, were sheep to be handled at our whims."

Short silence. Then from Thomas, "And you represent?"

The messenger laughed, a cruel sound. "Druids. The true masters of Magnus for centuries."

"Not possible," Thomas said. But Katherine heard a waver in his voice.

"Not possible?" the voice countered. "Ponder this. Magnus is an incredible fortress. A king's fortune ten times over could not pay for the construction of this castle and the protective walls. Yet to all appearances, Magnus is located far from the bases of power. Why go to the expense, if not for a hidden purpose?"

No! Katherine wanted to scream. *Lies!*

"And why has Magnus existed so long without being seriously challenged by the royalty of England? The earl of York leaves it in peace. So have the Norman kings. And the Anglo-Saxons before them. Would not even a fool decide great power lies within Magnus, great enough to deflect kings for centuries?"

No! Katherine raged. *Thomas must not believe this!*

"Why did the former lord, Richard Mewburn, take Magnus by the foulest treachery?" Thomas said with hesitation. "If you speak truth, it would seem to me that your circle would control this castle's destiny."

"Of course," came the snorted reply. "That's exactly why Mewburn was *allowed* to conquer Magnus. He was loyal to us. The earl before him . . ."

"Yes?" Thomas asked with ice in his voice.

"Don't be a child! We certainly know that his daughter raised you at that forsaken monastery. Can you not consider the possibility it was she who lied to you, not us?"

Katherine almost needed to force herself to breathe. She dimly felt her nails biting into her palms but did not unclench her fists.

Please, don't force me to be your executioner!

In the heartbeats that followed, Katherine agonized. Thomas did not know enough to make a decision, yet there was no way they could have risked giving him the truth.

"I have considered that possibility," Thomas said finally. "Logically, there is no reason against it. I was an orphan and depended on her. It would be difficult for a lost child to recognize the difference between truth or falsehood."

I now wish he had never looked into my eyes, Katherine told herself, *and had never raised hopes of love.*

"Good, good," the voice said. "We much prefer that you choose to live as one of us. You will share the mysteries of darkness, and anything you wish will be yours."

"It must have a price," Thomas said, almost defeated. "The rewards may be plain to see, but loyalty has its demands."

"Thomas, Thomas," the voice chided. "We wish only one thing as a test of your commitment."

"Yes?" Now the pleading of total defeat.

"Your hidden books of knowledge. We must have them."

If he agrees, Katherine told herself, *nothing will ease the pain of my duty. Yet he cannot lead them to the books. I must force my hands to betray my love for him, and tonight he will die.*

"Go," Thomas said with sudden strength and intensity. "Go back to the isle of the Celts!"

Katherine blinked in her darkness.

"Yes!" Thomas raged. "Report back to your murdering barbarian masters that Thomas of Magnus will not bend to those who brand the chests of innocent men."

"Yet—"

"Yet it appeared I might pledge loyalty? Only to see what it was you truly wished. Now, I shall do everything in my power to prevent you from that desire."

"Fool!" The word sounded as if it was molten iron, spat bright red from a furnace. "Magnus shall be taken from you as it was given. By the people."

"That remains to be seen," Thomas said steadily.

Behind her mask of bandages, tears of relief filled Katherine's eyes.

CHAPTER

23

A single night had passed since the Druid visitor had proclaimed his warning to Thomas, and Katherine's stomach still churned with fear. She knew the power of the barbarian Druids. Worse, the earl of York was expected to arrive in the valley with his army sometime in midafternoon. Katherine, better than anyone in Magnus, knew Thomas faced enemies both inside and outside the fortress of Magnus.

Suddenly an unearthly howl sounded, followed by a second. Within moments, a shrieking chorus filled Magnus.

Dogs—in the streets, under carts, in sheds—all moaned and howled and barked. People stopped and stared in amazement as the howling grew louder and more frenzied.

An unease filled Katherine. She wanted to hold her head and shake away the grip of something she couldn't explain.

Now cats. The high-pitched scream of yowling cats gradually became plain above the yipping and howling of dogs. All people stood where they were, frozen in awed dread. Rats scurried from their dark hiding places and ran headlong across the feet of shopkeepers and market people.

Then, unbelievably, bats! Dozens fell from the sky. A great swarm circled frantically a hundred feet above Magnus, dipping and swooping in a crazed dance.

Bats do not fly during the daytime, Katherine told herself, as she struggled to accept what her eyes told her. *They do not drop like a hailstorm of dark stones.*

Still the bats fell, and the thud of their landing bodies was lost among the howling and shrieking of cats and dogs. And into the noise came the screams of terrified peasants.

Then, like a snuffed candle, it stopped.

A final dozen bats dropped from the sky to quiver and shake in death throes. The dogs stopped howling. The cats stopped shrieking. And, stunned by the sudden end of noise, the terrified peasants stopped screaming.

Whispers began in the marketplace.

"A judgment from God," someone said.

"Yes," said another, more clearly. "We allow a murderer of monks to remain earl of Magnus!"

"The earl of York brings justice with his army!"

"God's judgment!"

"Yes! God's judgment upon us!"

The whispers became shouts of anger and fear.

Katherine forced herself to swallow, her mouth was so dry. *Thomas must hear of this . . . if he hasn't been informed already.*

Katherine, her face hidden in bandages, joined Thomas on top of the wall.

"The earl of York makes no effort to hide the size of his army," she observed.

"He has no need," Thomas replied. "Magnus, of course, cannot flee."

They shared the silence as they watched the faraway blur of banners and horses approaching.

Katherine ached to tell Thomas more, to tell him that he was not alone in his struggle with the Druids. But Hawkwood's warning echoed stronger than the inner voice that urged her to remove the bandage from her face.

"Will you see the earl of York?" she asked.

Thomas shook his head. "We will deal through messengers."

Unspoken was the thought neither could avoid. *Already, division weakens Magnus within. Thomas can ill afford to leave to conduct negotiations himself.*

"Whom do you trust?" Katherine asked several minutes later. "Robert of Uleran?"

"His dismay at the escape of the prisoners in my absence seemed real," Thomas said. "Upon my return, he offered his resignation. Now . . . now I have no other choice but to trust him. After the unnatural happenings, it is only his strong insistence that keeps many of the superstitious soldiers faithful to our cause."

Despite the afternoon sun, Katherine shivered at her memory of the uncanny events of the morning. Not a single peasant in Magnus believed any longer that Thomas was innocent of the murders. Not for the first time did Katherine consider the harm that a few well-placed rumors from Druid sources might cause. Yet how could they have called bats from the sky?

Soon the sounds of the earl of York's army drifted upward to them . . . grunting beasts . . . the slap of leather against ground as men marched in unison. . . .

When the army reached the narrow bridge of land that connected the island fortress to the land around the lake, one man on foot detached himself from the front of the army and slowly walked toward the castle.

Thomas spoke more to himself than to Katherine. "He holds paper rolled and sealed. I have little faith the message is a greeting of friendship."

Katherine reached the secluded grove long after the bells of midnight had rung clearly across the valley from within Magnus. It had not been easy to avoid an entire army camped around the lake of Magnus.

Bent and covered in shawls, she had more than once played the role of a disoriented servant, seeking her tent in the darkness. And each time she had faced a sentry, she had gripped tightly beneath her shawl a dagger. *Nothing must keep me from Hawkwood.*

As always, the old man was waiting. He wasted no time with greetings.

"What happens in Magnus?"

"As you foresaw," Katherine said, "those of darkness sent a messenger."

"And as *you* predicted," the old man said after some thought, "Thomas refused to be bullied or bribed."

"Yes, but how do you know of—"

"Katherine, had you been forced to be his executioner, nothing could have hidden it in your voice. Thus, I know he is alive. And alive only because he wants no part of the Druids."

"There is more," she said, and explained the morning's happenings, and the rumbles of fear within Magnus.

The old man mused for several moments. "Your fear is legitimate, my child. No matter what they wish us to believe, kings rule only by the consent of the people. History is scarred by revolutions against fools who believed otherwise."

"And Thomas grieves," Katherine said. "He is bewildered by the earl's declaration of war and by his fierce anger. He once believed they were friends as close as brothers."

She told him of the savage message delivered late that afternoon by the scroll: *Unconditional surrender or unconditional death.* "And Thomas wonders why the former lord of Magnus heard of the monks' deaths so much sooner than the earl of York."

"That, at least, is not a mystery," Hawkwood said. "On their journey to Magnus, Isabelle would have learned from Thomas of the monks' deaths and reported them accordingly."

He paused. "Then, I'm sure it was convenient for the Druids that only the reigning lord of Magnus know. Now, of course, it is convenient for the earl of York to know. It will be much easier for the Druids if the earl fights their battle in a misguided pursuit of justice."

Katherine nodded. "The dogs. The cats. Bats falling dead from the sky. Now that the people within Magnus believe justice must be served against Thomas, he may lose his earldom the same way he gained it."

"I catch doubt of his innocence even in your voice, child."

Katherine sighed. "Slight doubts only. How could our enemies call bats to hurl themselves from the sky?"

"It is a question not easily answered," Hawkwood agreed. "Let me think." He sat cross-legged and arranged his mantle over himself to fend off the cold night air.

Katherine waited in silence as the cold seeped into her and her tired legs grew to feel the soreness even more. Not until the gray fingers of false dawn reached into the valley did Hawkwood stir and finally speak.

"Close your eyes," he said to Katherine. "Do you recall seeing the smoke of a fire as the creatures howled?"

She did as instructed. Eyes closed lightly, at first she saw only the frantic movement of bats against the morning sky. Then, dimly, something snagged in her memory because it did not belong against that sky.

"Yes," she said with triumph. "Smoke from the bell tower of the church!"

Hawkwood let out held breath. "And you felt like shaking your head free from a grip you couldn't explain."

Did she imagine that a smile appeared in the shadows of his cowl?

"I believe I understand. I would have done the same were I they. As would Merlin himself." Hawkwood spoke slowly. "And I believe there is a way that Merlin would have countered those actions. So speak to Thomas tonight. As yourself, unencumbered with bandages. If he has courage, he can defeat the Druids."

She hoped for, watched for—and with thudding heart—saw the startled flare of recognition in his eyes.

"You!"

"Yes, Thomas. I bring greetings from an old man. One saddened to hear of your troubles."

"You! Impossible! Soldiers are posted at every turret."

Katherine repeated her greetings from Hawkwood—she was cool on the outside, but glad inside that her sudden presence had shocked him into not hearing her first words.

They stood in nearly the same position they had stood a day earlier, on the outside walls of Magnus—only then she had been disguised in her bandages. Fifty yards farther along the top of the wall a soldier stood posted at a square stone turret. Fifty yards behind, another.

Below and across the water were campfires of the sieging army, so close they heard the pop and saw the sparks whenever a log exploded in the heat.

Thomas groaned and laughed in the same sound.

"Why must I be tortured so? Is it not enough that Magnus rumbles with rebellion? That the most powerful earl in north Britain camps on my doorstep? That the sorcery of Druids threatens? That you haunt my dreams?"

The groan deepened. "And with all of that, you place in front of me the never-ending mystery of the old man."

He shook his head, and in light, joking tones said, "I pray thee tell me all."

"I cannot," she said. *Although I wish to.*

"For example," he said, "tell me how you arrived here, during a siege, on these walls during the night?"

She shook her head.

"Perhaps why you and the old man dog my footsteps?"

She shook her head.

"The identity of the old man?"

Another shake.

"The mission he wishes me to pursue?"

Again, Katherine shook her head silently.

In one quick, almost angry motion, he stepped across the space between them, and pulled her close enough to kiss her squarely on the lips. Then he pushed her away.

"And tell me if you enjoyed that."

Katherine's first response—and one too immediate to stop—was to slap him hard—open palm against open face—for taking such an action without permission or invitation. Her second response was regret at the first response.

A woman should not value lightly her first kiss, she thought. *Not if it is one never to be forgotten.*

"Milord?" one of the sentries had heard the slap.

Katherine could not help but giggle. "I didn't intend to hit that hard," she whispered.

"It's nothing," Thomas called back to the sentry. Then to Katherine, "Punishment justly deserved."

They stared at each other.

Stop, she told herself. *It is duty which brings you here.*

She spoke. "You talk of rebellion within Magnus, of the army across the water, and the sorcery of Druids."

Thomas nodded without taking his eyes away from hers.

She plunged ahead. "The old man wishes for me to tell you that there is a way to overcome all three."

"How is that?" Thomas asked.

She paused before answering, then said. "Ask for God's judgment. Trial by ordeal."

CHAPTER

24

Thomas, Robert of Uleran, Tiny John, and the disguised Katherine stood and waited at the end of the drawbridge.

At the other end of the narrow strip of land that reached the shore of the lake, the earl of York and three soldiers began to move toward them.

"Are you sure they'll not run us through with those great swords?" Tiny John asked, not for the first time that morning.

"The earl will not risk losing honor by treachery," Katherine replied. "Not after Thomas requested a meeting."

Her answer did not stop Tiny John from fidgeting as the earl of York moved closer.

Beside her, Thomas and Robert of Uleran stared straight ahead. Each wore a long cloak of the finest material in Magnus—this was not a time to appear humble.

For Katherine, the earl of York's march across the land bridge seemed to take forever. How badly she wanted it to still be the previous night, with Thomas listening to her words, half his attention on her face, the other half on Hawkwood's instructions. How badly she wanted it to be that single moment of farewell, with the awkwardness of Thomas not daring to hold her, yet hoping she would not disappear again. And how badly she wanted to be free of the bandages which now disguised her.

The earl of York was now close enough for Katherine to observe the anger set in the clenched muscles of his face.

"What is it that you want, you craven cur of yellow cowardice?"

"An explanation, perhaps, of this sudden hatred," Thomas said. "I understand, if you truly believe me guilty of those murders, that duty forces you to lay siege. But you called me brother once—"

"Treacherous vulture. Waste no charm on me," the earl said in thunderous tones. "Were it not for honor, I would cleave you in two where you stand. You called me here for discussion. Do it quickly, so that I may refuse your request and destroy Magnus."

Thomas stiffened visibly and kept his voice level and polite. "I ask for a chance to prove my innocence."

"Surrender the castle then. Submit to a trial."

Thomas shook his head. "I ask for a trial by ordeal."

The earl of York gaped at him. "Ordeal!" For the first time he showed emotion other than anger. "The church outlawed such trials more than a hundred years ago."

"Nonetheless," Thomas said, "I wish to prove to you and to the people of Magnus that I am innocent."

The earl rubbed his chin in thought. "Shall we bind you and throw you into the lake?"

That had been one of the most common ways of establishing guilt. Bound, and often weighted with stones, a person was thrown into deep water. If the person did not drown, innocence was declared.

Some chose the hot iron. The defendant was forced to pick up an iron weight still glowing from the forge. If, after three days in bandages, the burns had healed, it was taken as a sign of innocence.

"Not by water," Thomas said. "Nor by fire."

"What then?" the earl of York demanded. "How are we to believe you innocent?"

"Tomorrow, I will stand alone on this narrow strip of land," Thomas said. "Stampede toward me twenty of the strongest and largest bulls you can find. If I turn and run, or if I am crushed and trampled, then you may have Magnus."

Katherine stood among the great crowd at the base of the castle to hear and watch Thomas.

When he appeared, the rustling undercurrents of speculation immediately stopped. Thomas held their complete attention.

Katherine was grateful for her bandages. She smiled in admiration, and she wasn't sure she wanted Thomas to know how he impressed her.

"People of Magnus," he began, "today I face death. Because of you I undergo trial by ordeal. Magnus can withstand any siege, but only with your support. Some of you believe I am guilty of the charges laid against me. Today I will prove my innocence so that Magnus might stand."

Now his face darkened, the face of nobility angered. "And I tell you now, dogs will howl and bats will fall from the sky at the injustice of these false accusations."

Thomas spun on his heel and marched back into the castle.

From Katherine's position among the hundreds of citizens lined along the top of the fortress wall, Thomas appeared small, standing alone halfway across the land bridge.

He stood completely still and faced the opposing army. Between them, and where the land bridge joined the shore of the lake, a hastily constructed pen of logs roped together held huge and restless bulls. Dried bushes had been heaped at the back end of the pen.

Katherine frowned as the tension of the spectators began to fill her too. *Dear God,* she prayed, *let Hawkwood be correct in his calculations.*

Soldiers moved to the front of the pen.

Thomas crossed his arms and moved his feet apart slightly, as if bracing himself.

If he turns and runs, he declares his guilt. Yet it will take great courage to remain there as the bulls charge. The land is too narrow. Unless the bulls turn aside, he will surely be crushed.

A sudden muttering took Katherine from her thoughts. She looked beyond Thomas and immediately understood.

The bushes at the rear of the pen! Soldiers with torches! They mean to drive the bulls into a frenzy with fire! Thomas did not agree to this!

The vulnerable figure that was Thomas remained planted. Katherine fought unexplainable tears.

Within moments the dried bushes crackled, and high flames were plain to see from the castle walls.

Bellows of rage filled the air as the massive bulls began to push forward against the gate. Monstrous black silhouettes rose from the rear and struggled to climb those in front as the fire surged higher and higher.

Then, just as the pen itself bulged outward from the strain of tons of heavy muscle in panic, the soldiers slashed the rope that held the gate shut.

Bulls exploded toward Thomas in a massed charge.

Fifty yards away, he waited.

Does he cry for help? Katherine could not watch. Neither could she close her eyes. Not with the thunder that pounded the earth. Not with the bellowed terror and fury of churning hooves and razor-sharp horns bearing down on Thomas like a black storm.

Thirty-five yards away, Thomas waited.

Men and women around Katherine screamed.

Still, he did not move.

Twenty-five yards. Then twenty.

One more heartbeat and the gap closed to fifteen yards.

Screams grew louder.

Then the unbelievable.

The lead bulls swerved and plunged into the water on either side of Thomas. Within moments, even as the bellows of rage drowned out the screams atop the castle walls, the bulls parted as they threw themselves away from the tiny figure in front of them.

Katherine slumped. It was over.

No bull remained on land. Each swam strongly for the nearest shore.

Before excited talk could begin, the first of the bulls reached shore. As it landed and took its first steps, it roared with renewed rage and bolted away from the cautiously approaching soldiers.

Small saplings snapped as it charged and bucked through the trees lining the shore, through the tents and campfires beyond, and finally to the open land beyond.

Each bull did the same as it reached land, and the soldiers fled in all directions.

And behind the people, dogs began to howl in the streets. The men and women of Magnus turned in time to see bats swooping and rising in panic in the bright sunshine, until moments later, the first one fell to earth.

CHAPTER

25

All around Katherine was joyful song, the vibrant plucked tunes of six-stringed lutes, and the jangle of tambourines. Merchants and shopkeepers, normally cheap to the point of meanness, poured wine freely for the lowliest of peasants and shared the best cakes and freshest meats freely. People danced and hugged each other.

Today, the threat of death had vanished, and their lord, Thomas of Magnus, had been proven innocent. How could they have ever doubted?

Only the most cynical would have observed that much of the celebration was desperation. No one wanted to remember the uncanny howling of dogs and the death of bats that had followed Thomas's trial by ordeal. That was something to be banished from memory, something all would pretend had never happened.

Katherine moved aimlessly from street to street. Never in her life as a freak in Magnus had she felt like she belonged. This celebration was no different. Few offered her cakes, few offered her wine, and no one took her hand to dance.

Does it matter? she wondered. All those years of loneliness, years of serving a greater cause. She thought she had become accustomed to the cruelty of people who judged merely by appearance.

Yet today, the pain drove past the walls around her heart. Because of Thomas. Because she could remember not wearing the bandages. Like a bird freed from its cage, then imprisoned again, she longed to fly.

Thoughts of Thomas darkened her usual loneliness.

Yes, Thomas had proven his courage and defeated the Druid rebellion within Magnus. And yes, Thomas had turned away the most powerful earl in the north.

But the Druids had not been completely conquered. As well, the earl of York had departed as a sworn enemy—a mystery she knew both bewildered and tormented Thomas. Magnus was not free from danger.

Katherine was disappointed in her selfishness. So much was at stake, as her duty to Hawkwood proved day after day. Yet, she could barely look beyond her feelings—a frustrating ache—and beyond the insane desire to rip from her face the bandages which hid her from Thomas.

She sighed, remembering Hawkwood's instructions. *Until we are certain which side he chooses, he cannot know of you or the rest of us. The stakes are far too great. We risk your presence back in Magnus for the sole reason that—despite all we've done—he might become one of them. Love cannot cloud your judgment of that situation.*

Head down and lost in her thoughts, Katherine did not see Gervaise until he clapped a friendly hand on her shoulder.

"Dear friend," he said, "Thomas wishes you to join him."

"The Roman caltrops worked as the old man predicted," Thomas said in greeting. He stood beside the large chair in his throne room and did not even wait for the guard to close the large doors.

Strange. Thomas trusts me enough to reveal how he survived the charge of the bulls?

Katherine kept her voice calm. With only the two of them in the room, she could bluff. "Predicted? Forgive my ignorance, milord." After all, the person behind the bandages should have no understanding of caltrops or of Hawkwood.

"Katherine." Thomas chided. "Caltrops. Small sharp spikes. Hundreds of years ago, Roman soldiers used to scatter them on the ground to break up cavalry charges. Certainly you remember. After all, the old man gave you instructions for me. 'Go the night before and seed the earth with spikes hidden in the grass. Bulls are not shod with iron. The spikes will pierce their feet and drive them into the water.'"

"Milord?"

Behind her bandages, beads of sweat began to form on Katherine's face.

"Katherine . . ." He used the patient exasperation, a parent humoring a dull child. "We are friends, remember? You need not keep the pretense. After all, you're the one who told me how to bring dogs to a frenzy. How to force bats to their deaths in daylight."

Yes, but it was me unfettered with bandages, not hidden as I am now. How can you know we are both the same?

"Milord?"

"Come here," Thomas said sharply.

Katherine did not move.

So Thomas stepped toward her and lifted a hand to her bandaged face.

"No!" she cried. "You cannot shed light upon my face. It is too hideous."

Thomas dropped his hand. "These are your choices. Unwrap it yourself. Let me unwrap it. Or, if you struggle, the guards will be called to hold you down. They will also be witnesses . . . something I'll wager you do not wish."

Katherine whimpered, something she had learned to do well over the years. "Milord . . . the humiliation. How can you force me to—"

"I shall count to three. Then I call the guards."

He stared at her, cold and serious.

Katherine firmed her chin. "I shall do it myself."

It seemed a dream, to be within Magnus and finally removing the hated mask. Wrap by wrap, she removed the cloth around her face. When she finished, she shook her hair free. And waited, defiant.

"You did that in the moonlight, once," Thomas said, with wonder in his voice. "You loosed your hair and gazed at me directly thus. I shall never forget."

Do I feel anger or relief? She showed neither.

"Please," Thomas said gently, "sit and talk."

She remained standing. "How long have you known?"

He shook his head. "How long have I suspected? Since you arrived back as Katherine beneath those bandages. That is your name? Katherine?"

She nodded. He smiled.

He is not raging at the deception?

"Your disappearance the night after I conquered Magnus,"

Thomas began. "At first, I thought the soldiers had killed you and hidden the body. There could be no other explanation. After all, I had promised you anything if Magnus was won."

I remember that well, Katherine thought. *I remember wishing for something you could never give to a freak behind bandages—the love between a man and a woman.*

"When you returned unharmed much later, I could not think of a reason why you would remain away from Magnus so long, knowing I had conquered it. But I did not want to ask."

"You cut me short when I tried to explain."

"I had been lied to already," Thomas said, "by someone whose beauty nearly matches yours."

"Isabelle. You thought of her often while waiting in the dungeon."

"I did," Thomas said. "She was a lesson well learned. Mere admiration of beauty does not make love. Mere beauty does not make a person whole. I confess, however, to having learned feelings for you as the Katherine behind the mask . . ."

He stopped himself, and his voice hardened slightly. "I had been lied to by one person whose face could deceive. There was no way to know if you would do the same."

"Thomas—"

He did not let her continue. "And there was your unexplained entrance into Magnus. Since the night you disappeared, all guards at the drawbridge had instructions to watch for one whose face was hidden by bandages. I hoped always for your return. Yet, when you finally arrived, no guard noticed. Thus, I was forced to conclude you had entered as you are now. Unmasked."

Katherine did not protest. *Better that he did not know the truth.*

"So," Thomas said, "I pretended trust. I wanted to learn more about you, and playing the fool seemed the best way. The dungeon, as you know, had little effect in getting the truth from Isabelle. I thought honey would work better than vinegar."

He held up a hand to forestall her reply. "Finally," Thomas said, "as the midnight messenger, unhidden by bandages, you were able to appear within Magnus, even during a siege. Since it would be impossible for you to leave or enter with an army camped around us, I decided you had been here before the siege began. As Katherine."

Once again, she managed not to betray her thoughts. *He*

cannot know the truth about my escape, or my visit, then, to Hawkwood during the siege.

So she asked, "You are not filled with anger at my deception?"

Thomas smiled. "Not yet."

Katherine felt a skip in her chest. *Not yet.*

Sadness and joy tinged his smile as he spoke again.

"Katherine," he said, "I learned to know you before you spellbound me beneath a midnight moon. You are courageous, you love truth, you love God. And you brought me instructions which saved Magnus. It is much easier to believe you are not an enemy."

"I am not," she said quickly. "How can I convince you of that?"

"Tell me about the old man. Tell me about the mission he has placed upon my shoulders. Tell me why you endured endless years in the horror of disguise." His voice grew urgent, almost passionate. "Tell me the secret of Magnus!"

Many long moments of silence. Many long moments of wanting to trust, wanting to tell him everything.

But she could not. There were Hawkwood and his instructions. *Love cannot cloud your judgment of that situation.* And far too much was at stake.

Finally, and very slowly, she shook her head. "I cannot."

Thomas sighed. "As I thought. Even now, I cannot find anger."

She moved toward him and placed a hand on his arm. "Please . . ."

"No," he said with sadness. "I know so little. All I can cling to is the memory of someone who gave me the key to Magnus, and the reason to conquer. More important to Sarah than winning Magnus, was a treasure of . . . of . . ."

Books, Katherine thought. *Knowledge in an age of darkness.*

"Books," Thomas said. "I told you the night I conquered Magnus. It is a mistake I now regret."

"Regret?"

"I should have kept my secret. How I am to know you are not one of the Druids? Perhaps, by appearing to help save me from the earl, you deceive me into revealing what the Druids want most."

"Thomas, no!"

Still sadness as he spoke. "No? The Druids first caused dogs to howl unnaturally by rubbing crystal into sounds so high-pitched that the animals writhed in torment. The Druids first caused bats to leave their roosts by lighting a fire beneath, and poisoning them with the smoke of yew branches thrown on the fire. Then you reveal to me those secrets so that I can cause the villagers to believe in my innocence once again."

"No!" she pleaded again.

"How is it then you know what the Druids do? Even astronomy, as the old man proved with his trickery at the gallows? If you are not a Druid, who are you?"

That was the question she wanted to answer more than any other. But she could not.

Tears streamed down her cheeks as she shook her head again.

"I am sorry, milady," Thomas said. He lifted her hand from his arm, then took some of her hair and wiped her face of tears. "I cannot trust you. This battle, whatever it may be, I fight alone."

He lifted her chin with a finger. "Know this, Katherine. The God of whom you spoke, He let me find Him."

Katherine opened her mouth to ask. He placed his finger against her lips.

"No more," he said. "Remember, I shall not forget the Katherine—the real Katherine—who comforted me in the depths of a dungeon and told me of God. Because of her, I cannot and shall not hold you, the deceiving Katherine, against your will."

He turned away from her as he spoke his final words. "Please depart Magnus."

CHAPTER
26

MAY 1313
MAGNUS, NORTHERN ENGLAND

At the rear of the royal chamber, Thomas leaned casually against the large, ornate chair which served as his throne. He waited for the huge double doors at the front to close behind his sheriff, Robert of Uleran.

Thomas's last glimpse was of the four guards posted out front, each armed with long pike and short sword. As usual, it irritated him to be reminded that double guard duty remained necessary.

Thomas pulled one of the long, padded benches away from the tapestried wall and sat down. With a motion of his hand, he invited Robert of Uleran to do the same.

"Have our fifteen visitors been thoroughly searched?" Thomas asked.

Robert of Uleran froze his movement halfway into his sitting position, and turned his head to frown at Thomas.

Despite his worries, Thomas suddenly laughed. "Relax, Robert. You'd think I had just pulled a dagger!"

"You may as well have, milord," Robert of Uleran grumbled. "To even suggest my men might shirk their duty."

Thomas continued to laugh. "My humblest apologies. How could I *not* think they had been searched?"

Mollified, the big man finally eased himself onto the bench. "We searched them thrice. There is something about them which disturbs me. Even if they claim to be men of God."

Thomas raised an eyebrow. "Claim?"

Robert of Uleran nodded. "They carry nothing except the usual travel bags. A sealed vial. And a message for the lord of Magnus."

"Vial," Thomas repeated thoughtfully.

"I like it not," Robert of Uleran said with a scowl. "A vial which they claim holds the blood of a martyr."

Thomas snorted. "Another religious miracle designed to draw money from even the most poverty-stricken. To which martyr does this supposed relic belong?"

The sheriff stood and paced briefly before spinning on his heels. He looked directly into the eyes of Thomas, lord of Magnus.

"Which martyr?" Robert of Uleran repeated softly. "The man who listened to the cock crow on the dawn of the crucifixion of Christ. The man Christ called the rock of the church. St. Peter himself."

Thomas called for the doors to the royal chamber to be opened. Normal chaos reigned in the large hall. The huge fire to one side crackled and hissed as the fat dripped down from the pig roasting on a spit, and servants and maids scurried in all directions, preparing for the daily meal. On the high table at the far end of the hall on a raised platform were pewter plates in place. The rough wooden tables down the entire length of the hall were crowded with people, some resting as they waited to see Thomas, some there because of the liveliness of the hall. There were men armed with swords, bows, and large wolfhounds; some women were in fine dress, others in rags.

Standing to the side of all this activity, aloof to the world, were fifteen men garbed in simple gowns of brown. They did not bother to look up when the doors opened. When summoned by Robert of Uleran, two of the men broke away from the group, but walked as if they were bestowing a favor in agreeing to the summons.

Thomas noticed the posturing and gritted his teeth. He said nothing as the doors swung shut again, leaving the two monks alone in the chamber with him and Robert of Uleran.

The silence hung heavy. Thomas made it no secret that he was inspecting them, although their loose clothing hid much. He could not tell if they were soft and fat, or hardened athletes. He could only be certain that they were large men with the tops of their skulls shaved.

The first, who stared back at Thomas with eyes of flint, had a broad, unlined forehead and a blond beard cropped short. His nostrils flared slightly with each breath, an unconscious betrayal of restrained anger at the deliberate lack of civility from the lord of Magnus.

The second appeared slightly older, perhaps because his face above his scraggly beard was etched with pockmarks. His eyes were flat and unreadable.

Thomas fought a shiver and then forced calmness upon his own features.

Thomas had spent the entire winter learning and practicing swordplay. No man could handle a broadsword for hour after hour without developing considerable bulk. Thus, he no longer looked like an unseasoned puppy, but had the presence of a formidable man. That and his well-fitted, expensive clothing added to the poise earned from the responsibilities which he carried as lord of Magnus, and made him an imposing figure.

He did not smile.

Finally, the younger of the two men in front of him coughed. It was enough of a sign of weakness for Thomas to finally speak.

"You wished an audience."

"We come from afar, from—"the younger man began.

Thomas held up his hand and slowly and coldly stressed each word. "You wished an audience."

The older man coughed this time. "Milord, we beg that you might grant us a brief moment to hear our request."

"Granted." Thomas smiled briefly and without warmth. "Make introduction."

"I am Hugh de Gainfort," the dark-haired man said. "My fellow cleric is Edmund of Byrne."

Thomas stepped backward slowly until he reached his throne. He then sat upon it, leaned forward, and steepled his fingers below his chin in thought.

"Clerics?" he said. "You appear to be neither Franciscan or Cistercian. And representatives of Rome already serve Magnus."

Hugh shook his head. "We are from the true church. We are priests of the Holy Grail."

"Priests, I presume, *in search* of the Holy Grail?" But even as he asked, Thomas felt suddenly chilled by their smug certainty.

Hugh's next words came on the edge of his disdainful smile. "No. We *guard* the Holy Grail."

"Impossible!" blurted Robert of Uleran. "One might as well believe in King Arthur's sword in the stone."

For a moment, Hugh's eyes widened.

In shock? The moment passed so quickly that Thomas immediately doubted he had seen any reaction.

"The Grail and King Arthur's sword have much in common," Hugh replied with scorn. "And only fools believe that the passing of centuries can wash away the truth."

Robert of Uleran opened his mouth and drew a breath. Thomas held up his hand again to silence any argument.

"I am told that your procession brings a saint's relic," Thomas said. "Are you here among the people of Magnus to squeeze from them money and profit from the blood of St. Peter? Or have you requested audience merely to siphon directly from the treasury?"

Edmund clucked as if Thomas were a naughty child. "We are not false priests. *They* shall be punished soon enough for their methods of leeching blood from the poor. No, we are here to preach the truth."

"Yes," Hugh added. "Our only duty is to deliver our message to whoever has a hunger for it. We have coin for our lodging in Magnus, so we beg no charity. Instead, we simply request that you allow us to speak freely among your people during our stay."

"If permission is refused?" Thomas asked.

Hugh bowed in a mocking gesture.

"Enough of your villagers have already heard rumors of the martyr's blood that you dare not refuse." The priest's voice became silky with deadliness. "If you do, our miracles will become your curses."

CHAPTER

27

The priests of the Holy Grail waited until the afternoon of their second day to demonstrate their first miracle.

The low, gray clouds of the previous week had been broken by a sun so strong it felt almost like summer. To the villagers of Magnus, it was a good omen. These priests, it seemed, had banished the dismal spring chill.

The priests of the Holy Grail were quick to take advantage of the people's good spirits.

There were only five now, speaking at the corner of the church building which dominated the center of Magnus. The others rested quietly within nearby shadows. They took turns, constantly calling out and delivering selected sermons, answering questions, and warding off insults from the less believing.

Hugh de Gainfort was leading the group of five into the hours of the early afternoon. He spoke with power, and it was not unusual for twenty or thirty of the village people to be gathered in front of him.

He looked beyond the crowd into the shadows of the church, then nodded so quickly that any observer would have doubted the action had been made.

"Miracles shall prove we are the bearers of God's truth. And as promised for two days, one shall now appear."

His raised voice and his promise drew murmurs from the crowd in front, and attention from passersby.

"Yes!" Hugh continued in a near shout. "Draw forward, believers and unbelievers of Magnus! Within the quarter hour, you shall witness the signs of a new age of truth!"

"Go," he urged the crowd. "Go now and return with friends

and family! For what you see will be a sure sign of blessing!"

The other four priests began chanting, "The promised miracle shall deliver blessings to all who witness."

For several seconds, none in the crowd reacted.

Hugh roared, "Go forth into Magnus! Return immediately, but do not return alone! Go!"

An old man hobbled away. Then a housewife. Finally, the rest of the crowd turned and spread in all directions. Some ran. Some walked and stumbled as they looked back at Hugh, as if afraid he might perform the miracle in their absence.

Almost immediately, Edmund of Byrne left the shadows. He carried a statue nearly half his height and set it down carefully in front of Hugh.

"Well spoken, my good man." He patted the top of the statue. "Remember, Hugh, not until they are nearly in a frenzy should you deliver. Thomas of Magnus must suffer the same fate as the once-proud earl of York."

Edmund smiled with a savage gleam. "There is a certain sweetness in casting a man into his own dungeon."

Within half an hour, a great noisy crowd had filled the small square in front of the stone church. It was not often that such unexpected entertainment broke life's monotony and struggle.

Hugh de Gainfort raised his arms to request silence.

"People of Magnus," he called, "many of you doubt the priests of the Holy Grail. Some of you have ridiculed us, but we, the speakers of truth, forgive. After you witness the miracle of the Madonna, such insults will not be forgiven as those delivered from ignorance. After today, none of you will be excused for not following our truth!"

Hugh lifted the statue, and with seemingly little effort, held it high above him.

"Behold, the Madonna, the statue of the sainted Mother Mary."

The sun-whitened statue was of a woman with her head bowed behind a veil. A long flowing cape covered most of her body. The Madonna's face captivated with carved details of exquisite agony. Her eyes were deep crystal, a luminous blue which seemed to search the hearts of every person in the crowd.

"The Mother Mary herself knew well of the Holy Grail," Hugh said in deep, slow words. "She blessed this statue for our own

priests those thirteen centuries ago, our own priests who already
held the sacred Holy Grail. Thus, we were established as the one
true church!"

A voice from the entrance to the church interrupted Hugh.
"This is not a story to be believed! Only the Holy Pope and the
Church of Rome may make such claim!"

Hugh turned slowly to face his challenger.

The thin man at the church entrance wore a loose, black robe.
His face was white with anger, his fists clenched.

"Ah!" Hugh proclaimed loudly for his large audience. "A
representative of the oppressors of the people!"

This shift startled the priest. "Oppressors?"

"Oppressors!" Hugh's voice gained in resonance, as if he were a
trained actor. "You have set the rules according to a religion of
convenience! A religion designed to give priests and kings control
over the people!"

The priest stood on his toes in rage. "This . . . is . . . vile!" he
said with a strained scream. "Someone call the lord of Magnus!"

No one in the crowd moved.

Hugh smiled, a wolf moving in on the helpless fawn.

"The truth shall speak for itself," Hugh said. He turned back to
the people. "Shall we put truth to the test?"

"Yes!" came the shout. "Truth to the test!"

The priest felt the trap shut. He knew he could not defy such a
large crowd, and he felt fear at Hugh's confidence.

Hugh held up his arms again. Immediate silence followed.

"What say you?" Hugh queried the priest without deigning to
glance back. "Or have you fear of the results?"

More long silence. Finally the priest croaked, "I have no fear."

Hugh smiled at the crowd before him. He noted their flushed
faces, their concentration on his words.

Yes. He mentally licked his lips. *They are ready.*

"This Madonna," he said with a theatrical flourish, "blessed by
the Mother Mary herself, shall tell us the truth. Let us take her
inside the church. If the priest speaks truth, the Madonna will
remain as she is. However, if in this church resides falseness
against God, the Madonna will weep in sadness!"

Even as Hugh finished speaking, those at the back of the crowd
began to push forward. Excited babble washed over all of them.

None wanted to miss the test.

"When the truth is revealed," he continued in confident, deep tones, "the new and faithful followers of the priests of the Holy Grail will be led to the Grail itself!"

At this, not even Hugh's upraised arms could stop the avalanche of shouting. The legendary Grail promised blessings to all who touched it!

Hugh took the statue into his arms, turned to face the church, and marched forward. Without pausing to acknowledge the priest, he walked through the deep shadows of the church's entrance and into the quiet coolness beyond. He kept walking until he reached the altar at the front. He moved the lit candles and set the statue down so that it faced the gathered people.

Soon the church was full, every eye straining to see the Madonna's face, every throat dry with expectation.

"Dear Mother Mary," Hugh cried to the curved ceiling above, "is this a house worthy of your presence?" He fell to his knees, clasped his hands, and begged at the statue's feet.

"Dear Mother Mary," Hugh cried again, "is this a house worthy of your presence?"

For a dozen heartbeats, he stayed on his knees, silent, head bowed, hands clasped high above him. Then he looked upward at the statue and moaned.

"Behold!" he shouted. "The Madonna weeps."

Three elderly women in the front rows fainted. Grown men crossed themselves. Mothers wept in terror. And all stared in horror and fascination at the statue.

Even in the dimly filtered light at the front of the church, all could see tears glistening in the Madonna's eyes. As each second passed, another large drop broke from each eye and slowly rolled downward.

CHAPTER

28

Thomas greeted each dawn from the eastern ramparts of the castle walls. There, in the quiet of a new day, Thomas found great solace in prayer, opening his heart to the God who listened directly to each man and woman who called upon His name.

Yes, Thomas now took comfort in his faith, something he would not have believed possible a year earlier; but he still could not overcome his suspicion of the priests and monks who used their religion as a battering ram for their own selfish purposes.

For man, the church was more of a career than a way to serve God, and many abused their positions. The leaders in the church were as prone as the nobles to eat from plates of gold and silver. Clergy, using the hard-earned money of their peasant charges, often wore jewels and rings and kept fine horses and expensive hounds and hawks.

A test for clerical status was simple; because literacy and education were so rare, any man who could read a Latin text from the Bible could claim "benefit of clergy." This was especially valuable, for those in the church who had committed any crime from simple theft to blatant murder were given complete exemption from the courts of the land and tried instead by the church. At the very worst, a cleric might face a fine or a light whipping for even the most terrible of crimes.

Thus, Thomas lived in uneasy alliance with the priests of Magnus. More dreaded to an earl or king than a sieging army was the threat of excommunication. After all, if the mass of the people believed that a ruler's power was given directly by God, how could that ruler maintain power if the church made him an outcast?

Each Sabbath, Thomas entered the church to worship, as expected by tradition. Unlike most of the people of Magnus, Thomas could read and write. He understood Latin in its written form, and winced at the biblical inaccuracies spouted by priests too willing to deliver whatever message it took to ensure that ignorant peasants remain cowed by the threat of God's punishment.

It was with relief, then, that Thomas pursued the knowledge of God through his own reading and prayers.

And without fail, each morning following his prayers and each night before falling to sleep, Thomas would silently ask himself the questions that haunted him, in empty hopes that the asking might any day receive an answer.

An old man once cast the sun into darkness and directed me here from the gallows where a knight was about to die, falsely accused. The old man even then knew my dream of conquering Magnus. Who was that old man? How did he know?

A valiant and scarred knight befriended me and helped me win the castle that once belonged to his own lord. Then he departed. Why?

A crooked candlemaker and Isabelle, the daughter of the lord we vanquished, captured and imprisoned in the dungeons of Magnus, escaped in a manner still unknown. How?

And the midnight messenger, Katherine. She spent all those years in Magnus disguised beneath bandages as a scarred freak. Was she one of the false sorcerers who nearly won Magnus from me? Or was she truly a friend, now banished unfairly by my command from this kingdom?

What is the secret of Magnus?

On this day, less than a week after the arrival of the priests of the Holy Grail, Thomas now had other urgent questions and problems to occupy him.

Not even the enthusiastically squirming burden left in his throne room yesterday—Thomas smiled as he recalled how Tiny John had deposited the clumsy puppy on his lap—was enough of a distraction during these terrible days.

His only comfort was in knowing that there was one man in all of Magnus who had a gentle wisdom. It took little for Thomas to decide that this day required another visit and discussion.

"Five days of nonsense about the Holy Grail!" exploded Thomas. "Blood of a martyr which clots and unclots as directed by prayer! I am at my wits' end, Gervaise. It is almost enough to make me sympathize with the priests of Rome."

"Then the matter *must* be grave." The elderly man, on his knees in the rich dirt of the garden, chuckled without looking up from his task.

"Jest if you will, but do not be surprised if you find yourself without gainful work when the priests you serve are cast from this very church."

Gervaise merely hummed in the sunshine which bathed his stooped shoulders in pleasant warmth. He had thick, gnarled fingers, as capable of threading the most delicate needles as of clawing among the roots of the roughest bush, which he did now with great patience.

Carefully pruned bushes stood tall among wide, low shrubs, and lined in front of these were rows of flowers almost ready to bloom. The greatest treasures among these for Gervaise were his roses. He would coax forth each summer the petals of white or pink or yellow, all considered prizes by the noble women of Magnus.

Gervaise placed another weed on a rapidly drying pile. "The sun proves itself to be quite hot these days," he said in a leisurely tone. "It does wonders for these precious plants. Unfortunately, it also encourages the weeds."

Thomas sighed. "Gervaise, do you not understand what happens within Magnus? With these signs of miracles, the priests of the Holy Grail have almost the entire population of Magnus in their grip."

Gervaise straightened with effort, then finally turned to regard the young master of Magnus.

"I understand it is much too late to prevent what surely must happen next. The horse has escaped the stable, Thomas. Therefore, I will not worry about closing the gate."

Thomas stopped halfway through another stride. "So you agree with me," he accused. "And what do you believe will happen next?"

"The priests of the Holy Grail will replace those within the church now," Gervaise said mildly. "Then, I suspect they will preach sedition."

"Sedition? Rebellion against the established order?" Thomas exploded again. "Impossible. To set their hand against the church is one thing, but against the royal order is yet another!"

"Impossible?" Gervaise echoed softly as he walked to a bench half hidden by overhanging branches and sat. "Last summer you conquered Magnus and delivered all of us from oppression of our former master. Yet how have you spent your winter? Relaxed and unafraid?"

Thomas sat alongside the old man. "You know the opposite," he said slowly, realizing where his answer would lead. "Day after day, each meal, each glass of wine tasted first for poison. Each visitor searched thoroughly for hidden weapons before an audience with me. Double guards posted at the door to my bedchamber each night. Guards at the entrance to this garden, ready to protect me at the slightest alarm. I am a prisoner within my own castle."

"Thus," Gervaise said with no trace of triumph, "you are no stranger to rebellion. Why, then, do you persist in thinking it may not come from another source?"

"Mayhaps," Thomas countered. "Yet these are priests against priests, Holy Grail against those from Rome, each seeking authority in religious matters, not matters of state. . . ."

Thomas let his voice trail away as Gervaise shook his head and pursed his lips in a frown. "Thomas, these new priests carry powerful weapons! The Weeping Madonna. The blood of St. Peter. And the promise of the Holy Grail."

Gervaise paused, then said, "Tell me, Thomas, should the priests of the Holy Grail become your enemy, how would you fight them?"

Thomas opened his mouth to retort, then slowly shut it as he realized the implications.

"Yes," Gervaise said. "Pray these men do not seek your power, for they cannot be fought by sword. Every man, woman, and child within Magnus would turn against you."

Thomas leaned on the ledge near the window and waited until Robert of Uleran entered and closed the door to the bedchamber.

"Attack, beast!" Thomas called out. "Attack!"

With a high-pitched yip, the puppy bolted from beneath a bench and flung itself with enthusiasm at Robert's ankle.

"Spare me, milord!" cried Robert of Uleran in fake terror. "Spare me from this savage monster!"

The puppy had a firm grip on Robert's boot, and no shaking could free him.

Thomas laughed so hard that he could barely speak. "Tickle him behind the ears, good Robert. He's an easy one to fool."

Robert of Uleran reached down, soothed the puppy with soft words and a gentle touch, then scooped him up and dropped him in Thomas's arms.

Thomas rubbed the top of its head. "Would that all of Magnus could be tamed this easily."

Robert of Uleran nodded. "You seem far from ill, milord. The reports led me to believe I would find you half dead beneath the covers of your bed."

Thomas smiled. "I was that convincing, was I? Good." He grew serious very quickly. "Do not let the rumor rest. It serves our purpose for all to believe the fever grips me so badly that I cannot leave this room."

"Milord?"

"Robert, three days ago, with the miracle of the weeping statue, the priests of the Holy Grail won the mantle of authority in the church of Magnus. They now preach openly from the pulpit itself, and the former priests have been banished from the church."

Robert shrugged. "Let the religious orders fight amongst themselves."

"I wish I could agree," Thomas said. The puppy chewed on the end of his sleeve and sighed with satisfaction. "But I must be sure that there is no threat to the remainder of Magnus."

Robert of Uleran raised his eyebrows in a silent question.

"All winter," Thomas continued, "we have been hidden in these towers, away from the people. Aside from the servants in this keep, and those who request audience, I have almost been a prisoner."

"The Druids, milord," Robert of Uleran said in a whisper. "You cannot be blamed for precautions."

"Perhaps not. But now I have little idea what concerns these people in everyday life. How do they feel about these new priests? Someone must go among them and find out."

"I will send someone immediately."

"A guard?" Thomas asked. "A knight? Do you believe such a man will receive the confidence of housewives and beggars?"

Robert of Uleran slowly shook his head.

Thomas grinned. "I thought you might agree. Therefore, someone must spend a day on the streets in disguise, perhaps as a beggar himself."

"But who, milord? It must be someone we trust. And I am too large and well known for such a task."

"Whom do I trust more than myself?" Thomas countered. His grin widened. "And it has been a long and terrible winter cooped inside these walls."

Gone was the long, flowing purple cape Thomas wore as lord of Magnus. Gone were the soft linen underclothing, the rings, and the sword and scabbard.

In their stead were coarse, dirty rags for clothing, no jewelry, and—as Thomas had copied from his long-departed knight friend—a short sword ingeniously hidden in a sheath strapped between his shoulder blades. To pull the sword free, Thomas would only have to reach over his shoulders as if scratching his back.

With Robert of Uleran's help, Thomas dyed his skin several shades darker with the juice of boiled bark. He cut his hair short in ragged patches, and carefully scrapped dark grease beneath his fingernails. It was his plan to spend at least two days among the peasants of Magnus, and only the blindest of fools would fail to notice the improbability of clean hands on a street beggar.

To disguise his features, Robert of Uleran suggested an eyepatch. Many in the land were disfigured or crippled and forced to beg or die.

Thus disguised, Thomas let his shoulders sag and added a limp as he slipped unnoticed through the great banquet hall among the crowds of morning visitors.

He stepped into the spring air outside and rejoiced at his freedom as a beggar. For with his purple cloak and scepter, he had also left behind his responsibilities and the constant vigil against Druid assassination.

It took less than a minute for some of that joy to be tarnished.

"Step aside, scum!" bellowed a large man guiding a mule loaded with leather. When Thomas did not react instantly, the man shoved him rudely back into a crowd of people on the side of the street.

"Watch yourself!" another shouted at Thomas. Hands grasped and pulled at him, while others pushed him away in disgust. One well-placed kick inside the back of his knee almost pitched Thomas forward, and when he stood upright again, he knew it would not be difficult to pretend his limp for the rest of the day.

Thomas moved ahead, handicapped by the lack of depth vision because of his eye patch.

Still, he refused to be downcast. He was, after all, temporarily free. In two days, he would resume his position of authority— without regrets; for now, he could wander much as he did the first time he set foot in Magnus as a powerless orphan.

He smiled to remember that day. The streets, of course, looked identical. Shops so crowded the streets that the more crooked buildings actually touched roofs where they leaned into each other. Space among the bustling people was equally hard to find.

The streets were filled with the stench and mess of emptied chamberpots and the waste of sheep or calf or pig innards thrown there by the butchers. Pigs squealed, donkeys brayed in protest against heavy carts, and dogs barked, all a backdrop of noise against the hum of people busy in the sunshine.

Thomas sighed and turned backward to gaze at the large keep of Magnus dominating the center of the village. It was easy to rejoice in his new role as beggar, knowing he would be back in its quiet and safety by the next evening, and knowing he would not need to beg to feed himself.

To confirm that, Thomas reached for his hidden pouch which contained two silver coins. Beggar or not, he did not relish going hungry in the evening or on the morrow—

Thomas groaned.

Those grasping hands in the crowd! Only five minutes away from the castle and I have been picked as clean as a country fool.

Thomas sighed and resigned himself to a long two days among his people.

CHAPTER

29

"T is our good fortune the weather holds so well," the old lady cackled to Thomas. "Or the night would promise us much worse than empty bellies. The roof above us leaks horribly." Thomas grunted.

The old lady accepted his grunt as one of agreement. She moved herself closer and snuggled against his side in the straw.

Thomas grunted again, then fought the urge to laugh.

Which was worse? The cloying barnyard smell of the dirty stable straw, or the stale, unwashed odor of the old woman who sought him for warmth. His skin prickled; already he could feel the fleas transferring from the woman to him.

Besides, Thomas did not know if he agreed with her. It had been so long since he had known hunger, he almost would have preferred a rainy, cold night for the sake of being fed.

"I wonder," he asked, "why there are not more of us seeking shelter here. Do they fear the soldiers of Magnus?"

Thomas, however, knew well they did not. As lord, he had commanded his men not to harry the poor who commonly used the stables as a last resort. *So why are the stables empty?*

The old woman snorted. "The others choose the church as sanctuary."

"Ah," Thomas said. He maintained his role as a wandering beggar, freshly arrived in Magnus. "I hear the priests of Magnus will give food and a roof to any who pledge to work the following day." Thomas smiled to himself. He and Gervaise had set that policy themselves, to allow the penniless their pride and to stop the abuse of charity by the lazy.

Much to his surprise, the old woman laughed cruelly. "No

longer! Have you not heard? Those priests have been replaced by the men of the Holy Grail."

"Indeed?" Thomas replied.

"Indeed." The old woman explained the miracle of the weeping statue, and how the newcomers had ruthlessly used their newfound power to banish the former priests.

"You say the priests of old are not in the church. Where, then, do the less fortunate stay each night, if not here in the stables or at the church?"

"I did not say the church was empty," the old woman told him. "Only that the poor need not pledge a day's services in exchange for food and lodging. Instead, the priests of the Holy Grail demand an oath of loyalty."

"What!" Thomas sat bolt upright and bumped the woman solidly. He almost forgot himself in his outrage and forced himself to relax again.

"Lad," the old woman admonished, "I pray thee might give warning the next time. My old bones cannot take such movement."

"I beg pardon," Thomas said. "It seems such a strange requirement, the pledging an oath." He must keep his voice wondering instead of angry. "I thought an oath of loyalty could only be pledged to those who rule."

The old woman cackled again. "Are you so fresh from the countryside that your eyes and ears are still plugged with manure? These priests have promised the Holy Grail to their followers. With such power, how could they not rule soon?"

Once again, Thomas fought frustration at the invincibility of his unreachable opponents. When he felt he could speak calmly again, he pretended little interest.

"What do you know of this Grail?" he asked casually. "And its power?"

The old woman clutched Thomas tighter.

"Had you no parents, lad? Anyone to instruct you in the common legends?"

She reacted instantly to his sudden stillness.

"I beg pardon," she said softly. "There are too many orphans in the land."

"'Tis nothing." Thomas waved a hand in the darkness. "You spoke of the Holy Grail."

"The Holy Grail," she repeated. "A story to pass the time of any night."

Her voice became singsong, oddly beautiful as it dropped into a storytelling chant. As Thomas listened, the stable around him seemed far away.

"Long ago," she said softly, "at Camelot, there was a fellowship of knights so noble . . ."

So the story began.

The Holy Grail, she told Thomas, was the cup Christ had used at the Last Supper, the night before He was crucified. This cup was later obtained by a wealthy Jew, Joseph of Arimathaea, who undertook to care for Christ's body before burial. When Christ's body disappeared after the third day in the tomb, Joseph was accused of stealing it, and was thrown into prison and deprived of food. But he was miraculously kept alive by a dove which entered his cell every day and deposited a wafer into the cup.

"Yes," the old woman breathed, "it was in that prison cell that Christ Himself appeared in a blaze of light and entrusted the cup to Joseph's care! It was then that Christ instructed Joseph in the mystery of the Lord's Supper and in certain other secrets! It is these secrets which make the Holy Grail so powerful!"

"What are these secrets?" Thomas interrupted.

"No one knows" she said, "but it matters little. How can these secrets help but be marvelous?"

Yes, Thomas thought sourly, *despite the profound lack of truth in this legend, it is something to which the people want to cling. And oddly, again, I find myself sympathizing with the church as it struggles to counteract the ignorance around it in this age of darkness.*

Thomas did not betray that almost bitter reaction. He wanted the old woman to continue, wanted badly to know if the priests of the Holy Grail had managed to poison the people of Magnus entirely.

She told him the rest of the legend in awed tones, as if whispered words in the black of the stable might reach those priests of power.

After Joseph was released, he was joined by his sister and her husband, Bron, and a small group of followers. They traveled overseas into exile, careful to guard the cup on their journey, and formed the First Table of the Holy Grail.

"This table was meant to represent the Table of the Last Supper," the old woman said with reverence. "One seat was always empty, the seat which represented Judas, the betrayer. A member of the company once tried sitting there and was swallowed up!"

Thomas marveled at the woman's superstitious belief. Yet, he told himself, if one cannot read, one cannot combat the evils of ignorance.

"Go on," he said gently. "This takes place long before King Arthur, does it not?"

"Oh, yes," she said quickly. "Joseph of Arimathaea sailed here to our great island and set up the first Christian church at Glastonbury, and somewhere nearby the Grail Castle."

She sighed. "Alas, in time the Grail Keeper lost his faith, and the entire land around the castle became barren and known as the Waste Land, and strangely, could not be reached by travelers. The land and the Grail remained lost for many generations."

The woman settled farther. Her silence continued for so long that Thomas suspected she had fallen asleep.

"Until King Arthur?" he prompted.

"No need to hurry me," she said almost crossly. "I had closed my eyes to see in my mind those noble knights of yesteryear. Too few are the pleasant thoughts for a forgotten old woman."

Then, remembering the impatience of youth, she patted Thomas's knee in forgiveness. "Yes, lad. Until King Arthur. At the Round Table the Holy Grail appeared once, floating veiled in a beam of sunlight, and those great knights pledged themselves to go in search of it."

Thomas settled back for a long story. Many were the escapades of King Arthur and his men, many the adventures in search of the Holy Grail, and many the hours passed by people in their telling and retelling.

Thomas heard again of the perilous tests faced by Sir Lancelot and his son, Sir Galahad, by Sir Bors, Sir Percival and the others . . . how Sir Percival wandered for five years in the wilderness, found the Holy Grail, and healed the Grail Keeper, making the Waste Lands flower . . . how Percival, Galahad, and Bors continued their journey until they reached a heavenly city in the East, where they learned the secrets of the Grail and saw it taken into heaven.

His companion told it well, this legend which captured all

imaginations. But she did not finish where the legend usually ended.

"And now," she said, "these priests offer to us the blood of a martyr of ancient times, blood which clots, then unclots after their prayer. They offer us the weeping statue of the Mother Mary. And they speak intimately of the Holy Grail, returned rightfully to them, with its powers to be shared among their followers!"

Thomas felt his chest grow tight. Indeed, these were the rumors he had feared. "What must they do to receive the benefits of the Holy Grail?"

The old woman clucked. "The same as the poor must do to receive shelter. Pledge an oath of loyalty, one that surpasses loyalty to the lord of Magnus, or any other earthly lord."

Open sedition, open rebellion! These were the rumors which had not yet reached him, the rumors he had sought by leaving his castle keep. How much time did he have left to combat these priests?

Another thought struck Thomas.

"Yet you are here," Thomas said to the woman, "in the stable and not at the church. Why have you not pledged loyalty for the benefits of food and lodging?"

The old woman sighed. "An oath of loyalty is not one to be pledged lightly. And many years ago, when I had beauty and dreams, I pledged mine to the former lord of Magnus."

"Yet . . . yet . . ." Thomas stammered suddenly at her impossible words, "was that not the lord who oppressed Magnus so cruelly, whom Lord Thomas recently overcame?"

"You know much for a wandering beggar," she said sharply. "Especially for one ignorant of the Holy Grail."

"I have heard much in my first day here," Thomas countered quickly.

"So be it," the old woman agreed. "I did not swear an oath to *that* tyrant. No, my pledge of loyalty was given to the lord who reigned twenty years earlier, a kinder lord who lost Magnus to the tyrant."

Thomas marveled. This woman showed great loyalty to the same lord Thomas had avenged by reconquering Magnus. *I will reward her later, when I leave my disguise and resume my duties as lord of Magnus.*

He was given no time to ponder further. The nearby horses stamped nervously at a sudden rustling at the entrance to the stable.

"Hide beneath the straw!" the old woman hissed. "We'll not be found!"

She began to burrow.

While Thomas did not share her fear, he wanted to maintain his role, and a half-blind beggar in a strange town would do as she instructed. So he burrowed with her until they were nearly covered.

Many moments passed. Strangely, a small whimpering reached them.

Straw poked Thomas's ears and closed eyes. Despite his curiosity, he held himself perfectly still.

Somehow, a patter of light footsteps approached their hiding spot directly and with no hesitation. From nowhere, a cold wet object bumped against his nose, and Thomas nearly yelped with surprise. Then a warm tongue rasped against his face, and Thomas recognized the intruder was nothing more alarming than a friendly puppy.

Can it be—

"Thomas?" a voice called.

Tiny John! What meaning did this hold?

Thomas sat up and shook the straw free from his clothes. Yes, it was his puppy wriggling against him in joy.

"I am here," Thomas said from beneath the straw. He ignored the surprised flinch of the old woman. "What urgent business brings you in pursuit?"

"I followed the puppy to you," Tiny John explained. "Exactly as Robert of Uleran predicted in his last words to me."

Thomas stood quickly, a cold fear in his stomach.

"His *last* words? What has occurred?"

Tiny John's voice trembled. "The castle has fallen without a fight, milord. Few were those who dared resist the priests of the Holy Grail."

"That . . . cannot . . . be," Thomas uttered.

"I recognize you!" the old woman cried.

"The deception could not be helped," Thomas muttered, as his mind tried to grasp the impossible.

The old woman ignored him. "Dark as it is, I know that voice. Tiny John. He is a friend of the lord of Magnus! And a friend to the poor. Why, more than once he has raided the banquet hall and brought us sweet meats and flagons of wine. The boy could pick a bird clean of its feathers and not wake it from . . ."

The old woman's voice quavered, then faded. "What deception? You spoke of deception?" Then a quiet gasp of comprehension. "The boy called you Thomas! Not our Thomas? The lord of Magnus?"

"Aye, indeed. I am Thomas. And by Tiny John's account, now the former lord of Magnus."

The old woman groaned and sat heavily.

"Milord," Tiny John blurted. "The priests appeared within the castle as if from the very walls! Like hordes of rats. They—"

"Robert of Uleran," Thomas interrupted with a leaden voice. "How did he die?"

"Die?"

"You said that he spoke his last words."

"Last words to me, milord. Guards were falling in all directions, slapping themselves as they fell! The priests claimed it was the hand of God, and for all to lay down their arms. Robert of Uleran pushed this puppy into my arms and told me to flee, told me to give you warning not to return to the castle."

Thomas shifted the puppy into the crook of his left arm and gripped Tiny John's shoulder fiercely with his right hand. "You know not the fate of Robert of Uleran?"

"No, milord. There was great confusion."

Thomas then covered his face with his free hand, and bowed his head in sorrow.

CHAPTER

30

Thomas limped along the edge of the streets. It took little effort to add that limp to his step; yesterday's brutal kick was this day's growing bruise, and a sleepless chilled night had stiffened his leg considerably.

Beneath his rags, he carried the puppy in the crook of his left arm. There was comfort in the warm softness of the animal against his skin.

Thomas kept his gaze lowered on each halting step along the street. Whispers of the massive bounty placed upon his head had reached his ears: the priest of the Holy Grail had offered a brick of purest gold to the man who captured him. *If the wrong sharp pair of eyes recognizes me, despite the rags and eyepatch . . . if the old woman does not keep her vow of secrecy . . . if Tiny John is captured by bounty hunters . . .*

Yet Thomas could not remain hidden, cowed in a dark shadow somewhere within Magnus. To survive, he must escape the castle island. To escape, he needed help from one person he might trust.

And to reach that person, he must enter directly the lions' den. So Thomas limped to the church and prayed no Holy Grail priest would inquire too closely of the business of a starving beggar.

At the rear of the stone building, Thomas followed the same garden path he had walked only two days before in his purple cape as lord of Magnus.

He rounded a bend of the path and saw the familiar figure of Gervaise kneeling in the soil, pulling weeds with methodical delicacy. Thomas almost straightened and cried aloud in relief, but caught himself in time. Instead of a joyful call, Thomas continued to limp, and in that manner slowly reach the old man.

"Good sir," Thomas croaked. "Alms for the poor? I've not eaten in two days."

Gervaise yanked another weed free from the soil.

"Gervaise," Thomas hissed. "It is I!"

Gervaise didn't look up. "Ask your question again," he said, "as if I am deaf. And add insult to your words."

Thomas hesitated a moment, then raised his voice. "Are you deaf, you old cur? I've not eaten in two days."

"Do as the other beggars," Gervaise instructed equally loudly with acted impatience. "Enter the church and pledge allegiance to the priests of the Holy Grail."

"Within the church?" Thomas said quickly. Shock raised his voice another level. "Why would—"

Thomas stopped abruptly as Gervaise turned his head to look upward in response.

The mangled right side of the old man's face was swollen purple. Lines of dried blood showed the trails of cruel, deep slashes. His right eye was swollen shut, and his nose was bent and pushed sideways at an angle which made Thomas gag.

"The priests of the Grail know we are friends," Gervaise said calmly. "This was done to encourage me to deliver you into their hands. They observe me now from the church windows and from the trees behind you."

Thomas blinked back tears.

"If you do not go into the church shortly," Gervaise said in a low voice, "those watchers will suspect you and hunt you down. They may be within hearing distance. Ask me now which priest to see. Do not forget the insults."

Thomas hoped his voice would not choke as he forced the words into a scornful snarl. "Worthless donkey! Instruct me well the priest to seek, ere I add to your scars!"

"Enter the church without hesitation," Gervaise commanded quietly. "You *must* reach the altar. Then—" Gervaise looked past Thomas, then back at Thomas. "Spit upon me. Curse me as if I have not replied!"

"I cannot."

"Thomas, anything to deceive our watchers. It will purchase a few precious moments."

"May the pox blind you and your children," Thomas finally

blurted, then spat downward. "Feed my belly, not my ears, you miserable old man. May worms rot your flesh as you sleep if you do not help me."

Gervaise recoiled and bowed his head as if afraid.

But his voice continued strong. "Thomas, the panel beneath the side of the altar which holds the candles—kick it sharply near the bottom. Twice. It will open. Use the passage for escape."

"But—"

Gervaise then looked Thomas squarely in the eyes. Exhaustion and strain marked the other side of the old man's face. "After sixty steps, you must make the leap of faith. Understand? Make the leap of faith. You will find the knowledge you need near the burning water."

Thomas began to shake his head. "Burning water? What kind of madness do you—"

"Strike me across the face," Gervaise urged Thomas. "You must reach the altar. If they suspect who you are, Magnus and all its history are lost."

"Gervaise—" Thomas pleaded.

Gervaise sighed. "Show courage, my young friend. Strike me."

Thomas raised his right hand.

Gervaise nodded slightly without turning away. "God be with you, Thomas," he whispered.

Thomas swung down. The impact of hand against swollen face sickened him. And the grunt of pain from the old man brought a whine from the covered puppy in Thomas's other arm.

Gervaise crumpled beneath the blow.

Will that convince the unseen watchers?

Thomas stepped over Gervaise, then limped toward the entrance of the church. He kept his head low and wept.

At the wide doors to the church, Thomas discovered that some of his fears were unfounded. Instead of being a lone and highly noticeable figure, he was only one of many entering and leaving the building.

Once inside the church, Thomas stopped to let his stinging eyes adjust to the sudden dimness.

Men and women stood in a long line down the center of the nave. In the chancel near the altar stood a priest who briefly dipped his hands in a vessel, then touched the forehead of the person bowed before him.

"Move on, you bag of scum," a fat man growled at Thomas from behind. "This is no place to daydream."

Thomas fell in behind two women and slowly limped toward the front of the church. The measured pace of the line gave him time to look around. Vaulted stone ceilings gave an air of majesty and magnified the slightest noise. The nave where he stood was clear of any objects save pillars. Rumors had reached Magnus from London of churches holding long benches called pews for the worshippers, but no one believed such nonsense. People had always stood to worship.

There were at least four priests of the Holy Grail in the church—one at the front and three on the sides of the nave. Thomas tried to study their movements without betraying obvious interest.

Was it fear, or did he imagine they in turn studied him?

Thomas also wondered at his own lunacy. How much trust should he have placed in Gervaise? Had the blows to the old man's head addled him? What could exist beneath the altar? And how would the altar be reached—and kicked—without the notice of the priests?

Yet Thomas moved forward. He had no choice. Those behind him pressed heavily.

And even if he could turn away, what good would it do? There was no place to hide in Magnus.

His heart pounded harder as step by step the line advanced to the priest at the front. Thomas recognized him as Hugh de Gainfort. Garbed in royal purple robes, he dipped his hands in the liquid.

"Partake of the water of the symbol of the Grail," Hugh de Gainfort intoned, "and henceforth be loyal to the Grail itself and to its bearers. Blessings will be sure to follow. Amen."

The woman kissed his hand. "Thank you, father."

The line moved ahead.

"Partake of the water of the symbol of the Grail," said Hugh de Gainfort without acknowledging the woman's adoration, "and henceforth be loyal to the Grail itself. . . ."

The next person moved up.

Would the puppy in Thomas's arms remain quiet?

"Partake of the water of the symbol of the Grail. . . ."

Thomas wondered if the priest would hear the thumping of his heart long before he reached the front. Only ten people stood between him and Hugh de Gainfort, and Thomas could see no way to reach the altar beyond without drawing attention to himself.

What trouble had Gervaise cast him into?

" . . . And henceforth be loyal to the Grail itself and to its bearers. Blessings will be sure to follow. Amen."

The light of the sun through the reds and blues of the stained-glass windows cast soft shadows upon Hugh de Gainfort, so that if Thomas did not look closely, he would not see hatred glittering in those eyes, hatred he had felt during their brief audience in the castle keep.

Will I be recognized during the blessing? Thomas worried. *And if not, how to reach the altar? And even at the altar, what truth can there be to the old man's instructions? And if the passage reveals itself, how can I enter unnoticed?*

Thomas swallowed in an effort to moisten his suddenly dry throat. This was madness, and he was only one step away from a blessing which . . .

"Partake of the water of the symbol of the Grail . . ." Hugh de Gainfort's hand dipped automatically into the water. Wet fingers brushed against Thomas's forehead. " . . . And henceforth be loyal to the Grail itself, and to its bearers. Blessings will be sure to follow. Amen."

Thomas started to turn away. The movement drew Hugh's eyes briefly. Suddenly those black eyes widened.

"It is you!" the priest hissed. He opened his mouth to shout.

Thomas reacted with a fighting move he had been taught by Robert of Uleran, but had never been forced to use. He twisted his shoulders away from the priest, then spun them back to drive forward his right hand in a shortened swing. In that blink of an eye, Thomas managed to hit his target with his clenched fist, middle knuckle slightly protruding. The point of the knuckle found its target, a small bone between the ribs, just above the priest's stomach.

The air left the priest's lungs with an audible pop. He clutched himself and began to sway. It happened so quickly those behind Thomas were not sure what they had seen.

Before Thomas could decide how best to flee, a terrifying crash shattered the quiet church. One of the arched windows fell inward, burying a nearby priest. A large stone clattered across the floor. White light from sudden sun flooded the church and danced off rising dust. Hugh de Gainfort dropped to his knees, still winded so badly he could barely breathe, let alone draw enough air to shout.

Then another crash as the window farther down tumbled inward.

The destruction—it can only be Gervaise!

Thomas did not hesitate. Whatever sacrifice the old man had just made to create the diversion must not be wasted.

All eyes were focused on the western arm of the church building, and the third window cascaded inward, as if riding the high scream that entered with it.

Thomas darted to the altar.

What did the old man say? The panel beneath the candles—kick it sharply near the bottom. Twice.

Thomas glanced to see if Hugh de Gainfort had seen him, but the priest had sagged into a limp bundle. All others stared in horror at the sight of priceless stained glass in pieces. *If there truly is a passage, I may escape without witnesses.*

Thomas kicked once. Twice.

Soundlessly, the panel swung inward. It revealed a black square beneath the altar, wide enough for a large man.

Then another scream from outside the building. *What price has Gervaise paid?*

Thomas bit his lower lip. He must ensure the sacrifice was not made in vain. Thomas ignored the pain in his leg and sat quickly, so that his feet dangled over the edge. He pulled the puppy from beneath his arms.

"My friend, if you go to your death, so do I."

Thomas put both arms around the puppy to shield it, then let himself fall into the darkness.

CHAPTER
31

Thomas dropped for half a heartbeat. He closed his eyes and braced for the crush of impact to splatter him against the black unknown.

Then, incredibly, it felt as if arms began to wrap him, as a great resistance began to slow his fall. Thomas felt growing friction against his body and realized these were not the arms of a savior, but a giant sleeve of cloth tapered into a narrowing tube.

It slowed him almost to standstill as the tube grew so narrow that the fabric squeezed even against his face. Then, just as it seemed he had more to fear from suffocation than from splintered bones and shredded flesh, his feet popped into open air, and he slid loose from his cloth prison.

Even though the final fall was less than the height of a chair, Thomas was not able to see the ground in time to absorb the impact; the jarring of his heels against hard ground forced a grunt of pain. He recovered his breath quickly and strained to see around him.

"Wherever we are, puppy," Thomas said, glad in this darkness for the company of his whimpering friend, "let's pray it is a better alternative than what was in store for us above."

Thomas reached around to explore for walls. In the darkness, he could not even see the movement of his own arms. He pulled his eyepatch loose, but that did not help his vision.

Thomas forced himself to smile. "Ah, puppy, you do not answer. That is a good sign. For if I were mad, or dreaming, you would speak."

He set the puppy down and sobered immediately.

So much had happened so quickly. Only yesterday, he had

ruled the island castle of Magnus, and by extension, the kingdom around it. Today he was a fugitive, marked for death by the offer of a brick of gold for his head. Because of him, his friends had suffered equally. Robert of Uleran's fate was unknown, Gervaise was surely dead for his sacrifice of distraction, and Tiny John could only wander the streets and hope the priests of the Holy Grail would not place any importance on his freedom.

And now?

Thomas took a deep breath to steady himself.

Now he was in pitch blackness, somewhere below Magnus in a pit or passage he had never known existed.

To return to Magnus would endanger his life. Yet how long could he remain within the bowels of the earth?

A new thought struck Thomas with such force that he sucked air in sharply.

Gervaise knew. Gervaise knew of the trapdoor below the altar.

More thoughts tumbled upon Thomas. Warnings and whispers of evil and secrets within Magnus he had heard more than once. Warnings he had tried to ignore throughout a long winter of isolation within the castle keep. Warnings that had plagued him since first conquering the kingdom.

Surely this must be part of the mystery of Magnus. Yet if Gervaise knew, why did he not reveal it much earlier, before the arrival of the priests of the Holy Grail? And if Gervaise knew but said so little, is he a friend or foe? And if he is a foe, what lies ahead?

Thomas stopped his whirlwind of thought. *No, if Gervaise were foe, he would not have ensured this temporary escape.*

Thomas must believe. He had no choice.

He strained to remember the old man's words.

After sixty steps, you must make the leap of faith. Understand? Make the leap of faith. You will find instructions near the burning water.

Somewhere in this darkness, he would find the answer. But if there ever was a moment to delay the search, it was now. He paused for a moment of quiet repose and prayed.

Then he took his first halting step with a courage which resulted from three things—the calm from prayer, the promise of an explanation should he find the burning water, and, strangely, from the puppy, who blundered into his legs at every step. A companion, no matter its size, made the eerie silence easier to bear.

Thomas took his second step into a rough stone wall. His groping hand prevented any injury to his face, yet he recoiled as if he were struck. Any sudden contact, gentle or not, created awesome fear in this pitch darkness.

Thomas pushed himself away, then thought against it, and brought his right shoulder up to the wall again.

"I'll feel my way along," he told the puppy. "It will give me warning of twists and turns."

Thomas patted the wall as he followed it, grimacing at real or imagined cobwebs. He stubbed his fingertips against outcrops of stone and stumbled occasionally against objects on the ground. Twice he patted empty air—as much a fright as the original contact against stone—and each time discovered another turn in the passage. He counted every step, remembering the strange message about a leap of faith. The puppy stayed with him and did not complain.

Upon his sixtieth step, Thomas paused. There was nothing to indicate a leap of faith. *What did the old man mean?*

Two steps later, Thomas reached for the stone wall ahead of him and for the third time found nothing.

"Another turn," he muttered to the puppy. "Is this what he meant? Then why not warn me of the previous two?"

He slowly began to pivot right, when a low angry noise froze him. It took a moment, but Thomas identified the echoes as growls of the puppy at his feet.

"Hush," he spoke downward, then moved to take his step.

The puppy growled again, with enough intensity to make the skin ripple down Thomas's back.

"Easy, my friend." Thomas knelt to hold the puppy. The growling stopped.

Thomas stood and moved again. This time the puppy bit Thomas in the foot and growled louder.

"Whelp! Have you gone crazy?"

Thomas reached down to slap the puppy for its insolence, but couldn't find it in the dark.

He groped farther, patting the ground. First behind him, then to his side, then—

Ahead! The ground ahead has disappeared.

Thomas forgot the puppy. He patted the wall on his right,

found the edge of the corner, and slid his hand downward, finally kneeling to reach as low as possible. Where the corner met ground, it was no longer a corner, but a surface which continued downward below the level of his feet.

The skin on his back now rippled upward in fear.

"Puppy," he cried softly. A whimper answered him.

Thomas, on his knees and blind in the darkness, crawled backward two more paces, then eased himself onto his stomach.

Feeling safer on his belly, Thomas inched forward again, feeling for the edge of the drop-off with his extended right hand. When he reached it, he kept his hand on the edge, but shuffled to his left, determined to find the width of the unseen chasm.

Seconds later, he found it, joined to the left wall.

Thomas was too spent with jolts of fear to react with more than a moan of despair.

"How deep?" he asked the puppy. "How far ahead to the other side?"

Thomas crawled ahead as far as he dared. With his dangling hand, he reached down into the blackness. *After all, perhaps this drop is a mere foot or two. I could be stuck here forever, afraid to step downward.*

Thomas slumped. His exploring hand had found nothing. Even after drawing his sword and extending it to reach farther, he could not prove to himself that the drop was only a shallow ditch.

Long minutes later, he raised his head from the ground. He knew he had three choices. *Leap ahead and trust the chasm was narrow enough to cross. Drop into the chasm and trust its bottom was just beyond his reach. Or retrace his steps.*

He chose to reverse direction.

Sixty-two counted steps and two turns later, he was back to his starting point. Thomas looked upward, half expecting to see light where the priests might be peering downward from the trapdoor beneath the altar. But he knew that would not be. No one had seen his escape. And now he was trapped here, unless the other direction yielded better results.

He patted the ground and crawled ahead. Since he had passed his original beginning point, he did not know whether he should expect another sudden chasm ahead in the opposite direction.

Thomas did not travel far before the wall turned sharply, then sharply again. By now, as blind as if both eyes had been covered with patches, Thomas was accustomed to thinking with his fingers. He knew he had reached the end of the passage and was proceeding in his original direction, except along the left wall.

"Are you with me, puppy?" Thomas called. He wanted to be reassured by a familiar sound in the blackness. The puppy whined, and Thomas smiled through his misery. He had no choice but to proceed sixty-two steps back to the chasm and from there, debate his bleak prospects in a silence louder than any noise he had ever heard.

Unless . . .

Unless the passage split! After all, he had only traced the right-hand side of it. Perhaps the left-hand side broke into another passage and all he need do was find it by patiently continuing his blind groping.

Thomas called the puppy closer and tried to find its ears in the darkness. The puppy found his hand first and gently licked Thomas's fingers.

It was then Thomas realized the rawness of his broken skin and that the puppy was trying to lick away blood. In his fears, Thomas had not noticed the damage done by the walls to his fingers.

He moved ahead. Yes, the left wall must split into a new passage somewhere before the chasm. *It must.*

It did not.

Sixty-two steps and two turns later, Thomas was again on his belly, feeling ahead in the terrifying darkness for that drop-off.

He found it, retreated slightly, and with his palm banged the ground in frustration, uncaring of the new pain.

How could he possibly overcome this barrier?

Then a tiny flicker caught his eye. Thomas almost missed it, so much had he given up on using vision to aid his senses.

He blinked, then squinted. Five minutes passed. Another minute.

There! The flicker again. It brightened, then dropped to nothing. Thomas strained to focus and pinpoint its location. Ten agonizing minutes later, another flare, hardly more than a candle, suddenly snuffed.

It dawned slowly upon Thomas.

Burning water.

He was seeing the light of a far-off flame, light he had missed the first time here because it flared so rarely and softly, light which reflected and bounced through one or two more turns of the passageway.

Thomas lowered himself and sat, knees huddled against his chest. The puppy leaned against him, whining occasionally and then growling for no apparent reason.

A phrase echoed through his head. *Understand? Make the leap of faith.*

Why had the old man been so urgent with those words? Why had he repeated them and no other part of his instructions?

Make the leap of faith.

It reminded him of a conversation once held with Gervaise.

"One quiet morning," he said to the puppy, "Gervaise told me, 'No matter how much you learn or debate the existence of God, no matter how much you apply your mind to Him, you cannot satisfy your soul.'"

The puppy rested his chin on Thomas's upper thigh.

"Then the old man said, 'There must come a time at the beginning of your faith when you let go and simply trust, a time when you make the leap of faith, something much like a . . .'" Thomas faltered as he suddenly realized the significance of Gervaise's repeated words. *Something much like a leap into the darkness.*

"It is a leap into the darkness, Thomas," Gervaise had said. "God awaits you on the other side. First your heart finds Him; then your mind will understand Him more clearly, so that all evidence points toward the unshakable conclusion you could not find before; and after that leap your faith will grow stronger with time. But faith, any faith, is trust and that small leap into the darkness."

"No, Gervaise," Thomas said aloud. "I cannot do this. You ask too much."

Make the leap of faith. Understand? Sixty steps and make the leap of faith. Thomas had no doubt that Gervaise had meant he should do this now. Yet how could he blindly jump ahead? What lay on the other side? What lay below?

Make the leap of faith.

Thomas frowned. Then he finally allowed himself to decide what he had known since recalling the old man's words about faith.

He must leap into the darkness.

Ten times Thomas paced large steps backward from the edge of the chasm. Ten times he repaced them forward again, careful to reach down and ahead with his sword on the eight, ninth and tenth steps to establish he had not yet reached the edge.

"Puppy," he said, as he retraced his steps backward yet again, "if leap we must, I shall not do it from a standstill. Faith or not, I doubt our God or Gervaise enjoys stupidity."

Thomas had debated briefly whether to take the puppy. But only briefly. The extra weight was slight, and he could not bear to make it across safely and hear forever in his mind abandoned whimpers of a puppy left for dead.

Thomas squatted and felt for the line he had gouged into the ground to mark the ten paces away from the edge.

He rehearsed the planned action in his mind. He would sprint only eight steps, for he could not trust running paces to be as small as ten carefully marked paces. On the eighth step, he would leap and dive and release the puppy. His hands would give him the first warning of impact—he prayed for that impact—and at best he might lose his breath. The puppy would travel slightly farther, and at best tumble and roll. At worst, neither would reach the other side of the unknown chasm in this terrible blackness.

Thomas drew a deep breath. He hugged the puppy once, then tucked it into the crook of his right arm.

Make the leap of faith.

"God be with us," he whispered. Then he plunged ahead.

CHAPTER

32

On the eighth step, at full sprint, Thomas drove upward and left the ground.

In the blackness around him, he had no way to measure the height he reached, no way to gauge how far forward he flew, and no way to know how much he dropped.

It seemed to take forever, the rush of air in his ears, the half sob of fear escaping his throat, and the squirm of the puppy in his outstretched hands.

The puppy! In midair, Thomas pushed him ahead and released him from his hands. Before he could even think of praying for safety, the heels of his hands hit solid ground, and he skidded onto his nose and chin, then, as his head bounced upward, onto his chest and stomach. He could count his heartbeats thudding in his ears.

Was he across? Or at the bottom of a shallow ditch?

The puppy's confused whimper sounded nearby.

Thomas coughed and rolled to his feet.

"My friend," he said, "we seem to be alive. But across?"

Thomas answered his own question by turning around and crawling back. Moments later, his hands found an edge!

Thomas grinned in the darkness.

The next two turns in the passageway and the next eighty-eight steps took nearly an hour. Although the occasional flare of reflected light grew stronger, it provided little illumination. Thomas dared not risk another unseen chasm.

When he reached the turn, his reward was another flicker of light, this time, the flame itself! Not a reflection! It was straight ahead and far down the passageway. As Thomas drew closer, the rising and falling light provided more clues about the passage.

The walls were shored up with large blocks of stone, unevenly placed. He saw why his groping fingers had received such punishment in the total darkness.

The passage was hardly higher than his head, and wide enough to fit three men walking abreast. Other than that, nothing. No clues to the builders. No clues to its reason for existence. No clues to its age.

Thomas half ran the final few steps to the light.

Gervaise promised the knowledge I needed. It can only mean a message. And if Gervaise managed to leave the message, he also managed to leave here again, and there is hope in that.

Thomas noted the source of the light. It was imbedded in the wall, as if a hand had scooped away part of the stone. A wick of cloth rose above a clear liquid, and from it came the solitary tongue of flame. *Burning water!*

He did not examine the light for long, because the puppy whined and sniffed at a leather sack barely visible in the shadows along the wall below the flame. Thomas pulled the sack away before the puppy could bury its nose in it entirely.

He understood the puppy's anxiousness as soon as he opened it. Cheese. Bread. And cooked chicken legs. All wrapped in clean cloth.

Thank you, Gervaise.

Thomas suddenly realized how hungry he was. He ripped into a fat chicken leg, chewed a mouthful, then tore pieces free with his fingers to drop to the puppy.

More objects remained in the bag. Thomas pulled free a large candle. He dipped the end into the flame in the wall and immediately doubled his light. Then he pulled free a scrolled parchment, tied shut with a narrow ribbon. His fingers trembled as he pulled the ribbon loose and unscrolled the parchment.

> *Thomas, if you read this, it is only because the Druids disguised as priests of the Holy Grail have conquered Magnus. Yet, if you read this, it is because you dared make the leap of faith I requested, and in so doing have proved you are not a Druid.*

Druids! The shock was as of an arrow piercing his heart. Then Thomas rubbed his forehead in puzzlement. *To suggest I might be a Druid—how could Gervaise even dare to think the unthinkable? I have spent the entire winter in fear of their return.*

Yes, my friend, the chasm you leaped was a test. Were you one of the Druids, you would have known that these passages and halls—

Passages and halls? Thomas sighed. This message created more mystery than it solved. Did Gervaise imply that all of Magnus was riddled with secret tunnels?

—passages and halls are buried so deep in the island that anything more than several feet below their level would fill with water. As a Druid, you would already be familiar with this. As a Druid, you would have confidently stepped down and walked across, even without a light to guide you.

That you are reading this means you are not a Druid, for in that shallow, dry moat, I placed a dozen adders.

Adders! Snakes with venom so potent that only a scratch of poison could kill. *A dozen adders!* In the darkness, the puppy had not growled at the drop-off, but at what his nose had warned him about.

Thus, you now have my trust, Thomas. I regret I could not give it earlier. There is much to tell you, my friend, and I fear by the time you return to Magnus, I will not be alive to reveal to you the epic struggle between the Druids and Merlins.

Merlin! Mention again of the ancient days of King Arthur. For Merlin, King Arthur's adviser, had become a legend equaling the king himself!

I cannot say much in this letter, for who is to guess what others may stumble across it, should you not take the leap of faith. Let me simply ask you to consider the books of your childhood. It was not chance that they were placed near you, those books of ancient knowledge from faraway lands. It was not chance that one of us was there to raise you, to teach you, to guide you, to urge you to reconquer Magnus, to show you the way. It was not chance that I spread the legend of the angel shortly before your birth.

These new words were not the piercing of an arrow, but the bludgeoning of a club. *Gervaise knew of those precious books hidden near the abbey? Impossible!* At the significance of the message, Thomas could hardly breathe. He remembered the night he had conquered Magnus on the wings of an angel, how the entire population of Magnus had gathered enough strength from his arrival to overthrow its evil lord, simply because of a legend which all believed. *This had been planned before I was born?*

Yet none of this knowledge could I share, Thomas, much as I treasured our conversations. For too many years passed with you alone in the abbey. We did not know if they had discovered you and converted you. We did not know if you were one of them, allowed to conquer in appearance only, so that we might reveal the final secrets of Magnus to you, secrets so important I cannot even hint of them now.

You trusted me this far. I beg of you to continue that trust. Your destiny has grown even more crucial. We did not expect the Druids to act so boldly, so soon. Even now, perhaps, they have the power to conquer completely. As a born Merlin, you must stop them.

Thomas wanted to protest aloud. *I a born Merlin? Gervaise, how can you reveal so much, yet reveal so little?*

Follow this passage, Thomas. It will take you to safety. Return to the abbey of your childhood. Search for the answers among your books. Trust no person. Our stakes are too high. The Druids must not prevail.

CHAPTER

33

MAY 1313
PARIS, FRANCE

Katherine looked up, startled as a shadow crossed the pages of her open book.

"I'm sorry, my child," a soft voice reassured her. "The thoughts I interrupted, they must have been enjoyable. Your face showed much pleasure. And I was clumsy to—"

She blushed. "Frere Dominique, it is I who should apologize for daydreaming. The progress I have made with this Latin has not been remarkable."

"Katherine," Frere Dominique admonished, "it is not enough you have won an old priest's heart? And now you take advantage of it with beautiful helplessness that is merely acted?"

Katherine laughed. Little escaped the old priest. Although he was plump and graying and always wore a jolly smile, his eyes gleamed sharp in unguarded moments, or during the rough-and-tumble arguments in logic he and Katherine enjoyed to pass the time throughout the long winter here in the library of the royal palace.

Frere Dominique studied Katherine's face. He would miss the joy of admiring her fine, high cheekbones, the curve of her smile, the depth and innocence of her gaze.

"Yes, father?" Katherine asked his searching eyes. "Is something wrong?"

Frere Dominique nodded. "Only for me," he said. "I shall truly miss your presence here."

Katherine stood quickly. She took one of the priest's hands in hers and squeezed it tight. "He has returned?"

Frere Dominique nodded, then shook his head mournfully. "After an absence of six months, he refuses to accept the hospitality of a night's stay here. Even now, that scoundrel is in the stable, preparing a horse for you."

Katherine dropped the priest's warm hand. "Travel? So soon? Did he mention—"

Once again, Katherine blushed.

"England?" Frere Dominique finished for her.

Katherine nodded, watched the priest's face, and waited.

"Yes," Frere Dominique finally said. Then he smiled. "Your face again carries the look I interrupted moments ago. Who has captured your thoughts, Katherine? Were I three decades younger, I would be smitten with jealousy."

Katherine and Hawkwood rode for two days to reach the harbor town of Dieppe on the French side of the English Channel.

She knew Hawkwood was anxious. He did not question the price offered for their horses in Dieppe, although it was scandalously low. And half an hour later, he did not barter with the ship's captain for passage across the Channel.

Three days on a pitched and gray North Sea brought them to the cliffs of Scarborough. Once again, Hawkwood did not waste time searching for the fairest price of horseflesh, and paid double what he should have.

They rode thirty miles, directly to an obscure abbey north and east of the town of York, stopping only when the sun went down.

"Patience," Hawkwood said, "is well known as a virtue."

"Then I shall be nominated for sainthood," Katherine replied. "For nearly a week now, I have waited for you to inform me of the reason for our mad haste."

She waved at the land around them. "And now you ask me to sit here for hours, perhaps days, on the mere chance that Thomas might arrive in this remote valley."

"Keep your hands still," Hawkwood admonished. "He must have no hint of our presence."

"He will not arrive."

Hawkwood chuckled. "Your voice betrays your hope."

They had settled into the side of this hill barely half an hour earlier. Although they were near the exposed summit of the valley, Hawkwood had shrewdly chosen a vantage point among the shadows of large rocks. Downstream, trees guarded the tiny river which wound past the abbey.

Hawkwood had pointed at a jumble of rocks and boulders on the river, some as large as a peasant's hut. "There," he had said, "is hidden a dry, cool cave, invisible except to those who have been led to its narrow entrance among the granite and growing bush. That is his destination."

And now, long enough later so that the prickling of the sun's first heat had brought forth the ants which played in the dust in front of her, Katherine turned the discussion back to the questions she wanted answered.

"Not only shall I receive a sainthood for patience, but if ignorance is bliss, I shall be the happiest saint to walk this earth."

"I tell you little, but for your own protection."

"No," Katherine corrected. "For the protection of Magnus."

She then repeated the oft-heard words. "After all, I cannot divulge what I do not know."

That drew a sigh.

"Katherine," he said, "not even I know the entire plan. We all have our tasks, and we must trust to the whole."

Would it be fair, she wondered, *to push him for more?*

She hesitated. *Was it fair*, she countered, *to know so little?*

So she decided to ask, almost with dread at his anticipated anger. "Yes," she said softly. "There is truth in that. You fear that I might be taken by the Druids and forced to betray us. But if something should happen to you . . . how could I carry on our battle without more knowledge than I have now?"

Hawkwood dropped his head. Instead of anger, sadness filled his voice. "There is truth in that. And I've wondered how long it would take for you to use my sword of defense upon myself."

She waited, sensing victory, but feeling no enjoyment.

He continued. "In the cave below are books. In Latin, French, even Italian. But mostly Latin. Once, as you know, those of us in Magnus had the leisure to translate from all languages into that universal word."

"Books?" Katherine was incredulous. "Here in this valley. But that is treasure beyond value! Why here?"

"Indeed," he said, "treasure beyond value. More than you know. These are not books coveted by the wealthy for beauty and worth. In that cave lies knowledge brought from lands as far away as the eastern edge of the world. All for Thomas to use in his solitary battle."

"That is why you are so certain he will return," Katherine breathed.

"The messenger told me that Magnus had fallen. With no money and no army, Thomas has no choice but to seek power from the knowledge in that cave."

"As he did to conquer Magnus," Katherine said absently.

A sharp intake of breath from Hawkwood. "You know that?"

"Wings of an angel," she said simply. "How else could he have had such a secret?"

"Of course," he said. "You would not fail to see the obvious."

Should she feel guilty? Her answer was not a lie, but she had not told Hawkwood that Thomas had hinted to her of these books—and regretted it later as he banished her from Magnus.

Katherine now realized the immensity of the secret Thomas had held, not knowing she was one of his watchers. But her new information led to more questions.

As Katherine puzzled through more thoughts, she changed the direction of her query. "Why must we continue to watch? Surely he now needs our help."

Hawkwood shook his head. "Not until we are certain to which side he belongs. Our only word was that Magnus had fallen. Nothing else arrived from Gervaise to guide us further. In this game of masks behind masks, we can only wait."

Katherine finished for Hawkwood. It was a familiar argument. "For if he were a Druid, he would act as if he were not. Now, perhaps, it was convenient for them to assume open control of Magnus. And equally convenient to send him forth as bait."

He in turn finished her oft-used argument. "Yet, if he is not one of them, we can do so much good by revealing ourselves. Together, our fight will be much stronger."

They both sighed. It was an argument with no answer they could trust. Too much depended on Thomas.

When he arrived, they almost missed him.

He still remembered every secret deer path in the surrounding hills from his years of avoiding the nearby harsh monks. At times, Thomas would approach a seemingly solid stand of brush, then slip sideways into an invisible opening among the jagged branches, and later reappear farther down the hill.

His familiarity with the terrain, however, did not make him less cautious. It was only the loud caws of a disgruntled crow which warned Katherine and Hawkwood. Even then, it took them twenty minutes to see his slow movement.

From above, they watched Thomas circle the jumbled rocks near the river. Then he slipped into a nearby crevice and surveyed the area.

"He was taught well," Hawkwood whispered approval. "He has no reason to be suspicious, yet he still remains disciplined."

Minute after minute passed.

"He counts to one thousand," Hawkwood explained. "He was taught that this cave is the most important secret of all. Taught never to let anyone discover the entrance."

Thomas circled slowly once more, sometimes visible, sometimes not.

Katherine ached to see him, to discover if she still felt as she remembered. But she too had been taught discipline, and she held herself motionless, none of these thoughts crossing her face.

Then she noticed something.

"He walks awkwardly," she whispered. "Not from the bag he carries, but as if hunched."

Then she gasped as the hump on his back moved. And just before Thomas disappeared into the cave, she saw his burden poke its nose out from the back of his shirt.

"A puppy," she said in amazement. "An entire kingdom rides on his shoulders, and in its place he carries a puppy."

CHAPTER
34

Two days passed. During the long hours of waiting, Katherine could satisfy little of her curiosity through discussion, for Hawkwood insisted on silence. He also insisted on alternating watch duty. One must sleep while the other observed the rocks of the entrance.

The few moments they were both awake were spent sharing the sack of breads and cheeses they carried.

At night, they moved closer to the rocks by the river and settled into a nearby crevice in the hill. They could not trust the light of the moon to remain unclouded, and Thomas might leave at any hour. Twice already he had alarmed them with sudden appearances, only to fill a leather bag with water and return to the cave.

At night then, Hawkwood had told Katherine, their ears must serve as their eyes, for if they failed to follow Thomas to his next destination, the plan would surely be doomed.

Tell me more of the plan, Katherine had wanted to ask, but she did not. What Hawkwood knew of the plan would be revealed only when he deemed it proper.

She knew his urgency stemmed from reports that Magnus had again fallen, and she understood the need for action. *Without Magnus . . .* now she had been fully taught the history and tradition of the Merlins and hardly dared contemplate how many centuries of careful guidance were on the brink of destruction.

But why the importance of Thomas?

Deep as her feelings for him might run, warm as the skin on her face might flush as she remembered him, Katherine could force herself to remain objective enough to wonder why so much rested upon his shoulders.

Where are the other Merlins of this generation? Must Thomas combat the Druids alone and unaware of battles which have been fought for centuries?

And why the extreme urgency now? After all, until Thomas recaptured the kingdom, Magnus was under the control of the Druids for twenty years. Surely the passing of one month, two months, cannot determine the battle.

Surely—

"Katherine. Day is nearly upon us."

Katherine stirred, ready to pick her careful way back to the observation point.

"Wait!" came the soft whisper.

She froze. And immediately understood.

Below her, Thomas had finally moved out of the cave, and without the sack of food he had carried inside. Without the leather bag for water. Without the puppy.

He wore the plain brown garb of a simple monk.

They followed him along an isolated path in the forest south of the small Harland Moor abbey. Hawkwood went first, melting into the trees and keeping Thomas in sight. Katherine, a hundred yards behind and less adept at stealth, simply kept Hawkwood in her line of vision.

At times she lost sight of him completely. She marveled again and again at how silently he flitted from tree to tree, bush to bush.

An hour later, Hawkwood held up a hand of warning, then settled into a crouch. Katherine responded by doing the same.

Five minutes later, Hawkwood was up and moving ahead. This march of three continued for another half hour until they reached the road leading into the town of Helmsley.

Hawkwood waited for her at the side of the road.

"He is ahead of us," he told Katherine. "I have no doubt he is going to town."

Katherine raised an eyebrow in question. "His detour?"

"Gold," Hawkwood replied. "He has retrieved some of the gold he earned from the gallows in Helmsley and buried before leaving here with the knight for Magnus last summer. He has purchases in mind."

They next saw Thomas near the Helmsley stables where they had left their own horses a few days earlier. Watching discreetly proved no problem, with the usual crowds around the market stalls.

Thomas engaged himself in conversation with the ruddy-faced man who tended the stables.

Both nodded. The man disappeared inside the stable and returned with a middle-sized gray horse.

Thomas shook his head. The stableman shrugged. Another five minutes of conversation, this time with much animation.

The man again entered the stable, this time returning with a large roan stallion. Even from their vantage point, Katherine could appreciate its size and power.

A few more minutes of conversation. A snort of derisive laughter from the stableman. And yet again, he entered the stables. He brought out not a horse, but shabby blankets and saddlebags customarily placed on donkeys.

Thomas nodded, and the man departed. Instead of swinging onto the horse, Thomas threw a blanket over it and cinched on the saddlebags. He remained on foot and led the horse by its halter.

As soon as he was safely out of sight, Katherine and Hawkwood approached the stableman.

Hawkwood flashed a bronze coin.

The stableman grunted recognition. "The two of you." He looked at the coin and sneered. "I thought you'd both died. I've kept both your mounts in oats for three days. You expect bronze to pay the fare?"

"No," Hawkwood said. He pulled a tiny gold coin from deep within his cloak and handed that to the man, who bit the coin to test for softness.

"It's barely enough, but I'm not one to take advantage of strangers."

"It's a third more than you expected," Hawkwood said quietly. He then showed the bronze coin again. "And this is yours if you tell us what the little sparrow heard."

"Eh?"

Hawkwood fluttered his hand skyward. "The little sparrow flitting around as you spoke to that monk's assistant. What harm could there be in telling us words from a sparrow's mouth."

The fat man leered comprehension. "Ah, that sparrow. Now I

recall." He leaned forward and widened his leer to show dark stumps for teeth. "Unfortunately, that sparrow's a shy one."

A second bronze coin appeared in front of the stableman.

"The monk's assistant told me he wanted a horse that could outrun any in York," the stableman said quickly. "That was all."

"You spent ten minutes in conversation," Katherine protested.

The stableman looked at her darkly, then back at Hawkwood. "It's a sad day when a woman interrupts the business of men."

Katherine rose on her toes to answer, but caught the slight warning wave of Hawkwood's hand.

"I'll see she learns her lesson," he said. He then stroked his chin. "York? Hasn't its earl fallen from power?"

"It's what I said too," the stableman nodded. "I told him what even the deaf and blind know, that the earl of York now rots in his own dungeon." The man paused.

"Yes?" Hawkwood prompted.

"It's peculiar. When I said that, he told me that's exactly why he needed the horse."

Katherine knew Hawkwood had no appreciation for foolishness, so she waited an hour to ask her question. By then, they had traveled five miles along the road to York, and she had sifted through enough of her thoughts to know which question to ask, even if she would not start with it.

"We have not reached or passed Thomas yet," she began. "This means one of two things."

"Yes?" Hawkwood asked in good humor. It always lifted his spirits when Katherine applied her training.

"Either he mounted his horse as soon as he was out of sight of the town, and has ridden it fast enough to keep the distance between us as he travels to York. Or—"

"How do you know it will be the second and not the first?" Hawkwood interrupted.

Katherine smiled. "Because he wants to appear as a lowly monk's assistant leading a master's horse from one town to the next. He doesn't dare ride, because too many travel this road, and many would wonder at someone dressed so poorly mounted on such a fine horse. Since we have not yet reached him, he does not first travel to York."

Hawkwood clapped approval. "Instead, he has—"

"Thomas has undoubtedly returned to the abbey to retrieve what he needs from the cave to fill those saddlebags." Katherine paused at the thought and at what it meant. "He is arming himself."

"Yes, my friend." Hawkwood said nothing more, and they passed the next hundred yards with only the clopping of the horses' hooves to break their companionable silence.

She turned her gaze downward as the minutes passed. Not for the first time did she stare at the road and wonder at the Roman soldiers who had set these stones more than a thousand years earlier, even before the time of Merlin himself. York had been an outpost in the wild interior, while Scarborough forty miles to the east had been the coastal watchpost. From the high cliffs of Scarborough, the Roman sentries could easily spot enemy ships; the efficient road to the interior made it easy to shuffle legions of soldiers back and forth between Scarborough and York. And now, hundreds of years later, the road carried the everyday traffic between the two towns.

"Katherine."

She pulled away from her thoughts.

"What question do you have?"

"You can read me that well?"

"You had no need to impress me with your guesses. Except that I am sometimes impatient with meaningless prattle, and it seemed as if you sought to discuss Thomas more."

Katherine felt her face color at Hawkwood's tiny grin of comprehension and the twinkle in his eyes.

She also knew Hawkwood did not like false modesty or coy games, so she asked her question with no further hesitation.

"Why York?" she blurted. "Thomas knows—as do all—that the priests of the Holy Grail rule York as surely as they rule Magnus. Moreover, the earl of York, in chains or not, is a sworn enemy to Thomas. Why enter the lions' den?"

Hawkwood spoke so softly she could barely hear. "I've wondered that myself. Perhaps he has decided that if he frees the earl of York, they will swear a pact of allegiance and together fight the priests. Perhaps he simply wishes to observe the priests without fear of recognition by the townspeople, as would happen to him in Magnus. After all, he knows that the first maxim of warfare is simple. 'Know thine enemy.' "

Another hundred yards.

The riders swayed to the rhythm of the slow plodding. With less urgency now than during their previous travels, there seemed little purpose in taxing the horses.

The leaves of the oak trees lining the road had already burst forth, and dappled shade covered the two as they moved steadily along the road. Soon the leaves would be full and the road enough covered from the sun.

Have only four seasons passed since Thomas first entered Magnus? Only four seasons since I first spoke to him in a candlemaker's shop? Only four seasons since his long-predicted arrival captured my heart?

Another thought haunted her. *In another four seasons, will Thomas still be alive and the battle continued?*

"Your face is an open book, my friend." The gentle voice once again took her from her thoughts.

"Even if Thomas frees the earl," Katherine blurted, "or if he knows the priests of the Holy Grail as well as they know themselves, how can he prevail against their miracles? Blood of the martyr? The weeping statue?"

"The blood and statue I can easily explain," Hawkwood said. "How he is to prevail, I cannot tell."

"Please," Katherine said quietly. "I have great curiosity."

"Simple," Hawkwood said. "The blood is nothing holier than a mixture of chalk and water from rusted iron, sprinkled with salt water." He snorted. "Those false priests pray for the congealed blood to turn to liquid, but they help their prayers by gently shaking the vial. That's all it takes. And when it settles, it appears like thickly clotted blood."

"And the weeping statue?"

Another snort. "Those stone eyes weep water only when brought from the warmth into the coolness of the church. More sham and trickery."

"We too could duplicate those miracles?"

"And prey upon ignorant superstition? Never. And we choose to always remain hidden from the people."

"Thomas could expose those tricks for what they are!" Katherine said. "Surely, if enough see the truth, the priests would be known as frauds and lose their power to rule."

"No, Katherine. There is only one Thomas, and thousands upon thousands to convince. People treasure their misconceptions, cling to them, and never look beyond. Besides, how long could Thomas travel as a free man during his demonstrations against the priests?"

Katherine puzzled for several moments. "An army, then. Thomas can observe the priests, discover their weaknesses, and muster an army to strike as he sees best."

The old man shook his head. "With what money might he raise an army? With what allegiances? Moreover, the priests now maintain rule because all believe they are spokesmen for God. What man, what knight, dares raise a sword against the Almighty, when false miracles are so eagerly believed?"

They traveled much farther before Katherine spoke again. "There seems to be little hope for him. And for us."

"Perhaps Thomas is not meant to prevail," Hawkwood replied. "We still have no certainty to which side he belongs. They must know he is watched by us, even if they do not know the watchers. An apparent defeat of Thomas will lead us to trust him, and with trust, we might impart to him the final secrets they need so badly."

Katherine could only set her chin stubbornly as a means to hold back a sigh of sadness.

The never-ending logic of argument.

She closed her eyes and spoke to the sky. "This waiting is a cruel game."

CHAPTER

35

The next morning their wait at the massive gates to the town wall was rewarded as the bells rang Sext to mark midday. Unlike Magnus, the walls around the town of York did not have the advantage of a protecting lake. But they were much thicker, to better protect against battering rams. Indeed, so wide were these walls that atop were large chambers built from equally massive stone blocks.

Katherine and Hawkwood were so close to the west gate that almost directly above them, and built into the high arch above the entrance to the town, was one of York's prisons.

An open window had been cut into each of the four walls of the prison, hardly enough for a small boy to crawl through. Despite the thirty-foot drop to the ground, iron bars had been placed into the windows as a final barrier to prisoners with dreams of escape.

When Katherine looked up, she imagined the occasional dark shadow of movement through the window closest to her. She did not look up often, however. Imbedded into the stone walls were iron pikes. Upon three of them were impaled the heads of men who stared their silent horror on the town, as warning to others who might also become rebels.

Katherine watched as a noisy stream of peasants and craftsmen entered the town beneath those gateway prisons. This steady stream disappeared quickly once inside York, as the cobbled road twisted and turned its way into dozens of side streets.

Katherine and Hawkwood stood among the jostling people bartering for the wares of the cook shop. The aromas of the food did not make their waiting easy. Katherine could smell roasted joints and meat pasties—for a price double what one could expect to pay closer to the town center.

To amuse herself as she waited, Katherine tested her powers of observation by scanning the crowd for pickpockets. She saw two. One particularly clever pickpocket played the role of a drunk. He staggered and bounced into people, enduring their abuse and leaving with the coins he had dipped during the confusion of his fall against them.

Katherine hoped the jugglers would return. Yesterday, a half-hour had passed in the space of a drawn breath, so adept were these men with whirling swords and flames. Even Hawkwood had coughed admiration and thrown small coins in their direction.

Of course, sights like this were to be expected in York. After all, with its ten thousand inhabitants, only London exceeded it in size.

Katherine lapsed into her favorite daydream, the one where she was able to explain as much as she knew to Thomas. She imagined his face and tried not to hear his last words to her as he banished her from Magnus. She tried to picture his smile on the day he might finally understand why she had withheld the truth.

Hawkwood nudged her as the last of the Sext bells rang. "He approaches," he whispered. "Hide your face."

Thomas went no farther than the town gates. Hawkwood and Katherine were close enough to see the surprise on his face as the guard shrugged and pointed upward. They were close enough to see the discreet transfer of a gold coin from Thomas's hand to the guard's. They were close enough to hear Thomas's instructions to a boy standing just inside the town walls.

He left the boy holding the horse's reins and guarding it just inside the gate. Thomas then spun on his heels and half-sprinted back to the guard beneath the arch of the wall.

The guard nodded upon his approach, brought Thomas to the side of the arch, and led him through a door.

"Can it be?" Hawkwood said in hushed tones, as they watched from the shadows near the cook shop. Then conviction entered his voice. "Why did I not realize it before?"

"Yes?"

He pointed upward. "The earl of York is held there." He

pointed upward. "Not in the sheriff's prison. I should have asked the same question he did upon entering York. . . ."

Katherine caught the trace of self-doubt. "No," she said, as she patted his arm, "you should not have inquired. We do not want to draw attention to ourselves."

Hawkwood sighed. "Of course."

His sadness disturbs me, Katherine thought, as they resumed their watch in silence. *He has never allowed me to see it before.*

Following that sigh, none of her former distractions seemed enjoyable, and the waiting and watching passed very slowly.

Three-quarters of an hour later, Thomas stepped outside again, nodded at the guard, and marched back to his horse. He took the reins from the small boy and, without looking back, led the horse into the center of York.

Even before Thomas was lost to sight in the swirling crowds, Hawkwood pressed two coins into Katherine's hand.

"One to bribe the same guard he did," he explained. "The other to bribe the guard above."

He spoke with renewed vigor. An effort to restore her confidence? She did not comment but merely waited for more instructions.

"Reach the earl," he said next. "We must hear what Thomas plans."

"If the earl does not speak?" Katherine asked.

"Tell him it is the only way for him to remove the curse from his family."

Katherine paused. "I do not understand."

"He will," came the reply. "All too well."

Damp stone steps led upward in a tight spiral.

"'Tis money poorly spent for an audience, my sweet duckling," the guard had said to Katherine. "The earl's as powerless as a newborn babe."

Knowledge is power, Katherine told herself firmly, *and if the earl shares his, it will be worth every farthing.*

She reached the open chamber at the top of the stairs. As she arrived, a guard was unlocking one of the doors.

How does he know I wish to visit the earl? I have not yet placed a bribe in his hand, nor stated my request.

Her silent question was answered within moments as she saw a prisoner step through the low, opened doorway. That prisoner was not the earl of York.

"You've done well," the prisoner said to the guard. "It is no surprise that Thomas—"

He stopped suddenly as he noticed Katherine. The guard turned too, and they both stared at their quiet visitor.

The black eyes of the prisoner studied her sharply. His cheeks were rounded like those of a well-stuffed chipmunk. Ears thick, almost flappy. Half-balding forehead, shaggy hair falling from the back of his head to well below his shoulders.

Waleran. The spy who had shared a dungeon cell in Magnus with Thomas. Katherine had been there too, disguised beneath a covering of bandages around her face.

She bit her tongue to keep from blurting out her surprise at his presence.

Surely Waleran has seen Thomas, has already discovered him, within the hour of arriving in York!

Katherine fumbled for words, wanting to look as flustered as she felt. "I've brought this for the . . . the former earl," she said, extending the wrapped food that Hawkwood had insisted she carry. "To repay a kindness he once did my father."

Katherine bowed her head in a humbleness which she hoped hid her flush of fear. As she waited, her heart pounded a dozen times.

How can I warn Thomas? If I leave now, they will suspect!

The prisoner finally spoke to the guard. "Help this pretty creature. I need no escort. And time presses me."

It is Waleran who orders the guard!

The guard grunted agreement and began to unlock the adjacent door.

Katherine let her pent-up breath escape as the prisoner brushed past her and began to descend the stairs. She willed herself to move forward slowly, despite the sudden urgency.

The guard blocked her movement. Her heart leapt into her throat, but then he held out a grimy hand, and she understood. With concealed relief, she placed a coin in his palm. He bowed a mock bow and unlocked the door for her to enter the cell.

Before the door had latched firmly behind her, she started in a rushed whisper. "My good lord, there is—"

The former earl of York understood why she halted her words.

He touched his face lightly with exploring fingertips of his left hand. "The penalty of losing an earldom. It appears much more terrible than it is," he told her.

This was not the proud warrior who had stood beside Thomas in battle against the northern Scots. This was not the confident man of royalty who had later decreed that Thomas surrender himself and Magnus. Gone was the red-blond hair that spoke of Viking ancestors. His face was still broad but no longer remarkably smooth. The blue eyes that matched the sky just before dusk were now dimmed. And gone was the posture of a man at ease with himself and the world he commanded.

Below his shaved skull, his face was crisscrossed with half-healed razor cuts, so that it appeared a giant eagle had raked him with merciless talons. His right shoulder hung limp at an awkward angle, popped loose from the collarbone. And his feet were still in splints wrapped with bandages gray-red from dried blood.

"Please, my dear, smile," he encouraged her. "It would be a small gift well received."

Katherine did so, hesitantly.

He waved her to speak. "You had something to impart, and, it seemed with great speed."

Katherine nodded and swallowed. She did not yet know if she could trust her voice.

"Your visitor, Thomas," she said. "Would you still wish him dead as you did when he ruled Magnus?"

The earl leaned forward. "You knew the monk's assistant was Thomas of Magnus?"

"Yes, milord. And I fear so shall those who now hold York."

"Impossible," the earl said.

Katherine pointed to a vent in the wall. "Impossible that your voices might carry to the prisoner beside you?"

"Hardly," the earl snorted. "My conversations with him have kept me from losing all sanity here. Yet, even if he eavesdropped, there is nothing he can do."

"Unless he were a spy named Waleran." Katherine explained those days with Thomas in the dungeon beneath Magnus.

The earl clenched his fists. "The prisoner across the wall was one of them? A Druid?"

Katherine replied softly, "Then I need not explain the Druid circle of conspiracy?"

The earl shook his head. "No. Nor the darkness they have placed upon my family for generations. You know of the Druids too? What madness is this?"

Katherine nodded at his first question, and shrugged at his second. She wanted to learn what Thomas intended, but she dare not press the earl too quickly.

He shuddered. "Druids. We have always been at their mercy."

He darted a sharp look at Katherine. "This is strange, your sudden appearance. You are not one of them?"

She shook her head. "The Druids have already imprisoned you."

The earl gaped in sudden comprehension. "These priests of the Holy Grail are . . . are . . . Druids?"

"And Thomas, I pray, is not," Katherine replied. "Yet you swore his death. Until today."

"I swore his death because the Druids had forced it upon me, had threatened my sons would die a horrible death of worms eating their flesh as they lived, as once happened to a former earl of York. And now you tell me Druids pose as these priests who rule my kingdom?"

The earl shook his head weakly. "First Thomas with his rash promises. And now you. I feel so old."

Time. So little time remains. Those heads on spikes are a reminder of the price of failure.

"Rash promises?"

"He offered my kingdom back," the earl said.

"What does he ask of you in return?" Katherine asked. "How will he attempt this? Where goes he next?"

The earl stared strangely at Katherine. "It dawns upon me that you are privy to much, yet are a stranger. Why should you have more of my trust? Why should I believe the story of a spy in the opposite cell? Perhaps you are here to prevent Thomas from succeeding. After all, only a Druid could know what you do."

The earl gained more strength as his thoughts became more certain. "Only a Druid watcher placed at the gates would have known of Thomas's arrival so soon."

Time. Too little time remains. Yet can I betray a secret which has been kept from outsiders for centuries?

She thought of Thomas, of the heads outside this very prison. Even as she spoke in this prison cell, did Thomas walk unknowingly to his doom? Katherine made her decision.

"Few know of the Druids and the evil they pursue," she whispered. "None know there are those who seek to counter them."

The earl's eyes widened. "Another circle?"

Anguish ripped through Katherine for even hinting at that. Since birth, she had been trained to keep what secrets she knew, and had been permitted to grasp only the edges of the truth. It was a secret so precious that not even she knew much more than the existence of the Merlins, only that she was one of them and had been given much of their teaching.

How could she bring herself to go beyond that hint and betray even more? But there was Thomas. If he were not a Druid but, as she hoped, one like her, mere observation was no longer enough. Thomas now needed help.

Finally, Katherine forced herself to nod. "Another circle."

Those words hung while she waited until she could remain silent no longer. "Please. Thomas is in danger."

"I gave Thomas my ring," he said, unconsciously twisting his now empty finger. "He was to offer it at the castle keep to gain an immediate audience with the man who now holds York for the priests—the new earl of York."

"That is insane," Katherine blurted. "For what reason would he seek audience with the enemy?"

The earl's reply stunned her.

"Thomas believes he will be able to escape York with a ransom hostage."

CHAPTER
36

The sunlight blinded Katherine after the dim prison, and she almost stumbled in her rush to rejoin Hawkwood.

For a moment she felt panic, for she couldn't find him in the crowd. Then the familiar black cape appeared as he stepped from a nearby doorway.

Katherine knew he was troubled. Instead of waiting for her information with calmly folded arms, he reached out to grasp her shoulders and search her face.

"It is not good," Katherine answered his questioning eyes. "Thomas, it seems, seeks his own death."

She explained quickly. Later she would tell Hawkwood what she had had to reveal to the earl of York to get her news.

"We have little choice but to follow, watch, and pray," Hawkwood said. "Too much happens too soon." He turned to march down the street which led to the castle of York.

They reached the outer courtyard of the castle burdened with a sack of flour that Hawkwood had hurriedly purchased as they passed by the market stalls.

Servants scurried determined paths through the steady flow of noblemen and ladies who paraded in and out of the entrance with the assured arrogance that money and title provide.

Of Thomas or Waleran there was no sign. Then Katherine noticed Thomas's now familiar stallion tethered to the trunk of a sapling in the far corner of the court. Tending the horse was the same boy Thomas had hired near the town gate.

She tugged on Hawkwood's arm and whispered, "Thomas is already inside. Do we follow?"

He shook his head and kept his voice low. "If he succeeds, he must come this way. If not, we will bribe servants to tell us the story of his failure and make our plans in accordance."

"How can he hope to succeed?" Katherine asked.

"That is my question too," Hawkwood said softly. He motioned with his head for Katherine to stay at his side, and walked to the boy who tended Thomas's horse.

"The monk's assistant," Hawkwood said to the boy. "Has he promised to return soon?"

"He made a jest," the boy replied. "He said soon or not at all."

Katherine shivered. It seemed so futile, this direct attack by a single person. What could Thomas accomplish without an army?

"We have business to complete," Hawkwood continued as he pointed at the sack of flour that Katherine held. "Yet if he trusted you with his horse, he most surely will trust you with his purchase that we now deliver."

The boy shrugged.

"Place it in one of the saddlebags," Hawkwood instructed Katherine. "We shall leave it there as he requested."

Katherine complied, as puzzled now as when Hawkwood had bought the flour. When she finished, Hawkwood moved beside her to inspect.

"Keep the boy's attention," he said quietly.

That task was easy. A slight smile was enough to encourage the boy's full stare, and Katherine had no need to further distract him with conversation.

Less than a minute later, Hawkwood rejoined her and they strolled to another portion of the court. Little attention fell upon them. The noblemen and ladies were much too full of themselves and their gossip to look at mere townspeople.

"All that remains is the wait," Hawkwood said. "And the longer it takes, the poorer his chances."

Katherine closed her eyes and summoned the vision of her last meeting with Thomas. *I cannot trust you. This battle—whatever it may be—I fight alone.*

It was at least five minutes before Hawkwood spoke again. "He leaves the entrance."

Katherine opened her eyes wide and drew her breath sharply.

At Thomas's side was another, a person she recognized instantly.

Long slim body, long dark hair, haunting half-smile of arrogance now touched with fear. Isabelle Mewburn, the daughter of the former lord of Magnus. Isabelle, who had proclaimed love for Thomas as a means to assassinate him. Isabelle, once held prisoner by Thomas himself.

Katherine could not help but feel a stab of jealousy. She knew that Thomas had been captivated by Isabelle's royal grace and stunning features.

To a casual observer, it might appear that Isabelle merely accompanied the lowly monk's assistant. Yet, as Thomas descended the steps at Isabelle's side, Katherine could see strain etched across her face and the falseness of the smiles she offered passersby. For Thomas discreetly had hold of her elbow with his left hand. His right hand was hidden beneath his cape.

Katherine guessed he held a dagger, and that he had threatened her life at the slightest attempt of escape.

At the top of the stairs, two guards watched closely every move that Thomas made, and followed them both from ten yards behind.

Thomas guided Isabelle to his horse. The boy removed the reins from the tree and placed them across the horse's neck.

Isabelle balked as Thomas gestured upward, then slumped as he said something Katherine was unable to hear. A renewed threat to plunge the dagger deep?

She swung up onto the horse. At that, the idle chatter in the courtyard stopped as if cut by the knife Thomas most certainly had.

"How strange, how crude," the whispers began. "A royal lady mounting a horse in full dress."

Some pointed, and all continued to stare.

Isabelle remained slumped in defeat, until Thomas moved to climb up behind her. At the moment his grip shifted on the unseen dagger, she kicked the horse into sudden motion.

Thomas slipped, then clutched at the saddle. His dagger fell earthward.

The next moments became a jumble. Thomas strained to pull himself onto the now galloping horse. Isabelle kicked at his face and both nearly toppled from the horse. People threw themselves in all directions to avoid the thundering hooves.

And the following guards noticed the dagger now lying in the dust; Isabelle was no longer threatened. The first one shouted, "Stop him. He kidnaps the lord's daughter!"

Knights scrambled to their horses. Screaming and shouting added to the general panic.

Thomas now had his arms around Isabelle's waist. The horse was galloping in frenzied circles.

The speed of the horse was its only saving grace. Had its panic not been so murderous, Isabelle could have thrown herself free of the horse and of Thomas. Instead, she could only cling to the horse's neck.

Thomas finally reached a sitting position in the saddle and roared rage as he reached for the flapping reins. His hands found one, then the other.

"Raise the drawbridge!" the other guard shouted.

Thomas pulled the reins. The horse responded instantly to the bit. Thomas spun the horse in the direction of the courtyard entrance, then spurred it forward amid the shouting and confusion.

People once again scattered, except for a solitary knight with a two-handed grip on a long broadsword. The knight braced to swing as the horse approached him.

That iron will cleave a leg! Katherine wanted to scream.

As the horse reached and then began to pass the knight, arrows flew, three above Thomas and into the stone wall of the courtyard. The last struck the knight's right shoulder and he dropped in agony. The sword clattered, useless.

Thomas swept through the gateway and thundered toward the drawbridge.

Katherine scrambled with all the other people in the courtyard to catch a glimpse of what might happen next.

Thomas and the horse passed into the shadows of the gateway.

Already, the bridge was a third of the way raised!

Yet Thomas did not slow down. A clatter of hooves on stone, then on wood. Then silence as the horse leapt skyward from the rising bridge. In the hush of disbelief that followed, that sudden silence became a sigh.

Almost immediately, the thundering of more hooves broke the sigh of silence.

Four knights had finally readied their horses, and the first charged through the courtyard gate toward the drawbridge.

After seeing Thomas escape, Katherine had relaxed. Now, with a deadly group of four in pursuit, she clenched her fists again.

Thomas must escape. Yet we are so helpless.

She spun sideways in shock at Hawkwood's soft laugh.

"Look." He pointed from their vantage point at the front of the gathered crowd. "The drawbridge."

All four horses skidded and skittered to a complete stop in the archway at the drawbridge. The huge wooden structure was still rising!

Loud bellows of enraged knights broke the air.

"Fools! Winch it down!"

Hawkwood's delighted chuckle deepened. "Such a bridge weighs far too much to be dropped. They'll have to lower it as slowly as it rose. With three roads to choose on the other side, the open fields in all directions, Thomas will have made good his escape!"

Hawkwood touched her arm.

"Much has yet to be done," he said. "But if he truly is one of us, we could not ask for more."

Katherine tried to smile.

Yes, she could exult that Thomas still lived. And still lived in freedom.

But he was not alone. Another was at his side.

CHAPTER

37

"Our friend Thomas is free," Hawkwood said. "Yet, there is much that troubles me."

Katherine turned to him. *There is much that troubles me, too. I cannot shake my last vision of him. The reins in his hands. The stallion in full flight. And she . . . far too beautiful, and Thomas holding her far too close.*

Katherine did not voice those thoughts. Instead, she said simply, "I am sorry you are troubled."

They stood at the crossroads outside the town walls of York. Behind them the population buzzed with incredible news. *The lord's daughter has been taken hostage! Kidnapped in daylight beneath the very noses of the courtyard knights!*

Those same knights had already scattered in all directions from the crossroads where Hawkwood and Katherine and a handful of travelers now stood, each knight engaged in useless pursuit of a powerful horse long since gone on roads which would carry no tracks.

Hawkwood's head was bent even lower now, as he searched the hard ground of the well-traveled roads.

"Stay with me," he said softly. "We shall talk as we follow Thomas."

"Follow Thomas?" Katherine echoed with equal softness. "Half an army runs in circles of useless pursuit. If he has escaped them, most surely he has also escaped us."

Hawkwood laughed quietly. "Hardly, my child. Do you not remember the puppy he left behind with his secret treasure of books?"

Of course. In the excitement of his escape, Katherine had forgotten that Thomas must soon return to the cave.

"Yes," she said quickly. "He'll have to get back to his books within several days. And regardless of his plans, he will not let the puppy die of starvation."

Hawkwood chuckled again. "That only demonstrates once again that when you think of Thomas, you think with your heart. You wish him to have the nobleness of mind that would not let an innocent animal die a horrible death."

"Is it otherwise?" Katherine challenged, even though her face flushed at Hawkwood's remark.

"Perhaps not. But others might believe Thomas will return to his puppy merely because of the more valuable books nearby."

Katherine ignored that. "So we proceed back to the valley of the cave and wait." She did not want to think about the days which Thomas would pass in the company of such an attractive hostage, one who had once claimed a true love for him.

"Not so," Hawkwood replied. "That is far too long. We will find Thomas by nightfall." Hawkwood's head was still down, as he continued to examine the ground carefully.

"That shows much confidence."

"No," Hawkwood smiled. "Foresight."

They hurried ahead on the road which led to east Scarborough on the North Sea. Neither found it unusual that several of the strangers behind them followed the same road.

Several minutes later, Hawkwood stopped and tapped the ground at his feet with the end of his cane.

"There," he said. "Our trail to Thomas."

He rubbed the tip of his cane through a slight dusting of coarse, unmilled flour.

Katherine nodded, unable to hide her own sudden smile at Hawkwood's obvious delight in himself and the implications of that flour.

"I cut a small hole in his saddlebag and, of course, in the sack of flour. Unmilled and coarse, the flour that falls through is heavy enough to leave a trail wherever he goes."

A mile farther, Katherine remembered Hawkwood's words at the crossroads.

"What troubles you about the freedom Thomas so dangerously earned?" she asked.

Hawkwood's eyes searched ahead for the next traces of flour.

He answered without pausing in his search.

"Thomas should never have escaped York."

"God was with him, to be sure," Katherine agreed.

"Perhaps. But I suspect instead the Druids in York provided earthly help."

"He nearly lost his life," Katherine protested.

"Are you certain? Describe the events you recall."

Were the subject matter less serious, Katherine might have enjoyed this test of logic.

"He left the castle with Isabelle, a dagger hidden beneath his cloak and pressed against her ribs."

"Before that," Hawkwood said, with a trace of impatience.

"A boy watched his horse at the side of the courtyard."

"Katherine . . ." Now his voice held ominous warning.

Suddenly, she understood. And understanding brought a pain, as if her heart had twisted in her chest.

"On his arrival," Katherine said slowly, "he met with the earl of York. The spy Waleran overheard their entire conversation, then hurried away as I entered the prison."

"Continue," Hawkwood said. Satisfaction in her perception had replaced his rumblings of vexation.

"Much time passed as the earl of York told me what Thomas intended," Katherine said. "Enough time for Waleran to reach the castle and provide warning."

Katherine's heart twisted more at the implication.

With that much warning, how had Thomas succeeded? Unless those at the castle had not feared his actions. Unless he were one of them.

Another memory flashed. Of a knight blocking escape, with his huge broadsword raised high to cleave Thomas dead as the horse and its two riders galloped toward him. Until a stray arrow slammed through the knight's shoulder.

"It was no accident, then," she said slowly, "that those arrows missed Thomas and instead struck the one knight able to stop him."

"Nor," Hawkwood added, "that the drawbridge was not raised soon enough to hold him inside of the town. Then raised high enough to keep the knights from immediate pursuit."

"Yet why?" Katherine moaned. Her words were meant as release for the sorrow which gripped her. She already knew the answer.

"Our much-used argument," Hawkwood said. "The unseen Druid masters play a terrible and mysterious game of chess. Would they not prepare for any of us who had followed Thomas? The only thing they could not know is that you would recognize Waleran. And neither, of course, could he know. For bandages no longer cover your face. And had you not seen Waleran and known they had been warned, this escape would not have been suspicious."

"I've always said it could not be," Katherine murmured. "I could not argue with my heart. But a contrived escape can only prove he is one of them."

Hawkwood stopped and touched her arm in sympathy. It was a touch as light as the breeze which followed them down the road.

"Against the Druids, nothing is what it appears to be," he said. "They know we watch, even if they know not who we are. The more it would seem Thomas is not one of them, the more likely we might finally tell him the truth."

They walked farther in silence.

"What shall we do?" Katherine despaired.

"We shall play this mysterious chess game to the end," Hawkwood said grimly. "We shall tell Thomas enough for him to believe we have been deceived. And then arrange a surprise of our own. He shall soon be a pawn which belongs to us."

Katherine paused in the edge of darkness just outside the glow of light from a small fire in front of Thomas and his captive.

Thomas had chosen his camp wisely. He was flanked on two sides by walls of jagged rock, protected but not trapped. The light of his fire was low enough that intruders passing even within twenty yards would not notice; and his horse, tethered to a nearby tree, had been muzzled.

Katherine had prepared herself to remain cold of heart for this moment. She had told herself again and again since leaving York that she would not care how Thomas chose to react to his hostage. What would it matter if she stepped into the firelight and found the two gathered together side by side to seek warmth against the night chill, Isabelle's long hair soft against Thomas's face as she leaned on his shoulder?

It would matter, Katherine discovered. Her heart soared as she surveyed their makeshift camp. As much as she suspected Thomas of being a Druid, it filled her with relief to discover him far from Isabelle.

Thomas was seated on a log, leaning with two hands on the hilt of a sword propped point first into the ground, and staring into the flames. He seemed oblivious of Isabelle on her blanket near the fire. Her hands were tied together and her feet hobbled like a common donkey.

Hardly the signs of romance!

Katherine smiled, then felt immediately guilty for rejoicing in someone else's misfortune. *Besides,* she reminded herself severely, *we are forced to believe Thomas is one of them. Even if he is one of us, there is no surety that his heart belongs to me, as mine already does to him. Did he not once banish me from Magnus?*

So she set her face into expressionless stone and stepped forward. He would not get the satisfaction of seeing any delight in her manner.

At her movement into the light, Isabelle shouted. "Flee! He has set a trap!"

In the same moment, Thomas stood abruptly and slashed sideways with his sword.

Both actions froze Katherine, and a thought flashed through her mind. *A warming from Isabelle. They expected an intruder!*

Katherine was given no opportunity to ponder. A slap of sound exploded in her ears, and a giant hand plucked her feet and yanked her upward. Within a heartbeat, Katherine was helpless, upside down and her hands flailing.

She bobbed once, then twice, then came to a rest, her head at least five feet from the ground.

She swung upside down gently, and Thomas came forward to examine her.

Wonder and shock crossed his face.

"You!" he said.

"This intruder is an acquaintance?" Isabelle asked, her voice laced with scorn.

Thomas turned and replied, as if instructing a small child, "Your voice is like a screeching of saw blades. Please grace me with silence, unless you choose to answer my questions."

He turned back to Katherine. His face now showed composure.

"Greetings, my lady." He bowed once, then gestured above her.

"As you can plainly see, an arrival was not entirely unexpected. My traitorous captive, however, hoped to give you warning."

Katherine crossed her arms to retain her dignity. It was not a simple task, given the awkwardness of holding a conversation while blood drained downward to fill her head. "You may release me," she said. "I have no harmful intentions."

"Ho, ho," Thomas said. A smile played at the corners of his mouth. "You just happened by? It was mere coincidence that my saddlebag is nearly empty of flour?" He tapped his chin in mock thought. "Of course. You found a trail of flour and hoped to gather enough to bake bread."

"Your jests fall short of humor," Katherine snapped. "Are they instead meant as weapons in your bag of tricks?"

"You approve, then, of the hidden noose attached to a young sapling?" He savored her helplessness. "All one needs do is release the holding rope with a well-placed swing of the sword, and the sapling springs upward."

His voice sounded slightly bitter. "Another weapon from the faraway land of Cathay. Surely you remember our discussion of that matter in better times. Times of friendship."

Katherine regarded Thomas silently and bit her tongue to keep from replying. This oaf knew so little about the risks she had taken and the sacrifices she had made on his behalf. How could she ever have dreamed in confiding in him? Even if he offered her half a kingdom she would not tell him the truth.

"Without speech, now?" Thomas grew angry. "Magnus has fallen, and like magic you appear, dogging my footsteps when I have avoided all the soldiers of York. I demand answers."

"Thomas, Thomas," another voice chided from behind him. "Emotion clouds judgment."

He whirled to face a figure in black, head hidden by the hood of the dark gown.

"And you! The old man at the gallows!" Thomas said hoarsely. He raised his sword. "I shall end this madness now."

The figure said nothing.

"Before, I had questions," Thomas continued, the strain of holding back his rage obvious in his voice. "And you spoke only of a destiny. Then you disappeared." He advanced and threatened the figure with his sword. "Now speak. Give me answers or lose your head."

Still no reply.

Thomas prodded the figure with his sword. It collapsed into a heap of cloth.

"You have much to learn," Hawkwood said from the nearby darkness. "Had I chosen, you would have died a dozen times already."

Thomas sagged, and Katherine felt stirrings of pity for what must be going through him. Anger. Confusion. Desperation.

"By the knowledge that you are still alive, accept that we come here in peace," Hawkwood continued. "Cast your sword aside, and we will discuss matters that concern us both. Otherwise, the crossbow I have trained upon your heart will end discussion."

Thomas straightened and dropped his sword.

Hawkwood stepped into view. Unarmed.

He shrugged at the expression that crossed Thomas's face. "No crossbow. A bluff, of course. You are free to grasp your sword. But I think your curiosity is my best defense."

Thomas sighed. "Yes." He pointed to the clothes on the ground. "How was it done?"

Katherine coughed for attention. Men! Her eyeballs might pop from her head at any moment, and they were more concerned with techniques of trickery.

"Simple," Hawkwood replied. "It is merely a large puppet, a crude frame of small branches within the clothes, extended from a string at the end of a pole, with the darkness around it to hold the illusion."

Katherine coughed louder.

Thomas ignored her and nodded admiration at Hawkwood. "A shrewd distraction."

Hawkwood shrugged modestly. "You are not the only one with access to those books."

Thomas froze. "Impossible that you know!"

"Perhaps. Perhaps not." Hawkwood moved to a log near the fire and sat down. "Please release poor Katherine, and I shall tell you more."

Thomas retrieved his sword, stepped out of the low firelight, and approached Katherine where she hung.

He brought his sword back quickly, as if to strike her. A half smile escaped him at her refusal to flinch.

Barbaric scum. To think I once dreamt of holding you. Katherine did not give Thomas the satisfaction of letting him see her thoughts cross her face.

He slashed quickly at the rope holding her feet and she dropped, head first, letting out a yelp of fright. Somehow, he managed to drop his sword and catch her in one swift movement that cost him a grunt of effort.

For a heartbeat, she was in his arms, face only inches from his. And for that heartbeat, she understood why dreams of him had haunted her since her banishment.

In the heartbeat of stillness between them, she sensed a strength of quiet confidence. The total impression in that brief moment was much too enjoyable, and the rush of warmth she could not prevent as he held her became anger. After all, he had joined the Druid cause. She should not feel as she did to be in his arms.

Her response at the anger she felt toward herself—almost before she realized her left arm was in motion—was to slap him hard across the open face.

He blinked, then set her down gently, but did not take his eyes from her face.

"On this occasion," he said softly, "there was no stolen kiss to deserve such rebuke."

Katherine glared at him, shook the cut rope loose from her ankles, then strode over to rejoin Hawkwood.

Side by side, they faced Thomas across the tiny fire.

"You promised to tell me more," Thomas said. "And for that, I would be in your debt. Although it will take much to convince me of your good intentions. Your arrival here was no coincidence. Little encourages me to believe you will speak truth."

How can he pretend to be innocent? What monstrous deceit!

Just once, Katherine wished she had not been taught to hold her emotions in control. Just once, she wished she could stamp the ground in frustration and scream between gritted teeth.

She was conscious, however, that Isabelle was watching her closely. Too closely. So Katherine composed herself to stand in relaxed grace.

"We do have much to explain," Hawkwood said. "There was our first meeting in the gallows—"

Thomas interrupted. "Timed to match the eclipse of the sun. I wish, of course, an explanation for that."

Hawkwood nodded. "Then our midnight encounter as you marched northward to defeat the Scots—"

"With your vague promises of a destiny to fulfill. That too you must answer."

"And finally," Hawkwood continued, as if Thomas had not spoken, "Katherine's return to Magnus and her delivery of my instructions which resulted in the trial of ordeal that you survived so admirably."

Thomas shook his head slowly.

"You did not survive?" Hawkwood said. "I see a ghost in front of me?"

"Hardly," Thomas answered with no humor. "You spoke the word 'finally.' There is much more I need to hear. How do you know of my books? What do you know of the priests of the Holy Grail? Why the secret passages which riddle Magnus? How did you find me in York?"

Thomas paused and delivered his next sentence almost fiercely. "And what is the secret behind Magnus?"

Hawkwood shrugged. "I can only tell you what I know."

"Of burning water?" Thomas asked.

Neither Katherine nor Hawkwood was able to hide surprise, even in the low light of the small flames.

Thomas pressed. "Of Merlin and his followers?"

Hawkwood sprang forward over the fire and grabbed Thomas by the elbow.

"We have said too much," he whispered in a hoarse voice. "Your hostage is not as deaf as you once believed."

CHAPTER

How many times have I done this? Katherine wondered, as she stirred her gruel over the open fire.

Only this morning was different. Instead of Hawkwood resting in thoughtful contemplation of the day, it was the captured daughter of a powerful earl who stared at her with open hostility.

Katherine smiled to herself. At least she was not the only one who received those angry stares. Thomas too was marked for hatred by Isabelle's sullen rage.

Not for the first time since rising with the sun's light did Katherine glare at Thomas as he rested against a tree. *Even in the lowly clothes of a monk's assistant, he still appears as noble as the lord of Magnus he once was.*

She quickly turned her head back to the fire. *Stupid child,* she told herself. *Appearances are deadly illusions.*

Absentmindedly she tried to lift the pot away, then sucked in a breath of pain as the hot metal punished her for her lack of concentration.

How much does Thomas know? If only Hawkwood had not insisted on speaking with him privately last night. If only Isabelle had not been nearby, forcing Thomas and Hawkwood to walk far from camp and leave me behind as her guard.

Katherine consoled herself with the thought that it would all be explained later, when Thomas was fully in their control. For as Hawkwood had promised, a surprise for that coldhearted deceiver truly did wait ahead.

"The girl is expensive baggage," Hawkwood said, as Thomas began to roll up the blankets and pack his saddlebags.

"I agree," Thomas snorted, knowing full well that Hawkwood

meant Isabelle. "However, it was your decision to travel with her. And mine to depart from you both."

Isabelle laughed, but a dark look from Thomas cut her short.

"Merely as a hostage," Thomas said, answering Hawkwood's original question, "the earl's daughter is worth a fortune. To me, however, she is even more valuable. Little as the chance is, her captivity is my only hope to reclaim Magnus."

"Oh?" Hawkwood queried politely.

"Soon she will tire of her silence."

"Oh?"

"Her father rules York only by permission of the priests of the Holy Grail, so I am not fool enough to believe that the possibility of her death will frighten them into relinquishing power. But she has knowledge of those priests, and knowledge of the secret circle of Druids. When Isabelle tells me all, I can seek to find their weakness, or a way to begin to fight."

"Alone?"

"Despite what you said last night, despite the book you gave me, I cannot place my trust in anyone."

Hawkwood shrugged. "You still need help."

"After Isabelle speaks, she will then be ransomed for gold. That, along with what I have now, will fund a small army. And, as you know, I am not without hidden sources of strategy."

"She is still expensive baggage," Hawkwood commented. "Whatever knowledge she gives you is useless. Whatever army you build is useless. And whatever means of fighting you devise is useless."

Thomas tied down the last saddlebag. "For what you told me in privacy last night, I am grateful, if indeed it was truth. As for your advice this morning, I thank you too. But I must respectfully disagree."

He pulled Isabelle roughly to her feet and tied a rope from her bound wrists to the saddle.

"I am to walk?" she asked in disbelief.

"There are times when chivalry must be overruled by common sense," Thomas said. "You once planned to kill me. I cannot let you control the saddle while I walk."

He swung upward into the saddle and looked at Hawkwood, studiously ignoring Katherine.

"Thomas," Hawkwood said, "no amount of force will defeat the priests of the Holy Grail. Not now. As kings receive their power because the people believe they have a divine right to rule, so now do these priests begin to conquer the land. By the will of the people they deceive."

Thomas froze briefly, but enough to show he had suddenly comprehended.

"Yes," Hawkwood continued. "Is it not obvious? Think of how Magnus fell. By consent of the people inside. None dared argue with signs which seemed to come from God, no matter how false you and I knew those signs to be. First York, then Magnus. Word has reached me that four other towns have been infiltrated, then conquered by these priests. Soon all of this part of England will belong to them. How long before the entire land is in their control?"

Hawkwood paused.

What did they discuss last night? Katherine wondered. *This sounds like a plea for Thomas to return to us, to join with us and learn the truth behind Magnus, to help in a final battle against the Druids.*

At that moment, the cry of a loud trumpet shrilled through the forest. Dozens of men, on foot and on horseback, crashed toward them with upraised swords.

She relaxed.

The surprise has arrived as arranged, she thought in triumph. *Thomas will now be our pawn, regardless of his answer.*

Then she cried with horror. These were not the expected visitors! The attackers plunging toward camp wore the battle colors of York. These were knights of the priests of the Holy Grail.

Two lead horses galloped through the camp, scattering the ashes of the fire in all directions. Each rider reined hard and pulled up abruptly beside Thomas and Isabelle.

Within moments, the rest of the camp was flooded with men, some in full armor, some merely with protective vest and sword.

Katherine felt rough hands yank her shoulders. She knew there was little use in struggle, and she quietly accepted defeat. A man on each side held her arms.

Her attention had been on Thomas. Now she squirmed slightly to look around her for Hawkwood. The slight movement earned her an immediate prod in the ribs.

"Pretty or not, milady, you'll get no mercy from this sword," came the warning in her ear.

Katherine stared straight ahead and endured the arrogant smile that curved across Isabelle's face. Isabelle opened her mouth to speak, but the knight interrupted her.

"Greetings from your father," a knight said to Isabelle. "He will delight to see you safe."

"And you, I am sure, will delight in the reward," she said scornfully.

The knight shrugged.

"Shall my hands remain tied forever?" she asked.

The knight nodded to one of the men on foot, who stepped forward and carefully cut through her bonds.

Thomas, still in his saddle, had not yet spoken, nor moved. His eyes were focused on Katherine.

Rage and venom. She could feel both from Thomas as surely as if he had spoken.

Yet it was she who should be filled with rage and venom. He had lured them here and sprung this trap to capture them. But the shock of the sudden action had numbed her, and she was still far from the first anger of betrayal. A part of her mind wondered about Hawkwood somewhere behind her, surely just as helpless as she.

Their capture might end whatever hope there had been to defeat the Druids. Would Hawkwood see this as a total defeat? Was he also just beginning to realize the horror that waited ahead? For neither would reveal their secrets willingly. And both knew well the cruelty of torture which delighted the Druids. Katherine prayed she would die quickly and without showing fear.

"We have them all," a second knight grunted to the first. "The girl and her old companion."

He then spoke past Katherine's shoulder. "Someone see that the old man reaches his feet. We have no time to waste."

Reaches his feet?

This time Katherine ignored the point of the sword in her ribs and turned enough to see a heap of black clothing where Hawkwood lay crumpled and motionless.

"Sire, he does not breathe!" protested a foot soldier.

"Who struck him down!" the second knight roared. "Our instructions were—"

The first knight held up a hand to silence him.

"It was I," he said. "He leapt in my path, and my horse had no time to avoid him. I believe a hoof struck his head."

No! Katherine wanted to scream. *Impossible!*

Until that moment, she still had held no fear. Hawkwood had been her hope. He would devise a means of escape, even from the most secure dungeon. *He cannot be dead. For if he is, so am I.*

The second knight dismounted, walked past Katherine and knelt beside Hawkwood. He leaned over and checked closely for signs of life.

"Nothing," he said in disgust. "We shall be fortunate if our own heads do not roll for this." He glared at the men holding Katherine. "Bind her securely," he said, "but harm not a single hair. Her life is worth not only yours, but every member of your family."

Katherine could not see beyond the blur of her sudden tears. Rough rope bit the skin of her wrists, but she did not feel the pain. Within moments, she had been thrown across the back of a horse, but she was not conscious of inflicted bruises.

Hawkwood is dead. And Thomas is to blame.

"Sit her up properly," barked a voice that barely penetrated Katherine's haze of anguish. "She'll only slow our horses if you leave her across the saddle like a sack of potatoes."

Fumbling hands lifted and propped her in a sitting position and guided Katherine's hands to the edge of the saddle. She was too deep in her grief to care or to fight.

Her mind and heart were so heavy with sorrow that when her tear-blinded eyes suddenly lost all vision, it took her a moment to realize that someone had thrown a hood over her head. Now she had no chance to escape on the horse they had provided her.

Then came a sharp whistle, and her horse moved forward. Slowly it followed the others in single file down the narrow trail that led back to the main road.

Each step took her farther away from the final sight she would carry always in her mind, that of Hawkwood silent and unmoving among the ruins of camp.

Eventually, the tempo quickened and the steady plodding of her horse became a canter. Katherine had to hold the front edge of the saddle tight with her bound hands and sway in rhythm to keep her balance.

By the drumming of hooves she knew other horses were now beside her, which meant that the trail had widened. Soon they would be at the main road which led into York.

How far then?

She and Hawkwood—she felt sharp pain twist her stomach to think of him—had walked several hours along the main road yesterday. *That means less than an hour on horseback to York. There...* she shut her mind. To think of what lay ahead was to be tortured twice—now and when it actually occurred.

Would she have a chance to make Thomas pay for his treachery? Even if it was only an unguarded second to lunge at him and rake her nails down his face? Or a chance to claw his eyes?

As the horses picked up pace, her own anger and venom started to burn. Thomas had arranged this. He had trapped them and led Hawkwood to death. If only there might be a moment to grab a sword and plunge it—

Without warning, the lead horse screamed.

Even as the first horse's scream died, there were yells of fear and the thud of falling bodies and then the screams of men.

Because of the hood over her head, Katherine's world became a jumble of dark confusion as her own horse stumbled slightly, then reared with panic. The sudden and unexpected motion threw her to the ground.

A roar of pounding hooves filled her ears, and she felt something brush the side of her head.

Dust choked her gasp of alarm. More thunder of hooves, then a terrible crack of agony that seemed to explode her head into fragments of searing fire.

Then nothing.

CHAPTER

39

Katherine turned her head slowly. She could see. The hood no longer blocked her vision. She was sitting against a tree, rough bark pressing against her back. Her hands were free. She brought them up, almost in amazement at the lack of pain.

"The woman child wakes," a voice said.

Katherine tensed. The voice belonged to a stranger behind her. Before she could draw her legs in to prepare to stand, he was in front of her, offering a hand to help her rise.

"Milady," he said. "If you please."

If the man means harm, he would have done so by now, she told herself. *But what occurred to bring me here in such confusion?*

When she stood, she saw the aftermath of that confusion on the trail between the trees. Two horses, unnaturally still, lay on their sides in the dust. Several others were tethered to the trunks of nearby trees. She counted four men huddled at the edge of the trail. Their groans reached her clearly.

"It's an old trick," the man apologized, snapping her attention back to him. "We yanked a rope tight across the bend, knee high to their horses. These fools were traveling in such a tight bunch that when the leaders fell, so did the others, including you. I offer my apologies for the bandage across your head. We did not know you would be hooded."

Katherine gingerly touched her skull, and found, indeed, a strip of cloth bound just above her ears.

"It is not serious," the man said quickly. "The bandage is merely a precaution."

"Of course," Katherine murmured.

His eyes glinted good humor from beneath shaggy, dark

eyebrows. His nose was twisted slightly, as if it had been broken at least once, but it did not detract from a swarthy handsomeness.

Traces of nobility still showed in his clothes. The ragged, purple cape had once been exquisite, and his balance and posture showed a confidence instilled by money and good breeding. His shoulders, however, were broad with muscles borne of hard work, and the callouses on his hands had not come from a life of leisure.

He interrupted her inspection.

"Your friend Hawkwood, I presume, escaped?"

A spasm of grief crossed Katherine's face.

"That," he said gently, "is answer enough."

Someone called to the stranger from behind.

"Robert, come hither."

He beckoned her to follow, and turned toward the voice. Together, they moved deeper into the trees and entered a small clearing.

Katherine blinked in surprise. The remainder of the enemy horses were gathered. Isabelle sat on one, two enemy knights on others, Thomas on the fourth. Each was securely bound with ropes around their wrists. A dozen other men stood in casual circles of two or three among the horses.

"Robert, it is high time we disappeared into the forest," said a fat and balding man in a brown monk's robe.

"Yes, indeed," Robert replied. "The lady seems fit enough to travel." He paused. "Those by the road . . . they have the ransom note?"

The fat man nodded. "Soon enough they will find the energy to mount the horses we have left for them."

"They're lucky to be alive," spat another man. "I still say we should not bother with this nonsense about the earl's gold."

Robert laughed lightly. "Will, the rich serve us much better when alive." He motioned at Isabelle. "The daughter alone is worth three years' wages."

Then he turned to Katherine. "We did promise to help Hawkwood by capturing Thomas," he said in a low voice. "But we made no promise about neglecting profit. And although the arrival of these men of York has complicated matters, there is now much more to be gained by selling these hostages for ransom."

He lifted his eyebrows in a quizzical search. "After all, as the king's outlaws, we can't be expected to be sinless."

Their southward march took them so deep into the forest that Katherine wondered how she might find her way back to any road.

The man she knew as Robert led the silent procession of outlaws and captives on paths nearly invisible among the shadows cast by the towering trees.

As they traveled, she reviewed the morning's horror. *How did Thomas accomplish it? By prearranging his campsite so that the enemy knights knew exactly where to appear?*

Again and again, she fired molten glances of hatred at Thomas's back. *Of course he knew the saddlebag was leaking flour. To be followed so easily made his task of flushing us out that much easier. How he must have chuckled as he waited for us in his camp!*

Katherine needed to maintain the hatred. Without it she would have to face the numbness of the loss of Hawkwood, focus on the struggle ahead. Yet questions still troubled her.

With Thomas captured, what am I do to next? Without Hawkwood to guide, what hope have I of carrying on the battle against the Druids?

Eventually Robert halted the lead horse. He dismounted, then walked past all the others to reach Katherine.

"Milady," he said, "we will leave all the horses here and move ahead on foot. A precaution. We near our final destination. The marks of horses' hooves are too easy to follow." Robert gestured at the outlaw called Will. "He will lead the horses to safer grounds."

Katherine nodded, then accepted the hand that Robert offered to help her down from her horse.

"My apologies again," Robert said. "For you and the others must be blindfolded during the final part of our journey."

His grin eased her alarm. "Another precaution. As the king's outlaws hiding within the king's forests, it is only natural that we are reluctant to show hostages—or visitors—the paths to our camp."

As the shadows deepened with approaching dusk, small campfires appeared. At some there was low singing of ballads, at others, the games of men at rest—arm wrestling, storytelling, quietly laughing. The fire at the center of the camp was the largest. Beside it, turning the spit which held an entire deer, was the fat man in a monk's robe.

Katherine leaned against the trunk of a tree and watched the proceedings with fascination.

How did Hawkwood know of these outlaws? How did he contact them? Why did they agree so readily to help?

At the thought of Hawkwood, her tears began to trickle again. She blinked them away, then jumped slightly. The outlaw Robert had silently appeared in front of her.

"I would bid you join us in our eventide meal," he said. "Our venison will be ready soon. But first I have a message for you."

Katherine waited.

"Thomas seeks a private audience with you."

The outlaw noticed her posture stiffen.

"Do not fear, milady. He is securely bound, and a guard is posted nearby."

Katherine noted with satisfaction that her tears had stopped immediately at the prospect of venting her hatred upon Thomas. "Please," she said, "lead me to him."

The outlaw took her to a small fire a hundred yards away. As promised, a well-armed guard stood discreetly nearby.

Before departing, Robert said loudly, "Milady, don't hesitate to call if he disturbs your peace. A sound whipping shall teach him manners."

Katherine nodded, and Robert slipped away.

Thomas sat on a log, hands bound in front, a chain around his waist and attached to the log. Nothing about his posture indicated captivity, however. His nose and chin were held high in pride.

"You requested my presence," Katherine stated coldly.

"Yes, milady," Thomas said in a mocking voice. "If it doesn't inconvenience you too much."

Katherine shrugged.

As Thomas raised his bound hands and pointed at her, his voice lost all pretense of anything but icy anger.

"I want to make you a sworn promise."

"You seem in a poor position to make any promise," she answered with equally calm hatred.

"That will change," Thomas vowed. "And then I will seek revenge."

"Revenge?" she echoed.

"Revenge. To think that I almost believed you and Hawkwood

might be friends instead of Druids." He half stood and the chain around his waist stopped him short. "Hawkwood has already paid for his lies with death. And you too will someday regret the manner in which you betrayed my trust."

For a moment, Katherine could not get air from her lungs. She opened her mouth once, then twice, in an effort to speak.

"You . . . you . . . ," she barely managed to sputter.

She looked about wildly and saw in the underbrush a heavy stick. Rage pushed her onward. She stooped to the stick, pulled it clear, and raised it above her head.

She advanced on Thomas, who did not move.

"Barbaric fiend!" she hissed. "His life was worth ten of yours!"

She slammed the short pole downward. Thomas shifted sideways in a violent effort to escape, and the wood crashed into the log, missing him by scant inches.

It felt too good, the release of her pent-up anger.

She slammed the stick downward again and again. Each blow slammed the log beside Thomas, as she mindlessly directed her rage into the sensation of total release.

Thomas stared at her in a mixture of fear and awe.

She poked the splintered pole at his face and stopped it just short of his eyes.

"You craven animal!" she cried. "How dare you slur Hawkwood's name! He was the finest Merlin of his generation! He was the last hope against you and the rest of the evil you carry! He was—"

Katherine had to stop to draw air. She wavered in sudden dizziness. Then, as the last of her rage drained with her loss of energy, she began to cry soundlessly. She had nothing left inside her but the grief of Hawkwood gone. The tears coursed down her cheeks and fell softly at her feet.

Blindly, she turned away from Thomas.

His voice called to her. It contained doubt.

"A Merlin?" he asked. "You still insist on posing as a friend?"

"As *your* friend? Never." She could barely raise her voice above a whisper, yet her bitterness escaped clearly. "What you have betrayed by joining them is a battle beyond your comprehension. Yet you Druids shall never find what you seek. Not through me."

"*You* Druids!" his voice rose again with rage. "I am exiled from

Magnus. A bounty on my head! And you accuse *me* of belonging to those sorcerers?"

Katherine drew a lungful of breath to steady herself. "You knew we watched," she said. "Your masters sent you forth from York with the earl's daughter as bait for us."

"Set me forth? Your brains have been addled by the fall. I risked my very life to take her hostage."

Katherine managed a snort. "Pray tell," she said with sarcasm. "How convenient, was it not, that the drawbridge remained open for you, and not the pursuing knights? And explain how you managed to reach the earl inside the castle, even though he had been forewarned."

Thomas gaped. "Forewarned? You speak in circles."

Another snort. "Hardly. You pretend ignorance."

They stared at each other.

Finally Thomas leaned forward and asked in a low voice, "Who then forewarned the earl, if not you, the people who managed to follow me when none other knew my plans?"

Had it been less dark, Thomas would have seen clearly the contempt blazing from Katherine's eyes. "I was a fool for you," she said. "Caring for you in the dungeon of Magnus when even then your master, Waleran, was there. Then to discover him nearby in York—"

Thomas gasped. "Waleran? In York? How do you know?" He stiffened in sudden anger. "Unless you are one of them. Leading those knights to my camp."

More moments of suspicious silenced hung between them.

"Why?" Katherine then asked softly. "Why do you still pretend? And why did you betray us so badly? Is it not enough you were given the key to the secret of Magnus at birth?"

Thomas spoke very softly. "I pretend nothing. I betray no one. And this secret of Magnus haunts me worse than you will ever know."

He continued in the same gentle, almost bewildered tones. "Katherine, if we fight the same battle, whoever betrayed us both would take much joy to see us divided." He shook his head. "And if you are one of them, may God have mercy on your soul for your deceit."

"Milady, what plans have you for the morrow?" Robert asked. With dawn well upon them, lazy smoke curled upward from the dying fires.

Katherine huddled within her cloak against the chill. With visible effort, she pulled herself from her thoughts and directed her gaze at the outlaw Robert.

"Plans? I cannot see beyond today."

It was said with such despair that Robert gently took her elbow and guided her to the main campfire where the fat outlaw now stirred a wooden paddle in a large iron pot.

"Broth," Robert directed the fat man. "She needs broth."

A bowl was brought forth and filled to the brim from the pot, and Robert helped Katherine lift it to her mouth. When she tried to set it down after a tiny sip, he forced it to her mouth again.

Robert waited until she had finished two bowls before leading her to a quiet clearing away from camp.

"Tell me," he said, "what plans have you for the morrow?"

Katherine stood straighter now, and much of the wild hopelessness had disappeared from her eyes.

"None." She smiled wanly.

"I have discovered," Robert said slowly, "that to make plans, one must first decide one's goal. Then it is merely a matter of finding the easiest path to that goal."

Despite herself, Katherine chuckled. "Knowing the goal, my friend, presents little difficulty. The path to that goal? One might as well plan a path across open sky."

The outlaw shrugged. "The task is not that impossible. After all, birds fly."

"They are not armed with weapons to destroy."

"Milady, what is it you want?"

Katherine thought of the secrets she had shared so long with Hawkwood. With sadness, she said. "I cannot say."

The outlaw studied her face, then said quietly, "So be it. But if I or my men can be of service . . . ."

Katherine studied his face, as if seeing it for the first time. "Why is it that you offer so much? First to rescue me and capture Thomas? And now this?"

"Hawkwood never told you?"

Katherine shook her head.

"We were captured once," the outlaw said. "Captured and branded like slaves. Held in the dungeons of York . . . the rats and fleas our only companions. The night before our execution, all the guards fell asleep."

Robert's face reflected wonder. "Suddenly Hawkwood appeared among them. He unlocked our doors and set us free. When he sent word to us to arrange your capture, we were glad to pay our debt."

Katherine hid her smile. Child's play for a Merlin. A tasteless sleeping potion in food or wine. It did not surprise her that Hawkwood might release innocent men, nor that he would know how to reach them later.

"When?" Katherine asked. "When did this happen?"

"Some years ago," the outlaw replied. "We learned our lesson well. Since then, the sheriff's men have not so much as seen a hint of us." He grinned. "Except, of course, through the complaints of those we rob."

He went on quickly at Katherine's frown. "Only those corrupted by power. Those who will never face justice because they control the laws of the land."

"You will continue to be a thorn in the sides of those who reign now, the priests of the Holy Grail?"

"It will be our delight to provide such service."

A new thought began to grow in Katherine's mind. She spoke aloud. "My duty," she said, "is to fight them also. No matter how hopeless my cause might seem, I must strive against them."

Robert nodded. He understood well the nobility of effort.

"I have little chance to succeed," Katherine continued. "But what chance there is, I must grasp with both hands."

"Yes?" Robert sensed she had a request.

"Offer to battle Thomas. Set the stakes high. His life to be forfeit if he loses or his freedom if he wins."

"Milady?"

Katherine spoke strongly, more sure each passing second of what she must do in the next weeks. "Then," she said, "make certain that you lose the battle."

"As you wish, milady"—the outlaw bowed—"or my name is not Robert Hood."

CHAPTER

40

JULY 1313
ENGLISH CHANNEL

I repeat. Board this vessel alone or not at all."

Thomas merely shifted the puppy to his other arm. It was a deliberate act, done slowly to show he had no fear for the loud sailor. It was also a difficult act. The cloak Thomas wore did not encourage movement. Yet he would not ever consider traveling without the cloak. He understood well why Hawkwood had always worn such a garment. It concealed much of what he must always carry with him.

The sailor facing him jabbed a dirty finger in the air to make his point. "You and a dog with all its fleas. Hah! Might you be thinking this is Noah's Ark?"

The sailors around him laughed loudly.

"This puppy once saved my life," Thomas said quietly. "You will receive full passage for the creature."

The sailor squinted. "Eh? You'll pay double just to keep the mongrel beside you on the North Sea?"

Thomas nodded.

They stood on the edge of a great stone pier that jutted into the Scarborough harbor. More than twelve hundred years earlier, Roman soldiers had built a signal post behind a rough, wooden palisade, on the edge of steep cliffs directly north of the harbor. From there, they could see approaching warships and send messages forty miles inland to York for reinforcements.

In later centuries, Scarborough had suffered under the lightning-quick raids of the bloodthirsty Vikings. Time and again the Norsemen had sailed into this harbor, forcing the townspeople to scurry up the paths to the castle walls that lined the edge of the cliff above them.

But those Vikings had found the English land so rich that it defeated them with its luxury—eventually they began to settle and intermarry. Then, in the year 1066, the Anglo-Saxons suffered defeat by the Norman invasions. Through it all, Scarborough had served well as a harbor town, nearly as important as the major coastal city of Hull, a few days' travel to the south.

Now, as Thomas's nostrils informed him, Scarborough thrived through fishing and merchant boats. He prayed his thanks again for finding the *Dragon's Eye*, a merchant ship which was already near full with bales of wool from the sheep grown on the hills of the inland moors—and for finding one of the few ships not owned by the Flemish or Italians. Now he could at least barter his passage in English.

He looked directly into the sailor's eyes and repeated firmly, "Double passage." To prove his point, he dug into his small purse for another piece of gold.

The act of keeping the puppy beneath his arm while using the same hand to hold the purse proved tricky, however, and as the puppy squirmed slightly, it knocked the purse loose. A dozen coins spilled across the stone.

Thomas knelt quickly and scooped them into his free hand, but it was too late. When he stood, he faced greedy stares from all directions.

The sailor in front of him coughed politely.

"We welcome you aboard. And your companion. It would appear you both deserve to be treated like kings."

A deckhand led Thomas to the rear of the *Dragon's Eye*, chattering happily. "You picked a fine ship, you did. A cog like this handles the roughest seas."

The cog was over a hundred feet long, with a deep and wide hull to hold the bulkiest of cargoes. Thomas stepped around the bales of wool. Above him, he saw the single sail furled around the thick, high, center mast.

"It's not a fast or easy boat to maneuver," the deckhand continued, in the voice of one happy to have the chance to finally impart knowledge to someone who knew less than he. "But it's almost impossible to capsize."

He lowered his voice. "And its high sides make it difficult to be boarded at sea by pirates. Look about you," the deckhand continued. "The castle at the prow—" His voice became smug. "That's the fighting tower at the front—lets us fire arrows from above at any raiders who draw close."

He then waved at their destination on the cog, ahead of them by some fifty feet. "The sterncastle—the tower at the rear—is for important guests." He sighed. "A bed and privacy. What gold can't buy!"

Then he remembered he had superiority because of his knowledge and immediately began lecturing again. "We've got oars—we call them sweeps—should the gales be too rough or should we need to outrun pirates. You might be asked to man one."

Thomas said noting to stop the flow of words.

Dangerous gales and pirate attacks. What folly brought me here? Hawkwood's advice—words from one who betrayed me. And some vague references in my secret books. Such madness to begin the journey, let alone hope in its success.

Yet what else is there to do? The reward on my head has been increased, and with the priests of the Holy Grail controlling town after town, there soon will be no safe place left for me in northern England—unless I choose to live the uncertain life of an outlaw. My contest for life and freedom against that wily Robert Hood showed how dangerous that might be—

The deckhand interrupted his thoughts. "Here you are. The sterncastle. My advice is that you tie the dog inside. There'll be enough grumbles about a dog enjoying the shelter denied the crew without his presence outside as a daily reminder."

Thomas nodded.

The deckhand hesitated, then yielded to his curiosity. "Our destination is Lisbon. Will you go beyond Portugal?"

The scowl he received from Thomas was answer enough.

You and your friends stared at my scattered coins like wolves at a lamb. And I'm fortunate if we depart before you hear about the gold offered for my head. The less you know the better.

The deckhand stumbled back awkwardly to make room for Thomas to enter the dank and dark sterncastle.

Thomas ducked inside. *Most certainly the Druid spies will someday discover I escaped England on the* Dragon's Eye, *and eager will be the sailors to impart the information for the slightest amount of gold. They cannot know my destination is that of the last crusaders—Jerusalem, the Holy City.*

If the deckhand believes this to be luxury, Thomas thought with a sour grin, *then he and all the crew have my sympathy.*

As if in agreement at the squalor of the dark and cramped quarter, the puppy beneath his arm whined.

"You don't like it either?"

Thomas set the puppy down on the rough wood floor.

"They said two weeks to Lisbon if the weather is favorable," Thomas told his companion. "And crossed themselves when I asked how long if it isn't."

Another answering whine.

Thomas smiled. A week earlier, the puppy had first growled fearlessly as Thomas entered the cave after the absence of several days, the time spent captive among Robert Hood and his outlaws. But fearless growls had changed to yips of total joy as the puppy recognized the scent of Thomas returning.

Thomas had responded to the barking and jumping with equal joy, surprising himself. True, he had worried upon his capture that the puppy would die the slow lingering death of starvation; yet he did not want to be burdened with concern for anything except his goal of winning Magnus. Until that joy at their reunion had so surprised him, he intended to leave the puppy somewhere with peasants.

Instead, he decided not to abandon it, then spent two days in the cave, poring through the ancient pages of knowledge, uncaring of the aches which still battered his every move because of the fierce fight against the outlaw Robert Hood.

During those two days he puzzled his next move. Yes, Magnus seemed out of reach. But without Magnus to pursue, what else had he in life? So, despite the near impossibility of his task, he could not let it go.

And at the end of the second day, Thomas decided that the one chance of victory would be in uncovering the very reason that the books had been hidden where they were. The only clues he had were vague references to the last Crusade, written in the margins of two of the books. And simply because those were too similar to what Hawkwood had said during their midnight discussion before the betrayal, he realized he could not ignore what it meant.

A sudden wave nearly pitched him against the far wall of his quarters. Had he chosen the right direction for his search? Or was Hawkwood's advice merely bait? To be wrong meant a year wasted, one more year for the priests of the Holy Grail to add strength to their hold over the area around Magnus.

Despite the swaying of the boat, Thomas knelt and poured out his troubles in prayer. That quiet moment brought him peace. After all, in the face of the Almighty, the One who counts years as seconds and who promises love beyond comprehension for eternity, what mattered a man's gravest troubles when that promised eternity made any life on earth the briefest of flashes?

He opened his eyes and prepared himself for a voyage which gave him little hope of return to England, let alone a victory over the Druids who held Magnus.

CHAPTER 41

Shortly after dawn on the third morning at sea, Thomas wanted to die.

"Carry your own bucket out," snarled the sailor into the cramped quarters. "We've no time for softheaded fools."

The sailor half dropped and half threw the bucket in Thomas's direction, then slammed the door in departure.

Thomas could not even lift his head to protest. A small part of his mind was able to realize that the deckhand's prediction about resentment because of the puppy had been proven right. For two days, each visitor bearing food to his quarters—except for a small, dirty cook's assistant who had stooped to let the puppy lick his hands—had grumbled about the waste of food and space for a useless dog.

The larger part of his mind, however, thought nothing about the puppy or the resentment among the crew. Thomas truly wanted to die.

The cog rode the rough seas like a cork, tossing and bobbing on top of the long, gray swells of water as the winds slowly took it south, through the English Channel, and into the vast Atlantic Ocean.

Only once had Thomas been able to stagger to the door of his quarters to look out upon those green-gray waves. That sight had propelled him back into his quarters where he had fallen to his knees and emptied the contents of his stomach into a bucket.

The puppy seemed oblivious to the sea. Indeed, it seemed to delight in the pitches and rolls of the ship, and bounded around the small quarters with enthusiasm.

"Traitor," Thomas muttered, as the puppy now attacked the

food. "It is no wonder you grow like a weed, taking my portion with such greed."

The puppy did not bother to look up.

Thomas carried the slop bucket to the side of the ship and braced his legs to empty it over the side. He was so weak that it took all his energy and concentration to keep his balance and not follow the contents overboard.

As he turned back to retrace the few steps to his quarters, he nearly stumbled into the large sailor who blocked his path.

"By the beard of old Neptune," the sailor said with a nasty grin, "you would favor us all by becoming food for the fish yourself."

Thomas saw something as cold as the ocean in the man's eyes, and beyond the man's shoulder he saw two other sailors entering his quarters in his absence.

"I had feared pirates at sea," Thomas said. He had to swallow twice to find the strength to continue. "But I did not expect them aboard this vessel."

The sailor leaned forward, yellow eyes above a dirty beard. "Pirates? Hardly. We know the ship's captain charged too little by far for us to bear the insult of living so poorly while a dog lives so well."

Thomas sucked in lungfuls of cold air, hoping to draw from it a clearness that would rid him of his nausea.

"Rate of passage is the captain's realm," he finally said.

The sailor took Thomas' hesitation as fear, and laughed. "Not when the captain sleeps off a night's worth of wine!"

There was a loud yelp from the quarters, then a muffled curse. The other two sailors backed out.

"No signs of coin inside," one sailor said, dangling the puppy carelessly and ignoring its small whines of pain.

The other sailor squeezed his bleeding hand. "That whelp of Satan took a fair chunk from my thumb."

The yellow-eyed sailor turned back to Thomas. He dropped his hand to his belt and with a blur of movement, pulled free a short dagger. He grinned black teeth.

"Consider your choices, lad. You'll hand over the gold now, or lose a goodly portion of your neck."

In the sailor's yellow eyes Thomas saw a gleaming coldness which could belong to no sane man. Once they had the gold, he would die anyway. Alive, he would later be able to complain to the captain, or once ashore, seek a local magistrate. The sure solution for them was to make sure no one was watching and toss him—alive or dead—overboard. No person aboard ship would be able to prove their crime.

Show weakness, Thomas commanded himself. *Your only chance against three is to lull them into expecting no fight at all.*

He sagged, an easy task considering the illness that seemed to bring his stomach to his throat.

"I beg of you," Thomas cried, "spare my life! You shall receive all I have!"

The evil grin of blackened teeth widened.

"Of course, we'll spare your life," the yellow-eyed sailor promised. He jabbed his knife forward. "Your coin!"

All three laughed at how quickly Thomas cowered in reaction to the movement of the knife.

Then Thomas fumbled with his cloak. "I keep it in a pouch hanging from my neck," he said, not needing much effort to place an extra quaver in his voice. " 'Twill take but a moment."

Thomas had learned something about swordplay in the dungeon cells of Magnus with Sir William. *Reach for your neck, as if scratching a flea. Then in one motion, lean forward, draw it loose, and slash outward at your enemy.*

"The knot is awkward," Thomas said, fumbling with his right hand at his throat. He bent forward slightly, as if reaching behind his neck for a knotted string of leather.

In one smooth move, the sword drew free beneath his ducked head. Head still down, he struck the spot he had memorized before bending—the knife hand of the yellow-eyed sailor.

A solid thunk and squeal of pain rewarded him, even as he raised his head to give him a clear view of all three.

The sailor's knife bounced off the wooden deck.

Without pause, Thomas kicked fiercely, sinking his foot solidly into the man's groin. Then, even as the man fell forward in agony, Thomas charged ahead, slashing sideways and cutting into the flesh of the second sailor's shoulder.

The third sailor managed to step back half a pace, but even in that time he had brought his arm back to cast the puppy overboard.

He froze suddenly.

"I think not," Thomas grunted.

The sailor did not disagree. He slowly lowered the puppy, careful not to move in any way that might encourage Thomas to press any harder with the point of the sword pressed into the hollow of his throat.

"Let the puppy fall," Thomas said softly. "He'll find his feet. And you might not find your head."

The sailor opened his hand, and the puppy landed softly, then growled and bit the sailor's ankle.

"Obey carefully. This sword may slip," Thomas warned. "My balance on these pitched waves has proven difficult."

The sailor's eyes widened in agreement.

Thomas pointed left with his free hand, and the sailor slowly shuffled in the direction. Thomas kept the sword in place and shuffled right, and in that manner of a grotesque dance, they continued until Thomas had half circled and now faced the other two.

The puppy stood directly between his legs and growled upward at all three sailors.

"Listen to him well," Thomas said. All three were bleeding, the yellow-eyed sailor with the bones showing on the back of his hand, the second one with a gash through sleeve and shoulder, and the third from a torn ankle. "The next time, your greed will cost you your lives."

Thomas knew by the hatred in their eyes they would return. Yet he was helpless, for he would have to betray every instinct to kill them now in cold blood.

God help me, he prayed, *if they catch me unawares again.*

CHAPTER

42

Thomas grinned despite the bleakness of the forbidden sky and endless swells of water, for the dizziness and nausea had finally left him. After days without food, he was famished.

He carried the empty food bucket and swayed in rhythm to the motion of the ship as he walked to the edge of the rear deck. From there, he slowly studied the movements of the crew below.

Nothing seemed threatening.

For a moment, he considered seeking the ship's captain to set forth his accusations against the three. Then he dismissed the idea. Whose side would the captain choose? Certainly not his. With a crew of eighteen men—most of them unhappy with Thomas because of the puppy's comfort—the captain would never risk becoming the focus of anger by trying to discipline one-sixth of the crew.

Thomas could only pray that he had shown enough willingness to fight that the crewmen would not feel it worth the effort to provide more trouble.

Yet, Thomas felt that the sailor with the yellow eyes would return. And probably when all advantages were his. It would be a long, long journey, Thomas told himself, even if the cog were to reach Lisbon in the next hour.

A slow, small movement demanded his attention. The cook's assistant. Hat over eyes, shifting in sleep in a corner away from the constant menial work of preparing food.

Thomas whistled, low and sharp, and the boy raised his head and opened bleary eyes.

Thomas waved for him to approach the short ladder that led up to his quarters from the main deck of the cog.

"I beg forgiveness for waking you," Thomas began, "but I grow faint with hunger." He lifted his empty bucket and smiled. "You could earn yourself a friend."

The cook's assistant shrugged, face lost in shadows beneath the edge of the battered, leather cap, and took the offered bucket. When he returned, Thomas climbed down the ladder, reached into the bucket, and used his teeth to tear apart a hard biscuit. He swallowed water from a jug in great gulps, and then filled his mouth with the salted herring.

Thomas ate frantically in silence, half grinning in apology between bites. When Thomas finally finished, he wiped his mouth clean with the sleeve of his cloak.

"You have my gratitude," he said with good-natured fervor.

Once again, the cook's assistant shrugged, then held out his hand for the bucket.

"A moment, please," Thomas asked. "Have you any news of three crewmen in foul tempers?"

Another shrug greeted that question.

What face I can see is so dirty, Thomas thought, *hair so filthy that he is fortunate it is cut too short to support many fleas. And his clothes are hardly more than layers and layers of rags.*

"Of course." Thomas laughed at the silent response to his question. "All sailors have foul tempers."

A guarded smile greeted his joke.

"Three men," Thomas prompted, "with wounds in need of care. Has any gossip regarding their plans reached your ears?"

Another shrug. Then the cook's assistant touched his forefinger to his own lips.

Thomas understood. *Mute.*

The cook's assistant set the bucket down and cupped his hands together, palms upward. He then stroked the air with one hand above the other.

"Puppy?" Thomas asked. "You inquire of its well-being?"

The cook's assistant nodded, almost sadly.

"Its belly is fat with the food I could not eat." Thomas smiled. "At least only one of us needed to suffer."

The cook's assistant opened his hands wide.

"Why?" Thomas interpreted. "Why so much trouble for a puppy? That small, worthless creature saved my life."

Then, speaking more to himself than to his audience, Thomas said very softly, "And it is the only living thing I dare trust."

They attacked when the moon was at its highest.

Thomas saw every move of their advance. Crouched low, and silent with stealth, they slipped from bale to bale until reaching the ladder. There were only three.

Thomas smiled. Whatever code sailors had, it probably contained some of the rules of knighthood. Since Thomas had shown bravery by fighting earlier in the day, the other sailors had probably decided he should be left alone.

If the other crew members had refrained from joining the attack, however, they had done nothing to prevent these three from waiting until the stillest hour of the night to finish their crime.

Thomas could enjoy their deadly approach because he was far from his quarters, hidden in the shadows of bales of wool. Far too easy for an unwary sleeper to be trapped inside those quarters, and for a knife of revenge to be drawn across his throat. So he had chosen the discomfort of the open ship.

Seek what treasures you will, Thomas thought merrily. *Seek it until dawn. For what you desire rests safely with me.*

Within his cloak lay his gold. Warm against his side lay the puppy, squirming occasionally with dreams.

I shall rest during the day, Thomas silently promised the three sailors, *and spend my nights on constant guard among these shadows.*

Much to his satisfaction, angry whispers reached Thomas. There was a light bang of the door shutting and a grunt of pain. More angry whispers.

Then silence. Minutes of silence.

It began to stretch his nerves, knowing they were above him, out of sight, about to appear in silhouette at the top of the ladder at any moment.

Thomas wanted the warning, wanted to know as soon as possible when they were about to descend. But he did not look at the top of the ladder.

Instead, he chose to focus on a point beyond it. Night vision, he knew, caught movement much more efficiently at the sides of the eyes.

Silence continued. Now the creaking of the ship seemed to be the low, haunting cries of spirits.

Suddenly, Thomas's heart leapt in the terror of shock.

Directly above him, the edge of the deck detached itself!

He managed not to flinch, then forced himself to be calm; slowly, very slowly, he turned his head to see more clearly.

The black edge of the deck had redefined itself to show the black outlines of a man's head and shoulders.

These men are shrewd. Instead of choosing the obvious—the ladder—they now watch from above, hoping I will not notice and will betray myself with a movement.

Thomas told himself he was safe as long as he remained still. After all, he had chosen a deep shadow.

Yet, his heart continued to hammer at a frantic pace. *This is what the rabbit fears, hidden among the grass. I understand now the urge to bolt before the hounds.*

But Thomas did not bolt. What betrayed him was the only creature he trusted. The puppy, deep in dreams, yelped and squirmed. Within seconds, two of the sailors dropped to the belly of the ship. One from each side of the upper deck.

The puppy yelped again, and they moved with unerring accuracy to the bale which hid Thomas.

Moonlight glinted from their extended sabers. Thomas barely had time to stand and withdraw his own sword before they were upon him.

"A shout for help will do no good," came the snarl with the approach of the first. "The captain's drunk again, and the crew have turned a blind eye."

"For certes," a harsh whisper followed, "none take kindly to the manner in which you crippled my hand."

Thomas said nothing, waiting with his sword in front.

The puppy, now awake, pressed against his leg in fear.

Another movement as the third sailor scuttled down the ladder from the upper deck. He too brandished a saber.

I have been well trained, thought Thomas, *by Robert of Uleran, who fell in my defense at Magnus. I shall not disappoint his memory by falling without a worthy fight.*

The sailors circled Thomas, shuffling slowly in the luxury of anticipation.

Impossible to watch all three at once. From where will the first blow come?

Thomas heard the whistle of steel slicing air and instinctively stepped back. He felt a slight pull against the sleeve of his cloak, then—it seemed like an eternity of waiting later—a bright slash of pain and the wetness of blood against his arm.

"Ho, ho," the yellow-eyed sailor laughed. "My weaker hand finds revenge for the damage you did the other!"

"Gold and your life," the second sailor whispered. "But only after you beg to be spared."

Until that moment, Thomas had felt the deep cold of fear. He knew his blood would soak the rough wood at his feet. But their taunts filled him with anger, and his fear became distant.

"Beg?" Thomas said in a voice he hardly recognized as his. "If I die, you will die with me. This is a fight which will cost you dearly."

The yellow-eyed sailor mimicked his voice with a high-pitched giggle. " 'This is a fight which will cost you dearly.' "

That growing anger suddenly overwhelmed Thomas. He became quiet with a fury that could barely be restrained.

He lifted his sword and pointed it directly at the yellow-eyed sailor and spoke with compressed rage. "You shall be the first to taste doom."

The yellow-eyed sailor slapped his neck. As Thomas lowered his sword to protective stance, the sailor sank to his knees, then fell face forward onto the deck.

What madness is this?

Thomas had no time to wonder. As the second sailor betrayed himself by a movement, Thomas whirled to face him. Still carried by that consuming rage, he pointed his sword at the man's eyes.

The man grunted with pain, eyes wide with surprise in the moonlight. Then he too dropped to his knees and tumbled forward, to land as heavily as a sack of fish.

What madness is this?

Thomas answered his own bewilderment. *Whatever it might be, this is not the time to question.*

He spun on the third sailor, who staggered back in fear.

Thomas raised his sword and advanced.

"Nooo!" the man shrieked loudly in terror. "Not me!"

Then the sailor gasped, as if slapped hard across the face. His mouth fell open, then shut, and he too pitched forward.

That shriek had pierced the night air, and from behind Thomas came the sounds of men moving through the ship.

He gathered his cloak about him, scooped the puppy into his other arm, and fled toward the ladder.

CHAPTER

43

Thomas had fourteen nights and fifteen days to contemplate the miracle which had saved his life, fourteen nights and fifteen days of solitude to puzzle the events. For not a single member of the crew dared disturb him.

The three sailors had risen the next day from stupor, unable to explain to the crew members who dragged them away what evil had befallen them at the command of Thomas's sword.

Each day, the cook's assistant came with food and then darted away, without even the boldness to look Thomas in the eye.

While fourteen nights and fifteen days was enough time for the cut on his arm to heal, it was not long enough for him to make sense of those scant minutes of rage beneath the moonlight.

For fourteen nights and fifteen days, Thomas fought the strange sensation that he *should* know what had happened.

On the sixteenth day, he remembered. Like a blast of frigid air, it struck him with a force that froze him midway through a troubled pace.

No, it cannot be!

Thomas strained to recall words spoken to him in near panic the night Magnus fell to the priests of the Holy Grail. He was hidden in a stable, saved from death only because of his guise as a beggar. Tiny John had appeared and said, "The priests appeared within the castle as if from the very walls! Like hordes of rats. Guards were falling in all directions, slapping themselves as they fell! The priests claimed it was the hand of God, and for all to lay down their arms."

No, it cannot be, Thomas told himself again. Yet the Druids had posed as priests of the Holy Grail. They had mysteriously appeared within the castle—undoubtedly through the secret passages which only in his last hours there had Thomas discovered riddled Magnus— and had somehow struck down the well-armed soldiers within.

Guards were falling in all directions, slapping themselves as they fell. Yellow-eye had slapped himself, then fallen.

Impossible that a Druid was aboard this same ship.

Thomas had little time to search or wonder. An hour later, a shout reached him from the watchtower at the top of the mast. The port of Lisbon had been sighted.

To present myself as bait would be dangerous under any circumstance, thought Thomas. *But to be bait without knowing the predator, and to be bait in a strange town with no idea where to spring and set the trap, is sheer lunacy. Especially if that strange town is a danger in itself.*

Lisbon sat at the mouth of the wide and slow River Tagus, a river deep enough to bring the ships in and out of the harbor area. It was one of the greatest shipping centers of Europe, for the Portuguese were some of the best sailors in the world.

Thomas stood at the end of a crowded street that led to the great docks. He shifted from one foot to the other, hoping to give an appearance of the uncertainty he felt.

Which eyes follow me now? Impossible to decide.

Hundreds, nay, thousands of people flooded the docks of Lisbon. Swaggering men of the sea, cackling hags, merchants pompously wrapped in fine silk, soldiers, bellowing fishmongers.

It was confusion driven by a single purpose. Greed. Those canny enough to survive the chaos also thrived in the chaos. Those who couldn't survive were often found in forgotten alleys, never to receive a proper burial.

Thomas needed to find such an alley, to finally expose his follower. And he had only a few hours of sunlight left. For he knew he would need the protection of a legion of angels, should he be foolish enough to wander these corners of hell in the dark.

He moved forward, glad once again for the comfort of the puppy beneath his arm.

Thomas paused now and again, pretending to examine the merchants' wares—spices from Africa, exquisite pottery from

Rome, and strange objects of glass called spectacles.

Not once in his quick backward glances did Thomas spot a pursuer, yet he dared not hope that meant he was alone or safe. Not after the strangeness of the sailors collapsing because of an upraised sword.

During his wanderings, Thomas noticed a side alley leading away from the busy street. He discovered that it led—after much twisting and turning—onto another busy street. The alley itself held many hidden doorways.

So Thomas circled, an action which cost him much of his precious time. In the maze of streets, it was no easy task to find the original entrance to the alley again.

Once inside that tiny corridor between ancient stone houses, he smiled. Here, away from the bustle of the town, it was almost quiet. And, as with the first time through, it was empty of passersby. He could safely assume any person who traveled behind him was his follower.

Thomas rounded a corner and slipped into a doorway. He set the puppy down and fumbled through his travel pouch for a piece of dried meat, then set it on the cobblestone.

"Chew on that, you little monster," Thomas whispered. "I have no need for your untimely interference again."

Will it be fight or flight? Thomas wondered. He was well hidden in the shadows of the doorway. He could choose to let his follower move on and in turn stalk the stalker, or he could step out and challenge his unknown pursuer.

More seconds passed, measured by the rapid beats of his heart.

Thomas did not hear footsteps. His pursuer moved along the cobblestones so quietly that only the long shadow of the afternoon sun behind him hinted at his arrival.

When the figure appeared in sight, head and neck straining ahead to see Thomas, his decision was instant.

Fight. For the figure was barely the size of a boy.

Thomas reached out and grasped for the shoulder of the small figure. His reaction was so quick that Thomas only managed a handful of cloth as the figure spun and sprinted forward. But not before Thomas recognized the filthy face and hat.

The cook's assistant.

Thomas bolted from the doorway in pursuit.

The cook's assistant? Surely he is a mere messenger or spy. Yet his capture is my only link to his masters.

Thomas ignored the pain of his feet slamming against the hard and irregular cobblestones. He ducked and twisted through the corners of the tiny alley, gaining rapidly on the figure in front.

Thomas closed in, now near enough to hear the heaving breath ahead.

Three steps. Two steps. A single step away. Now tackle!

Thomas dived and wrapped his arms around the cook's assistant. Together, they tumbled in a ball of arms and legs.

Thomas fought and scrambled, surprised at the boy's wild strength. The cook's assistant scuttled sideways, but Thomas managed to roll over and reach around his waist and pull him back close into his body.

Then Thomas froze.

This is not what I should expect from a cook's assistant. Not a yielding softness of body that is more like . . .

Angry words from this mute cook's assistant interrupted his amazement and confirmed his suspicion.

. . . more like that of a woman.

"Unhand me, you murderous traitor."

Katherine's voice!

Thomas scrambled to his feet and grabbed her wrist to help her upward.

Even without the hat that had always cast a shade over her face aboard the ship, the layers of dirt and the filthy hair cropped short still made it difficult to recognize her. Yet it truly was Katherine. She glared hatred at him and spat on the ground beside him.

The puppy skidded to a halt between them. Thomas barely noticed.

"You . . . what the . . . how?"

Katherine looked over his shoulder and her eyes widened.

There was a slight rustle and the sound of rushing air. Then a terrible, black pain overwhelmed him.

When he woke, it only took several seconds to realize he was in a crude jail. Alone.

CHAPTER

44

Early evening light filtered through a tiny hole hewn in the stone wall, revealing a straw-littered floor, walls so confining that he could touch all four easily from the center of the cell, and a battered wooden door.

Thomas stood and groaned. He felt an incredible thirst. He staggered to the door and thumped it weakly.

What evil has befallen me now? Who threw me here, and why? Did that devil's child, Katherine, have others to help her?

Thomas thumped the door again. The impact of his hand against the wood worsened the throbbing of his head.

My cloak. My gold. The old man's book. My sword and sheath. Gone.

It finally dawned on Thomas that he had been stripped down to his undergarments.

"Release me," he croaked through a parched throat. "Return my belongings."

Faint footsteps outside the door reached him as the echoes of his words faded in the twilight of his cell.

Then, a slight scraping of wood against wood, as someone outside slid back the cover of a small partition high in the door.

"Your majesty," a cackling voice called in sarcastic English heavily accented with Portuguese. "Come closer."

Thomas did.

"Do you stand before the door?" the voice queried. "Beneath the window?"

Thomas looked directly above him at the hole in the door which permitted the voice to float clearly through.

"Yes," Thomas answered.

"Good. Here's something to shut your mouth for the night."

Without warning, a cascade of filthy water arched through the opening. Thoroughly drenched, Thomas could only sputter.

"And I've got buckets more if that doesn't instruct you on manners. Now let me sleep."

The partition slammed shut, and the footsteps retreated.

"Your majesty has a visitor." That heavy Portuguese accent interrupted Thomas's dreams.

Thomas opened gritty eyes to look upward at the face of a wrinkled old man. A toothless grin leered down at him.

The gnomelike man pointed back over his shoulder at the open doorway. "Why a common thief like you would receive such a visitor is beyond any mortal's understanding."

Thomas stared past the guard, transfixed by his visitor.

Katherine.

But not the Katherine covered with grime as a cook's assistant. A long cape of fine silk reached almost to her feet. Holding it in place was an oval clasp, showing a sword engraved into fine metal. Her neck and wrists glittered with exquisite jewelry. Her hair had been trimmed and altered to highlight the delicate curves of her cheekbones.

A slight smile played across Katherine's face, as if she knew his thoughts.

She would put a queen to shame.

He opened his mouth to speak, and she shook her head slightly to caution him against it.

"This most certainly is my runaway servant," she said sternly. "I shall see he is whipped thoroughly."

The gnomelike man nodded with understanding. "Feed them and clothe them, and still they show no gratitude."

"I have spoken to the authorities," Katherine continued. "The boy that this scoundrel attacked has not reappeared to seek compensation. Given that, and the fortune in gold that changed from my hands to the magistrate's, I have been granted permission for his return."

The jailer kicked Thomas. "Be sure we don't see your face again."

Thomas pushed himself to his feet. His back felt like a board from leaning against the cold stone; his legs ached from shivering,

and his head still throbbed. Now he was to play the part of
Katherine's servant?

Yet, what were his alternatives? He shuffled forward meekly.

Not until the jailer retrieved Thomas's clothing did he realize
how immodest it was to be standing there in his undergarments.
He seethed with frustration as he dressed under her smirking
gaze, stumbling awkwardly as he balanced on one leg and then
the other.

Then he followed Katherine through the narrow corridor into
the bright sunlight outside. They stood at the north end of the
harbor, and the noise and the confusion of men busy among ships
reached them clearly.

"You were arrested yesterday," Katherine began, "as you lay
there gasping like a stunned fish."

Thomas rubbed the back of his head. "What foul luck.
Certainly a harbor like this has only a handful of men who guard
and patrol for the townspeople."

"The guard was pleased to be such a hero," Katherine said.
"Rarely do such bold crimes occur in broad daylight. He also
seemed pleased at the accuracy of his blow." She paused. "It cost a
quarter of your gold to pay your ransom."

"My gold?" Thomas sputtered.

"Of course," Katherine said calmly. "I lifted your pouch as I
helped them drag you away. Had I not, the jailer certainly would
have. After all, did he not keep your sword and sheath?"

Thomas ground his teeth in anger.

"Fear not," Katherine said sweetly. "As the cook's assistant, I
spirited away your puppy. It remains safely waiting for you at
the inn."

"And my remaining gold?" Thomas spat each word.

Her voice remained sweet. "Much of it purchased this fine
clothing I needed to pose as a noblewoman retrieving an errant
servant. Besides, it would serve neither of us for me to remain as a
mere shiphand on our next voyage."

"*Much* of it? *Next* voyage?" he caught the implications. "*Our*
next voyage?"

"Yes."

"Hardly," Thomas vowed. "I have my own path to follow."

"Not unless you jump ship," Katherine said. "I need only say the word and you will be thrown in jail again. You are under my orders, you will board the ship of my choice."

"You have much to explain." Thomas clenched his fists in fury.

"Perhaps. But as my penniless servant, you are in no position to dictate any terms."

She favored him with another radiant smile.

"And my first command is that you bathe. You smell wretched."

Thomas stood on the gangway that led to the *Santa Magdalen*, an Italian merchant galley. This ship, unlike the *Dragon's Eye's* single mast with square sail, had two masts with lateens, triangular sails which, in the calmer seas of the mid-Atlantic and Mediterranean, enabled the ship to sail into winds with a minimum of tacking back and forth.

"You should find the servants' quarters somewhere below," Katherine said.

Thomas scowled at her, but discreetly.

She smiled back. Sweetly, of course.

He wanted to shake her by the shoulders and demand that she explain how she had followed him, how she had known his destination, to find passage on a galley that sailed to the Holy Land. Far worse, he wanted to stare into those taunting green eyes for every heartbeat for the rest of his life. His confusion only served to deepen his foul mood.

She is one of them, he forced himself to remember, each time their eyes met. *I should not feel this insane warmth.*

He growled surly agreement at her directions and began to march to the cramped and foul section of the ship which would be his home for several weeks.

In the hum of the activity of departure, Thomas moved unnoticed to the prow of the ship where Katherine stood. Spray cascaded against the wooden bow as the galley rose and fell with the waves, making it easy for him to approach her back without being heard.

"Have I not been tortured enough?" he asked.

She half turned and stepped back, not startled at his sudden presence. "I've hardly begun," she said. "But this is a long voyage, and I remember well your treatment of me as I hung by a rope."

"Do not hold those foolish dreams of revenge," Thomas said. "We are away from those wretched Lisbon watchdogs. I shall be my own man now."

She smiled. "If you glance over your shoulder, you will see unfriendly eyes watching closely your every move."

Thomas groaned. "Not so."

"Indeed," Katherine informed him. "Your gold has proven to work wonders with the ship's captain as well. He has promised to have you whipped, should you exhibit the same behavior which jailed you in Lisbon."

"My gold cannot last for an eternity," Thomas protested. "Silks, perfumes, rich food, passage, and now protection! I had planned to live for a year on that gold."

"Wool," Katherine said.

"Wool?" Thomas stared at her as if she had lost her sanity.

"Silks, perfumes, rich food, passage, protection. And wool. This merchant ship holds twenty tons of wool purchased with your gold. Even after the price of passage, I should profit handsomely with its sale when we arrive in the Holy Land."

"Impossible," Thomas said.

"Oh, no," Katherine assured him. "Wool is much needed in far ports."

"I . . . meant . . . impossible . . . that . . . I . . . had . . . enough . . . gold . . . for . . . twenty . . . tons . . . of . . . wool." Thomas could hardly speak now, so difficult was it to remain in control.

Katherine dismissed that with a cheerful wave. "Have I neglected to inform you that I borrowed heavily from the supply of gold you have hidden in England?"

His mouth dropped.

"Remember?" she prompted. "Near the cave which contains your secret books?"

A strangled gasp left his throat.

"It was child's play to follow you to Scarborough after your contest with the outlaw Robert Hood. All I needed to do was return to that cave and wait for your arrival."

She lifted an eyebrow and pretended surprise. "You expected that I would remain with the outlaws to share the ransom collected for Isabelle?"

Thomas closed his eyes briefly, as if fighting a spasm of pain.

"Thomas, Thomas," she chided. "Surely you don't believe it was your doing to win the contest with the outlaw?"

His eyes now widened.

"Robert Hood had been instructed to lose. I wanted you set free."

She moved closer to him and mockingly placed a consoling hand on his arm. "Take comfort, however. He admitted later the outcome was not certain, even had he wanted to defeat you."

Thomas slapped her hand away.

"Woman," he said fiercely, "you push me too far." He grew cold with rage. "My fight for Magnus was a deathbed promise to the nurse who raised and loved me more than a parent. Every pain suffered to fulfill that pledge is a pain I would gladly have suffered ten times over."

He stepped closer but did not raise his voice.

"Yet even after victory, the strange secrets behind Magnus haunted me. And each new secret glimpsed has had your face. I fight enemies I cannot see, and I fight enemies I wish I could not see. Too many good men have sacrificed themselves for this fight."

He advanced while she backed to the railing.

"Yet the reason for this fight—a reason I am certain you know—has been kept from me."

He paused for breath. "Your face and those secrets follow me here to the ends of the earth. And now I am your prisoner on a tiny ship in vast waters. You have stolen my gold. You have humiliated me."

He raised his forefinger and held it beneath her chin. "And now you mock me in tone and words. I will take no more."

Thomas stepped back and said in a whisper. "From this moment on, wherever you stand on this boat, I will choose the point farthest away from you. Threaten me, punish me, have me thrown overboard. I do not care. For I wash my hands of you."

He stared at her for a long moment, then let scorn fill his face before turning away.

She called to his back immediately.

"Forgive me," Katherine said. The mocking banter in her voice had disappeared. "Love leads one to do strange things."

He turned.

"*Que je ne peux pas* ne pas *t'aimer*," Katherine said.

Thomas was still stunned by her first words. So it took his

befuddled brain a moment to translate. *"I cannot* not *love you"*?
Why French?

"And I have loved you fiercely since I was a child," she was
now saying. Although he understood those words clearly, it took
Thomas another moment to realize her last sentence had been
spoken in flawless German.

Loved me since she was a child?

"I see by the light in your eyes," Katherine said, now in
English, "that you understand well my words. And that is part of
why I cannot not love you."

"Truth and answers," Thomas replied, using Latin. "Only a
fool would throw away love offered by you, but first I need truth
and answers."

She smiled and answered him in Latin.

"Can you not see we have received the same education? Have
we not been driven mercilessly by our teachers to be literate and
fluent in all the civilized languages, when few in this world can
even read in their own tongue?"

She moved to Thomas again, and placed again her hand on
his forearm. This touch, however, was tender, not mocking.
"And have we not been trained to fight the same fight against
the same enemies?"

She looked beyond Thomas and discreetly removed her hand
from his arm. "The ship's captain approaches. Tonight, let us talk."

The five hours until moonlight seemed as long as the entire
voyage from England to Lisbon.

Thomas had stood on the stern platform, staring at the
coastline directly eastward that became little more than a faint
haze with distance.

*I dare not trust her. Her vow of love is merely a trick. For if she
were not one of them, how else would I have been captured in my camp
the morning after her arrival with the old man?*

*Yet the old man spoke of Merlins, raised from birth to fight the evil
spawned by generations of a secret society of Druids. I almost believed
him, until my capture through their betrayal proved they were Druids
posing as Merlins.*

*And yet I must consider the alternative. If Katherine is a Merlin and
can truly explain the apparent betrayal, she is my only hope to*

recapture Magnus, my only source to the secrets which have plagued me. If she is a Druid, I will play the game to find what she really wants. So I must pretend to believe her, and refuse to let my heart be fooled as it so desperately wants to be.

Thomas remained on the platform until she appeared.

I cannot read her eyes. How dare I trust her word?

"You know by now that a secret war rages," she began without greeting. "Between Druids, who have chosen darkness and secrecy as the way to power, and Merlins, who battle back in equal secrecy."

Thomas nodded.

"You and I were born to Merlin parents," Katherine said. "But not even birth destines a child to be a Merlin. Some live and grow old unaware of their parents' mission."

Thomas held up a hand to interrupt.

"Certainly I know of the Druids," he said. "Their circle of evil is ancient. The Roman Emperor Julius Caesar observed them more than twelve hundred years ago, when they still reigned openly in Britain."

Katherine nodded. "Of course. You know that from your books in the cave. But of Merlins—"

"Of Merlins I know nothing more than their name, as mentioned by the old man and another I knew in Magnus. It is more than passing strange that they—we—bear the same name as King Arthur's wise man and trusted counselor."

"More than passing strange," Katherine agreed. "King Arthur and his knights ruled some hundreds of years after the Roman conquerors had taken Britain and forced the Druids into hiding openly."

"Hiding openly?"

"Openly. The safest way to hide. Blacksmiths, tanners, farmers, noblemen, knights, priests—during the day. But at night . . ." Katherine's voice trailed. "At night they would meet to continue their quest for power."

She shivered, although the air was warm. "Frightening, is it not? Any man or woman you might meet in England—a false sorcerer at night. And many strove for positions of power in society, the better to influence the direction of their secret plans."

Thomas spat disgust but said nothing. He knew too well the treachery of Druids.

"Merlin?" he prompted her.

"Yes. Merlin. Eight hundred years ago. The brightest and best of the Druids."

Thomas stood transfixed. The creaking of the ship passing through water, the clouds slipping past the moon, he was aware of none of it.

"Merlin a Druid?" he asked.

"It explains much, does it not? His powers have become legendary; some call him an enchanter. Equipped with the knowledge of a Druid—knowledge that is considerable and often seems magic to poor, ignorant peasants—he accomplished much through deception. And what better place for a Druid than at the right hand of Britain's finest king?"

He shook his head, trying to understand. "Yet he battled—"

"Yet Merlin battled the same Druids who raised him to such power. Merlin founded generations of the Druids' greatest enemies, each person equipped with the knowledge of a Druid. In short, he turned their own powerful sword upon themselves."

"Why?" Thomas asked softly. "Merlin had everything a man might desire. Why risk losing all by rejecting the same Druids who had given him that power?"

"It is legend among us," Katherine said, equally softly. "The Druids had waited generations for one of them to have the power in open society that Merlin did. With Merlin, there was finally one to set into motion the plan that would let them conquer the entire kingdom, a plan so evil that its success would establish the Druids forever. Merlin was the one man able to ensure success, until he became the one man to stop them. The legend is that a simple priest showed Merlin the power of faith in God by—"

"A bold plan to establish the Druids?" Thomas interrupted. "It failed with Merlin. It is the plan they follow now that Magnus has been conquered?"

"Yes," Katherine said quietly. "Merlin stopped them once. And since then, we have fought them, generation by generation, at every turn. We have held them at bay, until they finally discovered where we had hidden ourselves."

"What is at the end of this evil plan?" Thomas asked.

Hesitation. Then Katherine said, "I . . . I do not know. The old man always promised to tell me . . . but never had the chance."

Does she lie? Or are her faltering words because of grief for the old man?

Thomas paced back and forth several times, then asked. "The Merlins also hide openly?"

"Yes."

"And seek positions of power to counteract the influence of Druids?"

"Yes." Katherine smiled. "Sometimes we reach fame through these efforts. And we reach far. Generations ago, Charles the Great, king of the Franks, sent for educated people from all over Christendom. He wanted his people to learn again, from books."

Katherine paused, trying to recall the story. "The Druids had arranged to send one of their people. What better way to spread evil in other countries? We intercepted the orders and replaced that Druid with a man named Alcuin. He rose quickly within the royal court of the Franks and did untold good, spreading knowledge and even introducing a new style of writing."

She waved her hand. "There are others, of course, through the ages. We have all been taught the stories of our history."

Thomas frowned. "How many of us are there?"

Katherine sighed. "Before Magnus fell twenty years ago, hundreds. More than enough to keep the Druids from reaching their goal."

"And now?"

"I . . . I . . . do not know. I have only the stories they taught me."

She became quiet, the memory of the old man too hard to bear.

Thomas sensed her sadness and tried to occupy her with other thoughts. "Hundreds? How could hundreds be taught in secrecy? That would take hundreds of teachers!"

"Not so," Katherine replied, her voice not entirely free of sorrow. "Merlin devised a new method. He appointed his successor before he died. And each successor appointed another, so that Merlin's command was passed directly from generation to generation. Each leader was the finest among us. Each one selected teachers, who every generation shared knowledge with entire groups who sat together. One teacher had as many as thirty listeners."

Thomas whistled in appreciation. " 'Tis wondrous strange. Yet seems so simple. Now it strikes me odd this method is not followed elsewhere."

Katherine nodded. "Merlin called it 'school.' "

Thomas stumbled over the strange word. "School."

Katherine nodded again. "Our legends tell us he so named it because schools of fish reminded him of the way we gather to listen, but this I must believe is a story invented for only the youngest Merlins."

Thomas barely heard her last words.

Much now made sense.

Magnus. Isolated in the moors north of England, far from the intrigues and attention of reigning monarchs.

Magnus. With only moderate wealth, not a prize worth seeking.

Magnus. Hidden as it is, with the largest fortress in the north, a construction which must have cost a king's ransom, far more than the land itself could earn, even with the profit of centuries of income . . . yet with seemingly nothing to protect.

Magnus. Riddled with secret passageways.

Thomas understood. He stopped pacing abruptly and voiced his certainty to Katherine. "Merlin established Magnus. Obscure and well protected, it has been the training ground for every generation to follow."

"Yes," she said. "Merlin chose Magnus and had the fortress built. He retired to the island in that remote land. From there, he taught the others and sent them throughout the country to combat the Druids in hidden warfare. And Magnus served us well for hundreds of years. Even after the Druids finally discovered its location and purpose, it took generations for them to conquer it. I was not there when that happened, of course, but the old man told me that their surprise attack and ruthless slaughter twenty years ago all but destroyed the Merlins. Only a few survived."

She stopped, and in the dim light, Thomas could see she was trying to search his face.

"And, Thomas," she finally whispered, "you were appointed shortly after your birth, chosen as Merlin's successor of this generation to reconquer Magnus for us."

CHAPTER
45

Thomas stood and faced her, feet braced and arms crossed.

I want so badly to believe her.

"You weave a fanciful tale," he said scornfully. "Yet if it were true, why was I not told of this?"

"But you were, in a way," Katherine said softly. "Was it an accident you were hidden in that obscure abbey? Was it an accident that Sarah, your childhood nurse, gladly exiled herself there to raise and train you as thoroughly as if you had been raised in Magnus as son of the reigning earl?"

That startled Thomas into dropping his bluff of indifference.

"You jest! My father was a mason, a builder of churches. He and my mother died of the plague, but left behind money to pay for my education among the clergy."

"No, Thomas. Sarah was commanded to keep the truth from you. Your father was ruler of Magnus, the appointed leader of his generation of Merlins. It was crucial that no one ever discover your real identity, and it was feared that as a child, you might blurt it aloud in front of the wrong ears."

Thomas shook his head. "Sarah encouraged me to dream of reigning over Magnus, but she always told me it was her parents I should avenge."

Katherine disagreed, sadly. "Too many Merlins fell with Magnus. The old man often told me you were our only hope, that should the Druids discover the only son of the last leader of the Merlins was still alive, they would leave no stone in England unturned in their search to kill you."

Thomas took several moments to consider this staggering news. "My father reigned over Magnus? My father was the successor to

Merlin? It was my father's death at Druid hands that I was raised to avenge?"

"Yes."

Thomas raised his hands helplessly. "I should have been told this. I stumbled in the darkness." His voice became accusing. "Alone."

"You were too young to be trusted with that precious knowledge. The old man often told me that we could only trust Sarah's training had been a magnificent seed, that you would learn more from the books left with you, and that you would always remember Magnus."

Thomas shook his head again. "Yet I ruled Magnus for three seasons. Neither you, nor the old man, nor Gervaise revealed this to me then."

Katherine moved to the ship's rail and stared away. Thomas was forced to follow to be able to hear her words before they were swallowed by the breeze.

"We could not," Katherine said, still staring at the moon. "You had been alone at the abbey too long. We could not know if the Druids had found you and claimed you as one of their own."

"I conquered Magnus! I took it from them!"

Katherine sighed. "Yes. I argued that often with the old man. He told me that we played a terrible game of chess against unseen masters. They might have artfully arranged a simple deception, and the more it seemed you were against them, the more likely we might be to tell you the final truth, and in so doing lose this centuries-old battle in the quickest of heartbeats."

Thomas pondered her words and spoke slowly. "What is the final truth?"

The constant splash of water against the side of the galley was his only reply.

"The final truth," he demanded.

"Not even I was told."

She lies. I can sense that, even with her face turned away from me. Yet I must pretend to believe.

So Thomas said, "There is an undeniable logic in that. How could you ever finally believe that I was not a Druid, posing as one of you? So I was watched. By Gervaise, who posed as a simple old caretaker. And by you, in your disguise beneath the bandages."

"I am relieved you understand."

There is a simple flaw with this entire story. And it breaks my heart. Yet, I cannot leave it lie.

So Thomas spun her to face him and squeezed both her wrists with mercy.

"But explain," he said fiercely, "why you finally tell me this now. And explain it well, for otherwise I believe nothing, and I shall cast you overboard."

"No, Thomas," she begged. "You must let go!"

His response was to pull her closer to the edge of the ship.

She must believe this terrible bluff.

"Speak now—" he started.

Her eyes widened and she called out, "No!"

But her cry was not directed at Thomas.

He heard a scuffling of feet and turned his head. *Too late.* A familiar blackness crashed down upon him.

Thomas waited for his eyes to adjust to the dimness. The extent of his new prison made the cell in Lisbon seem like a castle.

His head felt it might split.

Uncanny, he thought with a twisted grin, *how they managed to hit me in the exact spot of my previous lump.*

He was able to contemplate this imprisonment for several hours before he had a visitor.

"No," he groaned at the scent of perfume. "Curse me with your presence no longer."

"Hush," Katherine said. "I risk too much even now. A real noblewoman saved from the attack of a rebellious servant would never grace him with a visit."

"You had us watched as we spoke," he accused. "And they believed I would harm you."

"Would you have?" Katherine asked.

"Then, no." He touched the back of his head. "Now, yes."

She smiled. "I have little time. Yet I wish to answer your question."

Thomas studied her face through the iron bars.

"In Scarborough," Katherine began, "you made an error. You sought advice from an old hag who sold fish, advice on how to reach the Holy Land."

Thomas shrugged. "I dared not ask any ship captain. I did not want him to know my destination. So I asked her, thinking she would never remember a passing stranger."

"A passing stranger with a tail sticking out of his cloak as he walked away?" Katherine laughed. "Thus I discovered your destination. There was only one ship in the harbor leaving for Lisbon. It was not difficult to sign on as a cook's assistant."

She took a breath. "I had intended merely to follow you on both ships. Until you lured me into the trap and had the misfortune to be arrested." She stopped, puzzled. "How was it you guessed you had been followed?"

"The manner in which three hardened sailors fell at the wave of my sword. It was the same mysterious manner in which my soldiers fell at Magnus."

Katherine giggled. "The surprise on your face as they fell!" Then she sobered. "A Druid trick. Short thick hollow straws. A puff of breath directs a tiny pellet coated with a sleeping potion. I was in the shadows nearby, watching, because I had heard the crewmen speak and knew you were in danger."

A Druid trick. She tells the truth and is a Merlin who knows much about the enemy—or she is the enemy. How do I decide?

Thomas nodded to conceal his doubt. There was yet the major flaw in her words. So he spoke the question aloud. "Why reveal what you did last night? Why now?"

"I will tell you now. And there is no need to threaten to throw me overboard," Katherine replied. "When you were arrested, desperate measures were needed. I had to help you, and could only do so by playing the role of a noblewoman. By then, I had also decided you were not a Druid. Not if you were going to the Holy Land by yourself."

She hesitates. What does she hide?

Katherine must have caught the doubt in his eyes. "Hawkwood is gone. If you are a Merlin, I need your help as badly as you need mine. It was a risk worth taking. If you are a Druid . . . I knew I was safe, protected by your gold as a noblewoman in Lisbon, and on this ship."

Perhaps. But there must be more. It is obvious in her manner.

Thomas nodded pretended satisfaction.

He thrust his hands through the gap between the iron bars and spoke softly.

"Love," he said. "Since childhood?"

She took his hands in hers. Although he had meant it as an appearance of trust, the touch of her hands in his filled him with warmth.

Do not trust her, nor your heart. Yet remember the first time you met her, and the instinctive reaching of your heart for hers, as if remembering a love deeply buried.

"Love. Since childhood and before you arrived in Magnus," she repeated. "I pray in the Holy Land that much more will be revealed to both of us."

A noise from behind startled her into dropping her hands.

"Thomas," she said quickly, "if it is possible to return safely, I will. Otherwise . . ."

She picked up the ends of her long cape and disappeared in the opposite direction of an approaching crewman.

Thomas did not see her again until the galley reached the harbor of St Jean d'Acre, the last city of the crusader in the Holy Land to fall to the Muslim infidels.

CHAPTER
46

LATE SUMMER 1313
THE HOLY LAND

Two crewmen brought Thomas to the deck of the ship as summoned by Katherine. He was weak from lack of proper food, and his ankles were shackled by chains of iron.

He stared at half-ruined towers, still magnificent and rising from the land at the edge of the Mediterranean Sea. St. Jean d'Acre was a town on a peninsula. Once while still in Christian hands, it had been protected by a massive wall that ran across the peninsula, so that the only approach for attack was by water.

The air around him was steamy with a heat he had never felt before. The sun seemed much larger than in England, and its glare was an attack of fury. The buildings that shimmered before his eyes as the galley grew closer were formed in unfamiliar curves.

At that moment, despite the heat, Thomas felt a chill replace his anticipation.

This land is so foreign, I am doomed before I begin. Muslims have fought Christians here for centuries, and I step onto their land, not even able to . . .

Thomas took a deep breath as that new thought almost staggered him.

I have been so intent on reaching the Holy Land, I have overlooked the single most obvious barrier to my success here. I do not speak the language!

The ship's captain approached Katherine.

"Milady," he said respectfully, "we all wish you Godspeed in the search for your relatives. Many were lost to fine families during the Crusades, and perhaps you will find one or two still alive among the infidels."

He paused, searching for a delicate way to impart advice. "This is a strange land with strange customs. Men take insult if a woman shows her face. To be sure, you will have no difficulty finding a buyer for your wool. Yet you must wear this during all times in public, including the times you negotiate with merchants."

The captain held out a black veil, and Katherine slipped it over her head. It stopped short of the clasp at her neck which held her cloak together.

"You have my gratitude," Katherine told the captain. "Would that all might have the grace and kindness which you have extended me."

He bowed slightly, then frowned at Thomas. "Shall we whip him once to ensure meekness ashore?"

Katherine removed the veil, held it in her left hand, and touched her chin with the tip of her right forefinger as she studied Thomas. A mischievous glint escaped her eyes.

"No," she said finally. "I think the shackles should suffice."

Thomas stood, unshackled, with Katherine in the crowded *fondulk,* a large open-square warehouse on the eastern waterfront occupied by hundreds of sharp-eyed Arab merchants. He could hardly believe his ears: The clamoring babble which surrounded him made sense.

"Don't trust his olive oil," one shout reached him clearly. "That merchant is as crooked as a snake's path!"

"Here for the finest salt!" another voice shouted.

"Silk from the overland journeys!"

I understand each word!

Katherine stood in front of him, her face hidden by her veil, bartering over the price of wool with an eager merchant.

In their language! Impossible!

He stood and watched the chaos around him with an open mouth. The harbor area of Lisbon now seemed like a sleepy town in comparison to this. Camels, donkeys, and gesturing men in long, white robes and turbans in all directions. Finely woven carpets, baskets as tall as men, beggars . . .

Katherine tugged on his arm.

"I have finished," she said in English. Satisfaction filled her words. "As predicted, I have doubled my investment."

"*Our* investment," Thomas felt the need to immediately correct her, although more pressing things engaged him.

He leaned forward. "Their words!" he said. "I understand."

"As well you should," Katherine replied. "It is—"

A beggar darted up to her and chattered excitedly.

"Lady, lady, from where did you get such a fine clasp?"

Katherine reached for her neck and touched it in response.

"Very fine!" the beggar cried. "I can find someone to give you an excellent price for it!"

"I am flattered, of course, yet—"

"Double what you had expected!" the beggar insisted. Then he stopped and looked at her coyly. "Or is it a family heirloom?"

Katherine nodded firmly from behind her veil. "It will never be sold."

Unexpectedly, the beggar darted away without another word.

"Strange," Thomas said. "About the language . . ."

"Of course," Katherine reassured him. "But first, we must purchase you clothing which lets you blend among these people. And a sword." She giggled. "And once again, you are in dire need of time in a public bathhouse."

Twenty-two years had passed since the last banner of any of the German, English, and French crusader knights had flown above the stone walls of St. Jean d'Acre. After nearly two hundred years as the main port to the Holy Land, the last of the crusader strongholds had finally fallen to Muslim infidels.

The city was now a mere shell of the trading town it had been. Its walls and high turrets were, on close inspection, war-ravaged and doomed to crumble to dust.

Few now were those in the town with fair skin and blue eyes, the sure signs of Northern European heritage. And none were those who dared display the colors of any knighthood among the Muslim infidels who so thoroughly dominated the entire land. It seemed prudent to dress in a way to conceal their identity.

"I no longer feel half dead." Thomas grinned beneath his turban. "A rest tonight in a bed that does not shift with the waves, some food, and I will be ready to conquer the world."

Katherine smiled back.

They gazed at each other in silence for several seconds, forming an island of privacy in the hectic motion of the market around them outside the bathhouse.

Don't let those eyes fool you. Remember, you will only remain with her until you discover the truths you need. There is nothing more to this situation.

To cover the flush he felt beneath her gaze, Thomas gestured at his robe and turban and sword at his side. "Do I not appear the perfect infidel? Especially after you tell me how it is I understand their language."

"Perfect," Katherine agreed lightly. "We—" She frowned. "Thomas, to your left. It is not the same beggar who approached me for this clasp?"

Thomas turned his head to see the beggar grasping the sleeve of two large men and pointing in their direction.

All eyes locked across the space between them. The beggar and his companions, each armed with a scimitar, and Thomas and Katherine staring back at them in return.

"I like this not," Katherine said. "We should return to the inn and see your puppy instead."

They backed away quickly. And soon discovered they were prey for the two large men.

In a half run, Katherine and Thomas darted around the market stalls and through crowds of people.

"This way!" Katherine cried.

"No . . ." But Thomas did not protest in time. Katherine had already started down a narrow alley.

Why have they chosen us? Thomas wondered as he ran. *Because we are foreign? Surely it cannot be because of the Druids. We have only just arrived.*

Thomas nearly stumbled on the uneven stone of the streets as he stopped and turned to run after her. His sword slapped against his side.

I pray I will not use this weapon. These men are larger and stronger.

The two men were familiar with the twists of the alley, and each second they gained ground. Thomas and Katherine were now in a full run, slipping beneath archways and around blind corners.

"Again! This way!" Katherine panted. "We are nearly there!"

"No . . ." Thomas moaned. He did not know the town at all,

but knew with certainty her path led them away from both the waterfront and the inn.

Without warning, Katherine stopped and pounded on a door hidden in a recess in the alley.

"That is not the inn!" Thomas warned.

"Behind you!" Katherine said. She banged the door with her fist

Thomas did the only thing he could. He drew his sword.

"You cannot avoid the assassins' pledge," the first man snarled, as he lifted his scimitar.

Thomas managed to parry the first blow, then stepped aside as the other swung.

I have only seconds to live, he realized.

"Katherine," he said quickly. "Run while you might."

In answer, he felt her presence plucked from his side.

The door has opened.

Another whistling blow. Thomas met it with his own steel, and the echoing clank was almost as painful as the jar of contact that shivered up his arm.

Thomas brandished his sword and prepared for a counterattack.

If I'm to die, they will pay the price.

Both men hesitated and stepped back.

"Cowards!" Thomas cried, in the full heat of battle.

"No," came a strangely familiar voice, from the very spot where Katherine had stood only moments earlier. "They are simply prudent."

Both men stepped back farther.

"Yes," the voice continued, now directed at the two. "This crossbow truly reaches farther and faster than one sword. Go back to the men who hired you. Tell them the blood they wish to spill is now under protection."

The swordsmen nodded and quickly spun around, then hurried to the nearest corner of the alley.

Thomas, still panting, turned to look at his rescuer.

"Well, puppy," he was greeted. "Must we always meet in such troubled circumstances?"

Thomas only stared in return.

Sir William. Sir William, who helped me conquer Magnus three seasons ago, then disappeared on his own private quest.

CHAPTER
47

Thomas found his voice. "You describe harmless gnats like those two as trouble? Truly, you must be growing old."

Now, as when the knight had bid farewell long ago in Magnus, Thomas fought a lump in his throat.

Then, an early morning breeze had gently flapped the knight's colors against the stallion beneath him. Behind them both had been the walls of Magnus. Ahead of them had been the winding trail that had taken the knight to a destination he could not reveal.

This destination.

St. Jean d'Acre, on the edge of the Holy Land.

The sorrow Thomas felt in remembering their farewell mixed like a sweet wine with the sorrow of a remembrance of Magnus. He blinked back emotion.

Sir William smiled, switched the crossbow to his left hand, and extended his right hand in a clasp of greeting.

The knight had changed little. Still darkly tanned, hair still cropped short, now with a trace of gray at the edges. Blue eyes still as deep as they were careful to hide his thoughts.

A sudden thought struck Thomas.

"You are one of us." Although it was a guess, Thomas spoke it as a statement. "A Merlin."

Sir William nodded. "And one unable to decide whether to be gladdened or sorrowful at your arrival in this fallen town of the last crusaders."

Thomas raised an eyebrow.

"This is perhaps not the circumstance I envisioned for a joyful reunion," Sir William said, as he beckoned them in and placed an iron bar across the inside of the door. "Yet when one prays for a miracle, one does not ask the Lord to make it a convenient miracle."

Katherine smiled as she unfurled the veil which covered her face. Thomas merely gazed about the room with undisguised wonder and awe.

"I have been here before," Thomas said, "many times, in strange and troubled dreams."

"Find comfort that you have reason for this familiarity. You spent a part of your childhood in this house," Sir William said softly. "Would that I had time now to explain."

The knight's face did not reflect his urgency, despite the too recent echoes of that iron bar slammed quickly into place.

Thomas shook away his trance and half laughed. "Explain? In this town less than half a day from stepping off ship, yet already I've been forced to flee assassins, only to have you appear as rescuer—you, a person I never expected to see again. Then you tell me that I spent part of my childhood here, in a land thousands of miles away from England."

Thomas stopped for breath. "Only a sane man would demand explanation of these mysteries." He shrugged and smiled to rob his sarcasm of insult. "However, no person could remain a sane man under these circumstances. So do not trouble yourself with tiresome explanations. Even if we had the time."

Any reply was interrupted by shouts from outside. Then, moments later, a crash into the wood of the door, as if a heavy shoulder had been applied.

Two more crashes, accompanied by shouts. The iron bar held secure.

"By the sounds, perhaps a dozen men," the knight said.

"Your crossbow will be useless at short quarters," Thomas said, nodding at the weapon the knight had laid on a nearby table. "Have we a place to our advantage in a sword fight?"

The knight shook his head. "Against infidel assassins, no place gives advantage."

"I will not die quickly," Thomas vowed.

"Who speaks of death?" the knight countered.

Sir William yanked an unlit lamp from a nearby shelf. He pulled the wick loose from the base and emptied the oil in a semicircle on the wooden furnishings of the room.

He then grabbed one of the three remaining lit lamps and shattered it on the ground.

Flames licked at the spilled oil, then burst into a small wall of fire. The knight nodded grimly as black smoke began to fill the room.

"Let them fight this instead."

Even as the flames began to roar around them, assumptions and conclusions raced through Thomas's mind.

The knight has an escape planned. He has no valuables to gather and protect. Thus, he has been ready to flee this house in an instant. He has anticipated this very moment!

How? Why?

The answers, Thomas vowed, would come later. Now, as shouting outside rose in response to the smoke which poured through the window openings, was the time to follow the knight.

Sir William gestured for Katherine and Thomas to follow. He led them through a narrow archway into another chamber of the house.

This chamber leads to two others. There will be arched windows in one. A statue of Mother Mary in the other. And, during the morning, sunlight will stream across the statue as it did so many times when I sat on the floor and listened to . . .

Thomas felt his heart skip a beat. Even in the haste of escape, the memories returned. This was no dream . . . no visit during sleep so that he woke with unexplained tears across his face.

I sat in this very house! My childhood nurse spent time with me in these very rooms! Yet, how could I have forgotten?

Sir William led them to the room which indeed contained the statue of the Mother Mary, then stooped suddenly and began to pry at the edge of a flat stone on the floor. Behind them, the heat of the fire as it spread into another chamber.

No words yet spoken . . . The stone moved aside . . . Below it, a large iron ring was recessed into the wood.

Sir William flipped the ring upward with both hands.

He grunted and pulled again. An entire section of the floor lifted. "Take a lamp," he instructed Thomas. "Descend and wait."

Thomas moved quickly across the room, grabbed the lamp base, and held it steady as he rejoined Sir William and Katherine. He looked into the darkness of the hole.

"Go quickly," the knight said. "There are steps. Katherine and I will follow."

Briefly, Thomas wondered if this was a trap. He did not yet trust Katherine fully. And by association, neither should he fully trust the knight.

He considered whether to hand the lamp to Katherine, to send her down first instead.

"Quickly," the knight urged. "They are breaking down the door!"

Thomas dropped down. Almost immediately, Katherine followed. With light in hand, it was not difficult now to see the downward path of the crooked steps.

Darkness closed over him as the trapdoor above was lowered. The flame flickered at the sudden rush of air, but Thomas protected it with his upper body, and the flame stayed alive.

He felt a hand on his shoulders. A soft touch.

"Thomas," Katherine whispered."Sir William is not with us."

Thomas set the lamp down, placed one hand on the hilt of his sword, and turned to move back past Katherine.

"No," she pleaded. "We cannot return."

"And let him die alone?" Thomas asked.

Katherine placed her hands on his shoulders as he attempted to push up the steps. "Or die together? He chose to remain behind. Our deaths up there will only make his sacrifice useless."

Thomas was that one step lower, and it brought his face directly to the level of hers. For an insane moment, Thomas forgot the fire, the mysteries, and the fight above. Katherine's scent filled him as surely as the softness of her hair against his face reminded him of the touch of her arms on his shoulders.

Her eyes widened in the faltering light of the lamp, as if she too were suddenly aware that time and circumstance had fallen away.

Thomas swayed slightly, closed his eyes, and moved close enough to feel the warmth of her breath on his lips. His hand left the hilt of his sword and, as if he had no control, moved to the back of her head to pull her even closer.

Insanity! She may be a Druid!

He opened his eyes. Her eyes were closed in trust. Such beauty. It brought him an ache of joy and sorrow to think of an eternity of her love.

Insanity! A friend above gives his life that we may flee!

She sensed his hesitation and opened her eyes, breaking the spell. "Milady," Thomas began to apologize.

"Thomas," she said in the same moment.

They both stopped in midsentence.

Awkwardly, Thomas stepped back and down from her.

"Surely this tunnel leads to escape," he said quickly. "Sir William would not have planned it otherwise. And the fire above will lead the town to panic. We must hurry to keep our advantage."

"And then?"

Thomas did not reply. He had no answer, and for that reason wanted only to concentrate on ducking through the low tunnel as he guarded the wick of his lamp from the water which dripped from the cool stone.

When they stopped to rest ten minutes later, Thomas was ready with his questions.

"Tell me," he said, determined to ignore the effect of her closeness, "of matters of my childhood."

"How is it I should know?" she asked, almost aloof.

"You . . . you are a Merlin." He had almost blurted that she *claimed* to be a Merlin. "As is the knight," Thomas finished. "Surely you and he have secrets in common."

"The fall of Magnus forced the few survivors into isolation. Sir William roamed the world while I remained in disguise among the Druids of Magnus. How much can I know of his part in our battle?"

Even now she holds back truth, Thomas thought with a trace of bitterness. *And I long to trust her and hold her and . . .*

He forced himself to concentrate on his questions.

"When the assassins pursued us from the marketplace," he said, "you led us not to the inn, but directly to the house where Sir William waited. Is that not proof of shared knowledge?"

Many heartbeats passed before she replied.

"Yes, indeed," she finally began. "When Magnus fell to the Druids, Sir William, your parents, and a handful of others barely escaped with their lives. England was no longer safe. So they fled here to the Holy Land, hoping . . . hoping to find help in fighting the Druids from the valiant crusaders."

Is her hesitation a shiver of cold? Or a lie? Thomas chose to remain silent, to wait for more.

"You and I," Katherine said, "were raised here, in the house that so troubled your dreams. Your father dared not return to England. Druid spies were everywhere. When the time was right, you and I—who never would be recognized—were smuggled back to England, I to serve in disguise as a spy in Magnus, you to receive training in that obscure abbey from Sarah, one of the most dedicated Merlins of her generation."

Thomas closed his eyes at the name of his childhood nurse. She had tutored him relentlessly, corrected him with endless patience. And in all those hours and days and years of instruction, she had favored him with the love deeper than any . . .

"It cannot be," Thomas whispered.

He faltered as he spoke. "I arrived at the abbey as a child. I was old enough so that now I can remember—dimly—those first days there. You tell me that the first years of my life were spent here. That I understand and believe, for is not my understanding of the tongue of this foreign country enough proof?"

He paused as another memory struck him . . . the memory of the first moment he saw Katherine's face in the moonlight when he and his army marched northward to battle the Scots. He had learned—from betrayal by the beautiful, dark-haired Isabelle—not to trust appearance as an indication of a person's heart. Yet in the shadows of the moonlight he had felt as if he had been long pledged to the woman with the mysterious smile in front of him. Katherine . . . known since childhood.

And later, on the ramparts of the castle, when he had first stolen from her a kiss, the same certainty. What a bond they must have forged as small children, laughing and playing here in St. Jean d'Acre, unaware of the roles they must later play in a battle against the very Druids who had slain so many of their parents' friends.

Was not the bond itself—and the foreign language of the marketplace which seemed so natural—solid proof of the time spent here? Yet how had those childhood memories been taken from him?

Thomas pushed those thoughts aside and pursued the one thought which had first caused his voice to falter.

"As a boy, I believed that I was an orphan, that Sarah was raising me in the monastery on the strength of money left to the church by my father, who had been a wealthy mason. You tell me, instead, that I was raised in secret a Merlin to be part of a centuries-old battle against the unseen Druids, and that both my parents were part of that battle."

Thomas shook his head. "I can scarcely take all of this in." His voice grew shakier. "My parents were alive then, not fallen to the plague. Could it be that Sarah, the nurse who guided and taught and loved me as truly as might a mother . . . could it be she *was* my mother?"

Katherine's silence in the darkness of the tunnel was answer enough.

Thomas did not wipe away his tears of renewed grief. To have lost a mother twice . . .

Katherine closed her eyes and shared quietly in his pain.

There was no chance for more conversation. For above the steady dripping of water against stone came the faraway echo of approaching footsteps.

Immediately, Katherine reached between them to pinch the wick of the lamp. Thomas grasped her wrist and held it steady.

"This light will betray our presence," she protested.

Thomas thought of another time, beneath the castle of Magnus, when blind stumbling through secret passageways had nearly cost him his life, so he did not release her wrist.

"How shall we light the lamp again?" he asked. "For without light, we might never leave this tunnel." He then smiled. "And did not your training as a Merlin teach you the words of a wise general now long dead?" He paused. "All warfare is deception."

The footsteps grew louder. Yet Katherine was more of a distraction for Thomas than the possible danger. It took effort not to reach upward and softly touch the curves of her face, as she looked at him with a steadiness that seemed to pierce his heart.

Thomas released Katherine's wrist, lifted the lamp, and carried it forty steps back in the direction from which they started.

He set the lamp down and rejoined Katherine in the darkness.

"Now," he said, "when our visitor approaches, he will expect us there, ahead at the light, instead of here in the shadows."

First, Katherine and Thomas saw an approaching glow, then the light of the visitor's lamp. The visitor's footsteps slowed, and stopped almost as soon as the light had appeared.

In the next moment, that faraway light disappeared.

The visitor chooses to approach now in darkness. From caution born of fear, or caution born of evil intent?

No longer could Thomas or Katherine hear footsteps.

This visitor must pass close enough to touch us. But now soon?

Thomas felt, rather than heard, the nearness of a stranger, as if the only hint of another person was air pushed ahead in the stillness of the tunnel.

Does this stranger walk with dagger or sword poised? Will I leap ahead into a sudden death?

Thomas did not answer his own silent question, for he had been taught that hesitation was the greatest enemy in the moment of action in any battle. He had also been taught the advantage of the terror of noise.

Thomas bellowed a rage that filled the tunnel as he charged into the stranger. His shoulder rammed a solid bulk. Hands were upon him instantly and Thomas punched back. Twice he hit only air, but three times his knuckles jarred against bone. Thomas continued to roar anger as he lashed out again and again at the unseen stranger.

The stranger was heavier, but Thomas was faster and more desperate.

Hands once managed to wrap around his neck, but Thomas lashed out with his knee to strike hard flesh, and the hands released with a grunt of pain, only to seek him again from the darkness.

Thomas felt a face and tried to dig his fingers into the eye sockets—anything to gain the advantage in a fight that meant life or death.

In response, a sudden blow pounded his cheekbone, and he fell back with flashes of light filling his eyes.

"Stop," Katherine was yelling. "Both of you stop!"

Thomas felt his opponent relax and roll away from him, so he too relaxed and struggled to his feet.

The voice which greeted him was all too familiar.

"Should demons ever assume earthly form," Sir William said, attempting a chuckle of humor, "that form would closely resemble Thomas of Magnus."

Thomas groaned and began to feel his body for broken bones. "And should humans ever assume the forms of ghosts," he said, as he probed his mouth for shattered teeth, "they would do well to imitate Sir William. For considerate humans would announce their presence to friends."

Sir William staggered slightly as he tried to straighten. "I saw the lamp, but no one near. I could only assume the worst, and wonder how best to approach the enemies who had captured you."

Katherine moved forward and examined Sir William's face for cuts. "We thought you dead," she said softly.

"My own face fares poorly," Thomas hinted.

She ignored him.

"What happened in the house? In the fire?"

"I'll tend to my own bruises," Thomas announced, but still Katherine ignored him.

Sir William took the lamp from Katherine's hand, returned it to his own lamp, and relit it. In the circle of renewed light, he sat and leaned against the tunnel wall with a moan.

"Join me," he said. "In the little time before the caravan leaves, I have much to explain, and here in the tunnel is much safer than above."

Katherine stepped forward, and Thomas limped closer.

"I wanted to lead them away from the house and the tunnel," Sir William began, "but I also feared if I explained my intentions to fight and flee by another door, neither of you would agree to accept the safety of this tunnel. So I fought briefly, escaped the house, led the assassins on a merry chase, then entered this tunnel by the hidden exit we shall reach soon."

He turned to Thomas. "As you might guess, this escape has been ready for years. The Merlins have been in possession of the house for generations—almost since the beginning of the Crusades—and have often used the tunnel for the arrival and departure of visitors who should not be seen in the town."

"But why here in St. Jean d'Acre?" Thomas asked. "We are across the world from Magnus. What significance has this town to the Merlins? Or to the Druids?"

Sir William nodded. "The town itself has significance only because it is the traditional entry for those bound to the Holy Land by ship."

He let that statement hang in the silence until Thomas spoke.

"You say then that it is the Holy Land which draws Druids as well as Merlins?"

Sir William nodded. "And their spies, as do ours, watch the ships as passengers enter the town. It is the symbol on Katherine's clasp so prominent on her cloak, I believe, which led them to discover you so soon."

Yes, had not that beggar in the market inquired of its value? The distinct sword engraved in the clasp, then, what is its meaning?

Thomas was given no time to ponder, for the knight continued to speak.

"Both sides seek a great secret lost here in the Holy Land centuries ago," Sir William said. "The search has stretched over generations. The side which first discovers that secret will have the power to destroy the other."

What strangeness this is, Thomas thought. *I am here beneath the streets of a town in the land where Christ walked, with remembered knowledge of a lost childhood, in quiet conversation with a knight who once saved my life and helped me win a kingdom, and—if Katherine's story during our sea voyage is to be believed—I have been destined to continue a centuries-old battle against a secret circle of evil.*

Thomas laughed softly.

Sir William glanced at him, puzzlement clear even in the flickering light of the lamps.

"You find humor in this?"

Thomas ran his fingers along the rough stone of the tunnel walls. "It is only because I feel the coldness of this stone that I can believe this is not a dream of madness," he said. "Laughter? How else might one face the storms of life?"

"Well spoken," Sir William said. "And this is indeed a storm. I have not yet heard what troubles have led you here to the Holy Land. Katherine, I am sure, will tell me the sad news later, during the long hours of travel that face us."

Thomas raised an eyebrow. "Katherine? Not I?" Instinctively, he dropped his hand to his sword. "Do you imply that I will not be there?"

Sir William groaned and raised a hand as if fending off attack. "Must you be so untrusting? Did I not with you secure Magnus from the Druids?"

"Trust is the one thing I wish I could possess," Thomas said softly. "While much has been explained, too little knowledge has yet been given me."

He stared directly at Sir William and Katherine, considering the reasons for his mistrust. "That day at the gallows long ago," Thomas challenged. "Why was the old man there, the same old man who so mysteriously appeared with Katherine as they followed me throughout England? And you too, Sir William. Why were you there at the gallows with the old man? I cannot believe in coincidence."

The knight answered, "We were there because of the songs Sarah taught you. Think back, Thomas. Had she not told you about a knight who would come from the land of the sun?"

Thomas nodded. He remembered that. He remembered her instructions. He remembered too the chant Sarah had taught him, the chant he had heard later from the people of Magnus, that the one to reconquer Magnus would arrive as if *delivered on the wings of an angel*. Thomas remembered how Sarah had again and again told him to wait for the one knight he would need to free Magnus.

And he remembered her love. *Sarah was my mother, and not once were we able to share that knowledge.* Thomas spun away from Sir William and Katherine and bowed his head as spasms of grief shook him.

Katherine rose quickly and placed a comforting arm around Thomas.

"No," he said, not harshly, as he straightened. "This is not a time for grief. This is a time for answers."

He drew a deep breath. His voice remained steady as he spoke again. "You expected me, then, to appear at the gallows that day?"

"Yes," Sir William said. "How else might we get you to come forth without exposing ourselves to unseen and unknown Druids?"

"Yet, had I not appeared," Thomas countered, "you would have swung from that rope."

Sir William shook his head. "The old man was there. Had you not appeared, he would have ensured my life, and we would have begun our search for you. After all, he had arranged the time of execution to match that of the darkness of the sun."

Thomas gaped. "The old man had such power?"

"Hawkwood is dead," Katherine said quietly to the knight.

"Dead?" The word was uttered in disbelief. "But you did not speak of—"

"Dead," Katherine repeated. "Magnus is in the hands of the Druids. They rapidly expand their power among the people of

Northern England, and the old man is dead."

The knight stood quickly. Urgency now filled his voice.

"Thomas, our continued survival is of utmost importance. All the more reason, then, that we separate now and travel apart. The assassins will be searching for three. And you, or Katherine and I must reach our destination."

Sir William turned to Katherine. "He shall go by caravan, you and I on foot. Tell me all during our journey. I must not delay in giving instructions to Thomas."

"Katherine," Thomas said. "That puppy. We cannot leave it to die at the inn."

"It shall be taken care of," Sir William said quickly, wanting the discussion to end. Then he took his lamp and began to lead them forward. Some thirty steps later—where he had first darkened his own lamp to approach with such caution—Sir William stooped to retrieve a package.

He gave it to Thomas.

"This must remain sealed. Guard it with every fiber of body and soul," Sir William said. "Too much of our battle against the Druids depends on its safe arrival—with you—in Jerusalem. After we visit Nazareth."

"Nazareth," Thomas repeated.

"Yes. For your father awaits you there."

CHAPTER

48

The tent flaps swirled open and a large figure entered, dark against the sunlight which streamed in behind his back.

It was the Arab, Muzzamar. Thomas had seen him briefly the night before, and then only in the light of a small torch, as he and Sir William bartered with great animation.

Although Muzzamar was fat, he moved with an athletic grace. His eyes were sharp; his gray goatee, well trimmed. The deep lines around his mouth showed years of laughter, yet no man reached his age and position without an ability to dispatch the most vicious enemy, and Thomas warned himself to be on his guard.

As Muzzamar lowered himself to sit on a stool near Thomas, great shrieking groans resounded outside the tent.

"Camels," Muzzamar explained. "Evil beasts. Smelly, stubborn. Put upon this earth to try men's souls. They will protest their load every morning until we reach Damascus."

"Damascus?" Thomas said. "Am I not to travel to Nazareth?"

Unconsciously he pressed his leg against the sealed package beside him beneath the blanket.

"Of course, of course," the man said. "From here, we travel to the Valley of Jezreel. Near Mount Tabor a road leads north to Nazareth. Some of my men will take you there as this caravan continues east to Damascus. Did not your friend explain?"

"Sir William had little time," Thomas said. "He cautioned me to avoid soldiers. He—"

"Good advice, indeed," Muzzamar said quickly, "something I cannot repeat enough. We travel in this land only by a pass of safe conduct granted by the Mamelukes. That safe conduct does not include passage for men from across the Great Sea. Should you be discovered, I cannot vouch for your life."

Muzzamar gestured behind Thomas. "There are clothes of the desert. The head veil will protect your face from sun and wind, of course, but also from curious Mameluke soldiers."

Muzzamar paused, then said, "I should not worry over-much about the soldiers, however. This caravan carries much wealth. On these roads, we face a much greater danger from bandits."

For the first few miles, Thomas marveled at the serene smoothness of travel on camel back. Except for the pressure of the small saddle, he had the impression he was floating far above the ground. And to think that these great beasts could go days without water!

Thomas idly wondered if it would be practical to take camels back to England, and that led to renewed memories of Magnus, which then led to his usual doubts and questions.

Even now, contemplating it for the thousandth time, Thomas felt an odd mixture of thrill and relief at his newfound knowledge. *I am a Merlin, engaged in battle against a secret circle of Druids.* That explained much of his childhood, much of the mystery behind Magnus, much about the precious books of knowledge, and much about the destiny given him by Sarah, his mother.

Sarah, his mother—each time that phrase entered his mind, Thomas forced it away. He would grieve, yes, but in privacy. Not among the men of this caravan that snaked slowly forward beneath the hot sun.

His new knowledge explained much of what had happened at the gallows so long ago. Yet new questions arose. Who was the old man with the power among ruling men to arrange a hanging on the day and hour that an eclipse would occur? What was this new quest in the strange Holy Land? The package he must so carefully guard?

Thomas felt dark suspicion, too. Both the knight and Katherine had said that the Merlins were unable to reveal themselves to Thomas because of an uncertainty of his true allegiance. This matter of their trust was important. They had hinted that through Thomas the Druids might find the one single secret they needed to end the centuries-old battle. *What is the secret they believe I hold? And what terrible end to the battle?*

His suspicions darkened more. *Having revealed so much, why not tell me all? Unless they do not yet trust me completely. And if I am not yet trusted completely, why reveal anything at all?*

Were the answers in the package entrusted to him? Not for the first time did he consider unsealing it.

No. Thomas repeated the arguments he had given himself. *Were Sir William and Katherine foes, they would have given me nothing that might benefit me. If they are friends, then unsealing the package will cost me their allegiance.*

Thomas closed his eyes briefly. Should he in return trust them? Enough strange events had occurred so he might full well believe *they* were Druids.

His only choice was to play this game to its end. The bait promised him was nothing less than the father he had long believed dead.

The caravan moved south along the flat road of the coastal plains. Each time Thomas wiped his face and exposed his skin to the scorching air, he breathed gratitude at the layers of fine cloth which trapped the cooler air close to his body. Long before the sun passed its highest point, one of the leather bags of water tied to his saddle was half empty.

Much more difficult than the heat was the evil of watching the slaves stumble alongside the camels.

They were marked by the single rope which attached one to the other. This rope was looped around each neck, so that when one fell, he risked dragging the others down. When one slowed, he risked strangulation.

Thomas noted that they had no skins of water, and vowed to ease their thirst as soon as he could.

Muzzamar, at the front of the caravan, finally raised his sword to call a halt when the lead camels reached a stand of trees which hugged a wide well.

Thomas did not dismount until he had loosened two of his water skins from the saddle. Ignoring the scowl of the slave master, he moved to the first of the slaves. He had been warned by both Sir William and Muzzamar not to draw attention to himself, but he knew the men on foot must be in agony.

"Take this," Thomas said as he held out the water skin, "then pass it along."

The slave lifted his head. Dark eyes, glazed with exhaustion, now opened wide with surprise. The slave hesitated, briefly, then snatched the leather bag from Thomas and gulped water.

Thomas waited, then realized the slave had no intention of ending his drink, so he gently grabbed the slave's wrists and pulled the skin away.

Thomas carried the water to the next slave, then to the next and the next, until he reached the last slave held by the rope. Unlike the other slaves, this one did not open his hands gladly to receive the water skin.

"You risk your life," the slave said, head still down.

Thomas stepped back in surprise. *The man had spoken English.*

"Among these nomads, it is considered a weakness to show mercy," the slave continued. "And we will be fed and watered at nightfall, for they have no wish to kill us."

"English," Thomas blurted. "You speak English!"

The slave redirected his stare from the ground to Thomas. His eyes were a piercing blue.

"I speak English because I am English," the man said in a low voice. "Find it not so amazing. Many of us are doomed in this strange land, those long forgotten from a forsaken crusade."

Thomas again pushed the water skin toward the slave. This time the water was accepted, with another shrug. The slave drank slowly, then returned the water.

"You are too young to have come with the last crusaders," the man said. "Yet your command of their tongue tells me you are not a new arrival to this land. And you are not among the slaves. Your story must be one of interest."

Thomas nodded.

"Do not attempt to help me escape," the man said calmly.

The advice had the impact of a physical blow. For indeed, Thomas was contemplating that same subject.

Before Thomas could protest, the man fixed him with those uncanny eyes and unhurriedly spoke more.

"We are fellow countrymen. And, methinks, men of the same breed, for cowards and ne'er-do-wells would not stray across a world to enter the Holy Land." The man raised his voice slightly. "Yet do not offer your help. Even should you succeed, with me you would become a hunted outlaw."

A deep laugh greeted that remark.

"Well spoken, Lord Baldwin!" the words came from behind them in Arabic, for Muzzamar had approached quietly. "Words spoken for my benefit?"

Muzzamar clapped Thomas on the back. "Lord Baldwin saw me, of course. But it is still advice worth heeding. You are a stranger among us, and I suspect you know little of our history."

Muzzamar took Thomas by his elbow. "Come with me. We have a little time before our journey resumes."

Muzzamar spoke as he guided Thomas back to the trees. "You know, by now, of the Mamelukes. Two centuries ago as slaves to the Egyptians, they overthrew their masters. Later they overthrew the foreigners who built fortresses and castles all across this land."

The trader pointed east. "In those hills stood the great crusader castles. The greatest, known as Saphet, commanded the very road we travel. The Mamelukes had laid siege, and they promised safe passage to the knights upon their surrender. Yet when the gates of the castle were opened, every knight was beheaded on the spot."

Muzzamar examined Thomas for his reaction.

"So you see," Muzzamar's smile was nearly a caress of cruelty, and Thomas understood with a chill how different these people were, "we cannot afford to anger the Mamelukes. To our enemies, we are equally ruthless. And neither we nor the Mamelukes show the softness of the English."

Muzzamar tapped the water skin Thomas still held.

"We do not provide comfort to our enemies, and we show no mercy to those who betray us." Muzzamar's smile did not change as the implied threat continued. "Perhaps you feel duty-bound to help another. Take the advice offered you by Lord Baldwin. Journey along your own path. I have guaranteed your safety because I have accepted gold. And I am no common bandit. I will deliver you as promised."

Muzzamar's voice then flattened with deadliness. "But should you become an enemy, you will have the choice of death or slavery. And death would be more pleasant."

CHAPTER

49

On the eve of the third day of travel, Muzzamar visited Thomas in his tent.

"My young friend," Muzzamar beamed, "tonight we shall feast."

The previous days of travel had been at a forced pace. Tents had not been raised at nightfall, nor cooking fires lit. Sleep had been short, and in open air. The entire caravan had always been ready to move.

"No danger of bandits tonight?" Thomas asked. "Nor of Mameluke soldiers?"

"We are well into the Valley of Jezreel," Muzzamar said. "The passage into this valley is well guarded by hills. It favors large groups of bandits. Naturally, we are able to protect ourselves, but only at great cost, and to tarry in those hills provides the bandits unnecessary temptation. But now . . ."

Muzzamar swept his arms wide. "Now we are in the open valley. And a caravan of traders on its way to St. Jean d'Acre has joined us in its passing. There is safety away from the hills, and safety in numbers. We shall rest here and feast. You will be welcome, for it is hardly likely that Mameluke soldiers will appear at night to inspect the caravan."

"How long will we rest?" Thomas asked.

"The road to your destination is only a day's travel," Muzzamar said, "well within sight of Mount Tabor. From there, two of my men will guide you north into the hills to Nazareth."

Muzzamar caught the darkness of uncertainty that crossed Thomas's face.

"Come, come, Thomas. Have no fears. We have successfully

passed through the dangerous country. You and my guides will easily avoid Mameluke soldiers on the road to Nazareth. Your arrival there is a certainty."

Thomas forced a smile. His fears were not of arrival, but of what might occur after.

Thomas groaned as he laid his head to rest. The sealed package he had sworn to guard for Sir William was wrapped in a blanket and served as his pillow. But how could he possibly sleep?

Muzzamar's promise of a feast had only been a hint of the events of the evening. There had been tambourine dancing by veiled girls, rich meats and sweets, and servants pouring wine and delivering food. The feasters from both caravans needed only sit and eat. Thomas himself had gorged, urged on by a servant who tended to him.

As he finally drifted into sleep, Thomas tossed fitfully. His dreams gave him little rest.

He stood upon a high hill, shrouded in gray mist. The mist swirled, then cleared, and rays of sunshine broke through from behind him, sunshine that lit an entire city across the deep valley, so that beams of light danced on the curved towers rising tall above whitened square houses that spread in all directions along the plateau of the mountain.

From the city walls came a dark figure, slowly moving closer until Thomas could see it was a large man.

The peace Thomas felt to behold this city of dreams began to disappear, and in its place arrived a trembling panic which grew stronger as the figure approached, stronger as Thomas struggled to identify the man's face.

"Thomas, my son," the figure called. "Are you a Merlin?"

Thomas tried to reply, "Father," but he could not speak. There was something so threatening about this stranger who claimed to be his father that Thomas tried to reach for the sword at his side, but his hands were powerless. He stood mute and frozen.

"Thomas! Are you a Merlin?"

The figure became a dragon. Yet before Thomas could scream, the dragon became Sir William, swirling out of the mists with sword upraised.

Thomas tried to lift his arm against the blow, and as the sword came down, there was a roar, for the sword had struck, not downward against Thomas, but behind him at a lion that now snarled defiance against death as blood ran from its severed throat.

As Thomas turned back to thank Sir William, he caught the scent of perfume. The knight was not there. Instead, it was Katherine, her hair a halo of brightness from the sun. She reached for Thomas, and he sobbed with relief.

Her arms pulled him close and she kissed him and a flare of ecstasy filled him, yet something was wrong. Her kiss was one of death, for now he could not breathe, and she would not pull away.

He struggled, trying to push her away, but his arms were still trapped at his side, and she only pressed harder.

Breathe, find breath, for he must live . . .

Thomas opened his eyes in panic. For a single heartbeat, he relaxed. It was only a dream.

Yet he still could not breathe. And above him, a giant of a man blocked the flickering light of the tent lamp.

In the next heartbeat of awareness, he realized a heavy open hand pressed down upon his mouth and nostrils.

"Silence or death," a voice whispered.

The figure placed the tip of a knife against Thomas's throat.

"Silence or death," the voice repeated. "Nod if you choose life."

Thomas nodded.

The hand over his nose and mouth was removed.

Thomas drew breath, but slowly, for he did not want the intruder to consider a gasp to be unnecessary noise.

Several more heartbeats passed before the figure eased backward and the pressure of the knife left Thomas's throat.

"We leave camp," the voice said. "You will not return. If we are caught, we both die."

Thomas nodded again. He dressed hurriedly, careful to place around his neck the long strap which held his pouch of gold beneath the clothing. When he was ready, Thomas reached for the sealed package that had served as his pillow, for even the threat of death did not take its importance from his mind.

"Do not forget your sword," the voice said. "For you shall travel alone and without friends."

Thomas took the sword, grateful that this stranger would not see it as a threat. And why fight now? For if the stranger had meant harm, Thomas would already be dead in his sleep.

The stranger turned and Thomas followed. They moved

between the tents. Something seemed unnatural, and it did not take long for Thomas to understand. The camp did not stir with the slight movements of guards at night, the occasional scurrying of servant girls, the restless muttering of slaves in their tortured sleep. Only the grunts and stampings of the camels showed any life.

The stranger led Thomas away from the edge of the caravan. To their left was the camp of the other caravan, the traders headed for St. Jean d'Acre. This camp too was unnaturally still.

The sky above was ebony black, studded with brilliant diamonds. The moon was high and full, and cast enough pale light for Thomas to see the outlines of the far hills.

Finally the figure stopped and turned.

"My name does not matter," the stranger said. "I was among the slaves, yet we were not slaves. Rather bandits, biding our time."

"Band—"

The stranger held up his hand. "I have little time until my absence is discovered. What I can explain is this. It is well known that Muzzamar's caravan has many riches and is too well guarded for attack. Instead of raiding, we chose to pose as slaves until Muzzamar believed himself safe. The cook was bribed before we departed St. Jean d'Acre, before we let ourselves be put into bondage. And this night? As planned long before, all of the food of the feast was drugged. It was great fortune that brought us the other caravan to be plundered as well."

The stranger smiled as a look of comprehension crossed Thomas's face. Time and again his plate had been filled before he could rise to join Muzzamar and the others with their feasting. And each time his plate had been filled by a large slave.

"Yes," the figure said, as if reading Thomas's thoughts. "I ensured that you were kept from the food that all others ate. They sleep now. It was a simple matter for the cook to release us from our bonds and supply us with their very own weapons. It is an easy way for us to plunder, much simpler than open attack from the hills."

"Those weapons shall be used against them?" Thomas asked. "Many in camp are innocent women and children."

"Only the men shall die. This is a harsh land."

Thomas said nothing. He pondered the merits of attempting to warn Muzzamar. Yes, he had seen men die, but always in battle, not as helpless sheep.

"Your silence says much," the slave said. "Yet there is nothing you can do to prevent this. The men are heavily drugged, and your return will only ensure your death, and mine for assisting you now."

Thomas realized this was so. For a moment, wildness tempted him. Useless as his death might be, to die in attempting to warn others might prove to be a lesser evil than a haunting guilt later. But ahead were Katherine and Sir William and his father, and the fight of the Merlins.

"My own life has been spared." Thomas said in a flat tone as he tried to force his emotions of conflict aside.

"You gave us water," the slave answered. "And I decided to repay you in kind. I wish I could give you a camel, but your absence will be undiscovered in confusion to come, the loss of a camel is too easily noticed. Our own leader is without mercy, and cannot know you have been spared."

Thomas absorbed this information. Others would die, and he was helpless against it. The stranger in front of him had risked his own life to save Thomas. The gift could not be discarded. He must leave.

"Truly," Thomas said, "there is no way I can repay you."

"I have heard of the man who walked this land, the man you blue-eyes claim was the Son of God. Did He not say we are all brothers? And did you not prove it with your kindness?"

The stranger extended his hand in a clasp of friendship. "Brother, may your God protect you. Shalom. Go in peace."

The stranger untied a full water skin from his belt, handed it to Thomas, and took a step away. "You must reach the hills by daybreak. It will cost us both our lives for you to be found."

Thomas reached for the stranger's arm at a sudden memory of a brave and noble face.

"The slave from my own land, Lord Baldwin?" Thomas asked. "Will he too be slain?"

The stranger snorted in irony. "During this journey, we have discovered the hell of slavery ourselves. All slaves in both caravans shall be spared and released."

Then a pause before the stranger spoke more soberly. "Whether they survive this land is another matter."

Thomas entered Nazareth at dawn. Behind him, three days of cautious travel, of slow movement along the roads at night, sleep in shadows of safety during the day. Behind him, the long and rolling hills of Galilee.

Thomas was not thirsty. His water skin was still half full from a well fifteen miles earlier; and travel during the night had spared him the searing daytime heat which sucked so much moisture.

He was hungry, for he had not dared to stop at any inns or allow himself to be seen during the day. Time and again Thomas had shifted his focus from his tightened belly to think of Nazareth. There he would reach Sir William and Katherine. There he would be in relative safety.

What if Sir William and Katherine had not survived their journey? Thomas dared not think of that for how, then, how would he find his father?

No, he must trust that the knight would arrive with Katherine. But he would not be foolish as he waited. They might arrive in a day or a week, or time enough for Thomas to be noticed by Mameluke soldiers or their assassins. Because of that, he would satisfy his hunger, then find a place in Nazareth to wait quietly as he surveyed arriving travelers.

Thomas chose a large boulder to use as support and leaned back to survey the buildings ahead. The dawn's light was still soft, and the town ahead lay motionless in the growing shadows. It seemed small and quiet and ordinary, hardly a place to be remembered by generations. Yet there was a timelessness about it, and Thomas let himself contemplate the burden of history that had given Nazareth and the rest of the Holy Land such significance.

Here Moses had climbed the hills to look across the Jordan River and fill his eyes with the awesome beauty of this promised land before his death. Here a great king named David had defeated invincible armies and had sung psalms of praise and love. And here, in the very town Thomas surveyed, a boy had played in the dust of the streets. Later, as the Messiah, He had allowed Himself to die cruelly on pieces of rough wood tied together in the shape of a cross.

Thomas closed his eyes in a prayer of thanks for his safety and a plea for continued help. That prayer led him to another vision, a scene far away in a land he hoped to see again. There, a woman had started every morning with her head bowed in prayer and a young boy at her side.

Thomas blinked back a tear. As that young boy, he had barely understood her daily silence. In this moment as he remembered, his hunger faded and he knew that now, after his journey and before Katherine and Sir William might arrive in Nazareth, now he could afford the luxury and demand of grief. Some instinct, the instinct that compels all peoples to formalize the departure of life in the ceremonies of death, told him he must perform his own ceremony for the woman who had given him so much in that faraway monastery so many years ago.

Thomas closed his eyes and again remembered Sarah.

How difficult to raise a boy, to love him as a son, yet not once—even when facing death—let the boy know the teacher was also mother.

Month after month, Sarah had patiently taught him in the ways of Merlins, unable then to reveal to him his duty.

Duty that required her to sacrifice her identity as mother, duty that had let her die so far from her husband, let her die without telling me of her love for me.

Thomas bowed his head and prayed, grateful that his faith allowed him to see beyond life on earth, and to realize that the pattern of the universe was so great beyond comprehension that all he could do was trust and live as well as possible. *In the way that my mother trusted and lived.*

Thomas sat there for two hours, holding the sadness without trying to deny it. His tears and his prayers were all that he could give to the memory of Sarah.

At last he stood. Ahead, he could give more to the same duty that had called her. For that, he would have to hide openly in Nazareth. He had already chosen the method for that.

He would bribe an innkeeper to give him a room and keep it secret. During the day, he would pose as a beggar at the town gates.

After two days of begging, Thomas saw Katherine and Sir William arrive at the city gates at midmorning. With them traveled the two Muslim assassins who had vowed to kill Thomas in St. Jean d'Acre.

CHAPTER

50

His first reaction was the stillness of shock and disbelief. *Do not betray your presence*, Thomas told himself. *Behave as would all crippled beggars at the town gates.*

He stole another glance.

On foot, Sir William led a mule on which sat Katherine, veiled from Muslim eyes.

Beside Sir William walked two large men whose faces were engraved in Thomas's mind. Only days earlier, these men had pursued Thomas and Katherine through the street markets of St. Jean d'Acre. Only days earlier, they had forced Sir William to barricade the house and set it ablaze.

Now, they walked at ease with Sir William and Katherine. There was nothing to indicate strain or tension, nothing to indicate that Sir William and Katherine were captives.

Thomas raised his head again and noticed that Sir William's sword was still at his side. *If they were captives, Sir William would not be armed.*

The beggars around him moaned for pity in respectful voices. Thomas did the same.

It warmed him little that Katherine insisted upon throwing tiny copper coins into each bowl. *This is the woman who now betrays me.*

Thomas ducked his head as they passed by and silently nodded thanks for the coin thrown in his bowl. He wanted to rise, to roar in anger at the evil of their deceit. He wanted to rush Sir William, to seize his sword and attack the knight and his assassin friends. There was trembling in his legs and dizziness in his head at such colossal betrayal.

Lies. So much of what they told me must be lies.

*How could I have been fool enough to believe my father is still alive?
How could I have been fool enough to believe the tales of Merlin and a
destiny to fulfill? And how could I have been fool enough to believe her
eyes, her promises of love, and the soft touch of her lips against mine?*

Despair overwhelmed him. He did not bother to wipe the tears
that fell onto the tiny copper coin in the bowl at his feet.

It was another hour before he found the energy to grasp the
cane at his side.

What to do next? Where to go?

A castle he had once conquered in the land of his birth no
longer belonged to him. He was friendless in a strange land,
involved in a battle he did not understand, a battle he had not
chosen or invited.

Yesterday, there had been hope. Hope of finding his father.
Hope of returning triumphant to Magnus. Hope of a trust in
Katherine that might lead to—he barely dared think it in his
bitterness—a love that would fill him with joy.

Today?

Today he must continue his disguise and walk away from these
town gates leaning on his cane as if crippled, lest the ones he once
thought friends discover he was in Nazareth.

Today, he had nothing. No hope, no dreams. He hobbled several
more steps. He did not know or care what he should do next.

Thomas arrived safely at the inn and retreated to his small
room. He placed his few belongings on a stool, then sat cross-
legged on the floor with his back against the wall.

First, he tore open the package. A parchment, promising
reward for its return. On the other pages, meaningless scrawls of
Latin. A priceless package? What jest was this?

Thoughts tugged at him.

Why had Katherine brought the light near in the tunnel while
he fought a supposedly unknown assailant? She should have
stayed beside him, ready to help in the fight. Now it made sense.
She knew it was Sir William and wanted the fight to end before
either was hurt.

But why practice such deception?

Thomas answered his own question immediately. What better way for a Druid to convince him of friendship than find a common enemy to fight—the supposed assassins. Then, give him the mysterious package with cryptic words to further the illusion of trust.

In sudden rage and pain at the renewed thought of betrayal, Thomas slammed the floor with his open palm.

Regard this as warfare. There are two choices. Attack or retreat. Either action requires surprise. Yet it cannot be certain that the bribe to the innkeeper will ensure that my presence here remains secret. Therefore, action must be taken soon or surprise will be lost.

Retreat? His presence was still unknown. Retreat, then, would be simple. In these vast tracts of land, it would be impossible to find him. And retreat gained him time, time to seek answers.

But what is it they seek from me? Exiled in a strange land, where would he find answers to questions he barely understood?

There were only two places to begin. St. Jean d'Acre, where he had been raised as a child. Whatever else Katherine and Sir William had told him that might be false, he could not deny a childhood spent in St. Jean d'Acre. Not with those memories, not when he knew the language of this land. In St. Jean d'Acre, he would find someone who knew something. The tiniest scrap of knowledge would lead him to another. And another.

It would be safer now in St. Jean d'Acre. After all, Katherine and Sir William would be in Nazareth, waiting for him. With answers, Thomas could return, and play their game by his rules.

Or, instead of returning to Nazareth after St. Jean d'Acre, he could go next to Jerusalem. So much pointed to it. The Holy City. Perhaps he would find answers there.

Thomas smiled to this silence of the room. He still had his life. He still had his health. His freedom. And enough in gold to sustain the search.

Two days later, as Thomas traveled a road that narrowed between large rocks on each side, bandits attacked.

His first warning had been a slight scuffle of leather against stone. As Thomas looked over his shoulder, he saw two men dropping from the top of a boulder, only thirty paces behind.

There was no mistaking their intent. Swords raised, scarred and dirty faces quiet with deadliness, they advanced toward him.

Thomas glanced ahead to determine his chances of escape. There, four more bandits stepped onto the road. Walls of rock blocked him on both sides.

More terrifying than upraised swords was their silence and slow, patient movement. These men had no need to bluff or bluster. They would not waste energy through haste; their victim could not escape.

A part of Thomas's mind noted this objectively.

Another part noted the terrain and evaluated his chances. The road wound downward from the hills of Galilee. The Valley of Jezreel was barely an hour ahead, but that fact helped little now. The huge boulders on each side of the road were too smooth to climb.

The bandits closed the circle on Thomas step by certain step.

Thomas drew his sword. One against six. His death was certain. Yet surrender was impossible. His sword would taste blood before he died.

He began to back against a boulder for the slight protection it offered, then saw a break in the rocks beyond the four men advancing on one side.

Use more than your sword. Thomas could hear the words of Sir William as he had coached him in the art of fighting. *Terrain, a man's character, and surprise—all are added weapons.*

Even in this situation, the thought of Sir William and betrayal brought bitterness to the back of his throat. It brought anger too, anger which Thomas could direct at these bandits. He dropped to his knees and, without taking his eyes from the four men on his left, he felt about for stones. He found two and stood.

Still, silence from the bandits.

They expect me to attempt a break through the weakest part of their wall—the group of two, probably the stronger fighters.

So Thomas did the opposite.

He lunged at the four men on his left, and at the same time threw both stones at head level. The bandits flinched and ducked, only for an instant, and the stones clattered on the boulder behind them.

But as they ducked, Thomas swung his sword in a vicious arc and plunged directly ahead. The suddenness of his attack, the distraction of the stones, and the swiftness of his sword bought

Thomas only a heartbeat of confusion. But it was enough to get him through their ranks.

Yet his intention was not to flee. What easier target than an open back? No, Thomas focused on the split rock ahead among the large boulders.

Was the split large enough? Yes! Thomas reached it only a step before the bandits.

He turned and faced them. Rock now protected him on three sides. The fourth side, open to the bandits, was wide enough to give him room to swing his sword, narrow enough to limit their attack.

The largest bandit spoke to the shadow which covered Thomas.

"Fool," he spat. "You think this saves you?"

Thomas did not reply.

"You succeed only in irritating us."

Thomas still said nothing, only kept his sword ready.

"Throw us your valuables, and we will leave."

For a moment, Thomas was tempted. Then he realized they would probably retreat out of sight and wait for him to reappear in the open. And if he did survive, without his gold, life in this strange land would be next to impossible.

So Thomas only started at the bandit. The stalemate continued for thirty seconds.

"Search the nearby hills," the leader of the bandits then called to his men without turning his head. "Find wood and dried brush."

Two of the men scrambled away from the road.

"You see," the bandit resumed his conversation with Thomas, "I have no intention of risking even one man in direct combat. Few travelers pass here; we have much time, and a fire will easily move you from your shelter."

The man's eyes narrowed. "I will promise this. The longer you delay us, the longer it will take for you to die." He smiled faint amusement and began to whistle tunelessly.

Thomas wondered if it might be best to bolt from his shelter. With two bandits searching for wood, his odds were now one against four.

Thomas noted the layers of scars across the bandit's forearms, the relaxed but ready stance of the other three bandits.

They are no strangers to battle. I will be sliced to shreds. But better to die fighting than as a helpless captive.

Thomas did not have a chance to consider further, for a short buzz interrupted his thoughts. And almost in the same moment, there was a light thud.

The bandit looked down at his right shoulder in disbelief. The head of a crossbow arrow, gleaming red with blood, protruded an inch from his flesh.

Another buzz. Another thud. One of the bandits fell to the ground, clutching the shaft of an arrow already deep in his thigh.

The leader half turned. The next arrow pierced his hand and he dropped his sword, his mouth open in a soundless scream of agony.

The two other bandits were already running.

"Thomas!" a voice called. "You are safe to join me!"

English! And the unseen attacker knows my name.

Thomas stepped into the sunlight.

Above him, a dark silhouette rose at the top of a boulder.

Thomas ignored the two men moaning on the ground and took another step closer to the man with the crossbow. The sun behind him was bright, however, and much as Thomas squinted, he could not see the man's features.

Then the man dropped to the ground. "During attack, always keep the sun at your back," he instructed. "It gives you much light and blinds your opponents."

The man grinned and kicked aside one of the fallen bandits to step forward and extend his right hand to Thomas in a weaponless clasp of friendship.

The voice and face belonged to the captured crusader Thomas had last seen struggling in the bonds of slavery alongside a caravan of camels.

"I hope you will consider this a debt paid," Lord Baldwin said. "The water you once offered a poor slave in return for your life."

CHAPTER

51

Katherine wished that she had been born deaf, for then she could not have heard the words which now pierced her heart. "Thomas has failed our test." The muscles around Sir William's eyes tightened as he spoke. "We must conclude he is not a Merlin."

The test. So long ago, it seemed, she and Thomas had reached St. Jean d'Acre. And while he was in the public baths cleaning away the stench from weeks in the brig of the ship, the beggar, a spy for Sir William, had taken her to the house she remembered from her youth. There, to her surprise and delight, Sir William had greeted her, and they had hurriedly devised a way to test whether Thomas was truly a Merlin. Two others of the cause, posing as assassins, would pretend an attempt on their lives as soon as she rejoined Thomas. Then they would escape the fire by using the tunnel while Thomas believed assassins lurked nearby. In this manner, Sir William and Katherine could hurry Thomas into accepting the need for separate travel. They could also give him something of pretended tremendous value. If he appeared in Nazareth with the parcel still sealed, he could be trusted. If he did not appear . . .

"Can we not wait one more day?" Katherine asked. "Perhaps Thomas has been delayed."

And, she added to herself, *to wait means hope that Thomas can be trusted and believed.*

Sir William resumed his pacing of the inn courtyard, as if he were indeed considering her request.

"No," he finally said. "We have waited two weeks. Each day, I too have told myself that he has been delayed, but it is only wishful thinking. We must force ourselves to accept the bitter truth. Thomas has deceived and betrayed us."

Katherine heard a tiny voice speak. "Mayhaps . . . mayhaps he is dead." She was startled to realize the tiny voice was hers.

How she was torn. For if Thomas were dead, there was the consolation that he had not betrayed them, and she could always love his memory. If he were alive, she would have to learn to hate him, even though she would always harbor the slightest hope that somehow he might be part of their cause, and that her love for him could against all odds be realized.

"He is not dead," Sir William said. "No matter how much I might wish to use that for an explanation."

"I know," Katherine sighed. A great reward had been promised to the finder of the parchment inside the package entrusted to Thomas. Had he been killed or found dead along a road, someone would have appeared to inquire about the reward.

Sir William stopped his pacing, moved toward her, and placed his hands upon her shoulders.

"Katherine, even a blind man could see how deeply you feel for Thomas. I have delayed my decision until now simply because of that."

A single tear trickled down her cheek.

"He has not returned with the package. It means he opened it, either because he is one of them, or because he will not be one of us. He is a fool," Sir William said softly. "A fool to choose evil, and a greater fool to walk away from your love. But that is his decision, and now we must make ours."

Katherine bowed her head and patted Sir William's hand where it rested upon her shoulder. Then she turned away and began to walk across the courtyard to her room.

The quiet acceptance of her grief and pain was much more powerful than if she had protested in anger. Sir William felt the urge to justify his decision. He called to her back.

"Tell me again," he said, "of the trouble in England."

She paused.

He took three strides and guided her to a bench in the corner of the courtyard. For a moment, Katherine said nothing, as the peace of the evening fell upon them.

"England," she said, almost in a whisper. "Tell you again of England?"

Sir William nodded.

"The Druids—once hidden among the people, have conquered Magnus by openly posing as priests," she replied. "They claim power through the legend of the Holy Grail and by demonstrating miracles which are false. Now, in a large circle outward from Magnus, in one town after the other, they slowly gain converts to their cause."

Sir William nodded again, then said abruptly, "Have you ever questioned *our* cause?"

The change of subject and change in his tone startled Katherine, and for a moment, she was at a loss for words.

"You have never once questioned the sacrifices you have made to be one of us, a Merlin?" Sir William persisted. "Not during the years hidden in bandages, forced to endure the pain of an outcast freak, simply that you might report to Hawkwood the activities of Magnus? Not when other young women your age were dreaming of love and children? Not once did you question your role?"

"I . . . I . . ."

"And now," Sir William pushed, "as I make the decision to turn our backs on the one you do love, are you at peace to be a Merlin?"

Katherine drew a breath and faced him squarely. "I question," she said. And waited.

"That is good," Sir William said, "for a faith tested is a faith strengthened. And a faith unable to stand questions is a weak faith indeed."

He stared at the brightening stars. "For your sake, I am glad mere words cannot describe the evil I have seen, when the Druids first conquered Magnus and forced us to flee England. Their ceremonies involve the ritual murder of the innocent." Sir William clenched his jaw at unwanted memories. He stood, paced, and sat again before he continued.

"As you know, King Arthur's Merlin was once a Druid. His knowledge of science and potions gave him seemingly magical powers among ordinary people. Then he turned his back on the Druids and founded Magnus all those centuries ago, an island castle in a remote corner of England. There he taught others the Druid skills that were used against them, dark skills, so dark that through hypnosis, for example, we can change a man's mind, much as Thomas was caused to bury his childhood memories so very deep. But these skills can also be used for good, and the new Merlins used them throughout the country to combat the Druids in hidden warfare.

"Magnus served us well. For hundreds of years, the Druids did not know of our existence, and time and again, from secret positions in society, we Merlins defeated them. Even after the Druids finally discovered our purpose, they could not locate Magnus, and when they finally knew of the castle of Magnus, it took generations for them to conquer it. Their surprise attack and ruthless slaughter twenty years ago all but destroyed us. Only a few Merlins survived."

Sir William closed his eyes against unwelcome memories.

"You must understand, Katherine. Generations of us have sacrificed all to fight the Druids—a terrible battle hidden from the people. Now that Magnus has finally fallen, the Druids boldly and openly begin to control the people. They now seek to complete the terrible act that Merlin fought to prevent through the founding of Magnus nearly eight hundred years ago."

"What is that act?" Katherine asked. "Hawkwood always said I must not be burdened with the knowledge."

Sir William searched her eyes and made his decision. "That act? You shall be told, although few Merlins are. And you shall be told as we travel to Jerusalem."

"What of Thomas?" Katherine asked.

"He holds the key to the battle," Sir William said. "And we were almost fools enough to tell him where lies the final door to be opened by that key."

He slapped his thigh in frustration and anger. "Tomorrow, when we travel, you will hear of the Druid evil. And then, like me, you will be able to bear the pain of the fate of Thomas."

Katherine pressed her hands to her face as the knight finished his anguished words.

"There are still knights of the Crusade hidden in this land. They will be told. Thomas must be executed on sight. By sword or arrow, he must die."

They traveled on donkeys in a staggered line. Umar, one of the men who had posed as an assassin in St. Jean d'Acre, ranged the dusty road several hundred yards ahead of Katherine and Sir

William. The other, Hadad, kept pace an equal distance behind. Both were alert for any signs of ambush and would cry warning at the first indication of a bandit attack.

It was not until they had departed from the high hills—so treacherous with hiding spots—and reached the road to Damascus in the Valley of Jezreel, that Sir William felt relaxed enough to drop his constant search of the land around him and finally begin conversation.

"Soon enough," he said, "we reach the valley of the River Jordan. There we will turn south and follow the river to Jericho, where another road will take us high into the mountains of Jerusalem."

"You know a great deal of this land," Katherine replied. A breeze swept through the valley, so that travel was almost comfortable. Were it not for the hard saddle and the uneven gait of the donkey, Katherine might have enjoyed the horizon against the pale blue sky. But even with physical comfort, her mind and heart grieved for Thomas, and half-clouded any joy she felt in the freedom of the wide expanse of the valley.

"I know little," Sir William contradicted her with a smile. "What I know comes from conversation from the two who guard and journey with us. For generations, their families have served the crusaders."

Katherine was not sure she wanted to discuss the matter which filled her with so much distress. Now that Sir William deemed conversation more appropriate than constant vigilance against bandit attacks, she wished to keep him from the subject of Thomas for as long as possible.

"Tell me," she asked, "how is it that knights of the Crusades still live in this land?"

"For two hundred years," he began, "the crusaders fought and struggled to keep this land. Many were the noblemen who had the opportunity to return to the homelands of their fathers, yet refused. The castles established here, after all, were their true homes.

"Then the Mamelukes swept the land, destroying the castles and all the power of the crusaders. For many who survived, it was impossible to return to Europe. For others, unthinkable. They began to wander the Holy Land, for as nomads, they could avoid the Mameluke soldiers easily—much as we do so now by traveling in a small group and in the native dress of the people who live here."

"These knights are not Merlins?" Katherine asked.

"No," Sir William said. "Would that there were now many of us to continue the fight. But we have no Magnus here in the Holy Land, no place to impart to them the secrets and knowledge we use to combat the Druids."

He smiled again. "However, the knights recognize fellowship, and here among enemies they have learned to assist each other where possible. You might be surprised at how quickly news can travel from outpost to outpost, through messengers trusted by these knights. I myself have many friends among them. Not Merlins, but good and capable men."

The conversation stopped, and the silence between them weighed heavy, for each knew the other's thoughts. *Good and capable men now seeking Thomas for the purpose of his death.*

The donkeys swayed and plodded their sure steps for several more minutes before Katherine dared speak aloud her next question.

"Yesterday," Katherine whispered, "you told me I would understand why Thomas must die."

And to herself she continued, *As if that is consolation for the pain I bear.*

"I am certain you know much of the politics of men," Sir William said. "For Hawkwood would have trained you as thoroughly as any Merlin in the old schools of Magnus."

Katherine nodded. What was there in politics that the man she loved would so coldly betray her? What was there in politics that demanded the man she loved be sentenced to death?

"There is also the politics of religion," Sir William said. "Something I wish were not so."

"Religion is a matter of God, is it not?" Katherine asked.

"I am not sure how Merlin himself might have explained it," Sir William said, "but these are my private thoughts."

Despite herself, and the dull pain of loss of hope in Thomas that made her ache every moment, Katherine felt intrigued.

"I prefer to think of faith as separate from religion," Sir William explained. "Faith is God-made, the joy and peace He gives us with our belief in His eternal presence and in His promises to us. Thus, faith is the private communication between God and each of us."

Katherine nodded. For had she not spent many hours in

prayer? Had she not consoled herself countless times with such faith in her God?

"Religion," the knight said, "religion is man-made. It is the necessary structure here on earth for men to learn and teach this personal faith. The church, then, through imparting the truths of God, is made and maintained by men. We have a pope who oversees bishops, who in turn oversee priests, who in turn oversee the common man."

Katherine nodded again.

"In this man-made structure of religion, there are many men of true faith. Thus, God ensures that faith is passed from generation to generation. Yet, because religion is of this earth and of men, it is flawed. Some men use the structure of religion for their own purposes and claim faith merely for the power it gives them within the structure. You have seen, I am sure, bishops fat and well clothed, while the poor starve naked before them."

"Yes," Katherine said. ""This troublesome fact leads many to doubt the truth in religion."

"Truth in *religion?* Is there truth in the stone walls of a church? No, the truth is in the contents of *faith*. One must look beyond the stone walls of the church to see it, just as one must look past the structure of religion." Sir William searched for words. "The structure in which God passes along faith is far from perfect, yet this does not mean the truth delivered by the structure is imperfect. The faith itself—the ultimate truth of God and His Son—is pure."

"I find pain in a philosophical discussion, while my heart grieves over the death sentence of Thomas."

"Yet that is my point," the knight said softly. "Because of religion, Thomas and the Druids are deadly dangerous. Can you not see what might happen in England?"

Katherine said nothing.

"Through the sham of false miracles, how long until the priests of the Holy Grail have convinced town after town to abandon one religion for another? How long until the priests of the Roman church are powerless?"

The knight closed his eyes as he spoke. "The king of England receives his power because the people believe he rules by the authority of the Roman church and by the authority of God.

What then, when the people no longer believe in that authority? What then happens to the nobility, men appointed by the king to rule the entire nation?"

By his tone she knew these questions were not meant for reply, so Katherine held her tongue.

"It is not enough horror that the Druids plan to take from the people their faith; they also plan to take total power through devastation of the land."

"How?" Katherine asked.

"How? Through a method that Merlin could not abide, a method that turned him against the Druids who raised him."

"How?" Katherine repeated.

"Do you remember the earl of York? How generations of his family followed the orders of any secret messenger who showed the ring of the Druid symbol?"

Katherine nodded. She had been told the story by the earl himself, from his place of imprisonment, a dungeon in the town he had once ruled.

"Do you remember what happened to the one ancestor who did not obey a messenger's commands?"

Katherine frowned, then said, "The earl spoke of a curse which killed his great-great-great-grandfather."

"Yes. Worms consumed that ruler's body, though he was still alive. It took seven days for him to die, seven days of screaming agony."

Sir William clenched his teeth. "The Druids have a simple method to cause such death. A potion to cause deep sleep. Then a small portion of honey placed in a man's ears, and small maggots dropped within."

Katherine nearly retched. For the ears led to the inside of a man's head. How deeply would those maggots burrow? As they grew and spilled forth later, it would appear as if worms consumed the man.

Sir William took a deep breath. "Katherine, imagine this. The masses of people begin to believe the priests of the Holy Grail. And at the slightest sign of rebellion, the firstborn of every family dies such a death. Mayhaps even before rebellion, the firstborn of the rulers die in such a way. No one would resist. England would be theirs."

He clenched his fists. "Our Merlin education gives us the

history of mankind. Five hundred dark years have passed, darkness when knowledge was scarce and all people held in chains by ignorance. Only now has the light begun to appear. Advances in medicine and science are upon us, and through the written word, are shared from man to man, country to country. Mankind now begins to advance!"

Sir William stopped to draw another breath. His voice was urgent. "Katherine, there may come the day when fair laws protect every man, when abundance of food and medicine lets average people live to be forty, yes, even fifty years of age! When it will be common to read, so that all receive the pleasure you and I do from books! When ignorance is overcome and leaders of society must respond to the will of the people! This may someday arrive, even if it takes generations after you and I have left this earth. A day when such abundance and ease of living causes nations to exist in peace."

Katherine found herself holding her breath to listen to Sir William's passion.

He stopped suddenly, then dropped his voice. "If the Druids conquer and begin to rule, they will bar the people from knowledge, for their own power is derived from the ignorance of the people. They will end this slow progress that has been made by the learned men of our country. And the ages of darkness—" He faltered. "The ages of darkness will be upon the mankind for centuries more."

CHAPTER

52

After five days, the small group of travelers reached the town gates of Jericho. The gatekeeper gave them only a passing glance—Katherine had veiled her face as was the custom for all women in public, knowing too that it served another purpose, to hide her striking blond hair.

Once through the town gates, she noted that the streets were extremely narrow and ran crookedly in all directions. She mentioned her observation to Sir William.

"Defense," he said. "Should invaders ever break through the gates, they face the confusion of the twisting streets. And not only that; streets this narrow force armies to advance in a column only four or five men wide. Thus, four or five defenders can halt the entire army, for those behind the leading ranks of the army are unable to fight. And"—Sir William gestured upward at the sun-bleached square buildings—"while the army is slowed on the ground, defenders on top cast down rocks or boiling oil."

Katherine nodded, and then, as custom dictated, she followed meekly behind Sir William and the other two men as they searched for lodgings.

At dusk, a lighted candle in his hand, Sir William moved to the opening in the wall that served as a window to their small room in the inn.

The fading afternoon sun cast a small shaft of light into the cramped room. The walls were gray, the room bare except for a pile of straw in one corner. Beside the straw were a pitcher with water and a bowl with figs and bread.

"This inn is known to many of the forsaken knights as a safe haven," Sir William explained. "Even so, I prefer not to have you sleep alone. The four of us shall share this room."

"That sets my mind at ease," Katherine answered. "For one night, it is no discomfort to be guarded in such a manner."

Sir William stepped back. Three lighted candles were now standing in the window.

"It may be more than one night," he said. "For now we wait until this signal is answered."

The knock on the door came during the second night.

It was a soft knock, yet enough to pull Katherine from deep sleep. She sat up quickly, and when Sir William opened the door, her eyes were clear and she was alert.

The man who slipped inside wore the long flowing clothing of a desert nomad. As the door shut, he pulled the wraps from his headband and rubbed his head lightly.

Katherine watched him with mild curiosity. His hair was dark, unlike the complexion of his skin, and his first words confirmed Katherine's immediate guess.

"I had despaired you might never arrive," he said in slow and measured English. "It was with great relief that I saw your signal."

He glanced around the room and nodded at the two other men, Umar and Hadad. His eyes stopped on Katherine.

Sir William stepped forward to make introduction, and Katherine took the cue and rose.

As the man stepped closer, she saw that his hair was tinged with gray at the temples. *A handsome man, indeed,* she thought. Another part of her mind noted sadly that handsome as he was, her mind could not release a vision of Thomas.

"This, sir, is Katherine. She is one of us."

So the man is a Merlin.

He took Katherine's hand, bowed, and lightly touched his lips against the back of her hand.

"I am honored," he said.

Katherine raised her eyebrows in question, and Sir William answered immediately.

"And this is a man with vast knowledge of the Holy Land. As one of England's great knights, he has proven a thorn in the side of Mameluke soldiers who have attempted his capture for years."

Katherine said, "It is a pleasure to make your acquaintance, Sir . . . Sir . . ."

"Lord Baldwin," Sir William supplied. "None other than Lord Hubert Baldwin."

"May we speak freely?" Lord Baldwin asked.

Sir William glanced at Umar and Hadad and spoke rapid words in their native language. They nodded in reply.

Then Sir William spoke to Lord Baldwin. "They will not resent you if you speak in English, a tongue they do not understand."

"And the lady Katherine?"

"She has proven herself repeatedly, Lord Baldwin. Now, with so few of us in these desperate times, she must be counted among our Merlin leaders."

High praise indeed. Katherine hoped her flush was not visible in the candlelight.

"I have heard news, of course," Lord Baldwin said. "The one known as Thomas must be killed. It should not be difficult to find him."

Katherine flinched, but forced her face to remain as stone.

"But I know little else," Lord Baldwin said. "Why must he be killed? Did he not reconquer Magnus? Was not his father the—"

"Yes, yes," Sir William said quickly, as if he wanted to spare Katherine the pain of more thoughts of Thomas's betrayal. "Katherine, perhaps you might describe all that has happened since I departed from Magnus."

Katherine took a deep breath and repeated what she had told Sir William earlier.

Lord Baldwin's frown deepened at each new piece of information.

"What can we do first?" he asked, when Katherine finished.

Sir William grinned. "Listen to the man," he said. "He says 'first.' He believes something can be done!"

Then Sir William sobered. "I too have news from England." He faced Katherine. "I withheld it from you because I believed it unfair to give you false hope. I did not know if Lord Baldwin would reach us. But now that the one knight we need is here . . ."

"Spare the flattery," Lord Baldwin growled. "Tell us what you have."

"A letter," Sir William said. He hesitated. "From Hawkwood himself. Given to a trusted messenger who delivered it to me in

St. Jean d'Acre after months of journey from France."

Sir William looked to Lord Baldwin. "It arrived barely a week before Katherine did. I had no time to send you word and inform you of its contents."

Lord Baldwin dismissed the apology with a wave. "I am here now," he said. "That is what matters."

Sir William reached for his travel pouch and withdrew a strange, pale material, folded flat into a small square.

Puzzlement at the material was as clear on Lord Baldwin's face as on Katherine's.

"It is called paper," Sir William explained. "Lighter and more pliable than parchment. The messenger informed me that all of Europe is now learning of its use from the Spaniards."

He handed it to Katherine. Gently, hesitantly, she unfolded it. *So much lighter than parchment*, she marveled. *And it does not crack when folded.*

Almost immediately, however, her thoughts turned to Hawkwood. For there, even in the low light, she saw his clear, strong handwriting.

"Read it aloud," Sir William urged.

She did so, in low, almost hushed tones.

From Paris this 3rd day of March, In the Year of Our Lord 1313—

Word has reached me that matters in Magnus are worsening. Our enemies have openly begun their final campaign. In less than two years from now, I fear, they will have gained enough power among the people to succeed.

We are yet unable to trust Thomas. Our friend Gervaise is still in Magnus and watches carefully, but from him I have received no word that Thomas is one of us. And without trust in Thomas, we cannot be sure we will regain Magnus. Without Magnus, our efforts in England will be doomed.

Katherine closed her eyes briefly. Bitter sadness took her breath away. From Paris . . . Hawkwood had written this before leaving with her for England. Thomas had yet to betray them. It had been a time of hope. . . .

"Katherine?" It was Sir William's voice, gentle and worried.
She smiled a tight smile and turned back to the letter, reading
with a steadiness she did not feel.

*Yet, even if England is lost to us, my friend, do not despair. It
was no coincidence that we chose to flee to St. Jean d'Acre when
Magnus first fell. While it has been commonly believed among us
that the reason for retreat to the Holy Land was because of the
crusading knights who might be of service, there is another, more
compelling reason, one known only to the leaders of each
generation of Merlins. A reason which forced me these last
months to travel to the ancient libraries of Europe, and a reason I
must pass on to you in this letter; because, should I die, the
secret must not die with me. If there comes a time when I trust
Thomas, he, as you are now, will be directed to the Holy Land.*

Again Katherine stopped. "Hawkwood *did* direct Thomas here
after the letter was written! How could he have trusted—"
Sir William placed a finger to his lips. "Still, Hawkwood was not
certain, for he did not give Thomas what remains for you to read."

*There was a story passed from Druid generation to generation
about the Roman general Julius Severus, who ruled Britain some
hundred years after the death of Christ. This general discovered
the Druid circle, but did not expose it. To let Rome know of the
Druids would also let Rome know of their wealth and almost
magical powers. Instead, Severus plundered the Druids in one
fell swoop, taking a great fortune in gold and the book of their
most valued secrets of potions and deception.*

*Many of the details were lost through the centuries, but what
Merlin knew was that Severus was summoned from Britain to quell
a revolt, a Jewish revolt in the land of Christ. Severus could not trust
his treasure to be left behind, so he arranged to take it with him.*

*That is all the Druids knew, for they were not sailors, and had
no way of following the Roman general and his troops across half
a world. That was all that Merlin knew, all that he could pass to
the one he chose to lead the next generation of his followers.*

Yet the Merlin leaders of each new generation were not idle. They anticipated the day that Magnus might fall, and each generation was given the task of adding to our scant knowledge of the stolen Druid wealth and secrets. When the Holy Land opened to the crusaders, we sent Merlins here to search. I have compiled as much as is known in a book which must be matched with this letter.

Katherine stared at Sir William. She remembered how the jailer in Lisbon had returned to Thomas his cloak, his sword, and . . . and a book. "Thomas carried a book. Remember how I told you that Hawkwood spent time with Thomas away from the campfire, that he remained in disguise as an old man and gave him instructions? Could he have given him the book then?"

"I had wondered," Sir William said. "Yet without this letter, the book is meaningless, only bait to draw Thomas here."

Katherine nodded. She began to read faster.

In the land of the Franks, I stumbled across a parchment which held the words of the Roman historian Cassius Dio, who wrote a brief notice of Julius Severus and his war against the Jews. The Romans destroyed nearly a thousand Jewish villages, and a half million were slain. The Jewish rebels were finally defeated in their last refuge—caves in the Judean desert, north of the Dead Sea.

Severus, Cassius Dio writes, was recalled to Rome almost immediately after his victory in the Holy Land. It would seem unlikely he would take his treasure with him, for discovery of it by Roman officials would mean his death. Shortly after arriving in Rome, he died of sudden illness, taking his secret to the grave.

Yet there remains a peculiar fact noted by Cassius Dio. During one skirmish against the Jews near these caves, General Julius Severus lost twenty men in battle against a handful of unarmed rebels. These twenty men, Severus reported, died as a portion of the cave collapsed upon them, and their bodies could not be recovered.

It is not more likely that these would be the twenty men who transported the treasure? For wealth that great would take such assistance. Is it not likely that the surest way for Julius Severus to guard his secret would be to kill those twenty in the cave where the treasure was buried? I believe so, and upon this now rests our hopes. Look to your friends in Jerusalem for guidance on the location of these caves.

Should Magnus be lost to us, and should you be able to recover what was so precious to the Druids, their wealth and ancient secrets may be used against them upon your return to England.

I pray this letter finds you in good health, and that the Lord God will be with us as we fight His enemies.

Katherine's fingers were trembling as she finished the letter.
"I have heard rumors of such caves!" Lord Baldwin said eagerly.
Sir William pursed his lips. "You will assist us in the search?"
"To my death," Lord Baldwin said. He fumbled with a wineskin which hung from his belt. "And let us drink to this new hope!"
Sir William found the crude goblets supplied with the room.
Lord Baldwin insisted that Umar and Hadad join them in the toast.
The wine tasted bittersweet to Katherine. But she had only a short time to give it thought, for immediately she became drowsy.
Odd, she thought, *I was not tired, not with such important news.*
Struggle as she might, her lips would not do her bidding, and she could not voice those thoughts to Sir William.
Instead, she sat heavily, then collapsed into a stupor of wild dreams, among them that she had opened her eyes to kiss Thomas. When she woke in the morning, she was bound and tied with rough hemp rope.

"Fools!"
Katherine struggled to sit so that she could turn to identify the speaker. She was conscious of the terrible taste in her mouth, the thickness of her tongue, and the pounding of blood in her head that hurt as badly as the rope tight around her hands and feet. She swung sideways to prop her back against the wall.
Sir William, Umar, and Hadad, were as securely bound as she. And sitting on the stool before the door was a man she recognized at once.
Waleran.

"Did you sleep like a princess?" he asked.

Katherine felt dirty under his leering gaze. She refused to satisfy him with a reaction to his biting words.

"You can release her. She is not one of us," Sir William said thickly, "but merely the daughter of a knight. One whom I have pledged safe passage across this land."

Waleran laughed, a short, harsh, mocking sound.

"Do you play me for as big a fool as you? She has spent time with Thomas; that I know from my spies."

Sir William swallowed hard, trying to work moisture into his mouth. "Thomas, as did I, served as escort. She knows nothing of his hidden reasons for remaining with her on the voyage to this land."

Another snort of laughter. "Fool. I was there in York when she entered the prison to speak to the earl. She has been involved since the beginning."

Waleran watched Katherine's face. "It was like stealing from a blind beggar," he said, "arranging to let Thomas escape York with the girl."

In spite of her determination to remain silent, a greater need brought words to Katherine's mouth; for in the passing of a heartbeat she had gained hope that Thomas was not a Druid, and she could not quench her love. "You arranged for Thomas to escape?"

"Are we so clumsy that he could march into a castle and steal from us in broad daylight? The entire matter was pre-arranged. From my cell beside the earl's, I heard every word. While you spoke to the earl, I made certain that all knew Thomas would shortly arrive at the castle."

Waleran smiled. "Had I known that you were with Hawkwood, I would have had you arrested right there in the prison. It would have saved all the effort of finding a way to ensure that Thomas would lead us to you."

Katherine's mind flew back to that afternoon in England, and much suddenly became clear. Thomas had been the bait to bring Hawkwood into the open. Waleran had only needed to let Thomas think he had triumphed, then follow. Thomas had not led the Druid soldiers to Hawkwood, but Hawkwood had followed Thomas, so the result was the same . . . capture the next morning, and Hawkwood's death.

She spoke her thoughts, now dreading the answer.

"Thomas is not a Druid?"

"Hardly. Were it so, I would not have taken such pains to trace his every step across the world."

Her heart rose in joy, then fell in defeat. For Sir William had passed a death sentence on Thomas. Now, unless they escaped, word could not be sent to end the sentence. And every hour in captivity was another hour closer to his death. He would die without knowing that she loved him.

"Waleran has explained," Sir William said to Katherine. "Although if your head pounds like mine, you hardly need to hear the name of the one who did betray us."

The wine. Lord Baldwin.

"Betrayal!" Waleran threw his head back and laughed. "This is a touching tale of woe. Thomas was waiting for you in Nazareth. Disguised as a beggar. He saw you with your two friends and assumed you had betrayed him."

Not only would Thomas die unaware of her love, but he would die believing she had betrayed him. Pain slammed her like a physical blow.

"How do you know of this?" Katherine demanded.

"Ahhh," Waleran said, his voice now like oil. "Concern? A concern of love? This knowledge may prove to be of use."

He steepled his fingers beneath his chin and stared at Katherine. "My dear, it is simple. Lord Baldwin was not far from St. Jean d'Acre as Sir William believed, but nearby. Word of your arrival was immediate, and once he had followed you to the house and witnessed your carefully acted assassination attempt, it was an easy matter for him to anticipate the use of the tunnel; for as a Merlin, he too knew of it. Lord Baldwin then followed you to the caravan. He needed only to bribe the caravan leader to let him travel as a slave. From this position, he stayed with Thomas, and later managed to earn Thomas's trust."

Katherine looked at Sir William. The knight closed his eyes and nodded. "You remember the hints we gave Thomas of a great secret? Lord Baldwin deduced from Thomas that our final destination was Jerusalem. As one of the forsaken crusaders, Lord Baldwin, of course, knew of the safe house in Jericho. He convinced Thomas to journey with him to Jericho, then to Jerusalem. Here in Jericho, Lord Baldwin suggested a rest, and hoped we might arrive soon. When he saw our signal, he prepared the wine, on the advice of this man."

Waleran responded to the pointed finger of Sir William with a bow. "Through Lord Baldwin and his messengers, I was informed of every single step Thomas took. Child's play, to anticipate your arrival here and arrange for the drugged wine. And what an unexpected and superb catch, that Lord Baldwin might also take possession of the letter you so stupidly revealed last night."

"And now?" Katherine asked. The letter was not on her mind. "Where is Thomas now?"

Katherine kept her gaze steady.

"Lord Baldwin has returned to Thomas," came the reply. "He has stolen a pendant from Sir William and will use that as proof that he is Thomas's father."

Waleran smiled a smile that brought a shudder to Katherine.

"You see, my child, because of your blunder last night, we now know of the Salt Sea caves. Lord Baldwin will lead Thomas there as further proof that he is not a Druid. With that trust established, they will return to England, and Thomas will finally give us what we seek there. With our treasure restored, and with the final key to our plan, our victory will be complete. And once triumph is assured, three things will happen, my child. You and the knight will die, for there will no longer be reason hold you as hostage."

Two more heartbeats passed before Waleran spoke again.

"Thomas too shall die. And England will be ours."

CHAPTER

53

"D id a slave girl strike your fancy?" Lord Baldwin asked
Thomas. "I feared you might never return from the market."
Thomas shook his head. *A slave girl? When the vision of
Katherine fills my heart in dreams by day or night?*

Despite his thoughts, Thomas returned Lord Baldwin's smile.
There was no need to burden another with his own grief.

"Not a slave girl. Merely sweets to sustain us on our journey."
Thomas held up a small square wrapped in cloth. "Combs of
honey. For if we depart Jericho today, I would not refuse small
comforts along our journey."

Thomas grinned wryly at the small room around them. "Not
that this is the height of princely luxury."

Lord Baldwin nodded. "Our donkeys await at the stable. And
our journey is long."

They had traveled barely five miles before they reached the
portion of the road that climbs the hills toward Jerusalem.

Without warning, the donkey beneath Thomas stumbled.
Thomas pitched sideways but twisted to bring his feet below him
quickly enough to stand.

Lord Baldwin chuckled approval.

"Well, done . . . son."

Thomas stopped dusting himself with frozen abruptness.

"Yes," Lord Baldwin answered the stare of amazement. "Son."

Thomas straightened.

"You . . . you are my father?"

"Just as you are a Merlin." Lord Baldwin dug beneath the layers
of clothes that protected him from the heat. "This is the pendant
that I have waited for years to give you."

His words were so unexpected that Thomas ignored the donkey as it sagged back to sit upon its hind legs. He reached for the offered pendant.

He studied it carefully, aware that Lord Baldwin's eyes were intent upon him. The delicate carvings in the pendant showed a sword stuck in a stone, with the silhouette of the castle of Magnus in the background.

"You . . . you are my father?" His tone was not startled disbelief, but questioning hope.

"It was not chance that I was able to rescue you from those bandits outside of Nazareth," Lord Baldwin said. "Nor chance that I was part of the caravan which accompanied you away from St. Jean d'Acre." He shook his head. "It was a cause worth my while, to be with you; yet I pray I need never be a slave again."

"You followed me?" Thomas said.

Lord Baldwin nodded. "I dared not reveal myself. Not in St. Jean. Not in Nazareth. Not with that treacherous Sir William nearby. It would have been a fight to the death, and too much is at stake for me to risk such an end. Not when I couldn't tru—"

Thomas tilted his head in quizzical amusement. "Not when you couldn't trust me?" Thomas paused. "Why now? Why choose this time to tell me?"

"Because—" Lord Baldwin had no choice but to stop, as the donkey groaned in pain.

Thomas scanned the road behind him, as if measuring the distance back to Jericho.

"Is this usual for such a beast?" Thomas asked. "At least we are within sight of the town. It is not too late to turn back and find another, should this one prove to be seriously ill."

"I confess this matter is puzzling." Lord Baldwin frowned as the donkey groaned again. "Never in this land have I seen a donkey behave so."

"Shall we wait?" Thomas suggested. "Perhaps the beast has indigestion. If we rest in the shade, it may recover."

Lord Baldwin nodded; Thomas hobbled both donkeys and reached for a pouch which hung from the donkey's saddle before climbing the rocks which led away from the road. After the climb, he stopped in the shade of a large boulder and waited for Lord Baldwin to sit beside him.

"*Father*," Thomas said, trying the word. "*Father*. It is strange. I do not know how to feel."

An ironic smile from Lord Baldwin. "Merlins are taught so much, but this is something even the best teacher could not anticipate."

Thomas stared at him. "You know of Merlins. You call Sir William and Katherine by name, although I told you only that two friends betrayed me. Because you know of them, I cannot doubt you are my father."

"We will have much to share, my son." Lord Baldwin slapped Thomas on the back and smiled his handsome wolfish smile.

Thomas opened his travel pouch and unwrapped a comb of honey which he offered to Lord Baldwin. The older man bit into the sweetness with an eagerness that prevented him from speaking for several more minutes.

"At first, I did not know if you were, like Sir William and Katherine, a Druid," Lord Baldwin began, after clearing his throat. "After all, how easy to pretend anger at the two friends of whom you made mention, cleverly concealing their names as if you did not know I was a Merlin. Anything to gain my confidence. But we have passed Jericho, and now I know you deserve my trust."

"Jericho?"

"My logic is thus. Sir William is a Druid. Were you a Merlin, it would not be to his advantage to tell you of the crusader safe house there known to the knights of this land, nor to your advantage to tell you that I am a Merlin. Were you a Druid, he would have told you of the existence of the safe house—and instructed you to meet him there to discuss more plans to continue the deception you and he would have plotted against me. When you first told me that you might seek Jerusalem after a journey to St. Jean d'Acre, I wondered if you really meant to meet Sir William in Jericho, the one town where all travelers to Jerusalem rest."

Lord Baldwin licked the honey from his lips. "In Jericho, you did not seek the safe house, so I can happily conclude you are not an ally of Sir William. You truly are a Merlin. I can welcome you as my son. I shall earn your trust by sharing with you the great wealth of a long-lost secret. Then, we can return to England, and with what you know, defeat the Druids there."

Silence, as they both pondered those words.

"The honey is sweet, is it not?" Thomas finally said softly.

"You are generous not to take some yourself. And you have my thanks for the sweetness I enjoyed."

"Yes, very sweet. As sweet as the lies you may have told," Thomas continued in the same soft tones. He held up his hand to forestall Lord Baldwin. "I am not the fool you take me to be."

Lord Baldwin winced, but not from words. He clutched his stomach, and his wince became a moan.

"If the honey does not settle well," Thomas said, "it is merely because of the poison it contains, the same poison that pains my donkey below."

Less than an hour later, Thomas was walking through the streets of Jericho. He did not hesitate as he approached his destination, a small inn tucked among the poorer dwellings.

When he reached the door, he did not knock. Instead, he pushed hard with his shoulder and popped the door inward. As he entered, he pulled his sword loose and slashed air.

There was no one to challenge him. All four occupants of the room were lying on mats, bound, gagged, powerless to react to his sudden appearance.

Thomas turned so that he could face the half-open door. He kept his sword ready in his right hand, and with his left hand pulled the bands of cloth from his head to reveal his face.

Only then did one of the occupants react with a widening of her eyes.

"Yes, Katherine," Thomas said. There was no warmth in his voice. "Thomas. Perhaps you remember me?"

Thomas glanced at the others. "Sir William," he said, with the same lack of warmth. "You prefer assassins as companions? Or do you miss my company?"

The knight only blinked. The other two men, Umar and Hadad, shook their heads.

"You have my sympathy," Thomas said to them, with no sympathy at all. "For you two shall remain here."

With that, Thomas stepped forward and, with a small knife, cut the gag from Sir William's mouth.

"One may return," Sir William warned him. "The one who guards us."

"Then he shall taste steel," Thomas said. "A fight will serve as a useful outlet for my anger. You and she and all the others have mocked me with deception for too long. Now I intend to find the truth."

Sir William merely repeated his warning. "Watch your back," he said.

Thomas ignored Umar and Hadad as he moved to cut Katherine's gag.

"Thomas . . ." she began, only to stop at the cold rage in his eyes.

"I will free you both," Thomas said, "under one condition."

He loosed a leather water bag from his belt. "The condition that you drink from this."

"Water?" Katherine asked.

"Perhaps," Thomas said. "Why ask with such suspicion? If I meant you harm, I would slit your throats instead of burdening myself with your presence as we travel."

Sir William spit remnant threads of the gag from his mouth. "Drink it, Katherine. If he insists upon such childish games, we must play. And quickly. For if our jailer returns—"

"I will drink," Katherine said calmly.

Thomas squatted to offer her the mouth of the water bag. He held her head to steady it as he poured.

This soft hair. Those deep-blue eyes. And the lips which drink.

He moved to Sir William to let him drink.

Then Thomas stood. He drank heavily from the water bag, then tied the mouth shut and hung it again from his belt.

"At the very least," observed Sir William, "let the other two men drink."

Thomas wiped his lips and shook his head.

"They mean you no harm," Sir William insisted.

Thomas shook his head again, then leaned over with the knife to begin sawing at the rope which held Katherine's ankles.

"It will not be a favor to let them drink," Thomas said. He grunted in effort as the hemp of the rope snapped apart. "For the water we shared contains a slow-acting poison."

Past Jericho, somewhere high in the hills—Thomas did not

know how far from Jerusalem—they stopped at dusk. Thomas began to build a fire as the others unburdened the donkeys and unrolled blankets. When they finished, they stood near the fire and watched Thomas in sullen silence.

"You see, perhaps, that I brought much food," Thomas said cheerfully. "And that our donkeys carry bundles of kindling. You may expect, then, many more nights like this."

Thomas stood, placed his hands on his hips, and regarded them. Lord Baldwin on one side, still pale with illness. Katherine and Sir William on the other, almost pressed together in mutual distrust of their other traveling companions.

"Come, let us eat," Thomas said in the same cheerful tones. "Then we shall talk of many things."

"Eat?" Lord Baldwin grunted. "Not your food. For what potion will you surprise me with next?"

"Come, come," Thomas said. "No trust?"

Thomas grinned at Katherine and Sir William. If it bothered him that they did not smile back, he did not show it.

"And you two," Thomas said, grin still wide, "you'll not trust my food either?"

They merely stared at him.

Thomas rubbed his hands together briskly, as a man might do content to be with favored guests. "Well, then," Thomas said, "let me propose this. You three cook. And I'll eat my share of the food. That way you can be assured I'll not poison you again."

Silence.

So Thomas continued, "Besides, as I'll gladly explain after our meal, the poison already within you is sufficient for your death."

The flames had died to the red glow of embers, low enough so that Thomas could see beyond the fire to the shadows cast among the boulders by the moonlight.

He grinned to remember the shock on Lord Baldwin's face as he had unbound him in the presence of Sir William and Katherine. The man had been as helpless as a baby sheep during his convulsions after the poisoned honey, and he had been easy to bind and leave in the shade of the rocks until Thomas returned with the other two.

"It is time to talk," said Thomas. "Katherine, you and Sir

William travel with assassins who tried to take my life. Lord Baldwin tells me he is my father and accuses you of being Druids, yet keeps from me his acquaintance of the two of you. Whom shall I trust?"

Thomas's voice was quiet and cold. "Merlins and Druids. Druids and Merlins. For too long now, I have been subjected to the whims of either side. For too long now, I have been uncertain of the identity of the people who so mysteriously appear and disappear in my life. That changed, however, in Jericho, and for that I owe much thanks to Lord Baldwin."

Lord Baldwin croaked from his side of the fire.

"Surprise? Or twinges of convulsions?"

The croak became a groan.

Thomas stood quickly, moved to the donkey, and returned with a wineskin.

"Drink," he ordered Lord Baldwin. "Three large gulps. No more. No less."

The knight hesitated.

"Don't be a fool," Thomas said. "If I wished you dead, I would have killed you earlier."

Lord Baldwin did as directed. Thomas took back the wineskin.

"Good," Thomas said. "Your stomach shall settle shortly."

Thomas patted the wineskin. "I expect Sir William and Katherine will be in need of this as well."

"You are vile," Katherine said tonelessly.

"The pot calls the kettle black," Thomas replied, with equal lack of heat. "And I have a story to tell."

Thomas settled again at the fire, and then gestured at Lord Baldwin. "This man spent every night of our travels in sound sleep. Until Jericho. Then, while he assumed I slept, he crept out. I followed. Much to my surprise, he reached an inn at the center of the town. I dared not remain too close, and it wasn't until he left your room that I was able to slip over myself and peer through the keyhole. Much to my surprise, I discovered he had visited a certain knight and woman who had once held my trust."

Thomas paused. "There was something unnatural in the manner of which those in the room were asleep. So I entered the room and discovered that they had been cast into a spell of sleep, I assumed by potion, a potion easily concocted with Merlin—

or Druid—knowledge."

Katherine sat straighter, a sudden movement that caught Thomas's eye.

He smiled inside. *Perhaps she does remember the long kiss I could not resist as I gazed at the perfect curves of her face in the candlelight. Perhaps I didn't imagine her eyes opening for a startled moment.*

Thomas did not let that memory interrupt his story. "I could only conclude one thing. Whichever side each claimed—and you have both claimed to be Merlins—one was Druid. For why else would Lord Baldwin do such a thing unless he opposed you? My question, then, became simple. Who is Druid? Who is Merlin?"

Katherine groaned and clutched her stomach.

Thomas stood and offered her the wineskin. "Three gulps," he repeated. "No more. No less."

She accepted the wineskin quickly. Thomas waited until she finished, then took the wineskin.

Before he sat, he offered the skin to Sir William. The offer was declined, and Thomas sat to resume the one-sided conversation.

"Who is Merlin?" he repeated. "A simple question which presented me a difficult problem. For lies are too simple, and I have been deceived again and again."

He tapped his chin, as if thinking through the problem for the first time. "It took many hours, but, armed with the knowledge of my own training, I found a solution."

"Poison," Sir William said. His voice was strained.

Thomas brought him the wineskin as confirmation, and waited while Sir William drank.

"Yes," Thomas said, when the knight finished. "Poison. There are many known to the Merlins and Druids. Some brutally fast. Some slow. And, as you know, there are many potions to counter these poisons."

Thomas smiled. "This poison proves to be the perfect answer. The convulsions strike once or twice a day and will worsen as death approaches. Unless the countering potion is taken."

Thomas stopped and drank from the wineskin. "As Katherine and Sir William know, I too shared the same poison. For two reasons. You need not suspect the countering potion if I drink it. And you will realize how important this countering potion is to your survival. For if we all need it, we will all stay together. One side"— Thomas pointed at Lord Baldwin, then shifted his finger to point at Sir William and Katherine—"must guard me from the other. For if I die, so do all of you."

"How so?" Katherine challenged. "With you dead, we can merely share the potion."

"And when it runs out?" Thomas asked. "How will you replace it? For the dozens of combinations of poison, there are dozens of countering potions. You will not live long enough to seek the ingredients."

Thomas held the wineskin high. "No, you will all guard me against the others. And you will all stay with me, for I shall continue to supply you with life."

Lord Baldwin snorted. "Thomas, my son, to what purpose must we remain with these two traitors?"

Thomas's face softened. "Would that I could believe you were my father."

Yet his heart urged him in the opposite direction. *If he is my father and a Merlin, then Katherine is a Druid. Can I bear that pain much longer?*

Thomas took a moment to gather new thoughts. "From Lord Baldwin's pouch I have taken the letter from Hawkwood," he said. "It speaks of a great treasure. Together, we shall find it. In so doing, we ensure that the true Merlins possess it."

"The letter," Lord Baldwin croaked. "Is it not proof that I am Merlin?"

"It has not your name in it, nor William's, nor Katherine's. That you possess it says nothing."

"Then how will you know which of us is Merlin?" Katherine asked softly. "For I will tell you now that Lord Baldwin is the traitor, but you have no reason to believe."

"Believe me," Thomas promised, "I shall know. And when I withhold the antidote, the final convulsions of death shall be punishment enough for the traitor."

CHAPTER
54

They approached Jerusalem shortly after dawn. For two hours they had moved along the road in the pale light that preceded sunrise.

When the sun rose high enough to cast long shadows in front of them, Thomas began to feel an inexplicable mixture of joy and dread. For these mountains and hills were as strangely familiar as the house of his boyhood in St. Jean d'Acre.

Behind him rode Lord Baldwin and Sir William and Katherine. Ahead, the Holy City. And, if he was wrong in his desperate plan, his death.

The donkeys plodded forward.

"It has been no easy task," Thomas said, "to find scholars with knowledge of a Jewish rebellion which occurred a thousand years ago. Not when I am forced to slink from street to street with my face hidden lest my light skin give away my identity among the Mamelukes."

"Two days in this cramped hovel, as we wait for you to return with food," complained Lord Baldwin. "Two days of wondering whether Mameluke soldiers will burst through the doors. Two days of watching the traitors opposite me, to ensure that all of us live. I have little patience for *your* difficulties. Especially because I ache to help you, to prove to you I should be trusted."

Sir William sighed with weariness. "Lord Baldwin, it is no different for us."

Thomas surveyed his captives. They looked exhausted.

"How long must this game continue?" Katherine asked. "It is to the point that I almost wish death would take me away from the nightly convulsions brought upon me by the poison."

"Did you not hear me?" Thomas asked. "I said it *has been* no easy task. Now it is completed. I have secured a map and"— he held up a sack—"provisions from the market, which will let us begin the last part of our journey.

"Please prepare to depart. In a short time, I shall be ready, and I wish to leave without delay."

He did not wait for their reply, but went through the curtain which served as a door to the other room. There he moved to the rough, wooden table where he removed the provisions from the sack. There were several dried roots, a handful of seeds, a vial of dark liquid, and a small clay bottle containing a fine, white powder.

Was there a movement at the doorway? Thomas glanced up quickly, but saw nothing. He began to shred the roots with a small knife, then froze at a startled scream cut short in the other room.

Before he could move, the curtain parted, and Sir William stepped through.

"You have no permission to enter," Thomas thundered.

Sir William stepped aside as Katherine half stumbled through the curtain.

"Nor you—"

Thomas stopped as he noticed the reason for Katherine's clumsy movement. A knife was held against her throat. And Lord Baldwin was pushing her forward.

"Do you wish her dead?" Lord Baldwin asked softly from behind her. His wolfish smile, which had been hidden for so many days, glinted again in triumph.

"No," Thomas said without hesitation.

"Then set your map to the caves on the table."

Thomas reached into his clothing and pulled out a small roll of parchment. He placed it on the table.

"You had impressed me," Lord Baldwin said in conversational tone. His voice hardened immediately. "William, if you make another movement, this knife slashes her throat."

Sir William froze.

"Excellent," said Lord Baldwin. "Now stand beside Thomas. That way I can see you both."

Sir William joined Thomas at the table.

Lord Baldwin kept his left arm wrapped around Katherine. His right hand, which held the knife sharp against her throat, was steady.

He resumed his conversation.

"Yes, Thomas, you had impressed me greatly . . . until your stupidity now." Lord Baldwin studied for several minutes the various items on the table. When he was satisfied he had identified each, he nodded. "What else would you bring back from the market but more of the necessities of a countering potion? Especially if we are about to embark on our journey again."

Thomas bowed his head. "Please forgive me, Sir William. It would only have taken a moment, but now . . ."

Lord Baldwin laughed. "Now I will know the ingredients. I have no reason to remain among you."

Lord Baldwin tightened his grasp on Katherine and nicked her throat. Two drops of blood trickled downward.

"Finish your task, Thomas," Lord Baldwin snarled. "Do not delay."

Within minutes, Thomas completed mixing the ingredients.

"Pour it back into the wineskin."

Thomas did so.

"Excellent." Lord Baldwin thought for several seconds. "My choice would be that you die by the sword. My sword. But once I release Katherine, I cannot be sure of the results of battle. Not against two."

He thought for several more seconds. "Thomas, take the leather strips with which you bound me on the road from Jericho and tie William's hands behind his back."

The task lasted several minutes.

"Now, Thomas," Lord Baldwin said, "take the remaining leather strips, place them in your hands behind your back, and walk backward until you reach Katherine. She will bind your hands. At the slightest movement of threat from you, her throat will be cut."

The new task took slightly longer, for Katherine could not move quickly with the knife exerting pressure against her neck. When she had finished, Lord Baldwin reached forward and slid Thomas's sword from his sheath.

"Again, excellent," Lord Baldwin said. He pushed Thomas forward with a rude kick. "Securely bound. I can kill you at my leisure."

"No," Katherine said.

"No?" Lord Baldwin asked. He released Katherine and stepped back, sword at the ready. "You make demands on me?"

"An offer," Katherine replied. "Their lives for my assistance."

Lord Baldwin snorted. "Your assistance? You are Merlin. I am Druid."

"As you travel," Katherine said, "it will be valuable to have a companion. I hardly dare kill you, not when you have the countering potion."

Lord Baldwin examined her and smiled. "A traveling companion . . . I like it." He stopped stroking his chin. "And if I refuse your offer and kill them, but take you anyway?"

"I will fight you to my death," Katherine promised.

Lord Baldwin began to stroke his chin again.

"I will accept," he said. "But only because it gives me greater pleasure to think of these two facing a slower death from poison. For who is there to release them once you and I depart?"

"Well, my friend," Sir William said in the silence that followed the departure of Lord Baldwin and Katherine, "death is not a pleasant prospect at any time. Yet I shall seek consolation in knowing you and I share the same fight."

Thomas sighed. "The actions of Lord Baldwin prove that we do. I am baffled, however. The assassins of St. Jean d'Acre. They traveled with you to Nazareth."

"Please forgive me," Sir William said. He explained to Thomas the reasons for their actions. Then Sir William asked in casual tones, "How long before we die?"

Thomas smiled at the knight. "Ask that question of God. Only He knows the time of a man's passing."

Sir William did not return the smile. "A poor jest, Thomas. God did not make me drink poison."

"Nor did I, " Thomas replied. "And it is difficult to resist the temptation to threaten you with death to learn my father's name."

"Merely *threaten* me with death? But the poison we drank! The nightly convulsions!"

"You may recall the predicament I faced in Jericho. Were you and Katherine Merlins? Or was it Lord Baldwin? One side claimed to be my father, yet met with you in secret. The other side—

you—had threatened me with assassins, yet had also been pursued in England by Druids. I knew I had to find a way for the Druid to be revealed."

"Yes, yes," Sir William said between grunts, as he too tested his bonds.

"I devised a test," Thomas said, "knowing that any Druid would gladly abandon a Merlin to die. As you can see, my logic has proven to be correct. For Lord Baldwin took the first opportunity given him. It was not stupidity, as he so quickly assumed, that led me to announce I had returned from the market. Rather, it was bait. Bait, I might add, upon which he pounced."

Sir William shook his head. "He could easily have killed us."

"I was desperate," Thomas replied. "And had he raised the sword, I would have announced that he still needed us alive."

"My head spins, Thomas. What could he need from us? He has Hawkwood's letter and book. He has the parchment maps to the cave. He has the countering potion."

Thomas smiled. "There was no poison. Each evening meal you ingested a small amount of the juice squeezed from an insane root. Only enough to upset the stomach for ten minutes. The convulsions would have stopped whether or not you received the countering potion, which, of course, was no countering potion, but merely sweetened wine and water."

"You ate the same food we did," Sir William argued. "And *we* prepared it."

Thomas winked at the knight. "Who was it who delivered the plates for each meal? Plates—except mine—smeared with tiny drops of poison."

The knight laughed. "Well done!" Then Sir William caught his breath. "But you said we held something of importance that would have stayed Lord Baldwin's sword from our throats."

"The map to the caves," Thomas said. "Knowing I wanted the Druid to take my bait, do you think I would also give him the map?"

Another laugh from Sir William. "The parchment he took is useless?"

Thomas nodded. He waited until Sir William finished laughing. "There is more."

Sir William echoed, "More?"

"Yes. I expect we will be free in minutes."

"Impossible. I have given thought to our release and know it will be difficult. Glad as I am we won't die from poison, it will take hours while I use my teeth on the knots of your bonds."

"That too had been the method I thought we must use. But since Katherine departed with Lord Baldwin, our task will be much less difficult."

"Less?" Sir William strained against his bonds. "I am forced to disagree. Once we free ourselves, we must begin immediate pursuit to rescue Katherine."

Thomas began to whistle the tune of a childhood rhyme.

"What is it?" Sir William demanded. "What other knowledge have you kept from me?"

Thomas continued to whistle.

"Thomas!"

"My father's identity?"

"I have sworn the secret."

Thomas resumed whistling.

"If my hands were free . . ." Sir William threatened.

"If they were free . . ." A new voice came through the doorway.

"Katherine!" Sir William blurted.

She stepped through the curtain of the doorway. She smiled at Sir William, but only for a moment, for her gaze turned almost immediately to Thomas. He stared back, hardly daring to let his face show the joy that consumed him.

Without breaking her gaze, she stepped forward and leaned over, as if to cut the bonds on Thomas's wrists with the small knife in her hand.

But she did not use the knife. Instead, she kissed him. Lightly at first as she stood leaning over him. Then she fell to her knees, dropped the knife, and held his face in both hands and kissed him again, longer this time.

How long?

Thomas did not know, for his eyes were closed and his mind was filled with her touch and scent and the feeling of her hands on his face.

Discreet coughing finally reached his ears.

Sir William coughed louder.

Katherine released Thomas, but only drew her face back several inches.

"Thank you, Thomas," she whispered. She kissed him lightly again on the tip of his nose. "Thank you, my love."

Thomas could only grin like a dancing fool. When he found his voice, he asked, "Where did Lord Baldwin fall?"

"Thomas!" Sir William's voice was a begging groan. "What has transpired?"

Katherine picked up the knife and, still on her knees, began to saw at the bonds around Thomas's wrist.

"I can explain," she said. "Lord Baldwin drank the countering potion as we began to find our donkeys. Before he could offer it to me, he fell backward, holding his stomach in agony."

"Yes, Sir William," Thomas finished for her. "My final weapon. From the market I brought back not the ingredients for a countering potion, but a vile poison."

"Your test, then, could hardly have worked more perfectly."

Before Thomas could modestly agree, Katherine interrupted. "Not so," she said to the knight, "for when Lord Baldwin fell to the poison, he rolled in such agony that he drew the attention of many passersby."

Thomas and Sir William frowned.

"Among those passersby were Mameluke soldiers," Katherine said. "They now search the city for us."

CHAPTER

55

It did not seem real, the stillness of the morning air and the pastel contrasts of ancient stone buildings against olive green and brown mountains, all framed by pale blue sky. It did not seem real, the background of babble on the streets beneath the gentle warmth of the sun. And it did not seem real, to be slowly and calmly walking among the people on the streets while soldiers hunted this quarter of Jerusalem from house to house, soldiers determined to capture them.

Thomas wondered if the pounding of his heart might give him and the others away.

Shouts of soldiers broke above the babble of the streets as they swept from house to house. *How far behind are the soldiers? And how far ahead are the gates?*

Thomas dared not lift his head to check their progress. His gray-blue eyes and fair skin would be too obvious to any onlookers. It was over a hundred years since crusader knights had held the Holy City. Now the infidel Muslim conquerors ruled, and Thomas needed to keep his face hidden by the cloth draped over his head and neck as protection from the sun.

The other two, Katherine and Sir William, walked in wide separation and far in front. To remain in a group of three would instantly give their presence away to any sharp-eyed soldier.

Thomas could understand why a rabbit might bolt under the strain of waiting beneath a hawk, even knowing that to bolt meant certain death. It took great effort to force himself to walk slowly, when every nerve shrieked at him to run.

The stakes were enormous.

He and the knight were to fight to the death, should they be discovered. Katherine was to escape while they fought, the scrolled map hidden in her travel pouch.

So much depends on escape from this city. . . .

Thomas had survived a cutthroat ship's crew and a bandit-infested trek through the Holy Land. He had survived betrayals and lies; now finally, just as he had established that he could trust the two with him, soldiers were in pursuit. Thomas shook his head.

Walk slowly and think not of the soldiers.

So he thought of Katherine . . . of the moment she had first lifted her face to his in silvery moonlight, and how his heart had caught as if they had been long pledged for the moment, and how later, in the Holy Land the mystery of that yearning had been explained. He thought of their first fleeting kiss, one of anger and frustration at desires neither could understand or trust. If he were to lose her now, after all they had been through . . .

Walk slowly and think not of the soldiers.

Thomas felt a tug on the edge of his cape.

"Alms for the poor?"

He looked down into raisin-black eyes. A boy, maybe six years old.

The boy's eyes widened as he noticed Thomas's coloring. His mouth opened as he drew breath to speak his surprise.

"Alms you will have, my friend," Thomas said quickly to forestall any exclamation. "But you must grasp my hand!"

The command intrigued the boy enough that he did so and remained silent.

"Your name?" Thomas asked, his head still low as he looked at the beggar.

"Addon. I am seven."

Thomas concentrated on walking slowly, holding the boy's hand as naturally as if they were brothers.

"Addon, as you observed, I am a traveler, now confused and lost in this great city of yours. It will be worth a piece of gold if you guide me to the nearest city gates."

The boy grinned. "Essenes Gate! For a piece of gold."

Essenes Gate. As Thomas well knew, it was guarded by only one tower. Less than five minutes away. However, if a piece of gold and a feeling of self-importance kept this child silent until they had left the city walls . . .

"After the gates, where shall I take you?" the boy was asking.

"That shall suffice." Thomas smiled. "For then I depart."

Addon frowned. "Did you not know that is impossible? The Mameluke soldiers have shut all the city gates. They guard them now."

"Addon, this is indeed your blessed day," Thomas said as slowly and calmly as possible. "For you shall earn enough gold to feed you for a month."

Addon grinned happiness, his teeth a crescent of white against dark skin.

"There is a man ahead of me," Thomas continued in low tones. "See him yonder?"

Thomas pointed at Sir William until Addon nodded.

"Approach him and tell him the same news you gave me. Tell him I shall wait here for his return."

Addon scampered ahead.

Thomas waited in the shadow of a doorway and watched Sir William's head bend as he listened to Addon, then watched with relief as the knight turned back. To any other but Thomas, it would have been impossible to notice that the knight spoke to a veiled woman as he passed her upon his return, for he did not pause and his lips barely moved.

"Thomas," the knight said softly when he reached the doorway, "news of the gates does not bode well for us."

Thomas drew deeper in the shadows. "The Mamelukes must know not only of our presence, but of the scroll and the Cave of Letters. Why else go to such measures to find us?"

Sir William's lips tightened in anger. "A sword across the throat of the man who betrayed us!"

"Think of *our* throats," Thomas retorted. "The city is sealed. Yet we cannot keep our faces hidden forever. It will be too difficult to remain unnoticed inside."

Sir William closed his eyes in thought. Moments later, he smiled. "Have you a thirst for spring water?"

"Water? We fight for our lives and—"

"Thomas, tell me of Jerusalem's history."

"There are soldiers all around! This is no place for—"

"Come, come," Sir William chided with a grin. "Surely as a Merlin you would have a glimmer of this knowledge."

Thomas snorted. "The city is as ancient as man. Its history

would takes hours to recite."

"Tell me, then," the knight said with a grin, "of King David."

Despite the danger he felt pressing upon them, Thomas grinned in return. How many peaceful hours of his childhood he had spent in the same tests and discussions.

"King David?" Thomas squinted his eyes shut in thought. "King David. He chose this as his capital because it sat squarely between Israel in the north and Judah in the south. Yet until David, the city had never been conquered, for it held a spring and no siege could bring it down."

"Yes," Sir William said. "The spring. Gihon Spring."

Gihon Spring. Then Thomas knew. He grinned. "We shall leave Jerusalem the same way it was conquered."

Thomas turned to Addon and spoke. "You must guide us to the inner city."

He did not finish his thoughts. The inner city . . . close to the palace and soldiers' quarters.

The imposing structure of the palace was in the background, and directly ahead was the circular area where three main streets joined. At the center of that large circle, the well. Thomas surveyed the bulwark of bricked stone that surrounded the well and groaned. He could not share his dismay with anyone, because the knight and Katherine had traveled separately the entire journey back into the center of Jerusalem.

"You wish a different well?" Addon asked. "Yet there is none more ancient—"

"No," Thomas said, "a better guide we could not have found."

That was truth. For Addon had led them through a maze of narrow and obscure alleyways which made detection by searching soldiers almost impossible. Ironic then, that the first soldiers they had seen were surrounding the well.

A dozen soldiers, all within a stone's throw. More ironic, none were there as guards. Instead, they stood or sat in relaxed enjoyment of the sun and gossip.

Gihon Spring. Long ago, the shepherd boy named David, who earned a reputation as military genius and united all of Israel, had sent his soldiers up this well shaft to invade and conquer Jerusalem. Was the shaft still clear after these thousands of years?

There was only one means of discovering the answer. But the soldiers stood between them and a desperate attempt at escape. Only a distraction could—

Shouts and the braying of donkeys interrupted his thoughts.

Thomas looked to his right in disbelief. Two donkeys plunged frantically through the small market on a nearby sidestreet. They careened through stands of fruits and beneath the awnings which provided shade. One donkey plunged back out again, draped in the blankets from a shop.

Angry shouts rose in response and men chased the donkeys in useless efforts. The soldiers turned to the confusion, at first amused, then concerned. They dashed to chase the donkeys.

"The well, my friend," came a voice from the other side of Thomas. "How long until the soldiers return?"

Thomas turned his head to look into Sir William's grin. Katherine was already halfway across the street to the well.

"How—"

"Misfortune, of course. Who could guess that a rag tied to a donkey's tail might brush against a lamp's flame?"

"Who indeed?" Thomas grinned in return.

The hubbub from the street grew. The smash of glass and roars of rage rose above the clamor.

"Addon," Thomas said. "Two gold pieces for your trouble." He paid the child, then sprinted to join Katherine and Sir William at the edge of the well.

Thomas squeezed his eyes shut and concentrated on small mercies. With the deep unknown below, he at least worried less about the soldiers.

A heavy rope was attached to a pole at the side of the well. The rope hung at the side and disappeared into the black hole; thousands of years of friction of rope against stone had worn the edges of the well smooth. The well itself was wide—toe to outstretched fingertips, Thomas could not have reached across.

"If the well does not lead to safety?" Thomas asked.

"What choice?" Sir William countered. "Gates sealed, city walls guarded, and, in all probability, a reward offered for our heads. We cannot hide among these people."

Katherine hastily tore the veil from her face and put it in a compartment of her cloak. She smiled once at Thomas, then without hesitation took the rope in her hands and lowered herself over the edge.

Thomas too wrapped his fingers around the rough hemp of the rope and rolled over the edge. Sir William waited until Thomas had disappeared into the darkness, then followed.

Despite their conversation, less than a minute had passed from the time of reaching the well to when all three were clinging to the rope and lowering themselves hand over hand. No commands or soldiers' shouts reached them—no one had seem them escape.

Thomas breathed a prayer of gratitude. They were safe from detection. He prayed they would survive the descent, and that the shaft would indeed lead outside the city walls.

For the first ten feet of the descent, they found themselves pushing away from the sides of the well. Then, without warning, the walls seemed to fall away.

Looking upward against the light of the sky as backdrop, Thomas saw that the well shaft actually widened as it deepened.

The night gave him a prickle of hope. Would not a city as ancient as this slowly build over the well through the centuries? Did this widening of the shaft not mean that perhaps there would be room to stand around the pool at its bottom?

It gave him enough hope to ignore the burning in the muscles of his lower arms.

"Thomas!"

"Yes, Sir William," he grunted. It took great effort to breathe normally, let alone speak.

"At the side of this wall. Rungs!"

Thomas grinned relief. The knight had spoken truly. A ladder of horizontal iron bars was imbedded into the stone walls of the shaft. At one time, this well had been meant for more than rope and bucket.

The rope began to swing.

"Katherine!" Thomas yelped. "This is no time for play!"

"If we . . . reach the . . . rungs," she said, "no person above . . . who seeks to . . . draw water . . . will pull against . . . our weight."

It felt dangerous, to be swaying at this dizzying speed an unknown distance from the bottom, but Thomas knew

Katherine's logic was correct.

They began to sway in unison.

Moments later, Sir William managed to grasp a rung. He steadied the rope for Thomas and Katherine. Then Sir William yanked hard to test the iron bar. It did not move.

"Dare we hope this fortune holds?" he asked. He did not wait for a reply, but released the rope.

Katherine had reached a lower rung. She too relinquished the rope and began to climb downward.

With Sir William's feet about to step on Thomas's head, there was no choice. Thomas took the rung in front of him and began to feel below for another that would hold the weight of his feet.

It took less than five minutes to reach ground, which was a small beach circling the pool of water. And after that, through a cool and dank passageway so low they had to walk bent forward like waddling geese, it took another five minutes to reach a pile of rubble which blocked further movement. Yet from the first moment inside the passage that led away from the wide pool at the bottom of the well shaft, Thomas knew it was the most joyful walk he had ever taken. Step by cramped step, he felt like singing because of the distant white light that grew brighter as they approached. Sunlight, sunlight, and the sound of birds.

They stopped at the rubble that blocked them.

Thomas fell forward and kissed the rocks, which brought forth laughter from Katherine. Sir William caught his enthusiasm and clenched his fist in a victory salute.

"The gamble reaped great profit!" Thomas said when he stood again. "I'll not mind shredding my hands to clear these rocks, for outside are the hills and mountains."

Thomas went to the top of the pile of rubble and threw some rocks backward. The opening increased slightly.

"No, it's—"

"Not another—"

Sir William and Katherine stopped themselves, for they had begun to berate Thomas in the same breath.

The result was the same. Thomas stopped.

Sir William bowed gravely. "After you, milady," he said.

Katherine smiled. Thomas knew he would never tire of watching that gentle smile.

"I was about to say," Katherine began. "No, it's time I received an explanation."

"Explanation?" Thomas asked.

She nodded. "We were about to leave the city until Sir William turned back and whispered for me to follow. Then he lit the tails of those donkeys and told me to descend the well. I thought you had both taken leave of your senses."

"Yet you descended," Thomas marveled.

She turned grave eyes upon him. "What is trust untried? Sir William I have always trusted. And only now, in Jerusalem, have I pledged trust to you. With trust, there is acceptance. So I obeyed."

She spread her hands. "But now . . ."

"Gihon Spring," Thomas explained. "Sir William reminded me of another battle fought in Jerusalem. King David himself won this city by sending men up the shaft of the Gihon Spring."

"You did not know for certain the passage still remained?" Katherine said.

"No, but we had little choice. And we were led to the most ancient well in Jerusalem."

Katherine nodded slow agreement, then reached upward for Thomas to help her to the top of the pile of rubble.

"Not another stone, please," Sir William said. "That is what *I* had been about to say."

"We cannot remain here," Thomas said.

"Of course not. Yet why should we expose ourselves in the light of day to flee in the heat? Tonight, while the city sleeps, we will depart. By morning, we will be far enough away to purchase horses, perhaps in Bethlehem."

Sir William turned his hands so that his palms were face up. "Feel this air. Cool and comfortable. We can rest here in safety and sleep until nightfall." He flashed a grin from a dirt-smudged face. "The treasure we seek has lain undiscovered for centuries. One day more matters little, does it not?"

CHAPTER
56

By midnight, they had cleared away enough rubble to escape. Behind them, the eastern city walls. Outlined against the moonlight were the silhouettes of sentry soldiers atop those walls. Although the soldiers were barely in crossbow range, Thomas and Katherine and Sir William stayed low and crept from tree to tree as they moved directly away from the city.

Thomas hardly dared whisper until long after they had straightened and begun to walk in long, rapid strides.

"Water?" he croaked.

"None," Sir William replied. "And I share your thirst. It seems that we moved a mountain!"

"Thirst . . ." Katherine said. "I would give a king's ransom to dive into a pool. Does the scroll I carry have locations of springs nearby?"

Thomas pictured in his mind the maps he had pored over with scholars in Jerusalem. "We must turn south," he finally said, "cross the plains, and then travel to the hills of Bethlehem. That will be our nearest water. It is a journey that will last until dawn."

They slipped among the shadows, using the receding outline of the city of Jerusalem high upon its hill to gain their bearings as they moved south. Thomas waited several minutes, then spoke again.

"Sir William, yesterday you informed me of a self-evident truth. Lord Baldwin is not my father."

"Lord Baldwin." Sir William spat. "He hid among the Merlins for years, claiming to be one of us. Were it not for your test, we might never have known."

Katherine slipped beside Thomas as they walked. Without speaking, she took his hand and intertwined her fingers with his.

The simplicity of her gesture touched him so deeply that he did not trust himself to speak.

Sir William continued. "Thomas, you have solved one mystery. Lord Baldwin—the traitor among us—and Waleran were responsible for the fall of Magnus before your birth, the fall that sent all of us into exile here in the Holy Land."

"But my father . . ." Thomas said. "Who is my father, if not Lord Baldwin?"

"What was that!" Sir William said sharply.

"Who is my—"

"No. I thought I heard movement."

They froze. Thomas and Sir William placed their right hands upon the hilts of their swords, instantly ready to fight. Yet only shadows sifted and teased their eyes, only the sigh of the breeze greeted them.

Sir William relaxed and began to walk forward again.

"Who is your father?" Sir William asked. "Tell me first what you know of your childhood and the Merlins, then I shall reveal what of the rest he has permitted me."

"I am a Merlin," Thomas said. Quiet satisfaction filled his voice to call himself such. "I was raised as an orphan in an obscure monastery, near the kingdom of Magnus, which once belonged to us. The nurse who trained me, Sarah, I now know was my mother. She taught me the ways of Merlins, the use of logic and knowledge to fight our battles against the Druids."

"Yes," Katherine whispered. "You *are* a Merlin. For so long we could not trust you. Sarah's death . . ."

"My *mother's* death," Thomas said. "I could not know her as such during her life. Please let me have that now."

As Thomas continued, he noted that the knight did not cease in his vigil of the shadows which surrounded them. Their conversation continued as they walked.

"My mother died before I was old enough to be told of Merlins and Druids and their age-old battle," Thomas said. "I set out to conquer Magnus with the knowledge I had been given, unaware of the hidden Druid masters of that castle and kingdom. And for the last year, I have felt like a pawn between both the Druids and Merlins in their unseen battle."

"There is more," Katherine said. "More and terrible things. Sir

William informed me of what the Druids truly intend, as they expand their power across England."

"It is a horror that sorrows me to repeat," Sir William said, moving briskly as if attempting to dispel anger.

"Thomas, you know full well that the Druids have begun to conquer in the most insidious way possible, by posing as priests of the Holy Grail, by proclaiming false miracles to sway the people. Through the sham false miracles, how long until the priests of the Holy Grail have convinced town after town to abandon one religion for another? How long until the priests of the Roman church are powerless?"

Thomas replied, "If that happens, the entire structure of the country is threatened! The king of England receives his power only because the people believe he rules by the authority of the Roman church and by the authority of God! If the people no longer believe in that authority, all the noblemen and the king will face rebellion!"

"To be replaced by the chosen of the Druid priests," Katherine finished for him. "But there is more at stake."

Now Sir William was clenching his fists, and he walked so quickly that Thomas and Katherine were pressed to stay in stride.

"If the Druids conquer and begin to rule," Sir William said, "they will bar the people from knowledge, for their own power is derived from ignorance. They will end this slow progress that has been made by the learned men of our country. And times of darkness . . ." he faltered . . . "times of darkness will be upon mankind for centuries more."

"This is the cause we fight," Thomas said, filled with joy at understanding the battle, and filled with dread at the enormity of the stakes.

"Yes," Sir William said. "Merlin himself founded Magnus in the age of King Arthur for this cause. An unseen battle has raged between Merlins and Druids for eight centuries, and you hold the final secrets to the battle."

"I?"

"Together, when we return to England, this secret can be unlocked, just as surely as we shall find the treasure shown on the scroll which Katherine carries. With both, we will have the chance to overcome their evil."

"Along with my father?"

Before Sir William could reply, shadows detached themselves from beneath the trees to glide and surround them.

The shadows became men, men with drawn curved swords that gleamed in the moonlight.

"Only fools travel at night," came the hoarse whisper. "Fools who pay for their mistakes with blood."

The knight reacted without hesitation. He withdrew his sword and lashed outward in a single movement so quickly that two men dropped to clutch their arms with shrieks of agony before any other bandit moved in the darkness.

Then three men swarmed the knight, swords flashing downward in the moonlight.

Sir William danced tight circles. He struck outward with a fury of steel against steel which sent sparks in all directions and, incredibly, managed to press attack against the three.

Thomas, mesmerized by the skill of the knight's swordplay, nearly paid for that fascination with his life. Had the moon been behind a cloud, he would not have caught the glint of movement at his side. But the silver of the moon saved him, and the shine of steel gave him barely enough warning to dodge backward as a great curved sword slashed downward.

The point of that sword ripped through his sleeve, and Thomas spun around, knowing the bandit would strike again.

A *vicious horizontal swing*. Thomas sucked in his stomach, bending forward to pull his lower body away from the arc of the sword. Again, the swish of fabric as his cloak parted to razored steel.

Another vicious swing. This one less close, for Thomas had adjusted to the rough terrain and moved with nimbleness of desperation.

Another attacker joined.

Thomas ducked, then sprinted to a tree. He struggled to free his own sword but was hampered by his ripped cloak.

Both attackers stayed in pursuit. Thomas edged around the tree, using it to protect his back as he fought to clear his sword.

Where is Katherine? How many bandits? Is Sir William still alive? Thomas's thoughts scrambled as he did. *We must survive! Duck this sword!*

Thomas felt the pluck of air as the sword whooshed over his head . . . A thud as the sword bit into the olive tree.

The bandit grunted at the impact and yanked at his sword to pull it free. Thomas took the advantage and, while the bandit had both arms extended to grip the sword, he kicked upward with all his strength. His foot buried itself in the softness of the bandit's stomach and sent him retching.

Another whoosh as the second bandit swung across. The sword bounded off the tree.

And still the clank of sword against swords echoed through the night air. *Sir William is alive. Where is Katherine?*

Thomas stepped away from another slash and fought to clear his own sword. The distraction was a deadly mistake, for Thomas stumbled. He recovered with a quick half step, but the off-balance movement threw his right foot into the arch of a root which curled above the hard ground. He frantically tried to pull free, and a bolt of tearing pain from his ankle forced him to grunt. *Jammed!*

Another frantic pull, despite the pain.

Nothing.

And the curved sword was now raised high. A snarling wolf grin from the bandit as he savored the certain death he was about to inflict upon Thomas.

"Halt!"

Katherine's voice, clear and strong, carried through the trees.

"Halt! Listen to my words!"

The sword above faltered but did not descend. Farther away, the clank of swords ended.

Thomas flicked his eyes away from the upraised sword and glanced at the bandit's face. It mirrored surprise.

A woman's voice has shocked them all into curiosity.

As if proving his guess right, the bandits craned their heads in all directions, trying to locate her voice.

"Here, in the tree," Katherine called. A shifting cloud broke away from the moon, and suddenly her silhouette was easy to see against the light. She stood balanced on a thick branch, far from the ground.

Thomas grinned. Katherine had found safety during the distraction of Sir William's instant attack.

His grin died at her next words.

"I promise you far greater treasure than the mere coins we carry! I carry a scroll which leads to great wealth," she called again. Her voice remained easy to hear above the quickening breeze. To confirm her words, she waved the narrow tube of the rolled parchment.

With the attention so focused on Katherine, Thomas considered making a move for his sword, then decided against it. Katherine had managed to bring a temporary truce. He would trust she had reason to reveal the scroll. Besides, he noted more shadows moving among the trees. There were now at least a dozen, with more joining every minute. Any fight would most surely be lost.

"We are not fools," the bandit who had first spoken replied, as he edged to the tree. "Why should we believe that the scroll leads to treasure?"

"Because we will remain your prisoners until we will lead you to this treasure," Katherine said evenly. "Otherwise, our lives will be payment enough for a lie."

"Yes, I understand," the bandit said. He moved again.

"No!" Katherine said sharply.

"No?" The voice faked hurt surprise.

"No. You will not be able to reach me soon enough to get the scroll," Katherine said. She began to tear the scroll into shreds, an action easy to see in the moonlight. Pieces of the scroll fluttered away with the breeze.

"We carry the knowledge of this treasure in our heads. Now you must let us live."

Long moments of silence followed.

"This is acceptable," the bandit said. "You have made a bargain."

The bandit raised his voice. "Men! Hold your swords!"

Thomas let out a breath he hadn't realized he'd been holding.

"Yet listen to my words, woman," the bandit finished with silky menace. "Should you not lead us to the treasure, you shall all discover how it feels to die, when your skin is peeled slowly from your bodies."

CHAPTER

57

"You *do* remember all those marks upon the scroll, don't you?" Katherine whispered to Thomas. "We *shall* find that treasure, shall we not?"

"Or die?" Thomas asked with a wry grin. "Last night I wanted to dance for joy that you had found a way to save our lives. This morning . . ."

He shrugged to indicate the busy camp around them. Growing sunlight showed evidence of at lease twenty men. That shrug brought a wince to his face. Hours earlier, the bandits had savagely bound his hands behind his back with strips of wet leather. Now dry, the leather bit even deeper into his skin.

Katherine interpreted his wince as doubt.

"I had no choice," she said quietly. "Your knowledge was our only hope."

"*Is* our only hope," Thomas corrected her. "And at the very least, you have gained us time—time we did not have last night as the swords clashed."

Any chance of escape seemed impossible. Thomas, Katherine, and Sir William were bound and well guarded in the makeshift camp, which was hidden in a small, dusty fold of the hill. The bandits watched them constantly. All of them were lean and wary, and they moved with fast, certain efficiency as they performed their tasks.

Men who hunted, Thomas thought. *And who have been hunted. They will not be easy to deceive.*

Rashim, their leader, paced long, unhurried strides toward the captives, wearing the long white cloth of a nomad accustomed to endless hours in the heat. His eyes flashed glittering black above a giant hooked nose. The lines around his mouth were etched deep, lines which had long since turned downward from constant snarls.

"This day has already burned long," Rashim said without preamble. "I have readied my men for travel. At this moment, finally, I will listen to you bargain for your lives."

"Last night—" Katherine began to protest.

"Last night only saved you until morning. Convince me first that the treasure exists; then we depart. If not—" Rashim shrugged. "The vultures will feast up on your bones."

Thomas began, in a low and calm voice, to explain. "The story begins sixteen hundred years ago—"

"Impossible!" Rashim exploded.

"Sixteen hundred years ago," Thomas continued as if he had not been interrupted, "in the land from whence we come, Britain. Before the Romans conquered, Druids ruled the land. They knew of secrets of science and astronomy and kept that power through secrecy."

Rashim's eyes narrowed in concentration as Thomas spoke.

"When the Romans occupied Britain, the Druid leaders formed a hidden circle within society, a circle with great wealth. Later, a Roman general discovered this Druid circle. The general, Julius Severus, did not expose what he knew of the Druids and their accumulated gold. To let Rome know of the Druids would also let Rome know of their wealth and almost magical powers. Instead, Severus plundered the Druids in one fell swoop, taking a great fortune in gold."

Thomas did not add that Julius Severus also managed to find the book of the most valued Druid secrets of potions and deception. A book to stagger the imagination with the power it might yield its owner.

"You have my interest," Rashim admitted. "But the story is centuries old, and in a land halfway across the world. How did such a treasure come to be hidden here?"

"You searched us," Thomas replied. "In my possession you found a small, tightly bound book of parchment. It contains the notes of many who searched through the centuries for clues to the treasure. It is meant to assist any who would hold the scroll which Katherine destroyed last night. Without the map, this book is useless."

"A book in your possession because . . ."

"That story is long and tedious." Thomas affected a sigh of weariness, hoping Rashim would not press him.

"Then make me believe that the gold did reach this land," Rashim demanded. "Force me to believe that it might still be hidden."

"The Roman general was summoned from Britain to quell a revolt of the Jews here in the Holy Land. Severus could not trust his treasure to be left behind, so he arranged to take it with him. Once here, he and his Roman soldiers destroyed nearly a thousand Jewish villages, and a half million people were slain. The Jewish rebels were finally defeated in their last refuge—caves in the Judean desert near the Dead Sea."

Rashim's eyes flashed greed. "The Caves of Refuge! I have always discounted them as myth, for stories were told of entire families living for months inside the earth."

"Severus was recalled to Rome almost immediately after his victory of the Holy Land," Thomas replied. "The treasure he had taken with him from Britain he could not take to Rome, for discovery of it by Roman officials would mean his death. And shortly after arriving in Rome, he died of sudden illness, leaving his secret in the grave."

"Why the caves?" Rashim persisted. "In this entire land, why are you certain the treasure lies in the caves?"

Thomas closed his eyes and recited what he recalled from the letter of a man now dead. "During one skirmish against the Jews near these caves, General Julius Severus lost twenty men in battle, against a handful of unarmed rebels. These twenty men, Severus reported, died as a portion of the cave collapsed upon them, and their bodies could not be recovered. Is it not more likely that these would be the twenty men who transported the treasure? Is it not likely that the surest way for Julius Severus to guard his secret would be to kill those twenty, in the cave where the treasure was buried?"

"Ahah," Rashim purred, but before he could speak next, a bandit, almost exhausted, ran into camp and called for him.

Rashim hurried away and spent several minutes with his head bent low, listening to the man. Several times Rashim glanced back at Thomas and Katherine. Then he returned.

For a moment, he did not speak, only stared downward at Thomas. Without warning, Rashim lashed out with his open hand and slapped Thomas across the side of his face.

"You have deceived us!"

Thomas tasted warm, wet salt. Blood from a split lip.

Another wild lash.

Thomas concentrated on the pain, resolving not to show any response.

"You have deceived us!" Rashim repeated. He raised his hand again, but Thomas did not flinch.

Rashim dropped his hand without striking. "You told us of treasure," he thundered. "You did not tell us of soldiers!"

"Neither did we tell you of the ocean. Or of the mountains. Or of birds. Or anything else that exists in this world. What significance is there in soldiers?"

Rashim half closed his eyes, as if exerting great control over his rage. He opened them again. "One is not followed by the ocean. Nor by mountains. And the birds which follow you may soon not have far to go. For they shall be vultures circling your dead body."

Rashim pointed past Thomas. "Soldiers have followed your tracks away from Jerusalem. They are nearly within sight of these hills. Barely an hour away."

"We did not know," Thomas said. "And it does not change the matter of the wealth promised last night. Moreover, if I am dead or my friends harmed, the treasure will not be yours."

Men scurried in all directions as they loaded donkeys.

"Indeed, indeed," Rashim's smile caressed Thomas with cruelty. "Fortunately for you, the soldiers' pursuit readily confirms there is truth in your story."

Rashim lashed out one final time, hitting Thomas with such force that it loosened several of his teeth.

"Take care we don't leave you behind to be crucified," Rashim said.

"His death means you forfeit the treasure," Katherine said. "He is the only one of us who studied the scroll."

Rashim laughed. "Perhaps there is different treasure to be had." He laughed again. "Your hand in marriage," he said, as he bowed to Katherine, "might be well worth the forfeit, even if an angel like you might spend our first months together mourning his early death."

On the morning of the third day of slow travel toward the Dead Sea, Thomas almost wished Rashim had removed his skin in small strips as he had threatened.

It was difficult for Thomas to stumble ahead with his hands bound behind his back. The pressing heat squeezed sweat from every pore. Despite the irritation inside his mouth, he refused to ask for water, and it was rarely given.

The path took them through twists and turns and difficult climbs and descents as they followed the course of the ravines. The bandits were hampered by their lack of knowledge of this forbidding terrain, and they could not race forward and risk trapping themselves in a ravine with no exit. Instead, scouts were sent ahead in various directions to report back the safest routes. They moved so slowly that it took the two full days to cover a mere twenty-five miles. On each of the two nights the bandits had set up camp without daring to seek the comfort of fires, because of pursuit by Mameluke soldiers.

Thus far, the bandits had made no efforts to cover their tracks. To do so properly would have taken too much time, a luxury they did not have with over one hundred soldiers advancing steadily behind them. The heat worsened each step closer to the bottom of the massive rift which held the Dead Sea, some thirteen hundred feet below sea level.

Now, early in the morning of the third day, the heat was already oppressive and progress was still slow. The bandits hugged the base of cliffs so tall on each side of the narrow valley that Thomas had to crane his head backward to see where the rugged edges met the sky. Ahead, where the valley broke to open horizon, was their destination, the Dead Sea.

Thomas wished he could speak with Katherine or Sir William, but Rashim kept them separated. He despaired. Hands bound, stripped of everything but his clothes, without water, and exhausted from heat and pain, his chances seemed hopeless. He knew the same applied to Sir William. While Katherine's hands had been unbound—Rashim treated her more gently—she too had nothing that would help them in a fight or in escape.

And they could not leave without the priceless books which had been taken from the Druids so many centuries earlier. Even if escape were possible now, they could not turn back.

Thomas reviewed what must lie ahead.

In Jerusalem, near the ruins of the temple which had been destroyed by the Romans twelve hundred years earlier, Thomas had visited a monastery which survived from the days of the Crusades. The scholars there, allowed to live by the grace of the Mamelukes, were shy and elderly, with flowing white beards that touched their chests. They had not been surprised to see Thomas, or the small book with its directions to their monastery. When Thomas had asked of the Cave of Letters and the Dead Sea, two of the scholars had stood immediately and retrieved ancient scrolls from nearby chambers. They had retraced the markings onto a smaller scroll, and then accepted quietly the gold offered by Thomas.

When you reach the Dead Sea, go south, the scholars had told him as they ran old, thin fingers across the scroll. *It is a land so bleak you will discover no towns on the edge of the shores. You will easily find the ruins of Engedi, for there are no other ruins, and this one is marked clearly by dozens of collapsed stone buildings. The Dead Sea will be on your left and deep ravines on your right. Do not enter the ravine that leads from the hills into Engedi, but travel farther. Do not enter the next ravine, nor the next. The fourth ravine will lead you to the caves of Bar Kokhba, where he and the last Jewish rebels died. Why is it you want to know, young one? How is it that you even have the knowledge to ask of a rebel as obscure as Bar Kokhba?*

As he walked each painful step across the scorching earth, and despite his despair, Thomas smiled to remember the unforceful curiosity which had shone from the luminous eyes of the Jerusalem scholars as they posed those final questions. Grateful that the Mamelukes found their work both harmless and useful, the scholars had no concern for politics, no concern for wealth.

From an old one such as yourself, Thomas had answered. *One who would have loved to spend endless hours poring through these scrolls with you.*

They had smiled mysteriously in return and nodded as Thomas left them in the quiet chambers of study.

"What cause have you to smile?" demanded Rashim.

Thomas had not noticed the attention of the leader.

"I think merely of the treasure which will buy our lives," Thomas replied after a moment, for he had been so engrossed in recollection that it was not easy to dispel the feeling that he was still in the dark, cool chambers of the Jerusalem monastery. "You will fulfill your end of the bargain, will you not? You will release us after we have led you to the wealth?"

"You have my word of honor," Rashim said.

They both knew the words were lies.

At that moment, anger surged inside Thomas. This man with the taunting smile of evil meant to take from him his life, and, far worse, take Katherine.

The anger so completely replaced his despair that Thomas forgot his helplessness, forgot that he had no weapons, no means of using any Merlin scientific secrets. Somehow Rashim would be defeated.

Long after Rashim walked away, the anger burned within Thomas, then became cold determination. He would return to England with Katherine and the knight.

A shout rose at the first sight of the Dead Sea.

Thomas gritted his teeth. The Dead Sea. It meant he had till nightfall to find a way to live.

"I have heard much of this sea," Rashim said, gesturing past the wide beach. "Were not the soldiers in pursuit, I would send one of my men to test its waters."

Thomas concentrated on his balance. It was difficult to slog through the sand along its shore. Without freely swinging his hands, the task was doubly hard.

"Yes," Rashim was saying, "I am told the water is so salty that men float in it like pieces of wood."

Just one more step, Thomas told himself, *one more step. And then another. We have traveled beyond Engedi. The next valley holds the Cave of Letters. Just one more step.*

Rashim grabbed Thomas by the arm as he stumbled.

"My friend," he said with a wide, false smile, "we cannot have you die."

Rashim whistled for a bandit somewhere behind them.

Thomas was too exhausted to lift his head.

Rashim impatiently called for water.

Within moments, Thomas was drinking deeply. He did not mind the musky leather-skin taste of water hot from hours in the sun.

Beyond Rashim was the beach that led to the flat, waveless water of the Dead Sea. Its waters appeared ghostly white from the glare of the sun. Wavering in the heat, yet somehow appearing close enough to touch, were the high hills on the opposite side of the sea, hardly more than ten miles away.

"Are we near our destination?" Rashim asked. "Already we can see the dust of the soldiers behind us. Their pace quickens now that they too have reached the shore."

Thomas nodded in a delirium of confusion. All he wanted to do was lie in shade, close his eyes, and, if it were his time, finally die. His mouth was swollen and cracked from the blows dealt by Rashim. His feet were blistered and his arms numb. Because his hands were bound so tightly, each jolting step seemed to pull his arms from his sockets.

"Where?" Rashim was saying. "Where from here?"

Thomas tried to mumble something.

It was not clear enough for Rashim's liking.

"Bring the girl," Rashim commanded the bandit who had brought water.

When Thomas opened his eyes again to sway where he stood, Katherine was there, in front of him.

It felt like a dream, as if all he had to do was push aside the curtains of white haze between them and he could reach out and touch her. But his arms wouldn't move.

A sharp crack brought him back instantly.

Rashim's hand had flashed to strike Katherine flat across her face. A red welt appeared, showing clearly the outlines of Rashim's fingers and hand.

Rage took Thomas again, brought to him final reserves of strength. He set his feet wider, and the swaying stopped.

"Where from here?" Rashim asked again, and raised his hand to strike Katherine once more.

Rage crystallized the thoughts which tumbled through Thomas's mind. One thought took hold and grew with his rage. A thought of hope.

"Send most of your men ahead," Thomas said firmly. "They must continue along the shoreline."

"Now you give commands?" Rashim asked.

"The soldiers," Thomas said. *This small chance may be all we will be given. I must convince him.*

"Soldiers?"

"Surely if all of us turn away from the sea into the valley of the caves, the soldiers will follow. And the valley has no exit. We will all be trapped."

Rashim squinted as he considered the advice.

"We send most ahead to draw the soldiers," he finally agreed. "And cover our own tracks as we go into the valley."

"Yes," Thomas said. "But Katherine and the knight must go with us."

Thomas held his breath. *What little chance we have can occur only if the bandits are divided. If Katherine or the knight continue on with the others . . .*

Rashim shrugged.

Thomas felt his stomach shrink with fear. *He agrees easily because he cares little what happens to us when the treasure is found.*

"As you say, the girl and the knight travel with us," Rashim said with a mock bow. "After all, I am a man who bargains fairly."

Thomas took a deep breath and looked around. Hands bound, he had no other way to point except with a jerk of his head in the direction of the rocky ravine just ahead. In his mind, the directions echoed clearly. *The fourth ravine will lead you to the caves of Bar Kokhba, where the last Jewish rebels died. There are five caves high on the sandstone walls. Bar Kokhba took his last stand in the fifth cave, the one farthest west from the Dead Sea.*

Thomas prayed it would not be the cave where he and the knight would join those rebels in the slumber of death.

One hour later, he and the knight and Katherine, along with Rashim and five of the largest bandits, stood at the top of a path near the dark circle of a cave's entrance.

CHAPTER
58

"M y good friend," Rashim said. "I am pleased to discover you did not deceive us about the caves. Perhaps now it is time for you to die."

Rashim nodded once. The largest of the bandits drew a scimitar high above Thomas's head and waited for another nod.

Thomas set his jaw straight and stared straight ahead.

I have done everything I can, he thought. *If this is how it must end, it is the Lord's will. I will not beg or show fear.*

In that timeless heartbeat, Thomas was overwhelmed by awe. And joy. The passage of time became meaningless. The peace within him expanded and rushed outward.

My God, he thought, *You are Master of all. How can I fear death?*

"No!" a voice reached Thomas. "Do not kill him yet."

Thomas blinked.

The pain of his swollen mouth returned. The throbbing of his blistered feet, the ache of his arms.

"Do not kill him *yet?*" Rashim said. "Yet?"

Katherine nodded.

"My decision is to be with you, Rashim. Alive," she replied. "Let Thomas die as he retrieves the treasure."

Rashim stroked his chin. "You intrigue me. Tell me more."

"Have the sword lowered," Katherine said.

Rashim nodded at the bandit, and the sword dropped from the sky.

"What if this is not the right cave?" Katherine asked. "Do we have time to search all the others? Will the soldiers remain in pursuit of your men indefinitely?"

Rashim pursed his lips together, still not fully convinced.

"And there remains this cave," she said. "If you and I are to share the treasure, I wish to see you unharmed. Send Thomas ahead. Let him be inflicted by vipers. Let him stumble into bottomless pits. Let him risk his life for us. If I am to be wedded to you, I wish to live in luxury."

Rashim thought only for a few seconds.

"Find brush for torches," he directed his men. "We shall let the knight and his friend direct our way."

He grabbed Katherine by the arm and pinched her cruelly. "This one remains with me as we follow. Should she—or they—falter, I will slice her throat."

Thomas and Sir William stood side by side, ten paces ahead of Rashim and Katherine and the five other bandits.

"The strength of your arm?" Sir William whispered.

"I can barely hold this torch," Thomas replied. His fingers were still numb, though the bonds had been cut fifteen minutes earlier.

"Begin!" shouted Rashim. His voice now reflected nervousness. This was a man accustomed to ruling other men, not searching for the tomb of dead Roman soldiers.

"Tell me when your strength has returned," Sir William whispered as they shuffled ahead.

Thomas focused on the ground just in front. The light was not strong enough to illuminate much beyond.

"We cannot attack," Thomas countered. "He holds a knife to Katherine's throat, and we have no weapons."

"Where we find treasure, we will find remains of soldiers," Sir William said. "Where we find those soldiers, we will find their weapons."

Yes! The knight was correct. It increased their odds, no matter how slim! His mind now raced. *We have succeeded in dividing this small army of bandits. Our hands are now free. We may have weapons soon. But how to get Katherine away from the knife at her throat?*

Another thought. *Will the sight of the treasure prove to be enough of a distraction? Will that give the knight the final edge he needs?*

The cave tunnel widened suddenly into a hall. Light gleamed from the metal at the far corner of their vision.

"How much farther?" demanded Rashim.

Thomas could hear Rashim's quickened breathing. *This fear will be to our advantage as well.*

"I cannot say," Thomas called back. "But look here. Signs of those who lived in this cave!"

The gleam of light off bronze became a wide bowl and intricately designed pitchers.

"Keep your distance from each other," Rashim warned.

The hall narrowed again, became one passage and then almost immediately divided into two.

"Which side?" the knight asked.

"Does it matter?" Thomas said. "This entire cave must be explored."

Thomas dared not voice his single biggest fear . . . that the treasure was already plundered. Obscure and remote as this cave was, what if another had solved the riddle?

Thomas sucked in a breath. Intent on watching the ground for snakes, he noticed something the knight had missed.

A footprint.

Then he relaxed. In this still air, a footprint would be preserved for centuries.

The tunnel widened again, and looking back at the torches of the bandits, Thomas could see that the other passage, the one they had chosen to ignore, had rejoined them.

They moved into another hall and discovered a basket of skulls, a tangled fishing net, and a large basin scooped into a wall.

"Water reservoir," Sir William whispered. "Dozens of people may have lived in this cave!"

"Move quickly!" Rashim called.

Thomas hoped Rashim's knife would not tremble against Katherine's throat with the nervousness now so obvious in his voice.

Farther on, they found a bundle of letters, the edges of the parchment so well preserved that Thomas relaxed. This parchment had withstood the centuries; a footprint would do the same.

The hall ended abruptly. Thomas and the knight carefully searched for another passage but found none.

"We return," Thomas announced to the bandits who still followed ten paces behind. "There is one other passage to explore. One where this hall began."

The bandits gave them ample room to move by. *Despite the threat of a knife at Katherine's throat*, Thomas realized, *despite their weapons, they still fear the knight's fighting ability.*

The realization gave him even more hope.

Now we must find the treasure. And the Druid book.

Twenty steps down the other passage, they did.

Thomas and Sir William held their torches out over the pit. The light did not extend low enough to show the bottom or the other side.

"What is it?" Rashim asked from behind them. "Why do you stop? What do you see?"

"Only darkness," the knight replied. "The darkness of a great pit."

Thomas lifted his light to survey the nearby cave floor. At the edge of the light, he saw a ladder made of rope. He retrieved it and lifted it part way so that Rashim could see it too.

"The treasure lies below," Thomas said with confidence he did not feel. *Why else would a ladder have been left nearby?*

"Hurry then," Rashim said. "Bring me a sample."

Thomas knew he must continue to act the role of one helpless with the fear of death. It was an easy role to play.

"But you will only kill me once the treasure has been proven."

"Better than a slow death," Rashim said. From behind the torch, his fierce face was filled with shadows.

Thomas bowed his head, as if he had been beaten. Then he noticed a small line of dark powder that followed around the edge of the pit.

He dropped the ladder, fell to his knees to retrieve it, and managed to smear some of the powder on his fingers.

Strange, he thought as he turned his back and touched the powder lightly with his tongue. *This bitterness has a familiar taste. And why a line that surrounds the pit as far as I can see?*

He had no time to ponder further. Two of the bandits were at his side, holding their hands out to grasp the rope ladder. They lowered it over the side. Another bandit prodded Thomas with the point of his sword.

With pretended reluctance, Thomas began to climb downward. The bandits were so large, and held the rope so steady, that the ladder hardly moved at all with his full weight on it.

Thomas took one final look upward to mark Sir William's position. *If I find swords below, I cannot falter upon my return. I must toss him one without hesitation.*

Sir William's strong face regarded him without changing expression. Then a slow wink, and Thomas felt strengthened.

Thomas lowered himself slowly, one hand holding the side of the rope ladder, another the torch.

How far down?

He counted twenty-five steps, then touched bottom.

"What do you see?" Rashim called down.

Thomas realized that from Rashim's position, there would only be the glare of the torchlight. No one on the edge above would be able to see below the torch to what Thomas now beheld.

There were piles of large leather bags stacked along one of the smooth vertical walls of the pit. The bags bulged as if filled with stones.

Gold?

He kicked at one of the bags. The leather, dried from centuries of cool air, broke open. Chunks of gold trinkets and scattered jewels fell on the floor.

"What is it?" Rashim called again.

Thomas did not reply. He cared little for the treasure, glad only that it could be used as a distraction.

I need to find swords.

Thomas moved again and nearly stumbled over a skeleton lying in a curled position, as if the soldier had fallen asleep, never to wake again.

The torchlight flickered over another skeleton. Then another. All in the same positions.

Horror hit Thomas as he realized how these soldiers had died. Someone above had taken their ladder away.

It made too much sense. They would have carried the treasure down, then been abandoned so that the secret of the treasure's location would die with them.

"What have you found?" Rashim was saying, breaking into Thomas's spell of horror.

"The price of greed," Thomas said in a choked voice.

He pushed beyond the terrible sight. There, stacked neatly against the wall, were swords.

Thomas took two and tucked them into the belt beneath his cloak. He hurried back to the leather bags and took a handful of jewels.

Then he dropped the torch and stamped the flame into extinction.
To rise out of the darkness will give an advantage.
"What goes there?" Frustration was evident in Rashim's voice.
"Treasure!" Thomas tried to inject excitement into his voice. "I cannot carry both the torch and gold."

He began to climb with the awkward one-handed grip he had used to descend, but instead of a torch, he held the only hope there was for survival—jewels and gold. As Thomas neared the top, he tried to block fear from his mind.

There is so little time, and but a single chance to save ourselves. One misstep and Katherine will die.

He stepped onto firm ground.

"Yes?' Rashim demanded.

Thomas threw the gold and jewels onto the floor of the cave. Sparkles of light flashed.

Bandits whose lives were built on greed would have been inhuman if they could have resisted the impulse to look downward at the glittering of wealth.

In that heartbeat, Thomas threw open his cloak, tossed a sword to Sir William, and without pausing, charged his left shoulder into Rashim's stomach. As his legs drove forward, Thomas was reaching into his cloak with his right hand for the second sword.

Rashim fell backward. His knife clattered against the ground.

"Run, Katherine!" Thomas shouted, then whirled, sword in front, to help Sir William.

At that moment, the world seemed to come to an end.

A great light exploded in Thomas's eyes.

He staggered and reeled as a wave of heat roared past him. If he screamed, he could not hear it among the screams of panic from the bandits.

Then, as the echoes of thunder died, and as his eyes began to adjust to the new darkness, he saw them in the light of the fallen torches. Phantoms. Twice the size of a man. Floating downward toward him.

The bandits fell face down on the ground in terror.

Dazed, Thomas barely realized that he still carried his sword.

Sir William, whose back was to the phantoms, reacted quickly to the sudden surrender of the bandits. He kicked their swords into the pit and stood above them, ready to strike any who might try to rise.

And still the phantoms descended in the dying light. Rashim began to babble in terror.

"Will . . . Will . . . William," Thomas finally managed to say. Although he had remained standing. The explosion and the appearance of the ghostly specters had taken away his voice.

Sir William turned his head as the first phantom drifted into him. He laughed and turned his sword into it. The weapon slashed through white cloth.

A voice reached them from the darkness. "Forgive me. I could think of no other way to prepare for your arrival."

Thomas thought of the footprint, the line of dark powder along the edge of the pit. That bitter taste! Charcoal, sulfur and potassium nitrate. Explosive powder.

He found himself grinning. Only a Merlin would have knowledge of this secret from the far east land of Cathay.

And the phantoms. Cloth supported by a framework of branches. Thomas himself had once been fooled by the same trick at a campfire in England. By an old man who had traveled with Katherine.

A protest of disbelief arose, then died unspoken in his throat. *The old man is dead*, Thomas wanted to utter. *The old man died the next morning by the campfire.*

But then a figure emerged from the darkness. A familiar stooped and hooded figure which had haunted so many of Thomas's dreams—the old man who had once seemed to know Thomas's every step.

Could it be true? That Hawkwood was not dead?

The answer came from Katherine, who ran past the prone bandits and threw her arms around the old man.

"Hawkwood! You are here," she said over and over again. "You are here and alive."

"My child," he soothed. "If only I could have sent word."

When their embrace finally ended, the old man stepped past Katherine to face Sir William and Thomas.

"It appears you had little need of assistance," he said. "I could have waited in St. Jean d'Acre for your return. The leisure would have served my bones much better than travel through this harsh land."

Sir William grinned. "Hardly. We had not yet won this sword fight. And an entire army pursues us. I had begun to wonder when you might appear."

"You knew?" Katherine cried. "You knew Hawkwood was alive and did not tell me?"

"In a way, I did, for what promise did you overhear me make to Thomas?" Sir William said. "But against the Druids, it pays well to keep some secrets close. What if you had made mention of Hawkwood in Lord Baldwin's presence?"

"The army," Thomas said. "We dare not tarry."

Hawkwood dismissed the danger with a wave of his hand. "Bah. An army in pursuit of us will be like a horse chasing a gnat."

He then pointed at Thomas. "Sir William, the young man has proven himself, as I predicted."

Thomas bowed his head in respect. Inwardly, he was not calm. Thoughts raced through his mind. Memories. Possibilities. Hawkwood had known their destination, this cave. He had been in the Holy Land the entire time. He knew with sudden certainty that the old man was . . .

Thomas barely dared to raise his head to ask. When he did, he found himself looking at a man not stooped, but standing with the solid strength of one barely older than Sir William. Thomas found himself staring at a gentle smile in a face that was eerily familiar.

Thomas did not have a chance to ask his question. For the man answered it as his smile widened with joy.

"Hello, my son," Hawkwood said to Thomas. "It has been a long wait."

CHAPTER

59

JULY 1314
LONDON

Katherine gathered her hair into a thick ponytail between her fingers. When she released the hair, she took satisfaction in feeling its weight fall upon her shoulders. *Barely a year ago*, she thought, *I borrowed shears to cut this ragged and short. Never again . . . one cannot pose as a lady while looking like a boy.*

Then, almost unconsciously she smoothed her dress with quick pats and tugs.

"Have no fear, milady," Thomas said. "You are a sight to ravage the hearts of men and to send jealousy quivering through the ladies of the court."

"Thomas," she scolded. "Must you peer at my innermost thoughts?"

"All these months of travel together . . ." He shrugged. "Not once have I seen you so concerned about your appearance."

Katherine softened. Indeed, all these months of travel together. Moments of extreme danger as they avoided Mameluke soldiers in the Holy Land, fought wayside bandits, survived the most vicious storms at sea. Hours of conversation during the quieter times—beside evening campfires or on a ship's deck shifting to the waves beneath starlight. How could they not know each other? Yet they had avoided talk of the one thing nearest their hearts—love for the other—because, she could only guess, they each feared what might come to pass in England should the Druids be victors. And now, they were about to take the first step into the final battle.

Behind them were London's narrow, twisted streets of

cobblestone. Ahead, across the moat, were a half-dozen buildings of smooth stone block. The forbidding wall encompassed an area the size of a small village, which in fact, it was. The royal residences.

A part of London yet separate, these majestic buildings sat on the north bank of the Thames River. Barely a month before, Katherine and the knight and Thomas and Hawkwood had finally arrived at the nearby London docks on the same river. As their ship had slowly moved upstream against the Thames, they had all stood on the deck, drinking in the sounds and sights of London. From that vantage point they had seen the top half of the most imposing building within the walls, the Tower.

This building, high and mighty with cramped windows cut into the stone, held the political prisoners of the King of England, Edward the Second, who himself lived in luxury less than a hundred yards away in his permanent residence. It was said that King Edward often enjoyed a stroll past the Tower after a meal, that it helped his digestion to hear the cries of agony and pleas for mercy from his enemies within.

Yet, it was not simply this awesome display of wealth and power that caused Katherine to wonder how she might appear to others. All of the people within sight were dressed in colorful silk finery. They strolled through the grounds, accompanied by their expensive greyhounds. It was a spectacle which gave Katherine little comfort. She shuddered at the prospect of dealing with the intrigue of the high court. But it had to be done, for it might take them days to accomplish what they so desperately needed.

They sought an audience with King Edward himself.

"Must this servant accompany you every day?" sniffed the slim courtier, as he pointed at Thomas. "Your beauty and dress show royal blood, of course, but your choice of a manservant . . ."

The courtier let his voice trail away with a sniff, then continued. "Each day for the last ten mornings, I've had to suffer this peasant's . . . this peasant's unspeakable coarseness in dress and attitude. What on earth will Duke Whittingham think of me when I present such a peasant along with a lady like you? After all, a chamberlain does not receive just anybody, and the Duke of Whittingham is no exception."

Katherine saw Thomas trying to maintain the sullen look of a dull peasant. She knew him well enough to catch the twinkle in his eyes and to understand what he thought of the courtier's yellow tights and effeminate manners and voice.

She was glad, however, that Thomas maintained the longsuffering expression of a servant accustomed to abuse. She smiled sweetly at the courtier. "This servant is my best defense as I travel through dangerous streets. Already he has killed three men with his bare hands."

The courtier jumped back slightly in alarm. Thomas growled, and the courtier scurried farther away and disappeared around a corner.

A moment later, only his head appeared, and he gasped out one last sentence. "The chamberlain will see you when the bells strike the next hour!" With that, he pulled his head from sight. The pattering of his feet retreating down the hallway drew a smile from Thomas.

"That is not a man," Thomas said. "It is a mouse. What kind of king have we who surrounds himself with the like?"

Katherine smiled. "Sir William warned us the royal court would have its share of groveling flatterers and shameless bribe-takers."

"This one is both," Thomas spat. "For all the gold you have given him, I cannot believe it has taken ten days just to see the king's administrator. What price to finally reach the king himself?"

"It matters little," Katherine said, as she sat straighter on the wooden bench. "Not many receive an audience with the chamberlain, let alone King Edward. We will only have one chance to present the reasons for an audience with the king. We cannot fail now."

"Have you the book?"

"Of course. You bear the burden of its weight every day as we bring it here."

"Then fear not," Thomas said. "It is proof enough for the king to take action against the Druids. No longer will we fight alone."

"Yet—"

"Yet it is enough. You will tell the chamberlain how we found the book and what it contains. The Druids will no longer move in secrecy, and without that secrecy—their greatest weapon—we will prove victorious."

Katherine knew Thomas spoke true. She had rehearsed again and again their urgent story for King Edward.

The church bells rang, a sound that echoed clearly in the silence of the hallway. Almost instantly, the courtier appeared at the corner and beckoned.

Katherine followed, with Thomas close behind.

Let my words impress, she prayed silently. *Let them strike truer than any arrows.*

The courtier led them through a maze of corridors, then stopped at an arched doorway. Two guards stood in the recess of the doorway and solemnly stepped aside at the impatient snapping of the courtier's fingers.

"Go in," the courtier said, as he pushed open the large double doors. "Expect no more than ten minutes of audience."

Katherine swept past him, smiling with quiet amusement to see how he kept ample distance between himself and Thomas. The doors shut behind them.

It was a large chamber, with a portrait of Edward the Second above the fireplace. Tapestries lined the other walls, and on the far side of the room, an upright divider hid the rear portion. A large chair with leather armrests and a footstool dominated the center of the room.

The doors opened, and a large, stoop-shouldered man in a purple cloak entered the chamber. He bowed once, then stood near the chair and placed one foot upon the footstool.

"You have begged audience," he said. And waited.

"For good reason," Katherine said. She drew a deep breath. "My servant carries a book which has lain undisturbed in the Holy Land since the time of the Roman soldiers. This book contains proof of a secret circle of sorcerers and their plot which now threatens England and the good King Edward."

The large man leaned forward, so that his elbow rested on the knee elevated by his stance upon the footstool.

"My dear child," the large man said. "If you meant to intrigue me with such a bold opening statement, you have succeeded."

"My lord," she said, "my words are truth."

She began her explanation much as Thomas had done in convincing Rashim that a treasure did exist. She told of the time before the Romans conquered, when Druids ruled the land. She told of the Druid secrets of science and astronomy, and of the Roman general who plundered their great wealth only to be summoned to the Holy Land, and of how the wealth lay hidden in the Cave of Letters for so many centuries. She explained how bandits had taken them, and how Mameluke soldiers had followed them along the shore of the Dead Sea.

The large man held up a hand glittering with rings.

Katherine stopped.

"How did you come into possession of this remarkable knowledge?" he asked, "and how is it you have just now returned with your story? We lost the Holy Land to the infidels a generation ago."

"My father was a crusader knight," Katherine said, "forsaken in the Holy Land when the infidels defeated our armies. I was raised there, hidden among the peoples."

She gestured toward her fine apparel and jewelry. "I do not have royal blood, as your courtier might have assumed. Rather, the treasure that my father found provided me with passage here, and with the clothes I needed to gain entrance into royal society."

The large man closed his eyes in thought. Without opening them, he said, "You and he found this treasure in a cave. You were held hostage by bandits and pursued by Mameluke soldiers. How did you escape with the treasure?"

"The bandits were overcome with greed," she said. "My father and this servant were able to overcome them. We left the bandits in the pit in the cave for the soldiers to find."

The large man opened his eyes in sudden surprise. "For the soldiers to find?"

"Yes." Katherine explained how the soldiers had been tricked into following the main party of bandits. "As we left the cave and trekked through the ravine back to the Dead Sea, we dropped pieces of gold and jewelry, so that there was a trail of treasure leading back to the cave. When we reached the shore of the Dead Sea, we turned north. Instead of pursuing us along the shoreline, the soldiers followed the treasure back to the cave, where they were rewarded by the bulk of the treasure and by bandits held helpless beside that treasure at the bottom of the pit."

"Splendid!" The large man clapped his hands. "Absolutely splendid!" His craggy face then became a frown of puzzlement. "Did you not feel dismay to leave such wealth behind?"

"Not when keeping it all would mean our lives," Katherine said. "Besides, what we could carry ourselves was enough. And . . ."

Katherine paused. This was the most important moment.

"And there was the book. The Druid book. It contains—"

"—nothing but the fanciful spinning of a fairytale!" came a booming voice from behind the divider.

The large man dropped his foot from the footstool and straightened to ramrod attention.

"Duke Whittingham," the large man whispered. "I did not know . . ."

"Think nothing of it," the duke said, as he stepped from behind the divider. "You had your instructions, to pretend to listen to these impostors. You could not know that I too wanted to listen. But I have heard enough."

Katherine barely registered his words, for the shock of recognition hit her like a sword blow.

"Waleran!" The uttering of his name was a low hiss, but it did not come from her lips, but like a curse from Thomas, as he too reeled with shock.

"You are dismissed," the Duke of Whittingham said to the large man.

"Yes, milord." He bowed quickly, then almost ran from the chamber. The doors slammed shut behind him.

Waleran. Not even now, dressed in royal robes, did he have a single redeeming feature to lessen his evil appearance.

"You would do well not to call me Waleran," he said. "Duke Whittingham is my title. And let me assure you, I have ways to punish those who do not address me properly."

Katherine opened her mouth once, then shut it. Her thoughts were in such disarray that she was unable to talk.

"That is better," Waleran said with a cruel leer, misinterpreting her silence as obedience. "You might have been able to escape me in the Holy Land, but you shall not be so fortunate again."

CHAPTER

6o

"You are such fools," Waleran laughed. His teeth were unevenly spaced and black with rot. "So easy to deceive."

"How . . . how can the king's chamberlain . . ." Katherine stopped, still nearly faint from surprise.

"How can the king's chamberlain be a Druid? Or how can the king's chamberlain accomplish so much as a Druid?"

Katherine nodded. Waleran here was not what they expected during the long months of voyage and planning.

"Should it not be obvious? It is I who oversee all the Druid actions. And who is better placed to oversee a kingdom than the right-hand man of the king himself? And why should you show such surprise? You know the Druids have penetrated all levels of society. Surely it would seem logical that a Druid attain the position of chamberlain, especially when all the previous chamberlains were Druids. The unquestioned authority of this position gives great freedom and—" Waleran snapped his mouth shut and dropped his hand to his sword.

"Young man," he said to Thomas with a voice promising death. "Sit. Yes, immediately. On the cold floor. From there, you shall have difficulty continuing your slow movement toward me."

Thomas hesitated.

"Do you think it was an accident that you were searched? I know you do not have a weapon, and mine"—Waleran unsheathed his sword—"is coated with poison." He paused. "Now, sit! Or watch Katherine die."

Thomas lowered himself onto the stone floor with great reluctance.

"Much better," Waleran cackled, then broke into a wheeze. When he recovered his breath, he moved to the large chair in the center of the room and placed his sword beside him on the armrest. "I shall satisfy your curiosity. In turn, you shall satisfy mine."

More likely, you shall gloat, Katherine thought.

"As you well know," Waleran said, "it was I who posed as a fellow prisoner in the dungeon of Magnus during the time that Thomas and Sir William spent in captivity. Yet I overheard nothing about that which we seek."

Katherine grinned inside. *Thomas kept his vow well. What still lies hidden in the monastery of his childhood might . . .*

"It was hardly worth my efforts for what little I gained in that prison." Waleran squirmed as if remembering the dank darkness and the flea-infested straw and the scurrying of rats. "Then a freak whose face was burned helped them escape."

Again Katherine found reason for hidden satisfaction. *He does not know it was I behind those bandages.*

"However, my time in York paid dividends, as you know."

Katherine bowed her head. *Waleran was in a neighboring cell as Thomas spoke to the captured duke of York.*

Waleran cackled again. "Yes. Thomas here thought he was so brave and noble, capturing Isabelle and holding her as hostage. Little did he know we had deliberately allowed that, so that he would lead us to—"

"You saw the old man dead," Thomas interrupted with bitterness. "Was that not enough?"

Katherine kept her head bowed, this time so that Waleran would not see the gleam of triumph in her eyes. Yes, Thomas had led Waleran's soldiers to her and the old man. But Hawkwood, in the confusion of the attack, had pretended death by swallowing one of the prepared pills he always carried among the herbs and potions hidden beneath his cloak, this one made from the dried and crushed bark of rhododendrons. It caused unconsciousness, coldness of the skin, and a vastly reduced heart rate. Yes, it had been a gamble, for any of the soldiers might have run him through with a sword, but a necessary gamble. Once the Druids were convinced that he was dead . . .

"Dead, and not a moment too soon," Waleran laughed. "His death made it easy to outmaneuver you two. Following you both to the Holy Land was child's play. And such simple minds." Waleran choked on his laugher, then recovered. "Should it not be obvious that if the Merlins had men in the Holy Land, the Druids also would have their spies?"

"Lord Hubert Baldwin," Thomas spat.

"None other," Waleran said. "One of your most trusted men and one of our greater allies. Without his help, Magnus might never have fallen as it first did."

Katherine felt frozen to the ground. *So many died then. A generation of Merlins wiped out. And now the Druids will be able to move openly against an entire country.*

She lifted her head.

"You gave Lord Baldwin his instructions in Jericho?"

"Of course, milady," came the mocking reply. "He is a man of strong arm, but limited intelligence. And I did not want to soil my own hands with such matters."

"You mean you did not want to risk your life," Thomas said. "Baldwin now rots in a Jerusalem dungeon."

"He was a fool to allow himself to be taken to Jerusalem." Waleran shrugged. "No matter. I needed to return immediately to England—as a chamberlain I have freedom, but not unlimited freedom—and the situation seemed to be in hand, especially since the Mameluke officials are not adverse to bribes."

Then Waleran grinned, an ugly, evil grin of smug triumph. "You have told the rest. What we failed to do, you accomplished. What we lost so many centuries ago, you recovered and, against all odds, returned to England."

He stood and rubbed his hands briskly. "I shall take the book now," he said.

With reluctance, Katherine nodded at Thomas.

"Not so, my dear," Waleran said. "*You* take the book from him and slowly hand it to me. He is young enough and strong enough to attempt an attack."

Waleran placed his hand on the sword hilt as he directed his words at Katherine. "And if *you* attempt anything, I shall run you through."

Thomas removed the book from its wrappings. Katherine took it with both hands and extended it to Waleran.

He merely smiled.

"You think I will reach for it and drop my guard? Not so. Place it on the armrest and step away."

Katherine did as instructed. When she had retreated to her

previous position, Waleran opened the book and glanced inside.

"Ahh, splendid," he said. "I see already many of the secrets we lost over the centuries."

He ran a soiled finger down one of the pages. "Here, a mixture of common garden herbs to induce madness . . . there, a prediction of star movement, knowledge to impress superstitious peasants."

Waleran paused. "But you already know these weapons. The eclipse during the hanging of the knight . . . that was masterful," he mused. "Of course, the old man is dead and I need not worry."

He slammed his fist down on the book, snapping Katherine's head upward in attention.

"Tell me—" His voice was no longer contemplative, but ugly and threatening. "What did you hope to accomplish with this book?"

Katherine bit her tongue.

"Tell me!" Waleran roared. "Silence gains you nothing!"

He leapt to his feet and placed the tip of his sword against Katherine's throat.

"I need only pierce the skin," Waleran said, in a voice unexpectedly silky, "and she dies. So tell me."

"At the back," Thomas said hurriedly, "at the back of the book is the Druid outline for means of taking a country. Key towns to hold. Key people to bribe. Although it is dated by the passage of centuries, it shows intent. Proof of a Druid masterplan, to be delivered to King Edward. That, and news of what is happening in northern towns now, is enough to consider a Druid threat in this day and age. With his help, we hoped to stop you."

"Children, children," Waleran said with insincere sympathy, as he stepped away from Katherine and sat once again in his chair. "What delusions you carry. King Edward himself is a pliable fool who relies heavily on my advice. And he is so distracted now with the war against Scotland that I am allowed to dictate our domestic affairs."

Waleran laughed. "Do you think it is an accident that a hopeless battle against Scotland preoccupies him? Hardly. Once again, my advice that he should continue the war. As I said, a useful distraction weakens the entire country."

Waleran stared into the distance. When he spoke again, it was with the voice of a parent lecturing a child.

"Thomas," he said, "my thanks for securing this valuable book.

But we need more from you. Give what we have always wanted, what you were entrusted to guard since birth."

Thomas sat silent.

"You have a simple choice," Waleran said. "Join us and gain the wealth and power of the land's most powerful earl. Or remain silent and see Katherine die."

"No!" Katherine uttered. "My life is nothing compared to what he seeks. Thomas, I die gladly."

"Thomas?" Waleran purred.

Still Thomas said nothing.

"A difficult choice?" Waleran asked. "Perhaps time in the torture chamber will loosen your tongue."

Waleran did not wait for a response. Instead, he raised his voice. "Guards!"

The door open instantly.

Waleran stood and pointed to Thomas and Katherine. "Take them to the Tower."

Katherine wept freely. Though she was not alone in the Tower cell, her cries went unheard. The other occupant of the cell was Thomas, who was unconscious. Moments before, two guards had dragged him in, his head sagging like a broken puppet. They had shackled his wrists to the wall.

Now, the chains kept him from falling forward completely. His hands, attached to the chains, were behind his back, and Katherine hardly dared guess how much it tore his muscles to have his entire weight straining so awkwardly against his chest and arms.

She reached for his face. She didn't need the clank of chains which followed her every movement to remind her that it was near impossible. Her wrists were shackled as well, and her fingers stopped inches short of Thomas's face.

"My love," she cried, "awaken."

He did not.

Tears streamed down her cheeks. Five days running, the guards had taken him away during midmorning. Five days running, they had returned him less than an hour later. Each time he had been placed unconscious in those chains. Each time it had taken him longer to return to consciousness.

She longed to touch his face.

"Thomas," she whispered again. "Please. Please wake up."

Thomas stirred. Groaned. Blinked. And slowly found his feet.

"Katherine," he croaked. Joy filled his voice. "You are still here."

She turned her head so that he would not see her tears. *How can he think of me when they inflict so much pain on him?*

"I am still here," she said, her voice muffled by the hair which clung to her wet cheeks.

"Thank our Lord," he said. "It is my worst nightmare that I will return and find you gone. I . . . I . . . could not bear this prison alone."

"Nor I," she said simply.

As they looked at each other, Thomas brought his hand up and they reached for one another, but the chains brought them short.

"I dreamed you called me 'my love,' " Thomas said.

"I did," Katherine replied. She waited long moments, as if debating whether to speak. "It is a subject we have avoided," she said. "My love for you. Yours, I pray, for me. My own fear was this—to declare love for you, yet be helpless against the Druids."

"We are not helpless," Thomas vowed. "For I have not revealed to the torturers the secrets of my childhood monastery. Not even its location."

"To save your life—"

"No. Sir William hinted that my knowledge could turn the final battle. To reveal it now means my life is worthless."

"Yet—"

"No, Katherine. There is no 'yet.' " He grinned. It was a flash of white from a pain-exhausted face. Blood trickled from one corner of his mouth. "We shall watch for escape."

Thomas raised his voice in anger. "I say it again . . . we shall watch for escape. Then we shall return to the monastery, and I will solve the final puzzle, find what it is the Druids so urgently seek! With that, they shall be defeated."

The effort of rage cost him his last reserve of energy. He sagged against the chains. "Then we shall talk of our love," he finished softly. "Then we shall talk of our love."

Katherine wept again, this time unable to hide her tears.

Thomas gritted his teeth. "Katherine," he said, "do not despair. We will see a chance for escape. All we need to do is reach the monastery."

A key turned in the lock.

A huge surly guard—the one who shoved food at them daily—kicked open the door. From behind him, a blare of royal trumpets.

"Make way for the king!" came a shout. A courtier dashed inside the prison cell.

Then, without further fanfare, King Edward the Second, the reigning monarch of all of England, stepped through the doorway.

He was a tall, powerfully built man with fair skin and reddish-blond hair. He carried the royal scepter, so brilliantly studded with jewels of all colors that his purple robes and white-furred collar seemed poor in comparison.

He stood still and stared at them, his face empty of all emotion.

Katherine felt a shiver go through her. *This man need only lift a finger, and we are free. Or dead. At his command, armies of thousands march upon towns and villages.*

"This is the traitor with the tongue of stone," King Edward observed.

"Your majesty, I—" Thomas began to say.

The courtier stepped forward and slapped Thomas across the face. "One does not address his majesty unless asked a direct question."

"I am not—"

Another slap. This one rocked Thomas back against the wall.

Katherine's eyes filled with tears again.

"I am not a traitor!" Thomas roared.

The courtier prepared to strike Thomas again.

"Enough," King Edward said.

The courtier stepped away. King Edward moved forward to examine Thomas.

"I am told our best men cannot break your spirit."

Thomas raised his head tall and met the king's eyes. "Innocence gives strength, milord."

"Indeed," King Edward said noncommittally. He turned to examine Katherine.

"And you," he said to her, "are as beautiful as the rumors say."

Then he walked away from them both and filled the doorway again.

"I have heard many declarations of innocence," King Edward said, "from men as brave as you. From men who have endured the very chains you wear. Indeed, I often think it takes greater bravery to be a traitor than to serve the king. For traitors know the terrible price they will pay."

Katherine's eyes were on Thomas. He opened his mouth.

"No." With the full weight of royal authority, King Edward's command halted any words. "There is nothing you can say to convince me. The Duke of Whittingham has told me enough, and if I cannot trust him . . ." King Edward shrugged as he made his jest. "If I cannot trust him, my kingdom is worthless."

Such irony. Katherine wanted to shriek, but she, like Thomas, knew that any talk of Druids and Merlins and kingdomwide conspiracies would sound like the ravings of lunatics. Without the book, they had no hope of presenting their case. In chains, against the word of the chamberlain, they had even less hope.

King Edward fixed Thomas and Katherine with a stare.

"Why am I here, you might well ask, when I refuse to hear your case?" King Edward paused. "Not for curiosity."

His voice became quiet with menace.

"My son has been kidnapped," he said. "I have many enemies, all linked to the Tower prisoners, and I am here to tell each prisoner the same, so that word may spread and my son be returned. My royal proclamation is this. My son, Prince Edward, is returned safe within a week, or all prisoners within the Tower shall be beheaded."

They were fed twice each day. In the morning, their guard brought a bowl of thin, fly-specked porridge. In the early evening, it was bread and a bowl of beans boiled to mush.

The guard was so large he had to squeeze sideways to get into the cell. He would jangle his keys for several minutes and fumble with the lock, then kick the door open and grunt his way into the cell.

That he always drank too much beer was evident by the foul breath which overwhelmed the usual stench of the cramped prison cell. Because he was so large, most of his movements meant collisions with Katherine or Thomas.

Three nights closer to the eve of their execution, Katherine and Thomas received their usual warning of his arrival.

The door clanged open and the guard struggled through. This time, however, he strained harder than normal to wheeze air into his lungs. His eyes were unfocused, and his entire face the red usually restricted only to his nose.

He bent to place one bowl at Thomas's feet, and barely managed to keep his balance. He then turned to Katherine. He smiled uncertainly and his breath made her choke. His large, stubbled face loomed closer, his double chins wobbled.

Her thoughts turned to sudden alarm. For the ugly face did not stop its approach.

This is not an attempted kiss!

It was not. The big man sagged forward and fell into Katherine. His bearlike arms engulfed her.

"Thomas!" she tried to shout, but the guard's weight suffocated any words which might have left her lungs.

She tried to beat her arms against his chest, but she was pinned too securely. Yet his weight was passive, as if he were not attacking, but had . . . *collapsed?*

He rolled downward and fell in a heap at her feet.

Katherine found herself staring at the ring of keys on his belt. She hardly believed this might be. Slowly, she reached down and tugged on the keys. The guard did not respond.

It took Katherine less than a minute to find the key which unshackled her wrists.

CHAPTER
61

H ome!" Thomas shouted. "I . . . am . . . home!"
His words echoed through the valley below where he and Katherine stood among the shadows of large rocks.

Katherine smiled at his enthusiasm. No matter what their troubles, this was a time to set them aside and enjoy the sunshine, the feel of grass against their ankles, and the babble of the tiny river which ran past the abbey.

Their first destination was not the abbey itself. Instead, Thomas moved directly to the river and stood at its bank.

"You know about the cave?" Thomas asked.

Katherine nodded. "Hawkwood and I once waited for you here. It was an agony, not to know if you were Druid or Merlin, not to be able to simply join you instead of follow you."

"We are together now." But he said it in such a dismissing way that Katherine knew Thomas did not want to discuss the reason for that mistrust; so she too lost herself in thought.

When Katherine looked at Thomas again, she saw his eyes were closed, his head bowed.

Minutes later, he lifted his head again. "She was a remarkable woman," Thomas finally said. "There is so much that I owe her."

Then to dispel the somber mood, he smiled and pointed past the abbey. "See that pond? Many were the times I could not be found by those wretched monks. Little did they know I was beneath the water, breathing through a reed."

He pointed at the massive gray walls of the abbey itself. "My bedchamber was there, that tiny window. I slept on a straw mattress placed atop a great wooden trunk. At nights, I escaped down those walls."

He laughed at the surprise on her face. "No, I was not a fly. There are enough cracks between the stones for a determined boy to find room for fingers and toes."

She laughed with him. And marveled at how his gray eyes seemed almost blue beneath the clear skies.

"We have stood here long enough?" Thomas asked. "Given our followers enough notice?"

She nodded.

Thomas turned and led her to the cave.

The knight will be waiting for us, Katherine assured herself, as they walked among the boulders. *Surely not everything we planned has gone astray.*

"Count to one thousand," Thomas suddenly said. They were still at the side of the river. Immediately to their left was the entrance, so well concealed it was difficult to see, even from ten feet away.

"Count to one thousand? Here? Now?"

Thomas laughed at the confusion that crossed her face.

"No. That was the rule I was taught by Sarah. 'Count to one thousand. Watch carefully. Then slowly, cautiously, enter. Let no person ever discover this place.'

"It was a game, I thought then. Sarah taught me patience, how to wait here and listen to the sounds of the surrounding forest until I was part of it."

Thomas closed his eyes and smiled in recollection. "Inside, so cool, so safe. We spent hours in there. She taught me to read, to understand mathematics, to apply logic."

Katherine smiled in her own recollections. *What joy to be lost in the wonder of learning. He, here in a cave in a tiny valley in the moors of northern England. I, in a sun-baked town on the edge of the Holy Land. Both of us with a path destined to bring us to this cave. Will all of it end today or—*

"Has a trampling army arrived?" The voice came from a large figure stepping into sight from the cave's entrance.

"Sir William?" The relief in Katherine's voice surprised her. She had been depending so heavily on his being here.

Sir William accepted Thomas's offer of an extended hand. "By the sound of your progress, I expected all of England to be outside. You make enough noise to wake the dead."

Then the knight rolled his eyebrows. "Of course, waking the dead is the least of my concerns. But if you wake the babe-in-arms inside, then all wrath will fall upon us, for his majesty is prone to tantrums of temper most unseemly for one of royalty."

"The child?" Katherine asked. "He is here? Safe? With his nurse?"

Sir William nodded.

"Follow me inside," the knight said. "I will introduce you to the heir of all England, the future Edward the Third."

It was not a natural cave. Instead, it resulted from the haphazard piling of huge slabs of granite over the large boulders that lined the river. The cave was barely deeper than the interior of a peasant's hut, and was lit by a shaft of sunlight that fell between the cracks of two of the largest slabs forming its roof. In the far corner an oily torch burned, its smoke carried immediately upward in a draft that escaped between smaller cracks in the ceiling.

On a rough stool sat a nurse shawled in a coarse garment. In her arms, wrapped in the finest linen, was a young child.

Prince Edward. Eyes closed in sleep. A wisp of dark hair matted to his forehead. Tiny fingers clenched.

"Did his majesty travel well?" Thomas asked.

Katherine didn't hear Sir William's reply. She was struggling with unfamiliar emotions.

She had been brought up a lonely child. The years in disguise behind bandages had ensured she did not meet other children. Never had she been allowed to hold a baby, or even come close to one.

Katherine turned to the nurse. "May I help? Does he need anything?"

The nurse shook her head without lifting her face to look at Katherine.

"May I . . . may I . . ." Katherine had become shy.

"Hold him?" the nurse asked.

"Yes."

The nurse nodded.

Katherine did not notice the amused glance between Thomas and Sir William. None of them noticed a visitor step into the cave, his shoes silent on the soft dirt.

Katherine was halfway to the child when the new voice stopped her.

"Oh, my," the voice taunted. "A touching reunion."

Katherine whirled.

Waleran. It is Waleran. As ugly as a nightmare, and leering the evil smile he had flashed as guards had taken Katherine and Thomas from his chamber to the Tower.

"Tsk, tsk," Waleran said, as Sir William reached for his sword. "This is no place for rudeness. As you can see, I do not carry a weapon."

Sir William ignored the comment and withdrew his sword.

Waleran released an exaggerated sigh. "Dealing with barbarians is so tiresome." He pursed his lips and shook his head. "William, William," he chastised. "Do you think I would be fool enough to enter this den of lions like a helpless lamb?" He answered his own question. "Hardly, William. Outside this cave is an army of twenty. All I need to do is raise my voice, and all of you will be dead."

"Twenty men," William said. "That matters little if I slit your throat now."

Waleran snorted. "And what will become of your friends? Once I am dead, so are they. Thomas . . . Katherine . . . this child—"

For a moment, the arrogant coolness of Waleran's face slipped. "That is Prince Edward! The entire kingdom is in an uproar. And you have him here!"

Surprise became a sly smile.

"I beg pardon. *We* have him here. Perhaps you've saved me a great deal of trouble."

Before Waleran could say more, Sir William sheathed his sword.

"You will live," Sir William said, as the sword hissed back into place. "But it would be more pleasant to share this cave with a half-rotted pig."

Waleran blustered until he managed to contort his face into a sneer. He pointed at Thomas, then at Katherine. "In the very least, a half-rotted pig has more cunning than these two combined."

"Oh?" Sir William asked, with the casualness of a man holding back rage only through supreme effort.

"They believed it was an act of God that their guard suffered a seizure in the midst of their cell, that it was a miracle to escape the Tower through the use of the guard's keys."

Waleran laughed until he coughed. "A miracle? Certainly. A

miracle the guard didn't die after the potion I placed in his beer. My biggest fear was that he would collapse before he reached their cell."

"You let us escape deliberately so that you could follow us here," Katherine said quietly. "Just as you once let Thomas escape York to see where that led him."

"Yes, my dear," Waleran said in a patronizing voice. "You catch on so *very* quickly. And would it surprise you that every word you said in the Tower cell reached the ears of a listener?"

Katherine blushed.

"Oh, yes," Waleran said. "Every word. Such a shame. The love you two professed for each other will never flower."

He waved that away as insignificant. "Thomas repeatedly made the mistake of telling you that all he needed was to return to the monastery of his childhood. That here would be revealed the final secrets which might overcome us."

"You overheard our conversations and let us escape, just to track us here?" Thomas sounded as if he were in shock.

"Of course," Waleran said. "Nothing less than routine for the genius mind of the right-hand adviser to the king."

The nurse stirred to comfort the baby, who had begun to whimper at the harshness of Waleran's voice. Her movement was slight, however; she appeared too frightened to look up at Waleran.

"This baby, Prince Edward," Waleran asked. "Why was he taken?"

"Desperation," Sir William said, after a long exhalation of breath. "There are so few of us Merlins. Messengers brought me word that Thomas and Katherine had been imprisoned. The plan to show the king the Druid book failed. I hoped King Edward would believe Druids had kidnapped his baby. It would get him to look closely at how the towns in the northern part of his kingdom have fallen to Druids posing as priests of the Holy Grail. With King Edward's help, we would stop you before you gained power."

Waleran chuckled. "What a surprise then, that I was there as the king's chamberlain. As you well know, King Edward will never hear of that proof. You are the last of the Merlins, and soon you will be gone."

Katherine shuddered.

"Already, we hold dozens of towns here in the north. Having King Edward's son now as hostage only makes our task easier. And within a year, Druids will reign supreme."

Sir William bowed his head in defeat and spoke. "We have truly failed. King Edward will receive no proof of your existence. You have his son as hostage. And now you know the location of this abbey."

Waleran rubbed his hands together.

"Yes," he said. "We have finally found the childhood abbey which hid Thomas for all those years. Even if you don't tell us what we need, it will be found."

"I suspect so," Sir William said sadly, head still bowed.

"Do not suspect. Consider it truth," Waleran said. "There are twenty outside now, and more to arrive."

"More?" Katherine asked.

"I have sent messengers to all parts of England. The highest members of our circle will gather here to direct the final stages of battle. England will be ours. This baby will be the heir to nothing."

Thomas finally spoke. His voice was tinged with bitterness. "Druid leaders will all meet in secrecy here?"

Waleran laughed. "You do see the irony. This obscure abbey was sufficient to hide you for years, even from the all-seeing eyes of the Druid web. How much better, then, for us to gather in the same remoteness?"

"All is lost," said Sir William. "The Druids have defeated us."

Katherine moved to Sir William and placed a comforting hand upon his shoulder.

"Please," Waleran said to Thomas, "save us both time and effort and tell me of what we seek."

Katherine took an involuntary look at the open chest across the cave. She quickly looked away, but not soon enough.

"Ho!" Waleran said. "Something I should not see?"

He strode to the torch, pulled it from its base, and walked to the chest.

"A single book?" Disappointment registered in his voice. "We have been searching for ten years for the great treasure the Lord Baldwin heard was rumored to appear among the Merlins, and all I find is a single book?"

"It is nothing," Thomas said quickly. "What you seek lies at the bottom of the pond."

"Play no games with me," Waleran warned Thomas. "Your

whimpering voice tells me perhaps this book is valuable."

"I would rather die than tell you."

"Tell him all, Thomas," Sir William said. "Mayhaps we can leave with our lives."

"Yes," Waleran said in oily tones. "Tell all."

Thomas blinked once, twice, as if trying to decide.

"Spare yourselves further agony," Waleran said, "and tell me of this book." His voice rose in volume with such impatience that the boy woke and began to cry.

"Shut that whelp's mouth!" he ordered the nurse.

"No," the nurse whispered calmly.

"No? No?" Waleran's face began to purple with sudden rage. "You dare defy me? A common peasant dares defy the Duke of Whittingham? Master of the Druids? The right-hand man of King Edward? You defy me?"

The nurse lifted her head and pushed her shawl away.

"I defy *you?*" she asked, as she stared Waleran directly in the face. "Ask instead if *you* dare defy *me.*"

Waleran staggered backward.

"Queen Isabella!"

"Indeed," she said. "The one person in England King Edward trusts more than you, his beloved Duke of Whittingham. And I have heard enough for you to hang."

She smiled. "And enough for the Druids to be wiped from the face of the earth."

CHAPTER

62

"I mpossible," Waleran said. The slate gray of his face showed, however, that he believed it all too possible. "How . . . how . . ."

Queen Isabella stood and gracefully moved to Katherine, while Waleran's jaw worked against empty air. Katherine accepted the offered baby with awe, and hugged him warm against her chest.

" . . . How is it I am here—the last place on earth a traitor like you would expect?" Queen Isabella drew to her full height and pulled the shawl away from her face. Her words were brittle and unforgiving.

The peasant's shawl still wrapped her, but her posture became unmistakably royal—her back straight, her shoulders squared, and her chin held high with dignity. The pale, smooth skin of her face contrasted with her dark, thick hair and full red lips. An aura seemed to grow around her as she once again became the woman accustomed to the power that ruled an entire land.

She fixed her terrible gaze on Waleran and advanced. "I am here because of a mysterious stranger who appeared in the royal bedchambers shortly before dawn barely a fortnight ago."

Waleran shook his head as he retreated until his back touched the cave wall. "No. Only one man would be capable of such a thing, and he is dead."

"His ghost, then, appeared," Queen Isabella said. "And at first, I believed it to be so. How could a mere man slip through the royal residence and avoid the guards?"

"But—"

"My first impulse was to scream. Yet something about the man's calmness . . ." Queen Isabella smiled in recollection. "This man informed me that my son Edward had been taken. King Edward was at the country estate, and I was alone, except for the guards roaming the castle, but I did not panic. There was a gentleness about this man.

"He invited me to see for myself if the baby was gone, that he would be waiting for my return to the royal chambers. He was not afraid, this man, for he said that if he had lied, I could call the guards. He told me if Edward truly had been taken, however, it would be in my best interest to hear the story. The baby was gone from the nursery, and I returned without calling alarm. And I listened.

"That mysterious stranger informed me of a plot against the throne," Queen Isabella continued. "A Druid plot. Understandably, I found the thought ridiculous. Druids were a myth, a superstition, I told him."

Baby Edward began to cry. Katherine rocked him, but to no avail.

Queen Isabella turned away from Waleran and held out her arms for the child.

"Sir William," she said over her shoulder, "my son needs me. If you would care to finish."

"With pleasure, milady."

Sir William had again drawn his sword.

"Waleran, or . . ." Sir William paused as he lifted the sword, "would you prefer the Duke of Whittingham, short-lived as I pray that title may be?"

Waleran sank until he was sitting, back against the wall.

"We knew that someone in the royal court was a Druid," Sir William said. "Thomas and Katherine were sent merely to force that Druid—you—into action. We knew that it would be of utmost importance to prevent the slightest hint of Druids from reaching the king's ears."

Waleran groaned. "You fully expected Katherine and Thomas to be thrown into the Tower."

"Waleran," Sir William said, "not once, but twice did you rely on knowledge gained from conversations you overheard in prison, in Magnus and in York. Once too, you used the trick of letting a foe escape, simply to follow. We thought it likely the same ploy would be used again."

"You knew I was the king's chamberlain?"

Sir William shook his head. "Thomas's father suspected. He had been traveling England for years as an old man."

"No!" Again a flash of fear. "I tell you, he is dead."

A tall man walked into the cave from where he had been waiting in the shadows of the entrance.

"If I am dead," he replied to Waleran, "then let me be your most persistent nightmare."

Waleran moaned. "I thought you dead when we conquered Magnus. Later, I knew you traveled in disguise, but I thought I'd finally beaten you outside York, when Thomas led my soldiers to your campsite."

"I am most definitely alive." Hawkwood bowed to Queen Isabella. "Your majesty . . ."

She smiled in return.

And how can she help but smile, Katherine thought. *For this man is as handsome as his son, Thomas, with the same hint of mystery and confidence, the same air of gentleness and compassion.*

"Lord Hawkwood," the queen said, "I am pleased to discover my trust in you was not misplaced."

"It was a near thing, was it not? For a moment, you nearly impaled me."

The baby was quiet now, and Queen Isabella turned her attention again to Waleran.

"Lord Hawkwood offered to place his life in my hands. In my royal chambers that dawn, he opened my palm, set the handle of a short dagger upon my skin, closed my fingers over the dagger, and brought my hand up so that the dagger touched his throat. He told me if I chose to disbelieve him, I could end his life right there. But if I believed, I was to arrange for a trip into the countryside, as if distraught over the kidnapping, and, unknown to King Edward, attend my own son here, while we waited."

"For me," Waleran blurted. "You expected me to arrive."

Katherine cleared her throat. "Yes. Thomas shouted at the entrance to this valley. We feared you might not have managed to follow. Then we waited at the river by the abbey, once again giving you time. Finally, we talked loudly in front of the entrance to this very cave. All to lure you inside."

Waleran lifted his head. An animal-like gleam, almost insanity, suddenly filled his eyes.

"My army outside! I may die here, but you cannot escape."

"You no longer have an army outside." By the softness of Thomas's words, Katherine knew he felt pity for the completeness of the destruction of their enemy.

"We expected you, did we not?" Thomas asked. "Many more than twenty of the finest men of Magnus were hidden in these woods. Your army has long since fallen to ambush."

They gathered—the five of them and baby Edward—in the abbey hall that evening.

Queen Isabella was given the chair closest to the fire. She and the baby were wrapped in blankets; for although it was July, the evening chill in the northern valley had a bite, especially in the abbey hall with a cold stone floor and no heavy tapestries to slow any drafts.

Sir William was pacing the room slowly, a man of coiled energy still restless after the day's events, even with Waleran and his army safely captured.

Lord Hawkwood crouched on his knees, poking an iron into the fire to rearrange the burning wood.

Katherine and Thomas sat next to each other, opposite Queen Isabella.

They had gathered at the request of the queen.

"What will draw the remaining Druid leaders to this valley?" she asked. The question was asked softly, yet Katherine sensed the steel behind it.

"Your majesty?" Lord Hawkwood expressed puzzlement, without shifting from his position near the fire.

"I have agreed to give as many men as you deem necessary to capture all the Druids who arrive in the next weeks, but I wish to know what they seek."

Sir William stopped his pacing and stood behind Thomas.

"It is the book in that cave, I believe," Queen Isabella continued. "And you all seek to avoid the subject. I find it both amusing and strange that so much has been revealed about the Druids and so little about yourselves, the Merlins."

She smiled, but it did not rob the strength of her implied command to tell her all.

"You see the last of the Merlins here in this room," Lord Hawkwood said without self-pity, "so there is little to say about us."

Katherine held her breath. *Will Queen Isabella press the issue?*

Lord Hawkwood continued smoothly. "However, as you have guessed, it is the book which is of utmost importance."

"You have a habit of intriguing me," Queen Isabella said. "Please, go on."

Sir William stood. "I have brought the book from the trunk in the cave. Perhaps now is the time to deliver it to her majesty."

When Lord Hawkwood nodded, Sir William left the room, and Lord Hawkwood closed his eyes to think as he spoke. "It begins with an explorer named Marco Polo. . . ."

"Yes." Queen Isabella nodded. "The name is familiar. He dictated a book—*Description of the World*, I believe—while in prison."

"It is remarkable that you know that," Lord Hawkwood said, eyes now open. "His book is gaining popularity only now."

"Not remarkable at all. Coincidence. The man who transcribed the dictation, a romance writer named Rusticello of Pisa, spent time under the patronage of King Edward, my father-in-law. Royal courts all over Europe have copies of this book."

Lord Hawkwood grinned. "Then, milady, you shall readily understand what follows. As you know, Marco Polo explored Cathay, the unknown lands of the Far East. His patron was the great Kublai Khan, ruler of the Mongols. Polo received a golden passport from Khan, and for twenty years traveled safely through that land, recording everything he saw."

Queen Isabella nodded impatiently. "He beheld wonders, to be sure. I am told the people there have yellow skin and slanted eyes, and are extremely intelligent."

She waited while Sir William rejoined them, a large, leather-bound sheaf of parchments in his hand.

"But what," she asked, "has Marco Polo to do with *your* book here, a book to draw Druids like flies to honey."

"Consider this, your majesty. What if Polo recorded other books, not merely fanciful tales of the exotic, but books with the most advanced science of this world, books with secrets so powerful that kingdoms might rise and fall upon them?"

"I find that difficult to believe."

Lord Hawkwood turned to Thomas. "Please bring some of the exploding powder."

Thomas left silently and returned several minutes later with a small leather bag. Lord Hawkwood reached in and removed a pinched portion of dark powder.

"Potassium, your majesty," he explained. "Sulfur and charcoal.

Ingredients easily obtained."

Lord Hawkwood poured a tiny trail of the powder onto the floor, near the fireplace. He twisted a twig loose from a nearby log, held it in the fire until it was lit, then touched that small flame to the line of powder.

Even though Katherine knew what to expect, she still marveled at the small, flaring explosion of light and sound.

Lord Hawkwood turned back to Queen Isabella. His face was blackened with smudge.

"Exploding powder. The people of Cathay invented it centuries ago, yet we in Europe have no knowledge of it. Marco Polo deliberately omitted it from his descriptions of that land, and for good reason. Imagine the possibilities. If such power would be harnessed by men of evil . . . "

"It saved our lives," Thomas said.

Queen Isabella shifted her eyes to him.

"In the Holy Land," Thomas said, "Father had lined a pit with it. When it flared in the darkness, all the bandits panicked. We succeeded in our attack."

Queen Isabella nodded. "I understand. This book of yours, if it contains many more such secrets, would be as valuable as a kingdom." Then she asked sharply. "How is it that you have it?"

"The Roman church confiscated it for fear of what it might accomplish and destroy," Lord Hawkwood answered. "In my own travels after the fall of Magnus, I heard rumors of it, and . . ."

Lord Hawkwood appealed to the queen. "I would prefer not to say how it was obtained, only that I had it sent here, to this abbey, where Thomas was to be raised, away from the eyes of Druids. He would need what he learned from the book to regain Magnus."

"I will not press you for that secret," Queen Isabella said. "There is enough pain in your eyes, and you are a man of honor."

Lord Hawkwood nodded thanks.

"And the book is now mine?" Queen Isabella asked.

"If you wish," Lord Hawkwood replied.

"Why would I not wish?"

"If it falls into the wrong hands . . ." Lord Hawkwood struggled for words. "Knowledge of such a book will drive many men to desperate measures to obtain it. As it did the Druids. And in the wrong hands, a civilization may be shattered.

"Examine the politics of our day. The balances of power from country to country are so delicately held. Your husband may choose to take the secrets of this book and fight more than just the Scots. Other kings may begin wars to obtain the knowledge. After all, men have fought before for much less reason . . . even this exploding powder can kill men by the dozens, while ordinary warfare is much more humane."

He pointed at the baby sleeping in Queen Isabella's arms. "Too many die to leave the fatherless behind. Perhaps we can delay the advance of knowledge which might be used by evil men."

Queen Isabella stared at Lord Hawkwood and said nothing.

The fire crackled and popped several times in the silence.

"You have done so much for us," she said. "King Edward, of course, will end the Druid uprising. In secrecy, of course. It would do little good for the people to be stirred by these matters."

She hugged her baby. "You have ensured that my son will inherit a kingdom, that revolt will not tear this land apart. And now, you offer this book—not copied, I presume, by any hands."

"You presume correctly," Lord Hawkwood said.

Queen Isabella looked from one to the other, gazing first at Katherine, then Thomas, then Sir William and, finally, Lord Hawkwood.

"Because of this secrecy, history will not record what you have accomplished, and that fills me with sadness. You are worthy of much more." She nodded at the book. "And we will engage in this final act of secrecy."

Several more heartbeats.

"Thomas," Queen Isabella then said softly, "cast the book into the fire."

CHAPTER

63

C ontrary to what you might think," Lord Hawkwood said with a smile at Thomas, "we are not ready to depart this abbey for Magnus."

Thomas innocently raised an eyebrow. "Oh? Queen Isabella was satisfied that no more Druid leaders would arrive. Surely there remains nothing for us here."

They stood along the river in front of the abbey hall, the midmorning sun warming their backs.

Much had been accomplished. Day after day in the last two weeks, solitary travelers had arrived in the valley. Without fail, when captured, each had pleaded innocent to the charges of Druid conspiracy; but Waleran, as part of a desperate bargain to save his own life, had identified each as a Druid.

The full horror of the Druid circle had been exposed in those two weeks.

Again and again, Queen Isabella had murmured shock and surprise. Many she knew from their positions of power—magistrates, sheriffs, priests, knights, and even earls and dukes. Now, all were stripped of their wealth and imprisoned. In one swoop, most of the Druids across the land had been taken.

Beyond that, Queen Isabella pledged to begin action against remaining Druids who falsely posed as priests in the northern towns. Not only would the spread of their power be contained, but the base they had established in the last few years would be eliminated.

"Thomas," Lord Hawkwood said in a mock stern voice, "were you raised a Merlin?"

Thomas grinned and nodded. He enjoyed knowing he could not, even in jest, fool the man in front of him.

Strange, he thought, *to one day suddenly be forced to consider a stranger as flesh-and-blood father. Especially a man accustomed to shrouding himself in mystery.*

Yet the bond had formed. And Thomas felt himself flushing at the implied compliment.

"Yes, I was raised a Merlin," he replied.

"Tell me then, instead of pretending ignorance in hopes of hearing me prattle, why is it that we are not ready to depart."

Thomas looked beyond his father's shoulder at the high walls of the abbey and at the tiny window he had so often used for escape in the days he believed he was an orphan.

"We are not ready to depart because there remains something for us here. Something we could not seek until Queen Isabella departed, for she should not know of it."

"Ummm." Lord Hawkwood was noncommittal.

Thomas grinned again in pleasure. As before, in his childhood. Exercises of the mind. Tests of logic.

"Sarah would have enjoyed this." The words came from his mouth even as they reached his thoughts. He stopped, suddenly awkward. Always, deep inside, there was the ache that she was gone.

"I grieve too," Lord Hawkwood said in the lengthening silence. "Perhaps that is the highest tribute . . . to never be forgotten."

A tiny roe deer moved from the nearby trees, hesitant at first, then confident that it was alone. Thomas clapped, and the deer scrambled sideways and almost fell. The effect was so comical that each snorted with laughter.

"Life," Lord Hawkwood said. "The past should not prevent us from looking ahead and drinking fully from life, from enjoying each moment as it arrives."

Thomas let out a deep breath. "Yes."

"And one looks forward to drinking deeply this cup with Katherine?"

Thomas coughed. "Our reason for delaying departure?" he said quickly. " You were testing my observations."

Lord Hawkwood did not pursue the subject of Katherine, and instead nodded.

"There had to be more reason for the Druids to arrive here than a single book," Thomas said. "For many of these men, it involved the risk of travel and the need to explain a lengthy absence. No, there must be more."

"An interesting theory," Lord Hawkwood said. "What might you guess?"

"Before I answer," Thomas challenged, "I have my own question for you."

Lord Hawkwood waited.

"What," Thomas began, "is the single most powerful weapon available to men?"

"Not swords."

Thomas nodded.

"Not arrows. Not catapults."

Thomas nodded again.

"Not any physical means of destruction. For with the invention of each new weapon, there will be a countering defense."

"So . . ." Thomas bantered.

"So, as you full well know, my son, our greatest power is knowledge. In warfare. In business. In the affairs of our own lives. In the defense of our faith. Without knowledge, we are nothing."

Thomas pointed at the tiny window high on the abbey wall. "Were we to wager today my odds of answering your question, I would have an unfair advantage. For last night, as I puzzled yet again what might draw so many Druids to this valley, I returned to the bedchamber of my childhood."

Lord Hawkwood straightened with sudden interest. "You have not discovered—"

Thomas grinned mischief. "Ho, ho! The student knows something the teacher does not. Surely you speak the truth that knowledge is power!"

"Thomas, tell me!"

"In the Holy Land," Thomas said, "Sir William informed me that I held the final secret to the battle. Yet I had no inkling of what he might mean.

"Sir William had returned from exile in the Holy Land to spend time in Magnus with me," he said. "Had the final secret been there, he would have claimed it then. Moreover, had this mysterious object of great value been there, the Druids, who held Magnus for a generation, would have claimed it. Instead, since my departure from this abbey, both sides—Druid and Merlin—have been intent on learning the secret from me, a secret I did not know I possessed. I can only conclude that whatever it is has lain here at the abbey."

Lord Hawkwood nodded.

"Indeed," Thomas continued, "if you yourself do not know where it is located, I must conclude that it had been sent to Sarah, along with the book she chose to hide in the cave."

Again Lord Hawkwood nodded.

"Whatever this secret is," Thomas concluded, "Sarah hid it before her death. Whatever this secret is, the Druids were willing—no, desperate—to each undertake a journey from their separate parts of England."

Thomas smiled. "Every night, Sarah would sit beside my bed and help me with my prayers, or sing quiet songs of knights performing valiant deeds. And every night, her final words as I fell to sleep never varied: 'Thomas, my love, sleep upon the wings of light.' Each night she would simply smile when I asked what that meant."

His focus shifted from the hills to his father's face.

Lord Hawkwood began to smile too.

"Yes," Thomas said. "Your words to me at the gallows, as a mysterious man hidden beneath cloak and hood, were almost the same."

"Bring the wings of dawn's light," Lord Hawkwood's voice was almost a whisper, "into this age of darkness."

"Knowledge," Thomas said. "The knowledge accumulated by generations of Merlins."

"Yes, Thomas," Lord Hawkwood said. "Merlin himself founded Magnus as a place to conduct our hidden warfare against the Druids. Yet he destined us for more. To search the world for what men knew. And to save that knowledge from the darkness of the destruction of barbarians."

Lord Hawkwood's voice became sad. "Time and again throughout history, gentle scholars have suffered loss to men of swords. Great libraries have been burned and looted, the records of civilizations and their accomplishments and advances wiped from the face of the earth. Few today know of the wondrous pyramids of the ancient Egyptians, of the mathematics and astronomy of the ancient Greeks, of the healing medicines of, yes, the Druids, and of the aqueducts and roads of the Romans."

In a flash, Thomas understood. "Merlins of each generation

traveled the world and returned with written record of what they had discovered."

"When Magnus fell," Lord Hawkwood said, "it was more important than our lives to save the books which contained this knowledge. That is why so many of us died. Your mother and I, Sir William, and a few others escaped with the books of these centuries of knowledge, while the rest gave their lives. Why did each Druid willingly undertake a journey here when given the message by Waleran? Each assumed, rightly, there would be spoils easily divided. Books beyond value. One, two, perhaps more books for each. Books which can be duplicated only through years of transcribing."

"Father," Thomas said quickly, because now, seeing the worry on his father's face, he found no joy in prolonging his news, "the books you sent to this abbey are safe."

"Yes?"

"Sleep upon the wings of light," Thomas said. "What better place to hide something than in the open? My mattress was placed upon a great trunk, placed so that its edges hid the lid. Anyone would think it only a convenient pedestal to keep a sleeping child away from nighttime rats. But on that trunk, I truly did sleep upon the wings of light."

EPİLOGUE

As Thomas knelt, he thrilled to the touch of the sword atop his shoulder.

It was a private and quiet ceremony in the uppermost chambers of the castle of Magnus, with Sir William, Lord Hawkwood and, of course, Katherine, who held the sword.

"This is our own form of knighthood," she said softly. "An unseen badge of honor."

"It is enough," Thomas replied as he rose. "Worth more than the knighthood granted by Queen Isabella, more than this kingdom officially given us by her royal charter."

Thomas felt a sorrow, however, for just as the continued existence of Merlins had been kept from Queen Isabella, so too must he keep this part of his life hidden from those who waited below in the great hall to begin a feast of homecoming for him.

Tiny John, now bigger than the rascal sprout Thomas remembered from before his exile. Robert of Uleran, the valiant sheriff of Magnus who had survived the imprisonment and resisted all promises of the Druid priests. The earl of York, joyful to have his earldom returned. Gervaise, a man of simple faith who had often comforted Thomas and provided him escape from Magnus at the price of a terrible beating by the Druid high priests. And a magnificent dog, the puppy Thomas had taken across half a world, then brought back again from St. Jean d'Acre.

"Our task is not complete." Lord Hawkwood interrupted Thomas's thoughts. "For I cannot believe that the Druid circle will not somehow, sometime, begin to rebuild."

He smiled. "But I believe that we as Merlins will now be able to continue our task, searching and keeping the treasures of knowledge, and passing that task to future generations."

His voice grew fuller as he spoke with passion. "There will be a day," he said, "when a renaissance, a rebirth of sharing of ideas, will take all of us forward into the dawning of a better age. Until then, let us ensure that Magnus stands quiet, unknown, and on guard against the age of darkness."

Sir William began to laugh.

"Well spoken, Lord Hawkwood," Sir William finally said, through a broad smile. "Bur first we need future generations. And I will not see our task complete until you and I become grandfathers."

Katherine giggled.

Thomas felt his jaw gape open. *To be sure*, he thought in confusion, *Katherine and I have pledged marriage, but we have not yet spoken of children.*

"What is this of which you speak?" he blurted out to Sir William. "If—"

"When," Katherine corrected.

"When," Thomas said, "our marriage results in . . . in . . . little ones, it strikes me that Lord Hawkwood alone will become a grandfather. Who is it that *you*, Sir William, expect to arrive with a babe in swaddling clothes to provide you a grandchild?"

Lord Hawkwood began to laugh in great gales. Sir William joined him, then Katherine.

Thomas fought bewilderment.

Finally, he roared to be heard above the laughter.

"What is it?" Sir William found his voice. "Thomas," he said, "you showed such insight into untangling the past, we all assumed you knew."

"Knew what?" Thomas snapped. Mirth had reddened all their faces, and he did not enjoy being the source of their amusement.

Sir William moved closer and embraced him, then stood back.

"Thomas," he said, "Katherine is my daughter. Born, as you were, during exile in the Holy Land."

"But . . . but . . . " Thomas sputtered.

"Yes," Sir William said. "It will be I who gives her hand away in marriage, as you two begin to reign over Magnus. And, Thomas?"

"Yes?"

"I could not think of another man I would welcome more as my son than Thomas, lord and earl of Magnus."

HiSTORiCAL ПOTES

For 2,000 years, far north and east of London, the ancient English towns of Pickering, Thirsk, and Helmsley, and their castles have guarded a line on the lowland plains between the larger centers of Scarborough and York.

In the beginning Scarborough, with its high North Sea cliffs, was a Roman signal post. From there, sentries could easily see approaching barbarian ships, and were able to relay messages from Pickering to Helmsley to Thirsk, the entire fifty miles inland to the boundary outpost of York, where other troops waited, always ready, for any inland invasions.

When their empire fell, the Romans in England succumbed to the Anglo-Saxons, great, savage brutes in tribal units who conquered as warriors and over the generations became farmers. The Anglo-Saxons in turn suffered defeat by raiding Vikings, who in turn lost to the Norman knights with their thundering war-horses.

Through those hundreds and hundreds of years, that line from Scarborough to York never diminished in importance.

Some of England's greatest and richest abbeys accumulated their wealth on the lowland plains along that line. Rievaulx Abbey, just outside Helmsley, housed 250 monks and owned vast estates of land that held over 13,000 sheep.

But directly north lay the moors. No towns or abbeys tamed the moors, which reached east to the craggy cliffs of the cold, gray North Sea. Each treeless and windswept moor plunged into deep, dividing valleys of lush greenness that only made the heather-covered heights appear more harsh. The ancients called these North York moors "Blackamoor." Thus, in the medieval age of chivalry, 250 years after the Norman knights had toppled the English throne, this remoteness and isolation protected Blackamoor's earldom of Magnus from the prying eyes of King Edward II and the rest of his royal court in London.

As a kingdom within a kingdom, Magnus was small in comparison to the holdings of England's greater earls. This smallness was its protection. Hard to reach and easy to defend, British and Scottish kings chose to overlook it; in practical terms, it had as much independence as a separate country.

Magnus still had size, however. Its castle commanded and protected a large village and many vast moors. Each valley between the moors averaged a full day's travel by foot. Atop the moors, great flocks of sheep grazed on the tender, green shoots of heather. The valley interiors supported cattle and cultivated plots of land farmed by peasants nearly made slaves by the yearly tribute exacted from their crops. In short, with sheep and wool and cattle and land, Magnus was an earldom well worth ruling.

In the period in which this book is set, children were considered adults much earlier than now. By church law, for example, a bride had to be at least twelve, a bridegroom fourteen. It is not so unusual, then, to think of Thomas of Magnus becoming accepted as a leader at an early age. Moreover, other "men" also became leaders at remarkably young ages during those times. King Richard II, for example, was only fourteen years old when he rode out to face the leaders of the Peasant's Revolt in 1381.

Those interested in ancient times should know that Magnus itself, as a fictional setting, cannot be found in any history book. Nor, of course, can Thomas be found, or Katherine, Hawkwood, Sir William, and others among Thomas's friends or foes. Yet many of the more famous people and events throughout the story of Magnus did shape the times of that world. Accordingly, here are historical notes on some of those people and events.

CHAPTER ONE

Although there is no specific mention of an eclipse at this time in historical records, it does not necessarily mean that the eclipse did not occur. Scientific observations were almost nonexistent, and a partial eclipse could well have briefly darkened that part of England without an official recording.

CHAPTER FIVE

Gunpowder had been used by the Chinese since the tenth century A.D., but it was not until the year 1313 that any European "discovered" its explosive power; credit for its invention is commonly given to a German friar named Berthold Schwarz. Is it possible, however, that knowledge of its ingredients may have been known to other Europeans shortly before that time?

CHAPTER SIX

Wades Causeway is a preserved stretch of Roman road which may still be traveled today in the Wheeldale Moor of the Yorkshire area of England. It was built almost 2,000 years ago by the first Roman soldiers to reach Yorkshire in the year A.D. 70, and probably reached all the way to the coast. One of the reasons for the great success of the Roman soldiers as they conquered all of England was their roads, which let them move their armies with great efficiency.

The number of fighting knights in England by the year 1300 has been estimated to be only 500 to 1,000. Other landowners were called knights because they owed military service to the barons and kings above them, but they were country gentlemen, not members of a military elite.

A barbican was an outwork of stone built to protect the gatehouse or entrance into the castle grounds. Sometimes it was a wall of stone leading up to the gatehouse; later, as barbicans became more elaborate with their own turrets and drawbridges, they actually became outer gatehouses.

Although some scholars disagree, it is commonly held that Sun Tzu, a Chinese general and military genius who lived hundreds of years before Christ was born, compiled a book of his military theories and philosophies. This book has survived relatively unchanged for over 2,000 years. It is probable that he is the "greatest general of a faraway land" to which Thomas refers in his thoughts. Today, readers may find Sun Tzu's military advice in a book titled *The Art of War*, a book which General Norman Schwarzkopf made mandatory reading for the troops during the Gulf War of 1991.

CHAPTER ELEVEN

Marco Polo is the Italian explorer who reached Cathay (now known as China) in the year 1275. He served the Mongolian ruler Kublai Khan for many years, and returned to Venice in the year 1295. During his travels, Marco Polo noted the Chinese custom of sending a huge man-carrying kite into the air before a ship set sail on a long voyage.

CHAPTER FIFTEEN

Even by the year 1312, York was already an ancient and major center in northwestern England. Located roughly eighteen miles south of Helmsley, the site of the gallows of Chapter 1, York was an outpost for Roman soldiers 1,250 years before the times in which Thomas of Magnus lived. Any single man given jurisdiction over this city and surrounding area would have considerable power.

The Scots posed a serious threat to the English King Edward II, who reigned from 1307 to 1327. Robert Bruce, crowned King of Scotland in 1306, nearly lost Scotland in his first battle against the English because of the leadership of Edward II's father, King Edward I. When Edward I died in July 1307, Robert Bruce was able to oppose the weaker Edward II, and began a series of successful battles. In the years 1312 to 1314, Bruce defeated a series of English strongholds, and the restoration of English power in Scotland became an impossibility. In 1318, the Scots finally captured the castle of Berwick on the English border and from there were easily able to raid as far south as the Yorkshire area.

CHAPTER SEVENTEEN

It may be of interest to note that in 1297, Edward I's royal army in Flanders consisted of 7,810 foot soldiers and 895 cavalry, of which only 140 were knights.

At that time, the knight carried shield, lance, and sword into battle. His basic armor was a suit of chain mail, reinforced with steel plates at the knees and shoulders. During the 1300's, plating gradually began to replace chain mail as protection, until eventually, in the 1400's, knights were slow and heavy with complete body plating, and shields were no longer needed.

While the concept of reinforced bows was definitely unusual to English archers during Thomas's time, other cultures, as far back as the ancient Egyptians, had experimented with bronze or bone plating, to add strength to wood.

CHAPTER NINETEEN

The isle of the Celts is known today as Ireland.

The earliest known records of Druids come from the third century B.C. According to the Roman general Julius Caesar (who is the principle source of today's information on Druids), this group of men studied ancient verse, natural philosophy, astronomy, and the lore of the gods. The principal doctrine of the Druids was that souls were immortal and passed at death from one person to another.

Druids offered human victims for those who were in danger of death in battle or who were gravely ill. They sacrificed these victims by burning them in huge wickerwork images.

The Druids were suppressed in ancient Britain by the Roman conquerors in the first century A.D. If, indeed, the cult survived, it must have had to remain as secret as it was during Thomas's time.

Today, followers of the Druid cult may still be found in England worshipping the ancient ruins of Stonehenge at certain times of the year.

CHAPTER TWENTY

The battle tactic which Thomas used to conquer a larger force was not new. Readers today may find in *The Art of War* the same tactic used more than 2,000 years ago by the Chinese military genius Sun Tzu.

CHAPTER TWENTY-FOUR

For hundreds of years before Thomas's time, it had been commonly accepted that God would judge the criminally accused through trial by ordeal or trial by battle. In trial by ordeal, the defendant was made to undergo a severe physical test, such as burning or drowning. In trial by battle, the defendant faced his accuser in combat, usually with blunt weapons; the loser would be judged guilty and would often be hanged as a result.

In the year 1215, trial by ordeal was officially banished by the church. It would not be strange, however, for the people of Magnus to accept a self-imposed trial by ordeal or its deemed judgment, especially the one dramatically proposed by Thomas. Superstition was never very far from the people, and trial by ordeals always promised great entertainment.

CHAPTER TWENTY-FIVE

Caltrops were four-pronged spikes, much like the modern day "jacks" (except much sharper) of a game sometimes played by children with a ball.

The British Museum in London does have caltrops on exhibit, remnants of the ones used by Roman soldiers to break up calvary charges.

Yew trees are found throughout the Northern Hemisphere. All but the red fruit of the plant is poisonous to humans. The poison contained is taxine. Symptoms of poisoning include nausea, giddiness, and weakness, followed by convulsions, shock, coma, and death.

Poison ingested in smoke from the yew tree, especially concentrated in the narrow upward tunnel leading into the belfry, may well have caused the "supernatural" daytime appearance and death of the bats, especially since low concentrations could harm the smaller mammals.

There is, however, another possibility, one which has interesting implications perhaps unknown to Thomas. The oleander, or Jericho Rose, a shrub which normally favors hot, southern climates, also releases a poisonous smoke when burned.

CHAPTER TWENTY-SIX

During medieval times, two main meals were served in the castle keep. Dinner was at 10 or 11 a.m., and supper was at 5 p.m. Forks had not been invented yet. Plates were not common; instead, thick slabs of bread called "trenchers" generally held the day's food.

Chapter Twenty-Eight

In the early part of King Henry II's reign, a certain clergyman in Bedford slew a knight. Despite overwhelming evidence, he was found innocent in the bishop's court, and had the gall to then insult a royal judge sent to investigate the matter.

Chapter Twenty-Nine

It is difficult for historians to agree on the historical King Arthur. Most scholars now regard Arthur's reality as probable; it is commonly held that he was born around 480.

Some argue that the castle of Camelot existed at Cadbury in southern England, while others choose nearby Glastonbury. Historians do agree, however, that the legends about King Arthur (known as the Arthurian Romances) were finally put to paper by various poets in the twelfth and thirteenth centuries, some seven centuries after the Round Table.

Most of what the old woman relates about the Holy Grail is part of the legend which historians today know circulated from the twelfth century on, as part of the Arthurian Romances.

As the old woman tells Thomas, the Holy Grail is thought to be the cup used by Christ at the Last Supper. Yet is must be emphasized the Holy Grail is legend, not biblical truth. There is no single, clearly defined image of the Grail, or evidence it ever existed. In fact, even its outward shape is debated. Is it a cup? A shallow dish? A stone? A jewel? Despite, or because of, the lack of historical truth surrounding the Holy Grail, its legend held much sway over the ignorant peasants of Thomas's time, much to the dissatisfaction of the church.

A discerning reader might express amazement that in an age of wide illiteracy, an old beggar woman might know so much about the Holy Grail.

This is not surprising, however. The legend of the Holy Grail was a well-established oral myth, and stories were commonly passed from generation to generation.

Indeed, the woman's surprise at Thomas's pretended lack of knowledge is more appropriate; but Thomas, of course, wanted to discover how much influence the false priests might have among his people.

In other versions of the legend, Joseph of Arimathea does not go any farther than Europe, and the cup instead is passed on to a man named Bron, who becomes known as the Rich Fisher. It was told that he received this name because he had fed many from the Grail with a single fish. Bron and his company then settled at Avaron, whom many identify with Avalon/Glastonbury.

CHAPTER THIRTY

Constructed of stone, Norman churches were often built upon the ruins of the earlier and wooden Anglo-Saxon churches. Early churches generally consisted of the nave where people stood for the services, and a small chancel at the east of the church for the altar and priest. As time passed, towers, aisles, priests' rooms, and chapels were often added. Thus, the quieter eastern end of the church building of Magnus held the original altar.

CHAPTER THIRTY-THREE

Katherine was correct to express surprise at the existence of books so far from the libraries of kings or of rich monasteries. Books could only be duplicated through laborious hand-copying. They were so rare and valuable that some historians estimated that before Gutenberg invented the press in the early 1400's, the number of books in all of Europe only numbered in the thousands—fewer than the number found today in a single standard elementary school!

CHAPTER THIRTY-FOUR

Even today, the religious miracle of unclotting blood is hailed each year in Naples, Italy, as it has been for more than 600 years. Believers there say a sealed sample of clotted blood of Saint Januarius (martyred in the year 305) has turned into liquid each year since 1389, and the event now draws thousands, as well as a television audience numbering in the millions.

Scientists, however, claim this jamlike gel may simply consist of a mixture of chalk and hydrated iron choride lightly sprinkled with salt, a substance they say could have easily been produced by medieval alchemists.

As for the weeping statue, it is probable that the effects of condensation brought on by quick changes from heat to cold were little understood by the illiterate masses of peasants.

CHAPTER THIRTY-FIVE

Modern day York in the North York moors is a substantial city; but its inner core is still marked by the thick walls of ancient York, walls which still bear some of the chambers mentioned in this chapter.

Beheading traitors and leaving their heads for all to see was common and, unfortunately, one of the more merciful ways of dealing with rebels.

CHAPTER THIRTY-NINE

Because of widespread poverty and because of the severity of prescribed punishments for theft, outlaws were common during these times. Many faced death for crimes no more terrible than poaching the king's deer. As a result, those who escaped often banded together and lived on the edge of desperation.

While historians cannot establish whether an actual historical character forms a basis for the many tales collected about him, it is not unbelievable that the outlaw Robert who rescued Katherine was indeed the legendary Robin Hood.

Several possible facts point to this. By the nineteenth century, some historians fixed Robin as one Robert Hood who joined Thomas, earl of Lancaster, in his 1322 uprising against Edward II. This fits with the first datable reference to Robin/Robert Hood, a Yorkshire place name. The Stone of Robin Hood is cited in a document of 1322.

The thirty-eight ballads about Robin Hood place him either in the forests of Sherwood, in Nottinghamshire, or in the Yorkshire forests of Barndale.

As with many heroes of legend, Robin Hood has been placed in various time periods in different ballads; some historians identify Robin Hood with the twelfth century King Richard I.

However, if the outlaw Robert Hood, so gallant to Katherine, is indeed the Robin Hood of legend, it is not improbable that in the late spring of 1313 he would reign over his band of men in the Yorkshire forests near York, some nine years before some historians place him farther away in Yorkshire's Barndale forests.

CHAPTER FORTY

As the Vikings lost control of the North Seas late in the eleventh century, sea trade grew safer, and merchants began to need roomier vessels to carry larger shipments. By the year 1200, northern shipbuilders had developed the cog, which was the standard merchant and war vessel for the next 200 years. One of the most dramatic improvements of the cog was the rudder, a new kind of steering apparatus attached to the rear of the boat, and much stronger and more efficient for directing the boat than oars.

As Thomas notes, it was common for the merchant ships to belong to foreign exporters of wool, such as the French, Belgians, or Italians.

CHAPTER FORTY-FOUR

Merlin, legend tells us, was first an adviser to the King Uther Pendragon, King Arthur's father, and then an adviser to King Arthur himself. Merlin was known as the prophet of the Holy Grail—perhaps not a coincidence in light of the Druid attempts to use the Holy Grail to gain power. Finally, Merlin was legendary as a court magician or enchanter, something not unlikely for a man with the knowledge of science available to the Druids. Through his advice to Kind Uther Pendragon, Merlin was responsible for the formation of the Knights of the Round Table.

Is it a remarkable coincidence that Alcuin from York is found in the history books as the educated adviser summoned by Charles the Great, or Charlemagne, the famous ruler of the Franks (Germany) in the late 700s? Alcuin helped teach all the monks and priests in Charles the Great's empire learn to read and write. He also introduced a new style of handwriting known as Carolingian Minuscule, which used small letters and was quicker and easier than writing in capitals.

CHAPTER FORTY-SIX

The Crusades were a series of religious wars from the First Crusade in 1095 to the Eighth Crusade in 1270. These wars were organized by European powers to recover from the Muslim infidels the Christian holy places in Palestine, especially the holy city, Jerusalem. Many of the crusaders believed that if they died in battle, their souls would be taken straight to heaven.

Gradually, towards the end of the 1200s, the Muslims reconquered all the cities which had been taken from them St. Jean d'Acre, the common destination for all ships bearing crusaders, was the last to fall to the Muslims and remained in Christian hands until the year 1291.

CHAPTER FORTY-EIGHT

A warrior race of Muslim Egypt, the Mamelukes were originally non-Arab slaves to Egyptian rulers. They overthrew their rulers in the middle of the 1200s. Not only did they prove to be too powerful for the crusaders, but they were the only people to ever defeat a Mongol invasion—in the year 1260.

CHAPTER FIFTY-ONE

Sir William's fear of a small group of men taking control to bring evil upon an entire country is not unfounded, especially in light of the horrible events of recent history. Adolf Hitler, for example, as a single leader atop a pyramid of power, delivered and preached a message of racial hatred that managed to manipulate thousands of ordinary people into assisting in the murder of millions of innocent Jews.

Probably because of his excellent Merlin education, Sir William is acutely accurate in his observation of the Dark Ages, the term commonly given to the years 500-1000 A.D. These were centuries of decline across Europe, mostly attributed to the fall of the Roman

Empire, which left a vacuum of power that encouraged civil wars and stifled classical culture. This lack of education among the common people and the suspicion between countries prevented the sharing of ideas, especially in the arts, science, navigation, and medicine. Interestingly enough, what culture there was remained preserved in remnants by monks of Ireland, Italy, France, and Britain. Not until the Renaissance (1350-1650) did modern civilization begin to flourish, as men across Europe began again to strive to learn and share ideas.

CHAPTER FIFTY-TWO

Papermaking was invented in China in 100 B.C., another Chinese invention that remained unknown to the Europeans for hundreds of years. The Arabs learned how to make paper by questioning Chinese prisoners of war in 768. From there, it spread throughout the Arab Empire, which at that time included Spain. From Spain, papermaking finally spread to the rest of Europe.

Historical record confirms Hawkwood's research and shows that the Second Jewish Revolt took place in 132 A.D. and lasted for three and one-half years. Cassius Dio, a Roman historian as noted in the letter, wrote a brief notice of the war which has survived to this day. In this notice, Dio relates that toward the end of the rebellion, Roman legionnaires were unable to engage the Jews in open battle because of the rough terrain, and instead were forced to hunt them down in small groups in the caves where they hid, and starve them out. Cassius Dio describes the final results this way: "Fifty of their [the Jews] most important outposts and 985 of their most famous villages were razed to the ground; 580,000 men were slain in the various raids and battles, and the number of those who perished by famine, disease, and fire was past finding out. Thus nearly the whole of Judea was made desolate." In the nearby slave markets, there was such a surplus of Jews to be sold as slaves that the price of Jews dropped lower than that of horses.

As also noted in the letter, the Roman general Julius Severus was summoned from Britain to end the rebellion. Despite the fact that the timing of Druid disappearance and the stolen treasure is so close as to be possibly regarded as more than coincidental, no historical notes regarding a Druid treasure have been found. A number of the mentioned Dead Sea caves, however, were discovered in 1951-52 and 1960-61.

CHAPTER FIFTY-FOUR

Insane root was widely known from Egypt to India. It is also known as "fetid nightshade," "poison tobacco," "stinking nightshade," or "black hengane." This plant contains the poisons hyoscyamine and atropine. Its seed and juice are deadly poison; even in small portions, it can cause death in fifteen minutes. Among the many symptoms are uncontrollable convulsions. It is probable that Thomas used extremely small doses of the poisons to produce the results immediately after meals. It would have given two advantages: it was difficult to taste, and the slight tremor of convulsions needed no countering potion to end naturally minutes later.

CHAPTER FIFTY-FIVE

Jerusalem's history stretches back for more than 3,500 years. Its fortified walls were destroyed by invaders more than once; the last occasion by order of the Roman emperor Titus in A.D. 70, because of the first Jewish rebellion against the Roman Empire. After the fall of the Roman Empire, Jerusalem passed into the rule of the religiously tolerant Muslims, fell again to the knights of the First Crusade in 1099, and was then taken back by the Mamelukes who rebuilt the walls and restored much of the city.

Readers of the Old Testament often forget how historically accurate is its accounting of Jewish history, as proven where modern-day archeology has succeeded in discovering the sites of such events. King David's assault via Gihon Spring is reported in the Old Testament (Samuel 5:6-10). While it is reasonable to assume that any occupants of Jerusalem since then would guard against another such assault, it should not be surprising that defenders might forget the spring could also serve as an exit.

Thomas shows an excellent sense of logic as he notes that the well's walls become narrower at the top. As ancient cities aged throughout the centuries, garbage and rubble contributed to the slow building-up of the ground. Some excavations reached thirty to forty feet deep, to reveal life of the past at certain layers of time.

CHAPTER FIFTY-EIGHT

It is not unreasonable to assume that The Cave of Letters would lie undiscovered for the centuries from the time of the Roman general Julius Severus until it was rediscovered by Thomas and the bandits. No mention of the treasure is found in historical documents, but Mameluke soldiers would have had great incentive to keep the discovery of such great wealth to themselves. That the caves could be so well hidden and unknown is demonstrated by the fact that modern archeologists did not discover these sites until five more centuries had passed, in the years 1951-52 and 1960-61. Among the artifacts found in these caves were a basket of skulls, keys, metal vessels, parchment of palms, and fishnet. At least sixty skeletons were found.

CHAPTER FIFTY-NINE

Readers may find it interesting that the courtier's promised "ten minutes of audience" was in those times a relatively new term. With the arrival of mechanical clocks at the end of the 1200s and the beginning of the 1300s, mankind for the first time had found a way to impose regularity upon time; until then, an "hour" could be measured only as a portion of daylight, which of course varied from season to season. By finally establishing an "equal hour," man gained control over the daily measure of time, and a "minute" first became a divided portion of that hour.

CHAPTER SIXTY

England's battles against Scotland were begun by King Edward I in 1296. King Edward II did continue those battles, but to little avail. Shortly before Thomas and Katherine appeared in London for a royal audience, Edward II had lost a disastrous battle against the Scots at Bannockburn. The politics of that time would have put great pressure on Edward II for this loss; it is no wonder that he might have had little grasp on domestic affairs. Scotland, unlike Ireland or Wales, never did succumb to the English. A truce was declared in 1323.

The poison contained in all parts of the rhododendron, an evergreen shrub common in Britain, is carbohydrate andromedotoxin. While normally it takes over an hour for its poison to work, it is not unlikely that other herbs were added to compound its effect. Both Druids and the historical Merlin were famed for their knowledge of the poisons and medicines of plants and herbs; unfortunately, little of what they actually knew has survived.

CHAPTER SIXTY-ONE

Queen Isabella, the daughter of France's Philip IV, married King Edward II in 1308 and gave birth to Edward III on November 13, 1312. Isabella later joined forces with Roger de Mortimer, the first earl of March, and they forced Edward II's abdication of the throne in 1327 to give power to Edward III. Ironically, Edward III later rebelled against Mortimer's power and had him executed.

There is no historical mention of Edward III's brief kidnapping. However, especially given the ultimatum by Edward II to put pressure on his political enemies, it might be possible that King Edward did not want to alarm the people of England during a time of instability made worse by his recent losses to Scotland. Supposing that such an event took place, Edward would have hoped to gain his son back without public knowledge of either the kidnapping or return.

Marco Polo, who left for Cathay China in the year 1271 with his father and uncle, was reputed to have a photographic memory. Because of that, the intensely curious and open-minded emperor Kublai Khan appointed Polo as an envoy, diplomat, and observer of an empire that covered half the known world.

For twenty years, protected by the Khan's "golden passport," Polo explored the culture, politics, and science of one of history's most dazzling yet secluded empires.

Long given up for dead, he was barely recognized when he returned to Venice with a fortune in jewels sewn into his clothing. Later, as a rich merchant, he was taken hostage in a sea war between Italian cities. From prison, he dictated a book of his recollections. This book inspired Columbus to sail for the new world nearly two centuries later.

To those who scoffed at his tall tales, Marco Polo insisted, even on his deathbed, that he "never told the half of what he saw." Yet what if he had told the other half? His first book led Columbus to discover a New World. Historians might find it curious that gunpowder—in use by the Chinese for four centuries before Polo's arrival there—is not mentioned in the published book. Yet, gunpowder was "invented" in Germany shortly after Polo returned from China. Does this suggest that some of Polo's knowledge was not made public, but rather described in other books, missing or stolen, of his voyages?

Days of Deception
Lee Roddy

Being a spy for the famous Pinkerton Detectives suits Laurel Bartlett's adventurous nature. During the Civil War, Laurel had used her charm and cleverness to penetrate Confederate lines and bring back military intelligence for the Union army as a way to avenge her brother's death. But the war casts a long shadow onto Laurel's future happiness.

On a train heading South through lawless lands, sparks fly when she meets Ridge Granger, a handsome former rebel cavalryman, and Laurel's secret past comes back to haunt her. When Laurel stumbles upon a murder scene, both their lives are threatened by an unknown killer.

ISBN: 1-56476-635-7
PAPERBACK

And these great titles,
from Chariot Victor Publishing,
by popular author Jack Cavanaugh. . .

THE VICTORS
Jack Cavanaugh

The seventh book in the popular adult fiction series, "An American Family Portrait," *The Victors* follows the path of a new generation of the Morgan family. Four siblings are caught up in the events of World War II, and each will handle the challenge differently. Nat, Walt, Alex and Lily must face life's worst before they find out what it really means to be "the victors."

ISBN: 1-56476-589-X
PAPERBACK

The Peacemakers

Jack Cavanaugh

Into the volatile backdrop of cultural and political turmoil of the '60s, the author sets the final chapter of this popular series. How will the thirteenth generation of the Morgan family in America tackle the challenges of the Vietnam War, hippies, social protest and assassinations? Will their faith in God, symbolized by the passing of the family Bible from generation to generation, remain strong and vibrant?

ISBN: 1-56476-681-0
PAPERBACK
AVAILABLE JUNE 1999

Jack Cavanaugh is a full-time free-lance writer and public speaker. He lives with his wife and their three children in San Diego, California. Jack's other books in this series have appeared on the ECPA best-sellers list, and the first book, *The Puritans*, was a Gold Medallion finalist.

If you liked this book,
check out this great title from
Chariot Victor Publishing . . .